The Complete Cookbook of American Fish and Shellfish

The Complete Cookbook of

American Fish and Shellfish

Jean F. Nicolas

CBI Publishing Company, Inc.
51 Sleeper Street   Boston, Massachusetts 02210

Acknowledgments

For their generous assistance, the author is especially grateful to:

The National Marine Fisheries Service

The Atlantic States Marine Fisheries Commission

The National Oceanographic and Atmospheric Administration

Texas Department of Parks and Wildlife

Florida Department of Natural Resources

California Department of Fish and Game

South Carolina Department of Wildlife and Marine Resources

Maryland Department of Natural Resources

And also to Robert Finley of the National Consumer Education Service.

Copyright © 1981 by CBI Publishing Company, Inc.
All rights reserved. No part of this book may be reproduced,
by any process or technique, without express, written consent of the publisher.

Production Editor: Patricia Cronin
Cover/Text Designer: Roy H. Brown
Color Insert Designer: Charles G. Mitchell
Illustrator: Mimi Turner
Compositor: Trade Composition

Printing (last digit): 9 8 7 6 5 4 3 2 1

Printed in the United States of America.

Library of Congress Cataloging in Publication Data

Nicolas, Jean F
    The complete cookbook of American fish and shellfish.

    Includes index.
    1. Cookery (Fish) 2. Cookery (Shellfish) I. Title.
TX747.N54   641.6′9   80-16554
ISBN 0-8436-2191-5

To my wife, Chantal, whose devotion, contribution, and constant support have been invaluable.

Contents

Foreword

Jean Nicolas is a native of France, a graduate of the Hotel School of Paris, a former instructor at the Culinary Institute of America, and currently employed as a highly valued private chef. He has had extensive experience in the finest restaurants of Europe, the French Embassy in Dublin, the Dorchester Hotel in London, as well as various foodservice operations in the Bahamas.

He has received numerous foodservice prizes and honors in many culinary salon exhibitions. He has co-authored THE ART OF GARDE MANGER, presently in use as a text for the Buffet Catering course at the Culinary Institute of America.

THE COMPLETE COOKBOOK OF AMERICAN FISH AND SHELLFISH is a comprehensive and informative book designed to give readers a whole new concept in fish cookery. Fish and shellfish have long been part of our basic diet, but this has been a relatively small part when you consider the high protein value and availability of seafood. This book includes numerous newly developed and pre-tested recipes. Information is so abundant it is hoped that this will be the first in a series of such volumes.

It is with great pleasure that I recommend THE COMPLETE COOKBOOK OF AMERICAN FISH AND SHELLFISH, not only to the established professionals in the trade, but also to the students and apprentices who will be our professionals of tomorrow.

Joseph Amendola
Senior Vice President
Culinary Institute of America

Introduction

In the United States, fish and shellfish are appearing more frequently on our tables. Statistics compiled by the National Marine Fisheries Service indicate that the consumption of commercially caught fish and shellfish is increasing each year. For example, in 1963, the per capita consumption was 10.7 pounds (4.84 kg); in 1971, it rose to 11.5 pounds (5.2 kg); and in 1972, 12.4 pounds (5.6 kg). By 1976, per capita consumption reached 12.9 pounds (5.84 kg), of which 8.1 pounds were fresh or frozen, 4.3 pounds canned, and 0.5 pound cured. Consumption is expected to rise even more dramatically in the future, due in part to our changing eating habits.

Fish is an excellent source of protein, minerals, and vitamins. In addition, the variety of seafoods available and their versatility in preparation are factors responsible for their increased acceptance. We are constantly reminded that eating too much meat can be hazardous to our health, whereas eating more fish can increase life expectancy. The per capita consumption of fish and shellfish in the Nordic countries is the highest in the world—and so is their longevity.

In 1978, six countries accounted for 55 percent of the world's catch. Japan led with 15.5 percent, followed by Russia and China with 11.5 percent each. Peru was fourth with 8 percent, followed by the United States and Norway with 4.5 percent and 4 percent of the total catch, respectively.

As we depend more and more on the foods found in our oceans, we must realize the dangers threatening our seafoods. Pollution and overfishing are major threats to the balance of life in our seas; the leaping pink *Salmonidae* can no longer struggle in our polluted waters; *Homarus Americanus* has lost the battle against greedy fishermen; mollusks have become health hazards; and the red tide is taking a share of our ocean crop.

Fortunately, some improvements have occurred on several fronts. For the past decade, experiments have been conducted with our most depleted fish and shellfish species. American lobsters have been hatched and reared at the Massachusetts State Lobster Hatchery in Oak Bluffs. Individual lobsters have been held for as long as ten years, and the next step may well be lobster culture.

In 1900, Americans could get their caviar for the price of a nickel beer. Today, at $130 to $160 a pound, caviar is the costliest food on our planet. Future generations are certain to experience a shortage of caviar, although the Iranians are stocking the Caspian Sea with sturgeon fingerlings, hoping to alleviate this problem. The Russians are trying to develop a synthetic caviar that will taste and look like the real thing.

The most dramatic improvement may be the return of Atlantic salmon to our rivers. The resourceful Pacific king and silver salmon are showing considerable progress in their new environment. Marine officials in Maine, New Hampshire, and Connecticut are trying to control their polluted waters; they predict that Atlantic salmon will return to their spawning grounds, and latest reports do indeed confirm this. Chinooks and sockeye fingerlings have found new homes in Lakes Erie and Michigan, as well as in New England. To restore a healthy balance in the fisheries of the Great Lakes, over 20 million hatchery-reared predator fish are released each year into the Great Lakes and their tributaries.

At Rutgers University, in New Jersey, scientists have worked for twenty years to restore the oyster crop in Delaware Bay. In 1959, a disease called MSX killed over 90 percent of the Chesapeake Bay oysters. Most of the oysters that survived were resistant to that disease, and today the annual yield has reached the 1950 level of ¾ million bushels.

In 1976, Bill No. 94-265 was signed extending American fishing rights from 12 to 200 miles off our shores, thus restricting foreign fishing. This bill primarily protects New England and Pacific northwest fishermen who want to keep foreign trawlers out of their waters. Above all, it helps to alleviate the depletion of our seafood stock. This may well be a major step in balancing our marine resources effectively.

As the fishing boom expands, statistics indicate that commercial landings of lobsters, salmon, halibut, and other fish are declining at an alarming rate. In the future, our diet will probably include delicacies like dogfish, squid, skate, and other fish now unknown to American tastebuds.

The decline of our fish stock is not always due to pollution or overfishing. Natural fluctuations that occur among marine resources, and environmental influences, such as changing wind strengths and shifting currents, can affect the food sources for fish. Nevertheless, a large variety of fish and shellfish is available throughout the country. Undoubtedly, we have to develop a taste for species still unknown to most.

Russia and other countries are tracking and exploiting the antarctic krill, a shrimplike crustacean about two inches (5 cm) long. Millions of metric tons of the creatures are available. It is probable that the United States will join the krill hunt in the antarctic. But it is not yet certain that this high protein crustacean will enjoy widespread use. Russians are as hesitant about the taste of the newly processed krill as they are about synthetic caviar. Most people eat familiar fish and are reluctant to try new species.

The Maine Department of Fisheries is publicly testing a peculiar, fried, scalloplike fish at prime spots, such as the New York Coliseum Hotel and Motel Exposition. The fussy public reportedly finds the new seafood (dogfish) tasty. This fish is often rejected because it belongs to the shark family. But it is certain to gain popularity on our tables, as it already has in Europe. Apparently, sharks have more to fear from us than vice versa.

As the large foreign trawlers were scooping fish at sea by the metric ton, the average seashore catch declined sharply in recent years. As a result, fishermen are thinking of selling "junk fish," which in fisherman's language is a fish that has no market. Haddock and Alaskan crab were once classified as junk fish. So, we are certain to hear more about squid, shark, skate, and other species. There are already unusual fish ("thrash fish") being sold in the form of frozen sticks concealed in breading and other mealy crumbs. The exploitation of new species of fish and shellfish will help alleviate our seafood shortage, providing the public accepts and acquires a taste for the new fish products.

In addition, the potential catch of underutilized species is staggering. In United States waters, the squid, Pacific mackerel, small red crab, and

Jonah and cancer crabs could yield as much as the total existing United States fish catch.

The United States has a harvest of over 2,400 million pounds for human food. Although some species are on the decline, our Continental shelf is far from empty. New England fishermen caught over 32 million pounds of American lobsters in 1976. The oyster yield was 56 million pounds of meat, salmon landings were 230 million pounds, and scallops yielded 7 million pounds of meat.

Shrimp, the most valuable United States seafood, remains with tuna the highest in volume—387 million pounds each. Our favorite flounder family yielded 230 million pounds, an increase of 13 million pounds, but landings of haddock, halibut, and cod declined. If the laws governing our seas are obeyed, there is no reason why we cannot continue to enjoy our favorite fish and shellfish at reasonable cost.

I. Purchasing and Preparation

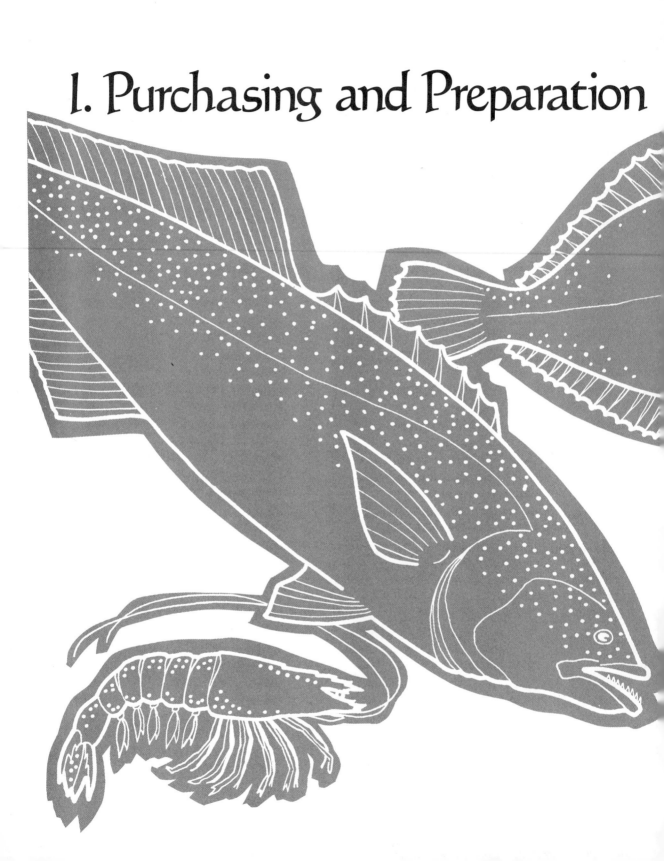

CHAPTER 1

Seafood and Health

Only recently has some light been shed on the nutritional and dietary values of seafood. We now realize that fish and shellfish not only satisfy our appetite and taste, but also provide valuable protein and minerals.

There is growing evidence that seafood plays an important role in our diet. Dr. Benjamin S. Frank, in his book *No Aging Diet,* emphasizes the role of seafood in our daily life when he says, "Grow younger eating seafood seven times a week."

Nutrition:

A Key to Good Health

Fish and shellfish can furnish most of the nutrients that are required by the body—and in generous amounts. When properly prepared, fish and shellfish can be delicious and satisfying, thus contributing to the simple enjoyment of eating.

The Nutritional Characteristics

of Fish and Shellfish

There are many reasons why the nutritional characteristics of seafood should be of vital interest to the consumer. Dietitians must provide balanced and appealing meals, at economical prices, for large numbers of people. Certainly, fishery products are highly nutritious and an excellent source of dietary essentials like protein, minerals, and vitamins. Moreover, the cost per pound of edible flesh from most fish is no more, and is often less, than that of many cuts of meat from domestic animals.

Consumers may be concerned about the caloric content of foods. The fat content of fish varies greatly among species, but those with low amounts of fat are particularly suited for weight-control diets. Moreover, the fat in fish contains a high proportion of polyunsaturated fatty acids. Because polyunsaturates in the diet may help to decrease the incidence of atherosclerosis, heart specialists are particularly interested in the nutritional quality and composition of fishery products. Many doctors now recommend generous portions of fish in the diet to increase the intake of polyunsaturated fatty acids, while insuring an adequate intake of protein.

Fishery products are also easily digested. Thus, they are valuable in the diets of young children and elderly people, where ease of digestibility is critically important.

Custom-tailored Diets

Like people, fish come in many sizes and shapes, and can be classified as lean, medium, or fat. By properly selecting fat or lean species of fish, you can tailor your diet to your particular needs. Of course, fat is only one major component of fish; the others are protein, minerals, and water. In

3

general, an inverse relationship exists between the fat and water content of fish, and these two components account for approximately 80 percent of the weight of fish.

Most fish and shellfish contain low amounts of fat and high amounts of protein. Some examples are tuna, halibut, cod, flounder, haddock, pollock, herring, rockfish, carp, whiting, crabs, scallops, and shrimp. Tuna and halibut are particularly good sources of protein. Some fish that contain both high amounts of fat and protein are anchovies, oysters, mackerel, salmon, and sardines.

For many centuries, fish and shellfish were considered easily digestible. Recent research proves that 90 to 100 percent of fish protein is digestible. This digestibility of seafood protein is considered slightly higher than that of beef and chicken.

Because fishery products are easily digested and well utilized, they are included in many special diets for people with digestive disorders. Fish and shellfish are used liberally in diets recommended for convalescent ulcer patients.

Since fishery products contain low amounts of connective tissue and fibrous components, they are especially suitable for low-bulk, bland diets. Here, the goal is to minimize the amount of undigested food in the digestive tract and still provide a nutritionally adequate diet. Often, fishery products are included in diets for people with digestive disorders to provide a wider variety of main dishes that are flavorful and appealing, but still suited to special dietary needs.

Fish and Shellfish: Excellent Sources of High-quality Protein

Scientific studies have shown that fish and shellfish contain protein of excellent quality, clearly placing them in a unique and enviable class. There is no mystery surrounding the attributes of the protein in fish. Simply stated, the protein in fish and shellfish contains generous amounts of compounds called amino acids, which are needed to construct body protein. Moreover, fish protein can be easily and almost completely digested.

A serving as small as 4 ounces of lean fish will supply about half the total amount of protein required daily by the body. The other half can be supplied easily by a normal intake of nonanimal protein. Although total protein content varies between lean and fatty fish, the amino acid composition and quality of the protein is remarkably constant. Thus, the quality of the protein is high whether it comes from lean or fatty fish.

Fish is often referred to by food faddists as brain food. There is no basis for this claim. In fact, no such thing as brain food exists. As we have pointed out, fish is a particularly good source of high-quality protein. When included in a balanced diet, it provides nourishment to all body tissues and shows no special preference for any particular part of the body.

Certain shellfish contain protein that is especially high in quality. Oysters, for example, are extremely beneficial for humans and are frequently used in therapeutic diets. Although the protein content of oysters is low, compared to that of most other fish and shellfish, the quality of oyster protein is superior to that of most fish and beef. Although oysters are excellent food, we have no scientific basis for the popular view that generous amounts increase sexual potency.

Oil in Fish and Shellfish

A great deal of attention has been given recently to the relationship between the amount and type of fat in the diet and the incidence of heart disease. This relationship has not been established conclusively, but evidence does suggest that a high intake of animal fat may be a predisposing factor contributing to heart disease. Because the fat in fish and shellfish has a unique chemical nature, fishery products are often recommended in diets designed to minimize the risk of heart disease.

Two dietary modifications are often recommended to reduce the incidence of heart disease among vulnerable groups. The first is to reduce the fat content and the total caloric content of the diet. The second is to substitute polyunsaturated fatty acids for some saturated fatty acids. Many studies have shown that the ingestion of oil containing large amounts of polyunsaturated fatty acids tends to suppress the blood cholesterol level and lower the incidence of atherosclerosis. Few people, however, want to consume oil directly. A much more palatable method is simply to include generous portions of fishery products in the diet. To illustrate, some salmon average nearly 15 percent oil. A 6-ounce serving can furnish nearly an ounce of oil rich in polyunsaturated fatty acids.

Fish not only contain high proportions of polyunsaturated fatty acids, but they also contain relatively small amounts of cholesterol. Certain cuts of beef and some egg products contain up to ten times as much cholesterol per ounce as is found in fish and shellfish.

Reducing the total intake of calories in the diet, however, is often as important to health as including liberal quantities of polyunsaturated fatty acids. In this case, fish that are low in oil will reduce the total caloric intake and still provide adequate protein to meet the body's requirements. Low-fat fish and shellfish normally contain less than 100 calories per 4-ounce serving. On the other hand, a 4-ounce serving of good quality beef may supply well over 300 calories. For those who are calorie conscious, seafood offers a distinct advantage over meats that are high in fat. (For more details on fat and lean fish, see Table 1.1.)

Vitamin Content

Fish products are good sources of several vitamins. The thirteen common vitamins can be divided into two major groups, fat-soluble vitamins and water-soluble vitamins. In fishery products, fat-soluble vitamins are found in the oil; water-soluble vitamins are found in the water content. In the history of vitamins, it was recognized early that fish liver oil was a rich natural source of fat-soluble vitamins, especially vitamins A and D. The flesh of fish, however, contains relatively small amounts of fat-soluble vitamins.

Fish oil generally has a higher content of fat-soluble vitamins than the fat of animals. In turn, fatty fish contain more of these vitamins than lean fish. Some fatty fish are excellent sources of vitamin D; lean fish contain very small amounts. The vitamin A content of the flesh of most fish is relatively low. It has been noted, however, that swordfish and whitefish contain high amounts of vitamin A.

As for water-soluble vitamins, four of the eight members of the vitamin B family can be supplied in adequate amounts by fish and shellfish. These four vitamins are B_6, B_{12}, biotin, and niacin. The remaining four B vitamins are found in fishery products, but generally not in appreciable quantities. Larger amounts of B vitamins usually are found in high-fat fish than in low-fat fish. Also, the B vitamin content of the dark meat of fish is many times higher than that of the white meat. The B vitamin content of fish and animal meat is about the same.

Table 1.1.   Fat and protein content of seafood

Species	Category A (low oil, high protein)	Category B (medium oil, high protein)
Abalone	x	
Anchovy		x
Bass, sea	x	
Buffalo fish	x	
Butterfish	x	
Carp	x	
Catfish	x	
Chub, lake		x
Clams	x	
Cod	x	
Crab	x	
Croaker	x	
Flounder	x	
Haddock	x	
Hake	x	
Halibut	x	
Herring, lake	x	
Lobster		x
Mackerel		x
Mullet		x
Mussels		x
Ocean perch	x	
Oysters	x	
Pollock	x	
Rainbow trout		x
Red snapper	x	
Rockfish	x	
Sablefish		x
Salmon, Atlantic		x
Salmon, chum		x
Salmon, king		x
Salmon, pink		x
Salmon, silver		x
Salmon, sockeye		x
Sardine, Norwegian canned		x
Scallops	x	
Scup (porgy)	x	

(cont.)

Table 1.1   (cont.)

Species	Category A (low oil, high protein)	Category B (medium oil, high protein)
Sea bass	x	
Sheepshead		x
Shrimp	x	
Smelt		x
Sole	x	
Spot	x	
Squid	x	
Swordfish	x	
Tuna, canned with vegetable oil added	x	
Whiting	x	
Yellow perch	x	
Yellow pike	x	

Seafood is a Valuable Source of Many Essential Minerals

Fish contain relatively large amounts of phosphorus, potassium, and iron. Conversely, the sodium and chlorine content of fish is relatively low.

With the advent of low-sodium diets, attention has focused on the sodium content of fish and shellfish. Occasionally, doubt is expressed about the advisability of using fish in low-sodium diets prescribed for people suffering from hypertension. This doubt is unfounded, even in the case of salt-water fish. With the exception of most shellfish, fish are low in sodium and can be used freely in low-sodium diets. Fresh oysters and soft clams are also low in sodium. Other shellfish often contain higher amounts of sodium and are not recommended for low-sodium diets. Also, if salt is added during processing, sodium levels will exceed the maximum permissible level. Since fish vary considerably in flavor and texture, they add variety and diversification to low-sodium diets.

Fishery products are noted for a high content of micro-minerals, or trace minerals, such as iodine and fluoride. Because trace minerals perform vital functions, fish and shellfish are viewed with special interest. Most essential trace minerals are present in seafood in amounts at least equivalent to those in meat, and usually in much higher amounts than in vegetables and dairy products.

Fish and Shellfish Contribute to the Enjoyment of Eating

Over 150 varieties of fish and shellfish—either fresh or processed—are available to the consumer. With this multiplicity of choice, it is possible to please even the most discriminating palate. Seafood, however, is a most delicate food and must be handled with care from the time it is caught until it is placed on the table. Natural goodness and taste are easily lost if improper preservation and processing techniques are used. Whereas meats tend to improve with aging, fish and shellfish are best when fresh.

The methods used in cooking fish and shellfish are especially important. Good fish can be easily spoiled if improperly cooked. The flesh of fish can be likened to egg white and should be cooked only until the flesh "sets" and is easily flaked from the bones.

Fish can be baked, broiled, boiled, or fried. Certain types of fish are more suited to particular methods of cooking. For example, fatty fish are considered better for broiling and baking; lean fish are more appropriately broiled, boiled, or steamed. The important point is that overcooking must be avoided to preserve the natural texture and flavor.

Fish and shellfish can be delicious and prepared with ease. They are more than a substitute for meat and can be used as an appetizer, a first course, or the main attraction. Even the connoisseur can find the right seafood to suit a particular purpose and taste. When cooked and flavored with appropriate herbs and spices, and consumed with vintage wine, seafood can be a truly enjoyable experience in eating.

Table 1.2. Food values of beef versus seafood

1 pound, 453 grams raw, meat only	Grams of Protein	Grams of Fat	Calories
Beef, rib roast	67	170	1,818
Cod	79	1	354
Tuna	112	14	603
Haddock	83	1	358
Pollock	92	4	431
Flounder	76	4	118
Ocean perch	88	18	535
Whiting	83	14	476
Hake	74	2	336
Halibut	95	5	454
Cusk	78	1	340
Mackerel	86	55	866
Herring	79	51	798
Butterfish..................	82	46	767
Scallops...................	69	1	367
Scup	86	15	508
Swordfish	87	18	535
Tilefish....................	80	2	358
Striped bass	86	12	476
Bluefish...................	93	15	531
Mussels	65	10	431
Hard clams	50	4	363
Soft clams	64	9	372
Squid.....................	74	4	381
Crab	79	9	422
Lobster	77	9	413

CHAPTER 2

Buying, Handling, and Storing Seafood

Meat must be aged to improve in taste, flavor, and tenderness. Fish and shellfish are perishable foods. As soon as they are exposed to warm air temperatures, they deteriorate rapidly. Fresh seafood, handled properly from landing to cooking, has an unmistakably good flavor and odor. Any error in handling and storing results in poor quality seafood.

Buying Quality Fresh Fish

When buying fresh fish make certain that:

1. The flesh is firm and elastic, not separating from the bones. In buying fillets and steaks, look for a fresh-cut appearance and color that resembles freshly dressed fish.
2. The gills are bright red in color.
3. The odor is fresh and mild. A fish just taken from the water has practically no "fishy" odor.
4. The eyes are bright, clean, transparent, and full.
5. The skin is shiny and bright in color.
6. The scales adhere tightly to the skin.

Handling and Storing Fish and Shellfish

Seafoods spoil more rapidly than any other food product and should be handled and stored with utmost care. Freshly caught fish or shellfish that is brought to the pan quickly is in a class by itself. The flavor of seafood diminishes if processing, storing, or cooking are mishandled.

Fresh fish should be cleaned and gutted to preserve freshness. The removal of the intestines, liver, heart, and gills will eliminate the major sources of bacterial contamination. This is the most important step in retaining the freshness of fish. Occasionally, the gills are not removed when fish are cleaned by distributors. However, the complete removal of gills is necessary to preserve the full freshness of fish. Red snapper, which has a delicate meat, will spoil three to four times faster if the gills are not removed completely within a few hours of the catch.

Fresh fish should be refrigerated on ice at 35°F to 40°F (1.5°C to 4.5°C) as soon as they are received. Seal the fish if necessary before placing on ice. Use a separate refrigerator, if available, or at least a section of the refrigerator avoiding contact with other foods. Fish should not be exposed to air unnecessarily as oxidation may alter the flavor. Fillets of fish lose their flavor more rapidly than whole fish and should be processed without delay. Purchase whole fresh fish if available. Eviscerate as soon as possible and process into fillets, steaks, sticks, or other forms shortly before cooking. This method of preparation guarantees the full flavor of fish. For more details on preparing various types of fresh fish and shellfish, see Chapter 5.

9

The source of supply is an important factor when purchasing fish and shellfish. It is therefore necessary to select a reliable fish dealer. Beware of fish sections in many supermarkets that display smelly and stale fish and shellfish. There is no bargain in buying stale fish at any price. Numerous supermarkets in the United States have the reputation of selling the best quality meat and the worst quality seafood.

One can never achieve a culinary triumph with poor quality fish. A freshly cooked fish has a sweet taste; if the fish has been stored improperly, it will have a "fishy" taste. A strong rancid flavor indicates that the raw material was poorly handled before or during the freezing process. Rancidity is caused by oxidation of the fish oil. As a rule, fish containing less than 5 percent oil freeze and preserve better than those that contain higher oil percentages. (Refer to Table 2.1.) Mackerel, lake trout, shad, and smelt are likely to become rancid faster than yellow perch, halibut, red snapper, or lobster. The Atlantic salmon, king salmon, and silver salmon keep exceptionally well when frozen, even though their oil content is very high. Yet the comparatively lean pink salmon, called humpback in British Columbia, becomes rancid and discolors after a relatively short period of freezing. This species of salmon is mostly canned.

Different environmental conditions can cause a particular fish to have different flavors. Apart from the problems caused by water pollution, several species of fish found in northern waters have a palatability superior to the same species caught in southern waters. A bass or perch caught in muddy warm water is inferior to the same species caught in clear cold water. The same applies to hatchery trout, which seldom have the delicate flavor of wild brook trout.

Refrigerated smoked fish should not be placed in contact with ice. Smoked fish, especially trout, salmon, finnan haddie, and herring, should always be well sealed with wax paper and foil to contain their penetrating odors.

The Handling of Frozen Fish

Fish to be frozen should be wrapped and sealed in moistureproof and vaporproof material. Do not freeze fish that are wrapped only in wax paper or polyethylene materials. Fresh fish may be frozen in a block of ice or by glazing, both of which prevent moisture loss. To freeze fish in a block of ice, place the fish in a container large enough to hold the fish and cover with water. Then freeze until solid.

Glazing is as effective as block freezing and takes less freezer space. To glaze fish (dressed, steaks, or fillets), place in a single layer on a tray.

Table 2.1 Freezer storage life

Types	Species	Months
fat fish ..	mackerel, salmon, (king, silver) tuna, herring, et cetera	3
lean fish .	haddock, cod, redfish, red snapper, swordfish, et cetera	6
	lobsters, crabs (meat)	2
	shrimp	6
	oysters, scallops, clams (shucked)	3 to 4

Wrap and freeze. As soon as the fish is frozen, remove from the freezer, unwrap, and dip quickly in ice-cold water. A glaze will form immediately. Repeat the dipping process three or four times. A thick coat of ice will result from each dipping. If necessary, return the fish to the freezer between dippings if the glaze does not build up after two or three consecutive dippings. Handle the fish carefully to avoid breaking the glaze. When glazed, wrap the fish tightly in freezer wrap or aluminum foil and return to the freezer. Glazing may need to be repeated if the fish is not used within one or two months.

Commercially packaged frozen fish products should be placed in a freezer, in their original moisture and vaporproof wrapper, immediately after purchase to maintain quality. Store at 0°F (−18°C) or lower. At temperatures above this level, chemical changes cause the fish to lose color, flavor, texture, and nutritive value. Storage time should be limited in order to enjoy the optimum flavor of frozen fish. It is good practice to date the packages for easy rotation.

The Handling of Shellfish

Fresh shellfish should be stored at approximately 33°F to 34°F (1°C to 2°C) and used within a day or two. Never store in water.

Clams and oysters in the shell are alive when the shells are tightly closed or close when lightly tapped. Gaping shells indicate that the shellfish are dead and not edible. Shucked oysters should be plump and have a creamy color and mild odor.

Cooked crabs and lobsters in the shell must be bright red with no disagreeable odor.

Fresh shrimp have a mild odor and meat that is firm in texture. Cooked shrimp have a red-colored shell and the meat has a reddish tint.

Scallops have a sweet odor and should be free of excess liquid when packaged.

To freeze shellfish, process the same way as frozen fish. Specific instructions for oysters and blue crabs follow.

To prepare oysters for freezing:

1. Wash shell thoroughly.
2. Open and remove meat. Place meat in a strainer and save liquid. Wash meat with a cool, 2 percent salt solution and remove loose shell particles.
3. Place in container with liquid and salt solution to cover meat. Label and freeze immediately.

To prepare live blue crabs for freezing:

1. Boil whole crabs for freezing. Boil whole crabs for 15 to 20 minutes in 5 percent salt water. Cool rapidly.
2. Pick meat from body and claws. Keep lump meat, claw meat, and flake meat separate, if desired.
3. Pack in moisture and vaporproof containers. Label container and freeze immediately.

Frozen Fish and Shellfish
Storage Life

Fish products of good quality, that were handled correctly from catch to freezer, should remain in good condition for the period indicated in Table 2.1(at temperatures ranging from 0°F to −10°F or −18°C to −23°C). Good quality fish products, frozen under the best conditions, will not be discolored or display freezer burns (a very white, dry appearance around the edges). Ice crystals inside the package indicate moisture loss from fish flesh, which could be the result of thawing, refreezing, or insufficiently low temperatures. For complete details on fatty fish and lean fish, see Table 1.1.

Cooked seafood Cooked seafood can be stored in the refrigerator or freezer. If stored in the refrigerator, cover the seafood and hold no longer than two to three days. If stored in the freezer, package the seafood in a moisture and vapor-proof material and hold no longer than three months.

Canned fish products Canned seafood should be stored in a cool dry place for no longer than one year.

Thawing Fish Products

Schedule thawing so that fish or shellfish will be cooked soon after thawing. Thawed seafood should be held no longer than one day before cooking.

Place the package of frozen seafood in the refrigerator to thaw. Allow 18 to 24 hours per pound for thawing a package. If quicker thawing is necessary, place the package under cold running water. Allow 1 to 2 hours per pound. Do not thaw fish at room temperature or in warm water, as it loses moisture and flavor. Thawed seafood should not be refrozen. Some frozen seafoods, such as breaded frozen fish products, can be cooked without thawing. Any leftover, uncooked fresh seafood, scallops, oysters, clams, fish fillets, and sticks can be breaded and frozen. The breading preserves the freshness of the seafood. In addition, frozen fish fillets can be cooked without thawing, if additional time is allowed. The cooking time for frozen seafoods is double that for the same product, fresh or thawed.

How Quality is Lost

The primary causes of quality breakdown in fish products are oxidation, dehydration, enzymatic action, and bacterial growth. When oxidation occurs, the oil or fat in the fish flesh can cause the fish to become rancid. Do not expose fish products to air unnecessarily, and wrap tightly before freezing. Dehydration is caused by improper packaging. Excessive drying out in frozen fish is known as freezer burn. Enzymatic action in the flesh of fish causes deterioration. Low temperatures slow enzymatic action and preserve the original quality. Bacterial growth increases mainly when the storage temperature is too high and when sanitation in handling fish is poor.

Emergencies

If power failure occurs but is not expected to exceed 24 hours, keep the freezer closed to prevent thawing. When power is restored, turn the thermostat to the highest setting until the freezer temperature is reduced to 0°F to -10°F (-18°C to -23°C).

If the freezer is likely to be off for more than 24 hours, use dry ice to keep the food frozen until power is restored. Once fish products are thawed, they should not be refrozen.

How Much to Buy

The amount of fish or shellfish to purchase varies according to portion size, the type of recipe, and the marketing form of the fish product. On the average, allow approximately 3 ounces of cooked, boneless fish per serving. The following is a fish and shellfish buying guide with the approximate amount listed for 6 servings.

Edible Portions of Fish and Shellfish

Servings of fresh and frozen fish products generally are based on portions of one-third of a pound (150 g) to one-half of a pound (225 g) for each person. The edible portion varies with the market form, the variety of fish, and the production area. Among all fish available commercially, salmon has the best yield. The edible percentage of drawn salmon is 70 to 75 percent.

The following approximate percentages indicate how much of the market form of each fish product is edible.

Table 2.2   Amounts to buy

Fish, whole	4¼ lbs. (2. 040 kg)
Fish, dressed or pan dressed	3 lbs. (1.360 kg)
Fish, fillets or steaks	2 lbs. (900 g)
Fish, portions	2 lbs. (900 g)
Fish, sticks	1½ lbs. (680 g)
Fish, canned	1 lb. (450 g)
Clams, in the shell	3 doz.
Clams, shucked	1 qt. (1 l)
Crab, cooked meat	1 to 2 lbs. (450 to 900 g)
Lobsters, live	5 to 7 lbs. (2.260 to 3.170 kg)
Lobster, cooked meat . . .	1 to 2 lbs. (450 to 900 g)
Oysters, in the shell	3 doz.
Oysters, shucked	1 qt. (1 l)
Scallops, shucked	1 to 2 lbs. (450 to 900 g)
Shrimp, headless	2 to 3 lbs. (900 to 1.360 kg)
Shrimp, cooked meat . . .	1 to 2 lbs. (450 to 900g)

Table 2.3   Edible fish products

Fish	Production Area	Edible Percentage
Whole or round	all	43 to 47
Drawn (eviscerated only)	all	46 to 50
Dressed (eviscerated, head and fins removed)	all	65 to 69
Steaks	all	84 to 88
Fillets	all	100
Sticks and portions	all	100
Shellfish, Live in shell		
Clams:		
Hard	New England	14.5
"	Chesapeake	10
"	Middle Atlantic	14
"	South Atlantic	9.5
"	Pacific	25

(cont.)

Table 2.3   (cont.)

Fish	Production Area	Edible Percentage
Clams (cont.):		
Soft	New England	22.7
"	Chesapeake	18.5
Surf	Middle Atlantic	20
Oysters:		
Eastern	New England and Middle Atlantic	11
"	South Atlantic	6.3
"	Gulf	6.5
Pacific	. . . .	11.3
Cooked in shell Crabs:		
Hard	Atlantic and Gulf	10 to 18
Dungeness	Pacific	22 to 26
Lobsters	New England	35 to 37
Shucked clams, oysters, bay and sea scallops	all	100
Headless, raw shrimp	South Atlantic and Gulf states	50 to 60
Cooked meat crabs, lobsters, and shrimp	all	100

CHAPTER 3

Marketing of Fish Products

Each year, about three billion pounds of fish and shellfish are caught commercially for food in the United States. The ocean's harvest is brought into United States ports nearly every day of the year. The highest landings occur generally from June through September, peaking in the last two months. Many species of fish and shellfish are then available at their lowest prices. Many shrewd food operators take advantage of the large supply of popular fish products and stock for months ahead.

Fresh fish is sold on the market in a number of forms:

1. whole or round
2. drawn
3. dressed or pan dressed
4. steaks
5. fillets

Whole or round fish are marketed just as they come from the water. Before cooking they must be scaled and eviscerated. The fins are removed but the head and the tail may or may not be removed, depending on the type of recipe and the presentation of the dish.

Drawn fish are marketed with only the entrails removed (see Fig. 3.1). They need to be scaled and washed before cooking.

Dressed and pan-dressed fish are both scaled and eviscerated. Usually, head, tail, and fins are removed to ready them for cooking (see Fig 3.2).

Smaller pan-dressed fish usually have the head and tail left on when readied for cooking.

Steaks are cross section slices of larger dressed fish. They are ready to cook as purchased (see Fig. 3.3).

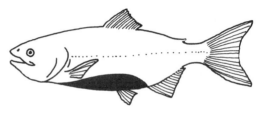

Figure 3.1

Figure 3.2

Figure 3.3

Fillets are the sides of dressed fish, cut lengthwise away from the back bones (see Fig 3.4). Fillets are usually boneless, may be skinned, and require no preparation before cooking. Butterfly fillets are the sides of the fish held together by the uncut belly skin or by the back, and are usually boneless. For more details on butterfly fillets, see page 106.

Figure 3.4

How Frozen Fish Products are Marketed

Frozen fish products are marketed as steaks, fillets, fish portions, and fish sticks. Fish portions are pieces of fish cut from the frozen fish block into uniform portions weighing no less than 1½ ounces (42 g) and up to 6 ounces (170 g). Fish sticks are pieces of fish cut from frozen fish blocks into uniform portions, usually about 1 inch (2.5 cm) wide and 3 inches (7.5 cm) long. They weigh up to 1½ ounces (42 g).

How Shellfish are Marketed

Fresh shellfish, such as oysters, clams, and some varieties of crabs, should be alive when purchased in the shell. Shucked shellfish are those that have been removed from their shells. Clams, oysters, and scallops are often shucked. The term *shrimp* refers to the fresh whole (heads on)

shrimp that are sold mainly near product points. *Headless shrimp* are the edible portions with the heads removed. The term *green shrimp* describes raw shrimp, in the shell, with or without the head. *Peeled shrimp* are headless; *deveined* shrimp have the intestinal track or black vein removed.

Cooked shrimp are available fresh, frozen, dried, or canned and are usually sold peeled, deveined, and ready-to-use. Shrimp in the shell are marketed by size—jumbo, large, medium, and small—or by the number to the pound—21–25's indicates 21 to 25 shrimp to the pound, U 10's means under 10 shrimp to the pound.

Oysters are sold live in the shell, shucked, breaded, frozen raw headless, frozen fried, or canned (whole or as stew). Live oysters in the shell can be purchased by the barrel, part barrel, bushel, half bushel, et cetera. They are marked by size.

Crabs are sold in several forms. If purchased live, they should be alive and active at the time of cooking. Crabs cooked in the shell should be bright in color and free of disagreeable odors. Cooked crabmeat is available fresh or frozen and is picked from the shells. Canned crabmeat is ready to serve or use as purchased.

Scallops are marketed shucked or breaded. The large adductor muscle that opens and closes the shell is the only part of the scallop that is marketed as scallop meat. Breaded scallops are available frozen raw or frozen fried. Shells can be purchased for serving scallops and other fish en coquille (in the shell).

The six principal species of clams available on the market are butter, hard, little, razor, soft, and surf clams. They can be purchased live in the shell, shucked, breaded raw or cooked, or canned.

Lobsters can be purchased live in the shell or as fresh or frozen cooked meat. Frozen meat is marketed in 14 ounce (400g) cans and packed in a salt-water solution. Live lobsters keep best when covered with seaweed or heavy paper. Excessive cold can make them appear inactive and sleepy when they are not. Lobster must be live when cooked. The flesh of dead meat flakes and falls apart. Fresh meat is firm and white with pink tinges. If the tail of a boiled lobster springs back when straightened out, it indicates that the lobster was alive before cooking. The shells of live lobsters vary in color, depending on their habitat, from dark bluish green or nearly black to mottled shades of brown and dark green. During cooking, the shells turn bright red. The moulting season for lobsters occurs generally in late July and early August. At that time, lobsters shed their hard shells and start new ones. In the soft-shell stage, lobsters are extremely perishable, lose weight, and have less meat than hard-shell lobsters.

The Seafood Market's Unique Characteristics

An average of 62 to 65 percent of the frozen seafood distributed in the United States goes to restaurants, institutions, and service operations. Only 35 to 38 percent is distributed through retail outlets. About 90 percent of frozen trout goes to the institutional market. On the other hand, frozen fillets are split almost evenly between the institutional and the retail trades. By way of contrast, the institutional trade received only about 26 percent of frozen poultry products and 40 percent of all frozen foods distributed in the United States.

The range of frozen seafood products marketed in the United States is extensive. It is interesting to note that it was in Gloucester, Massachusetts, in the mid-1920s, that Clarence E. Birdseye

developed and perfected a method of quick freezing that has had a tremendous impact on the entire food market. Only a little over twenty years ago, Birdseye developed frozen fish sticks, which have had a revolutionary effect on fish marketing. John Kaylor, veteran food technologist at the NMFS Atlantic Fishery Products Technology Center in Gloucester, points out that many of the 6000 or more items now sold at many supermarkets, especially fish products, were unheard of as recently as five or ten years ago.

Valuable information pertaining to a specific fish or shellfish listed in this book can be found in chapter 4. It includes the availability fresh, the best average weight, the market size, the quality, and the disposition for most species of fish and shellfish sold commercially.

The landings of fish and shellfish vary considerably; some months are more productive than others. Wind storms cut into fishing time; migratory fish, such as whiting, mackerel, and bluefish show up only in warm weather months; and at times one species experiences a population explosion and another species goes into decline. Purchases of fresh fish and shellfish should be planned accordingly.

Recently, the National Marine Fisheries Service created the Fishery Market News service. Fishery Market News reports the current information on prices, market conditions, production, imports, exports, cold storage holdings, and market receipts of seafood products in major fish trading centers in the United States. Information is collected by market reporters, and reported to, compiled, and disseminated by Market News offices in Boston, New York, New Orleans, Terminal Island, and Seattle. Each office issues the information in two-to-four-page reports. The information aids United States buyers and sellers of fish products in making intelligent marketing decisions.

The reports also establish an equal bargaining basis for everyone in the marketing system. The tri-weekly report or the weekly summary can be ordered from the National Marine Fisheries Service in Washington, D.C. In some parts of the country, automatic telephone message devices are used for rapid relay of current information on fish and shellfish landings, exvessel prices, and other market conditions. Telephone numbers for these Automatic Telephone Message Centers are:

Boston, Mass.—617-542-7878
Gloucester, Mass.—617-283-1101
New Bedford, Mass.—617-997-6565
New York, N.Y.
   a. Landings/prices—212-620-3577
   b. Frozen prices—212-620-3244
Hampton, Va.—804-723-0303
Chicago, Ill.—312-353-8484.

United States Inspection Programs

Bringing the harvest of the seas to consumers is often a complex operation. The Department of Commerce, The National Oceanographic and Atmospheric Administration (NOAA), and the National Marine Fisheries Service (NMFS) provide inspection programs to meet various needs. Fish and shellfish are naturally nutritious, appetizing, and varied. But unless these products are properly handled during processing and distribution, they will not retain their goodness and quality.

According to Gene Cope, Consumer and Trade Education Specialist, Fishery Product Inspection and Safety Division, NOAA, "Unlike other food areas that fall under the watchful eye of mandatory federal inspection programs, the fish industry has been given scarcely a supervisory glance." He adds that the only reason for this is that such an inspection program was never deemed necessary. Whether it is confidence in product quality or in a company's reputation that has led to this consenting opinion is guesswork. For those who purchase fish products without inspection or grading markings, the trust in a particular processing plant or distributor is commendable. There is no denying that quality products induce repeat business. Indeed, there is no reason to doubt quality if past product quality has always been satisfactory. Processing plants take pride in offering the best fish products available, despite the absence of federal watchdogs. The objectives and guidelines of most distributors of fish products are often as stringent, and more so, than federal regulations. But the option of federal inspection does exist for fish products, and the public should be aware of this alternative. The United States Department of Commerce (USDC) inspection and grading seal offers a product guarantee with no guesswork involved.

Inspection and Grading

There are two separate but related parts to the federal inspection program—inspection and grading. Inspection is the examination of fish products by inspectors to make certain that the products are safe, pure, and properly labeled. The plant, equipment, and food-handling personnel must also meet adequate and appropriate hygienic standards. Products that pass inspection may bear the Federal Inspection Mark or statement, "Packed Under Federal Inspection," on the brand labels.

Grading is an added step in which the quality

Figure 3.5 The Inspection Mark identifies fish products certified by federal inspectors to be safe, clean, wholesome, and properly labeled. The United States Grade Shield indicates the quality level of graded products. All products that bear Grade Shields have been federally inspected.

level of certain products is determined and certified by the inspector. In general, high volume fish products for mass feeding and direct consumer markets are subject to grading. Graded products bear a United States Grade Shield that shows their quality level.

Types of Inspection   There are three types of inspection: contract inspection, lot inspection, and miscellaneous inspection.

Contract inspection enables processing plants to have inspectors oversee preparation, processing, and packaging operations. Inspectors monitor the quality of raw materials and examine samples of the finished products. Producers and packers primarily use this service.

Lot inspection is performed on specific lots of a product. Lots are usually located in processing

plants, warehouses, cold storage plants, or terminal markets. Primary users are brokers, buyers, and others with a financial interest in the product.

Miscellaneous inspection and consultation services include plant surveys, sanitation evaluation, new product evaluation, and label and product inspection reviews. Processors, packers, and brokers use these services.

The Roles of Inspectors   Inspectors fill five roles that are tailored to the type of inspection desired by applicants. In general, these roles are:

1. Sanitation expert—pinpoints unsanitary conditions in the plant and recommends ways to correct them.
2. Quality control adviser—makes certain that the quality of the raw materials and all ingredients will produce a wholesome product. Helps establish procedures that result in a uniform product.
3. Quality control assessor—samples and grades the finished product.
4. Observer—keeps a careful watch on the overall operation of the plant.
5. Reporter—reports noted problems to plant management for resolution.

Inspection Benefits Consumers   Inspection services make an important contribution to the four principal areas of consumer concern about food products: quality, health, hygiene, and economy. Grade marks identify the product quality levels to enable wise consumer choices. Inspection assures the safety and purity of fishery products. It also assures that the product was produced, processed, and packaged under sanitary conditions. Finally, inspection helps consumers select foods that are truthfully and informatively labeled and packaged.

United States Grade Standards
for Fish Products

United States Grade Standards are an important aid to orderly and efficient fish marketing. As a part of voluntary federal inspection, grading provides useful standardized information for trade transactions in fish products.

Are Grade Standards Desirable? Grade standards identify the relative value, utility, and quality of each unit of fish product. For example, a product marked "Grade A" is of higher quality than "Grade B" or "Grade C" products. Fishermen, wholesalers, processors, distributors—all those involved in the production of fish products—use grade standards to buy and sell products of known and accepted quality. Consumers can rely on grading as a guide to quality products.

Products that Bear Standards The National Marine Fisheries Service assigns United States Grade Standards to many high-volume fish products for direct mass consumer markets. These standards cover such products as: frozen fish fillets and fillet blocks; frozen raw fish portions and fish steaks; frozen raw breaded and precooked fish portions and fish sticks; frozen raw headless shrimp and raw breaded shrimp; and frozen raw and precooked breaded scallops.

What Grade Standards Do Grade standards reflect different quality levels of products; form a basis for sales and purchases; provide guidelines for in-plant quality control; and establish a basis for official inspection.

The Meanings of Grade Standards Grade A means the top or best quality. Grade A products are uniform in size, practically free of blemishes and defects, in excellent condition, and possess good flavor for the species. Grade B indicates good quality. Grade B products may not be as uniform in size or as free of blemishes or defects as Grade A products. Grade B can be termed a general commercial grade, suitable for most purposes.

Grade C means fairly good quality. Grade C products are just as wholesome and generally as nutritious as higher grades. Grade C products have a definite value as a thrifty buy when appearance is not an important factor. Consumers will not find products labeled Grade B or Grade C in the marketplace because these products are usually marketed without any grade designation.

Inspection Reinforces Grading

Product grading is more valid when done by a neutral and unbiased party. The National Marine Fisheries Service provides voluntary federal inspection on a fee-for-service basis, paid by the plant under inspection. Officially graded and certified products from such plants are eligible to carry the inspection mark and/or the prefix U.S. on their grade marks (U.S. Grade A, for example). Products that bear only the inspection mark must be at least Grade B, and most are Grade A. Consequently, knowledgeable consumers consider inspection an added service by concerned processors on behalf of consumers.

Grading by Eye at Time of Purchase

Grade standards help maintain fish product quality from the seas to the kitchen. Knowledgeable consumers also check for the following indications of proper handling at the time of purchase. Packages of frozen fish should be solid, not soft.

They should be stacked well below the frost line or load line of the store's display freezer. Containers and wrapping should be intact. Packages should be free of "drip" or ice, which may indicate that the contents have thawed and been refrozen. Cello-wrap packages should not be discolored or show other signs of freezer burn. Breaded fish products should remain separated in the package. If poor quality products are purchased inadvertently, they should be returned to the store at once.

Consumer interests are a major concern of the fish industry. Much care and attention go into the production and distribution of fish products. Grade standards, inspection, and wise purchasing habits help consumers buy wholesome and nutritious seafood products at their best.

Federal Inspection Marks

Federal inspection marks are official marks approved by the Secretary of Commerce and authorized for use on brand labels of fish products. When displayed on product labels, these marks signify that federal inspectors from the Department of Commerce inspected, graded, and certified that the products met all the requirements of the inspection regulations and were produced in accordance with official United States Grade Standards or approved specifications.

They Serve Two Functions   The distinctive inspection marks signify two distinct but related functions in guiding the consumer to safe, wholesome products, produced in a sanitary environment and packed in accordance with uniform quality standards under the supervision of the United States Department of Commerce's voluntary inspection service. The inspection marks are "U.S. Grade" and "Packed Under Federal Inspection."

Fish Products that Bear Federal Inspection Marks   Many brand-name fish products carry either one or both inspection marks on their labels. The following is a list of fish and shellfish products, made from a variety of species, that bear inspection marks:

frozen raw fish fillets, portions and sticks
frozen fried fish fillets, portions and sticks
fresh and frozen whole or dressed fish
frozen raw breaded shrimp
frozen whole cooked crabs and crabmeat
fried fish and seafood cakes
raw and fried fish dinners
fried clams and clam cake dinners
fried scallops and fried scallop dinners
raw breaded scallops
frozen fish steaks
raw peeled and deveined shrimp
cooked crabmeat, legs and claws
fish and shellfish in sauce dinners

CHAPTER 4

A Comprehensive Survey of American Fish and Shellfish

Fish

Salt-water Fish

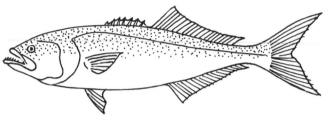

Figure 4.1 Bluefish

Anchovy

The anchovy is a small marine species of the herring family. It has a long snout and a large mouth. It is blue green on top and silvery on the sides and belly. The northern anchovy is usually 5 to 6 inches (12 to 15 cm) long with a maximum length of 9 inches (22 cm), and ranges from Baja, California to Washington. The striped anchovy is abundant from Delaware Bay through the West Indies.

Anchovies are not usually eaten fresh or whole, but they contribute a distinctive rich flavor to a variety of foods when pickled and salted. The fillets are usually cured in salt and olive oil. Anchovy paste is also available commercially. Most of the anchovy production is cured in fillets and canned.

Bluefish

Other name. Blue runner.
Appearance. The bluefish has a stout body with a bluntly pointed snout and sharp canine teeth. The coloration is blue green on the top fading to near silver on the belly. The bluefish is a dogged fighter with an insatiable feeding habit. Due to their exceptional appetites, they are capable of tripling their size in a single year.

Source. New England to the Gulf states.
Availability fresh. From May to November, bluefish are abundant in the northeast; in the winter months, in the Gulf states.
Average weight. Three to six pounds (1.360 to 2.7 kg).
Quality. Bluefish has a dark meat with a delicate flavor. However, the meat is fatty (10 to 14 percent).
Disposition. Bluefish do not freeze well. Commercially, they are sold mostly fresh, in fillets. Poor handling will render the flesh unpalatable, with an oily and strong flavor.

Butterfish

Other names. Dollarfish, harvest fish.
Appearance. The butterfish is a small silvery fish with a very thin, deep body.
Source. It is common on the northeastern coast.
Availability fresh. The fishing season in Chesapeake Bay runs from May through November. Butterfish are abundant in the coastal waters of

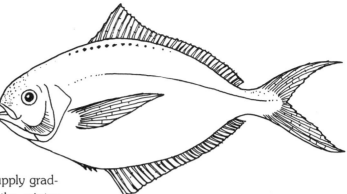

Figure 4.2 Butterfish

New England during summer. The supply gradually disappears in November and the winter months.

Trade size. Small—5 or less to a pound

Mixed—5 to a pound and over

Large—¾ pound (340 g) and over

Quality. A fatty, fine flavored fish of excellent food value. Butterfish is one of the best pan fish found on the Atlantic coast.

Disposition. Fresh, frozen, and smoked.

Cod

Other names. Atlantic cod, codfish.

Appearance. The Atlantic cod, a member of a large family of marine fish, is considered one of the most abundant fish in the United States. The cod is a heavy-bodied fish with three dorsal fins and a broad, nearly square tail. Cod vary in color from shades of gray to green, brown, or reddish tints, depending on the background (they are capable of changing color to match their surroundings). The back and sides are covered with roundish brown or red spots and there is a distinct, lighter colored lateral line.

Cod are differentiated from haddock by this pale lateral line, and from pollock by the large barbel and the projected upper jaw.

Source. Cod range in Atlantic waters from Newfoundland to New England, the chief ports being Boston, New Bedford, Gloucester, and Provincetown, Massachusetts, and Portland, Maine.

Availability fresh. Fishing for cod is a year-round industry. However, cod are most abundant from March to September. The price is usually higher from October to March.

Average weight. Ten pounds (4.5 kg). The best size is 6 to 8 pounds (2.7 to 3.6 kg).

Trade size. Scrod—1½ to 2½ pounds (680 g to 1.130 kg)

Market—2½ to 8 pounds (1.130 kg to 3.6 kg)

Large—8 to 20 pounds (3.6 kg to 9 kg)

Extra large—over 20 pounds (9 kg)

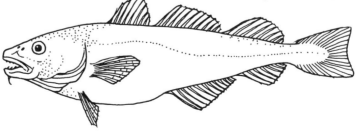

Figure 4.3 Codfish

To conserve the "beef of the sea," an international law is now in effect banning the use of otter trawl nets with a mesh size smaller than 4½ inches (11.25 cm). The law affects both the cod and haddock fisheries. Another step that is certain to help the repopulation of Atlantic cod is the 200-mile (320-km) limit law extending American fishing rights.

In 1976, the annual landing of Atlantic cod was over 55 million pounds; the Pacific cod recorded a harvest of 12 million pounds.

Quality. Cod is an excellent food fish with flaky, lean (0.5 percent fat) white meat.

Disposition. Fresh and frozen
>Fillets—raw and breaded (raw and cooked)
>Steaks
>Specialties—breaded (raw and cooked) cakes and patties; croquettes; fish and chips; in sauce
>Canned—cakes, flaked and salted
>Salted
>Smoked
>Sun-dried (in hot sauce)
>Lutefisk (alkaline-cured fish)

Scrod

In New England, fish called scrod may be immature cod or haddock weighing 1½ to 2½ pounds (680 g to 1.140 kg). Sometimes the term is applied to cusk of about the same weight, or to pollock weighing 1½ to 4 pounds (680 g to 1.8 kg). When fishermen use the word, they are usually referring to gutted small haddock.

Pacific Cod

Other names. Cod, sea bass, true cod, gray cod.
Appearance. The Pacific cod is a close relative of the Atlantic cod, and one of the 59 members of the *Gadidae* family of cod species. Several Pacific fish called cod are not true cod but only related. These are rockfish (rock cod), greenlings (tommy cod), sablefish (black cod), and lingcod (cultus cod). The practice of placing cod in the common names of many species serves to confuse the different species and families.

The presence of three, soft-rayed, well-separated dorsal fins, the single barbel on the lower jaw, and two anal fins distinguish the Pacific cod from its relatives. These fish range in color from brown to gray, fading to white to grayish white on the sides.
Source. From California to northern Alaska.
Average weight. From 5 to 10 pounds (2.3 to 4.5 kg).
Quality. The Pacific cod has a mild flavor with very soft, white meat that flakes apart easily when cooked. The meat is marketed as fresh and frozen fillets, and frozen portions and sticks. Some of the catch is also marketed as whole fresh fish or smoked, dried fillets. Fresh Pacific cod is available all year in the markets of the Northwest, where it is labeled as true cod to distinguish it from other fish that have cod in their names.

Salted Cod

The amount of salt used to cure cod varies greatly with the weather conditions, the humidity, the time of year, and the type of curing or brine. The results range from a lightly salted, moist cod to a heavily cured, dry fish. Excessively cured cod has little moisture and requires a longer time to soak. The flavor, therefore, is often impaired.

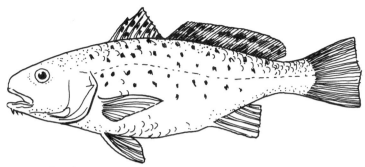

Croaker

Other names. Atlantic croaker, crocus, hard head, king billy.

Appearance. A member of the drum family, the croaker is a small pan fish characterized by a lateral line that extends onto the caudal fin, barbels on the lower jaw, and a concave tail. The upper part of the body is covered with many small dark specks.

Source. Available from Texas to Massachusetts, but abundant in Virginia, North Carolina, New Jersey, and Chesapeake Bay.

Availability fresh. Although available all year, the biggest landings occur from March to October.

Average weight. The market size is between ½ to 2 pounds (225 to 900 g).

Trade size. (round)

       Pins—under ½ pound (225 g)
       Small—½ to ¾ pound (225 to 340 g)
       Medium—¾ to 1½ pounds (340 to 680 g)
       Large—1½ pound and up (680 g and up)

Quality. A good quality, lean pan fish, ideal for frying and broiling. It has a high food value, containing 17 percent protein in a 3-ounce (85 g)

Figure 4.4 Croaker

serving, which is nearly 25 percent of the recommended daily amount for adults. It is also exceptionally high in potassium, a vital trace element.

Disposition. The moderately priced croaker is available fresh or frozen, and pan ready. A new product, called "flaked croaker," comes in 3 or 4 ounce (85 to 110 g) raw and precooked breaded portions. It is being readily accepted by the American consumer.

Cusk

Other names. Tusk, torsk.

Appearance. The cusk is a cold-water ground fish with an elongated body, a small barbel on the lower jaw, one long dorsal fin, and a rounded tail. The coloration varies from greenish brown to pale yellow fading to a cream color on the ventral side.

Source. Mostly New England states, rarely as far as New Jersey.

Availability fresh. February to July.

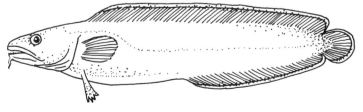

Figure 4.5 Cusk

Average weight. Cusk can reach 30 pounds (13.5 kg). The best weight is 5 to 10 pounds (2.270 to 4.5 kg).

Trade size. (drawn weight)

       Scrod—1½ to 3 pounds (680g to 1.360 kg)

       Medium—3 to 7 pounds (1.360 to 3.170 kg)

       Large—7 to 15 pounds (3.170 to 6.8 kg)

       Jumbo—15 pounds (6.8 kg) and up

Quality. The cusk, marketed under the name deep sea whitefish, has a soft, white delicate lean flesh.

Disposition. Fillets, fresh and frozen.

Dolphin

Other names. Dorado, mahimahi.

Appearance. This is not the friendly mammal we all know, but the brilliant color-changing, rainbowlike fish called mahimahi in Hawaii. Two commonly known relatives are the pompano dolphin, which reaches a length of 2 feet (60 cm) and a weight of 5 pounds (2.270 kg), and the slender dorado, which can exceed 50 pounds (22.650 kg), although most catches are between 5 to 15 pounds (2.70 to 6.8 kg).

Source. Dolphins are found in areas influenced by the warm waters of the Gulf Stream. They have been caught as far north as Nova Scotia, but only rarely. Commercial landings of dolphin center around Hawaii, where an average of 100,000 to 120,000 pounds are caught each year.

Quality. Dolphin is a gourmet's delight, probably among the top ten of the best fin fishes. On most restaurant menus, the fish is sold under the Hawaiian name, mahimahi.

Disposition. Dolphin is usually marketed fresh, in fillets.

Eel

Other names. American eel, silver eel.

Appearance. The American eel is a catadromous fish, spending the major part of its life in fresh water and returning to sea to spawn. It is closely related to the European eel, *Anguilla Vulgaris*.

The eel is elongated, almost snakelike in appearance. The dorsal fin originates far behind the pectorals, a characteristic that distinguishes it from the conger eel on which the dorsal fin originates slightly behind the tip of the pectorals. The eel has a pointed snout and a large mouth. Its color varies with the habitat and the spawning season, ranging from gray to olive to black.

The reproduction of the American eel and the European eel has remained a mystery for many

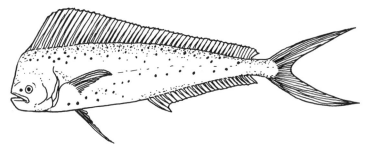

Figure 4.6   Dolphin

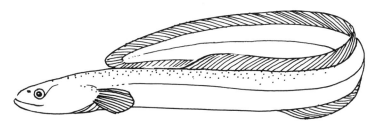

Figure 4.7   Eel

years. It is now known that adult eels travel from estuaries, tidal marshes, rivers, and lakes to spawn thousands of miles away, south of Bermuda and a thousand miles east of Florida and the Bahamas. Eels die after their single spawning. The larvae return to the coastal waters after a journey lasting one year or more.

Quality. The eel is not America's favorite food fish. But in Europe and Japan, the demand for eels exceeds the supply. Eel farming is a well-organized business in Japan. In the United States, there is a market for eel around the Christmas holidays, particularly among families of European origin.

Availability fresh. All year, but abundant during November and December.

Source. The principal points are the St. Lawrence River in Canada, Cape Charles, Virginia, and Chesapeake Bay. Eels are shipped live by aerated trucks to major fish markets on the East coast, Chicago, and New York.

Disposition. Dressed frozen and smoked.

How to Skin an Eel   Eel should be skinned before cooking. To remove the skin, tie a string around the head and secure the string to a nail. Cut the skin around just below the head. Peel back the skin, using a pair of pliers if necessary. In a quick motion, tear off the skin the entire length of the eel. Remove the head, cut the fish open, and clean. Remove the fins with a pair of scissors.

Depending on the recipe, fillet the eel or cut into sections.

Flounder

Flounder, an important year-round food fish, is one of a large variety of flatfish. They are abundant in Atlantic, Gulf, and Pacific coastal waters. The most common flounder are:

blackback or winter flounder
fluke or summer flounder
yellowtail flounder
dab of plaice
starry flounder

Most food operators list the above species under the general term *fillet of sole;* establishments of good reputation, however, often specify the type of flounder served on the menu since the taste, texture, and flavor vary.

The Title 50 Code of Federal Regulations lists the following species for the United States Standards for grades of frozen flounder: blackback, yellowtail, dab or plaice, starry flounder, and fluke. For more details on United States Standards for grades of frozen flounder, see page 20.

In general, the fluke is considered one of the finest table fishes. The winter flounder or blackback is also an excellently flavored fish, with thick fillets. The yellowtail, slimmer than the winter flounder, is marketed in large quantities and has a good flavor. The fillets are quite thin and the meat is flaky. The dab, once considered unpopular and undesirable, has a sweet flesh with a distinctive flavor and texture. It has thick layers of flesh on both upper and lower sides.

Blackback

Other name. Winter flounder.
Appearance. This species, best known to anglers, is a righteye fish. It has a small mouth like the yellowtail flounder, but differs in its straight lateral line with no arch over the pectoral fin, its thicker body, and widely spaced eyes.
Source. Blackback occur from Labrador to Georgia, commonly from the Gulf of St. Lawrence to Chesapeake Bay. The centers of abundance include the coastal waters of Massachusetts, Rhode Island, Connecticut, New York, and New Jersey.
Availability fresh. During the fall and winter months.

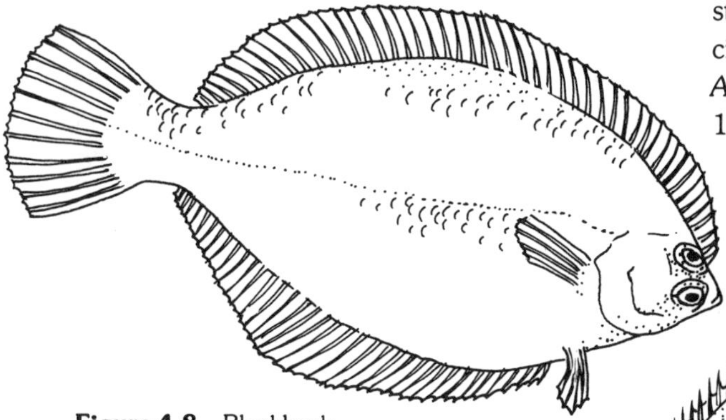

Figure 4.8   Blackback

Average weight. Usually 1 to 2 pounds (450 to 900 g), sometimes reaching 5 pounds (2.270 kg).
Trade size.   (round)
> Small—under ¾ pounds (under 340 g)
> Medium—¾ to 1½ pounds (340 to 680 g)
> Large—1½ pounds (680 g) and up

Quality. Winter flounder is an excellent table fish. It has white, firm, delicately flavored meat.

Fluke

Other name. Summer flounder.
Appearance. The fluke is considered one of the finest table fish. It is easily recognized by its large mouth and sharp teeth, and the eyes on the colored left side. The fluke usually has ocellated spots on its body.
Source. Ranges from Maine to South Carolina, but mainly off New England.
Availability fresh. Throughout the year. In some states, the angler's catch surpasses the commercial catch.
Average weight. Usually 2 to 4 pounds (900 g to 1.8 kg).

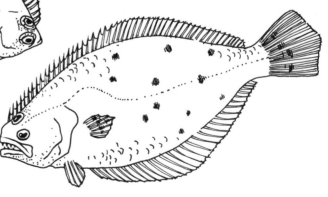

Figure 4.9   Fluke

Trade size. (round)

> Medium—1½ to 2 pounds (680 to 900 g)
>
> Large—2 to 4 pounds (900 g to 1.8 kg)
>
> Jumbo—4 pounds (1.8 kg) and up

Quality. One of the finest table fish, with lean white meat. Although the summer flounder is a fast grower (11 inches, 27.5 cm, when a year old), the commercial harvest has declined markedly. Fishermen have noticed a decrease in the size of the flounder and in their catches, a sign of a high fishing rate.

Yellowtail Flounder

Other name. Rusty dab.

Appearance. This righteyed species is characterized by its small mouth, pointed snout, and thin body, which has a definite arch in the lateral line over the pectoral fin. The body shape is nearly oval. Its color varies from grayish olive green to reddish brown, with large irregular rusty spots. The tail fin is yellow, hence its name.

Source. The species is found from Labrador to Virginia.

Availability fresh. Abundant from June to December.

Average weight. Usually 1 pound, (450 g); seldom exceeds 2 pounds (900 g).

Trade size. (round)

> Small—under 1 pound (450 g)
>
> Large—1 pound (450 g) and over

Quality. This is an excellent very lean food fish.

American Plaice

Other names. Dab, sanddab.

Appearance. This species is distinct from the European plaice. The American plaice is plain reddish to gray brown in color, lacking the red spotting of the common European plaice.

Source. The species is abundant on both sides of the Atlantic, occurring from Cape Cod to the Grand Banks.

Average weight. Ranges from 2 to 3 pounds (907 g to 1.350 kg).

Trade size. (round)

> Small—under 2 pounds (900 g)
>
> Large—2 pounds (907 g) and up

Quality. This species, once neglected, is an excellent pan fish. It has a thick layer of flesh, free from bones, on both the upper and lower sides. The meat is sweet and lean with a distinctive flavor and texture.

Figure 4.10   Yellowtail Flounder   **Figure 4.11**   American Plaice

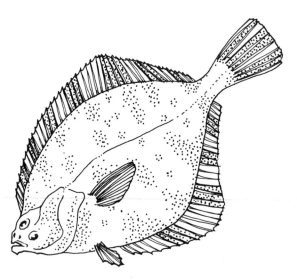

Figure 4.12   Starry Flounder

Starry Flounder

Appearance. This species is easily recognized by the alternating pattern of orange white and dark bars on the fins. The fish has a small mouth and a nearly straight lateral line. Although a lefteyed form, it may have the eyes on the right side. The body is rough, covered with spinous plates on the eyed side. It is dark brown to black with mottlings on the eyed side.
Source. Central California to Alaska.
Average weight. Usually 5 to 10 pounds (2.270 to 5.4 kg), reaching a weight of 20 pounds (10.8 kg).
Quality. Excellent food fish.
Disposition. Fresh and frozen
       Fillets—raw or breaded (raw and cooked)
       Steaks, breaded raw
       Specialties—breaded (raw and cooked), stuffed, cooked
       Salted
       Other—au gratin, in sauces

Other Flatfish of Commercial Importance

On the Pacific coast, the California halibut and the arrowtooth halibut are both available commercially. The California halibut weighs an average of 4 to 10 pounds (1.8 to 4.5 kg) and is sold mostly in fresh boneless fillets.

The arrowtooth halibut occurs in California and Alaska. It is sometimes marketed as turbot or French sole, and is sold mostly whole, frozen and gutted.

The imported turbot, closely related to the brill (known in French as *barbue*), is a flatfish at least as superior as the English Dover sole. These two fish are not related to the Pacific "turbots" that are inferior in quality. On the United States market, turbot is available frozen whole or in quartered fillets and steaks.

Grouper

Other name. Red grouper.
Other varieties. Black grouper
             Yellow fin grouper
             Nassau grouper
             Gag
All are marketed without distinction as to species.
Appearance. The red grouper is one of the most common species in southern Florida and the tropical American Atlantic. It has dark bars on its head and body, and sometimes scattered spots. The grouper is a member of the sea bass family.
Source. Abundant in Florida and the Gulf states.
Availability fresh. April to December.
Average weight. Ranges from 4 to 6 pounds (1.8 to 2.7 kg). In the Gulf states markets, 5 to 15 pounds (2.270 to 6.8 kg).

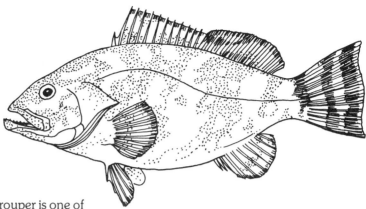

Figure 4.13   Red Grouper

Quality. Excellent lean fish. Red grouper is one of the most important commercial groupers in the United States.

Disposition. Fresh and frozen

       Fillets—raw and breaded raw

       Steaks—raw

       Specialties—fingers, breaded raw

Haddock

Haddock, which was once considered junk fish when other species of fish were abundant, increased in popularity between 1925 and 1930, when an estimated 1 billion pounds were harvested in the United States. The smallest catch occurred in 1972 (11.8 million pounds). Since Canada and Russia accounted for over 25 percent of previous harvests in Georges Bank, it is certain that United States landings will now increase as a result of the 200-mile (320-km) extension of American fishing rights.

Appearance. The haddock is closely related to the cod, and belongs to the same family of fish as the pollock and hake. The haddock is usually smaller than the cod, with a dark lateral line and a black patch on the shoulder known as the "Devil's thumb print" or "St. Peter's mark."

Source. Haddock are found only in the North Atlantic. They range principally from Cape Cod to Georges Bank and the Great Banks off Newfoundland.

Availability fresh. All year, but abundant during the months of March and April with supply falling off in November. The smaller supplies during the winter months usually cause a rise in price.

Average weight. Ranges from 3 to 4 pounds (1.360 to 1.8 kg).

Trade size. Scrod—1½ to 2½ pounds (680 g to 1.140 kg)

       Large—2½ pounds (1.140 kg) and up

Trawl nets with a mesh size smaller than 4½ inches (10.25 cm) have been banned in a conservation measure designed to protect young fish not yet of marketable size. As a result, snapper haddock and small scrod are not available.

Quality. Very lean white meat of excellent quality.

Disposition. Fresh and frozen

       Fillets—raw or breaded (raw and cooked)

       Specialities—au gratin, dinners, patties, et cetera

       Smoked

       Canned (finnan haddies)

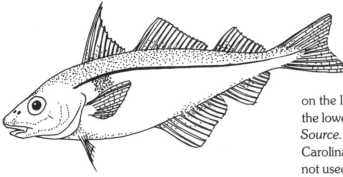

Figure 4.14   Haddock

Finnan Haddie

The smoked haddock, known as finnan haddie, became a popular item accidentally when a fire in a fish market in Findon, Scotland, smoked some fillets of haddock—hence the name finnan haddie. Today, one must be cautious when buying smoked haddock as the substitution of other fish and the addition of coloring and unnecessary preservatives result in poor quality smoked fish.

Hake

Other names. Ling, Boston hake, white hake, black hake, mud hake, king hake. Commercially, four species are recognized (but not separated) on the market: squirrel, white, long finned, and spotted. Squirrel hake and white hake make up most of the catch.

   Like many ground fish, hake is sometimes substituted for haddock or even cod, especially when salted.

Appearance. The hake is a member of a large family of marine ground fish. It has two dorsal fins and one long anal fin. Most species have one elongated, filamentlike ray on the first dorsal fin, except for the king hake (also known as spotted hake). Like the Atlantic cod, the hake has a barbel

on the lower jaw; the upper jaw projects beyond the lower.

Source. From the Gulf of St. Lawrence to North Carolina. Also abundant on the Pacific coast, but not used much as food fish.

Availability fresh. June, with peak harvest in August and September.

Average weight. Ranges from 1 to 8 pounds (450 g to 3.6 kg).

Trade size. Scrod or red hake—½ to 2 pounds (225 to 907 g) White hake (small—2 to 6 pounds (907 g to 2.7 kg); (large—6 pounds (2.7 kg) and over).

Quality. A white meat of good quality. The flesh is lean and softens quickly if not strictly fresh.

Disposition. Fresh and frozen fillets and steaks
           Salted
           Smoked

Halibut

Other names. Atlantic or eastern halibut, North Pacific halibut.

Appearance. The halibut, the largest member of the flatfish family, has a large mouth and sharp curved teeth. The eyes are on the right side of the head. The tail is concave; the anal fin is shorter than the dorsal and starts at the pectoral fin. The English thought highly of halibut and served it on holy days, calling it "holy-day-butte" (*butte* was the Middle English word for flatfish or flounder). Over the years, holy-butte evolved into halibut.

Source. East and west coasts of the United States. Atlantic or eastern halibut are caught off the coast of New England. North Pacific halibut are taken off Alaska and the shores of Washington.

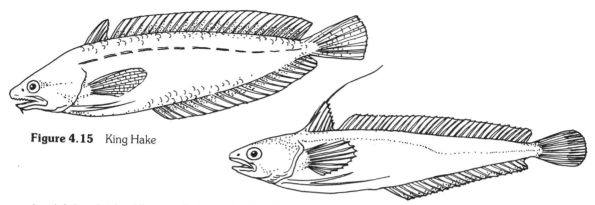

Figure 4.15   King Hake

Figure 4.16   Squirrel Hake

Availability fresh. All year, but most abundant from March to August.

Average weight. Ranges from 10 to 60 pounds (4.5 to 27.2 kg). Some specimens weigh from 150 to 200 pounds (68 to 90 kg) or more.

Trade size. (eastern, drawn)

    Snapper—under 7 pounds (3 kg)

    Chicken—7 to 12 pounds (3 to 5.4 kg)

      Medium—12 to 60 pounds (5.4 to 27.2 kg)

      Large—60 to 125 pounds (27.2 to 56.6 kg)

Whale—125 pounds (56.6 kg) and over

(western, drawn)

Chicken—5 to 10 pounds (2.27 to 4.5 kg)

    Medium—10 to 60 pounds (4.5 to 27.2 kg)

    Large—60 to 80 pounds (27.2 to 36.2 kg)

Whale—80 pounds (36.2 kg) and over

Quality. Halibut is an excellent source of high-quality protein and minerals, but low in sodium, fat, and calories. The true halibut, which has a white, tender flesh with a mild flavor, should not be confused with other species of flatfish that are sometimes sold as halibut.

Disposition. Fresh and frozen

    Fillets—raw and breaded (raw and cooked)

    Steaks, raw

    Cheeks

    Specialties—au gratin, patties, and in sauce

Preparation. Halibut can be cooked in a variety of recipes (see Sole). Halibut steaks are broiled, poached, or grilled, and served with a hot sauce.

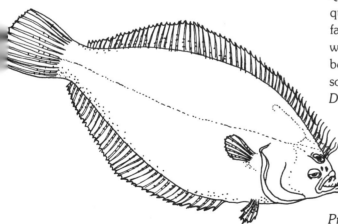

Figure 4.17   Halibut

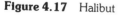

Herring

Herring, other than those canned for sardines, have never been consumed to any extent in the United States. The New England Fisheries Development Program, prepared by the New England Fisheries Steering Committee, states that a major problem faced by the industry has been the holding quality of the fish, which has made it impossible for our fleets to fish more than 4 to 5 hours from port. The New England Program addressed this problem by developing, testing, and demonstrating the technology needed to assure quality fish when landed. As a result of these program efforts, herring has gained in popularity in the United States.

A sex sorter!   Herring roe is highly marketable. During the roe-bearing season, a large amount of herring are "firmed" in brine (the roe must be firmed before removal from the female). Since the firming process renders the flesh inedible, males were wasted. Now a sex sorter has come to the rescue of the fishing industry. This unique machine separates roe-bearing females from males; as a result, 50 percent more fish are being used as fresh fillets for the market instead of waste or fertilizer.

The machine, designed by Canadian engineers, has a separation efficiency of 95 percent and a production rate of 2 tons (1.8 metric tons) per hour. An added advantage is that when the roe-bearing season is over, the sex sorter can be used as an automatic feeder for filleting, or for scaling such small fish as smelt, anchovy, and perch. It is estimated that a $20 million industry would exist for herring if they were all processed for human consumption.

Herring are processed in many forms. Several European countries export various types of pre-

served, pickled, smoked, or cured herring that are available at consumer levels.

Bismarck herring. Herring fillets cured in vinegar, salt, onions, and sugar.

Rollmops. Fillets of Bismarck herring wrapped around pickle slices and secured with wooden picks. They are usually preserved in vinegar and spices.

Schmaltz herring. A fat herring that is skinned, cut into sections, pickled, and preserved in a brine.

Soused herring. A British term to describe herring pickled in vinegar, white wine, and spices.

Matjes herring. A juvenile herring, bigger than the sardine, that is skinned, filleted, and cured in sugar, salt, vinegar, and spices. This is a European specialty, mainly Dutch.

Kipper. A butterflied herring, brined and cold smoked. Marketed fresh, frozen, or canned. The fish, gold in color, is usually artificially colored.

Other forms of herring are available commercially, such as herring in sour cream, hard salt herring, marinated herring roe, and pickled herring.

Lingcod

Other names. Blue cod, buffalo cod, cultus cod.

Appearance. As the Indian name *cultus* (meaning "false") indicates, lingcod is not a true cod but one of a number of species commonly called greenlings. For such a highly prized fish, its appearance is both deceiving and detracting. Its highly variable coloration is closely associated with its habitat. Basically, lingcod has subdued coloration ranging from a mottled brown to bluish green with cream colored undersides. The spots or blotches are brown, green, or tan, outlined in orange or light blue. The lingcod has a large protruding mouth armed with large caninelike teeth.

Source. Lingcod range from Baja, California, to

northwest Alaska, but are most abundant in the cold waters of the north.

Availability fresh. All year. In California, best from April to October; farther north, the fishing is best from October to May.

Average weight. Ranges from 5 to 20 pounds (2.270 to 9.10 kg). Some fish can weigh up to 40 pounds (18 kg).

Quality. Fresh lingcod is available along the Pacific coast, but sold frozen in other areas of the country. It is a fine eating fresh fish and is marketed dressed, in fillets, and in steaks. Smoked lingcod is another delicacy found in the markets.

The uninitiated sometimes avoid lingcod due to the unusual green or bluish green color of the flesh. The color is not harmful and disappears when cooked, producing a delicate, white, tender flesh very low in fat. Some of the preferred methods of preparation for lingcod fillets and steaks are broiling, butter sauteing, and poaching. Whole fish can be baked or poached. For broiling, small fish can be split down the middle and the backbone removed. An increasingly popular method of preparing lingcod is to pan- or deep-fat-fry for "fish and chips." Most of the lingcod produced now goes into the rapidly expanding commercial fish and chips market.

Mackerel

Mackerel are commercially important in the United States (landings totalled 67.5 million pounds in 1976). The Atlantic mackerel is superior in quality, followed in order by the Spanish, king, Pacific, and Pacific Jack mackerel, which is lowest in quality and sells rather cheaply in cans.

Spanish Mackerel

Appearance. Spanish mackerel is a member of a large family including tuna and other mackerel. They are beautifully colored fish. Their slender graceful bodies are dark blue on the upper part, paling to almost silver on the belly. Many small yellowish or olive oval spots occur above and below the wavy lateral line.

Source. Spanish mackerel are found from Massachusetts to the Gulf coast, and as far as Brazil. They are abundant from Florida to Chesapeake Bay. On the Pacific coast, they range from San Diego, California, to the Galapagos Islands.

Availability fresh. In New York, from November to May; in southern Atlantic states, from June to September; and in the Gulf states, during the winter months.

Average weight. From 1½ to 4 pounds (680 g to 1.8 kg). The best size is 1½ to 2 pounds (680 to 900 g).

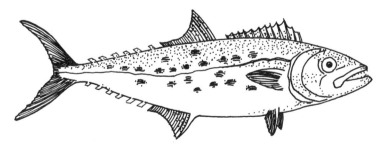

Figure 4.18   Spanish Mackerel

Trade size. Small—½ to 1 pound (225 to 450 g)
Large—1½ to 3 pounds (675 to 1.360 g)

Quality. A fatty fish with excellent flavor. The flesh is firm and much lighter than the dark meat of the Boston mackerel.

Atlantic Mackerel

Other name. Boston mackerel.

Appearance. The Atlantic Mackerel have smooth, tapering heads, streamlined bodies, and brilliant coloration. A distinguishing characteristic is the series of 23 to 33 wavy dark bands above the lateral line. There are also 4 to 6 finlets behind the dorsal and anal fins.

Source. The Atlantic mackerel is an important commercial fish on the Atlantic coast. Most mackerel fishing is done off New England but some occurs in the Middle Atlantic region. Massachusetts ports receive most of the commercial catch.

Availability fresh. The run is from April to early December, with heaviest landings in midsummer. Spawning season occurs during May and June, at which time the flesh may not be as good. Mackerel caught in gill nets are "drowned"—they have a mark around the neck, are considered inferior, and sell for less.

Average weight. From ½ to 2½ pounds (225 g to 1.140 kg).

Trade size. Small or spike—under ½ pound (225 g) round
Tinker—½ to 1 pound (225 to 450 g)
Medium—1 to 2½ pounds (450 g to 1.140 kg)
Large—2½ pounds (1.140 kg) and over

Quality. A fatty fish (7 percent polyunsaturated fat) with dark meat high in protein, vitamins, and minerals. Best when consumed fresh.

King Mackerel

Other name. Kingfish.

Appearance. The king mackerel lacks the yellow spotting of the Spanish mackerel, but has a similar shape with fewer spines on the first dorsal fin. Kingfish range from 5 to 25 pounds (2.270 to 11.30 kg) and over.

Source. Florida to Massachusetts. The largest catch occurs in Florida and the other Gulf states.

Availability fresh. November to March.

Trade size. Small—under 5 pounds (2.270 kg)
Medium—5 to 8 pounds (2.270 to 3.6 kg)
Large—8 to 12 pounds (3.6 to 5.4 kg)
Jumbo—12 pounds (5.4 kg) and up

Quality. A fatty fish with fine flesh. It has an excellent flavor like the smaller Spanish mackerel.

Disposition. Fillets and steaks, frozen
Canned, paste and spreads
Smoked

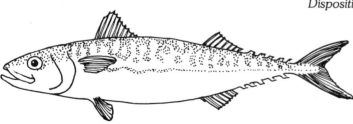

Figure 4.19 Atlantic Mackerel

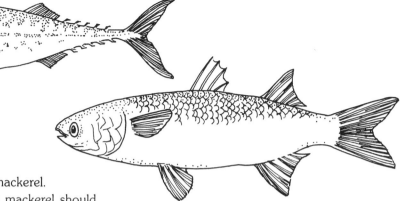

Figure 4.20   Pacific Mackerel

Pacific Jack Mackerel

Other name. California horse mackerel.

Appearance. The Pacific Jack mackerel should not be confused with the Pacific mackerel. It has no detached finlets behind the dorsal and anal fins. The Pacific mackerel resembles species of mackerel found in American Atlantic waters. The curved and the straight laterals of the Pacific Jack mackerel have enlarged scutes.

Source. From Baja, California, to southern Alaska. It is commercially important with landings of 38.5 million pounds in 1976.

Availability fresh. This species of fish is mostly canned. Only a small percentage is sold fresh.

Average size. From 1 to 2½ pounds (450 g to 1.140 kg).

Quality. The Pacific Jack mackerel lacks the quality of other members of the mackerel family. Most of the harvest is canned or smoked.

Mullet

Other names. Striped mullet, Florida mullet, black mullet.

Appearance. These versatile fish, sometimes called jumping mullet, are moderately sized. The bodies are elongated and rather stout. They have a dark bluish color on the top and silvery sides. The head and mouth are small. Mullet have large scales with dark centers that give an appearance of dark horizontal stripes.

Source. Mullet are the most important food fish in

Figure 4.21   Mullet

the South Atlantic and Gulf states, with an annual harvest of 30.5 million pounds. Florida produces about 75 percent of the mullet caught in the United States. They also occur in southern California.

Availability fresh. In the Gulf states, all year; abundant from April to November, with the heaviest run usually in September.

Average weight. From 2 to 3 pounds (900 g to 1.360 kg), occasionally up to 6 pounds (2.7 kg).

Trade size. Small—1 to 2 pounds (450 to 900 g)
  Medium—2 to 3 pounds (900 g to 1.360 kg)
  Large—3 pounds (1.360 kg) and over

Quality. This is the favorite fish of commercial fishermen. The tender, firm-textured flesh has a mild nutlike flavor. The iodine content of mullet is hundreds of times higher than that of the best grade beef. It is also rich in minerals. Fatter mullet are smoked; lean mullet are marketed fresh, whole or in fillets.

Disposition. Fresh and frozen
  Roe
  Fillets
  Split for curing
  Smoked

Ocean Perch

Other names. Atlantic coast: redfish, rosefish, deep sea perch, red perch. Pacific coast: longjaw rockfish.

Appearance. Ocean perch range in color from orange to flame red, occasionally grayish or brownish red, with a lighter red on the belly. The eyes are large and black, contrasting with the brightly colored body. The ocean perch has spiny projections on the sides of the large head as well as on the back fin. The Pacific coast rockfish numbers about 50 varieties, very similar in appearance to their relatives in the Atlantic but with numerous color variations.

Source. Ocean perch are found in the deep offshore waters of the Atlantic from southern Labrador to the Gulf of Maine. In the Pacific, they range from the Bering Sea to southern California.

Availability fresh. Almost the entire catch is filleted and frozen. Ocean perch is sometimes available fresh during the peak season of May, June, and July.

Average weight. From ½ to 2 pounds (225 to 900 g). Specimens over 5 pounds (2.270 kg) have a coarse texture and are unpalatable.

Trade size. Mixed, round—½ to 3 pounds (225 g to 1.360 kg).

Quality. Excellent food fish, with firm, lean, white flaky flesh.

Pollock

Other names. American pollock, Boston bluefish.

Appearance. Pollock are ground fish related to the cod and the haddock. The white lean flesh of pollock is in class with the hake and the cusk. Pollock is used as a substitute for cod and haddock in salting.

The head of the pollock is more pointed than the haddock's, the lower jaw projects, and the white lateral line is never black. Pollock usually have a deep olive or brownish green color above, paling to yellowish or smoky gray on the sides, and to silvery gray on the belly.

Source. American pollock range in cold Atlantic waters from Nova Scotia to Virginia.

Availability fresh. About 80 percent of the annual pollock landing occurs during October, November, and December.

Average weight. From 4 to 12 pounds (1.8 to 5.4 kg).

Trade size. Scrod—1½ to 4 pounds (680 g to 1.8 kg).

Quality. A lean fish with a good texture when fresh. However, the flesh softens quickly and becomes fibrous. The fish rates high nutritionally with easily assimilated protein, vitamins, and minerals. Pollock fillets hold up well under freezing.

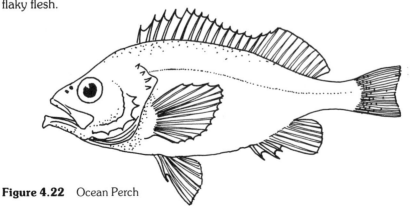

Figure 4.22   Ocean Perch

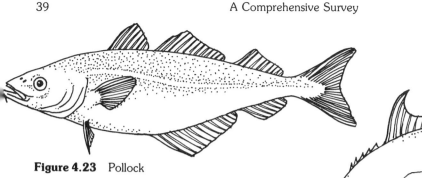

Figure 4.23　Pollock

Pompano

Other names. Cobblerfish, butterfish, palmenta.

Appearance. The Florida pompano is the only commercially important species. It is a thin, deep-bodied fish with a deeply forked caudal tail and dorsal fins. It has a silvery body, shading to metallic blue above and to golden yellow ventrally. Some experts contend that the Florida pompano is a member of the butterfish family rather than the Pacific or the California pompano family.

Source. Commercial landings of Florida pompano occur from Virginia to Texas, but most of the United States catch is from Florida waters.

Availability fresh. Pompano are caught all year round but major fishing occurs in March, April, and May.

Average weight. Ranges from 1½ to 4 pounds (680 g to 1.8 kg).

Trade size. Gulf states market (round): ½ to 4 pounds (225 g to 1.8 kg).

　New York market (round):

　　Small—under ¾ pound (under 340 g)

　　Medium—¾ to 1¼ pounds (340 to 565 g)

　　Large—1½ to 3 pounds (680 g to 1.360 kg)

Quality. Florida pompano is incomparable in taste to any other salt-water or fresh-water fish. Pompano has a firm white flesh and is moderately fat. It is easy to fillet, to handle, and to cook, and it freezes well. It is distributed frozen in fillets.

Figure 4.24　Pompano

Porgy

Other name. Scup.

Appearance. Porgies or scup are members of the vast perch family. The porgy has a body about half as deep as it is long. The color is dull silver and iridescent, darker above than below, and white on the belly. The head is silvery with dusky blotches, and the eyes are rather small. The front dorsal fin points forward. The scales are rather large, thick, and firmly attached, and the tail is crescent shaped.

Source. Porgies or scup range in Atlantic coastal waters between Cape Cod, Massachusetts, and Cape Hatteras, North Carolina.

Availability fresh. The major scup population moves northward in the spring and south in the fall. They are abundant from April to June in New England; as they migrate south in the fall they are caught in the Middle Atlantic states.

Average weight. The average size is 1 to 2 pounds (450 to 900 g).

Trade size. (whole dressed)

　　Small—under ½ pound (225 g)

Medium—½ to 1 pound (225 to 450 g)

Large—1 to 2 pounds (450 to 900 g)

Quality. Porgies or scup are known as the saltwater pan fish and are tender and fine eating.

Disposition. Usually whole dressed; seldom filleted.

Preparation. Porgies are best sauteed meuniere and pan fried. See cooking techniques, chapter 6.

Redfish

Other names. Channel bass, red drum, red bass.

Appearance. The upper half of the body is reddish bronze and the large scales are silvery around the edges and coppery in the center. One or more black dots appear at the upper base of the tail.

Source. Abundant in the South Atlantic and the Gulf states where annual landings average 3 million pounds.

Availability fresh. All year, but abundant from November through February.

Average weight. From 2 to 8 pounds (900 g to 3.6 kg). Above 10 pounds (4.5 kg), the fish loses in quality.

Trade size. (Gulf states market round or drawn)

Rats—1½ to 3 pounds (680 g to 1.3 kg)

Medium—3 to 8 pounds (1.3 to 3.6 kg)

Bulls—8 pounds (3.6 kg) and up

Quality. Excellent eating fish with a light firm meat.

Disposition. Fillets, frozen.

Red Snapper

Other name. Mexican snapper.

Appearance. Bright and gaudy best describes the red snapper's coloration. There is a rosy red hue on the upper part of the body, fading to a pink, then a white stomach. A very distinguishing feature are the eyes, which are always red.

Source. Red snapper range along the Atlantic and Gulf coasts; they are abundant in the Gulf of Mexico.

Availability fresh. All year, but abundant during the summer months.

Average weight. From 2 to 8 pounds (900 g to 3.6 kg). Some species, weighing over 15 to 20 pounds (6.7 to 9 kg), are available and make incomparable buffet displays served cold.

Trade size. (drawn)

Small—under 2 pounds (900 g)

Medium—2 to 5 pounds (900 g to 2.270 kg)

Large—5 pounds (2.270 kg) and over

Quality. Delicate, lean white meat with excellent taste. The red snapper is the most important commercial snapper in the United States. Do not discard the head of the snapper as it makes an unexcelled base or stock for fish fumet, chowder, bouillabaisse, et cetera. The throat flesh is the most delicate and the richest tasting part of the entire fish; it is taken from the ventral side of the head, reaching down to the border of the gill flaps.

At least three distinct families of fish, including the mangrove or gray snapper that takes on a reddish color when dead, have been sold as red snapper. They include the "hambone" or blackfin snapper, silk snapper, red grouper, yellowfin grouper, and black hind.

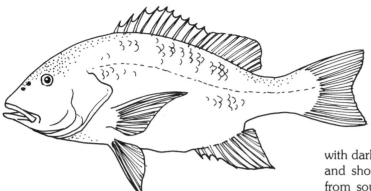

Figure 4.25   Red Snapper

Rockfish

More than 50 varieties of rockfish live along the coasts of Washington, Oregon, and California. Many of them are excellent for eating.

Appearance. The rockfish family, as a group, is distinguished by stout, heavily constructed bodies. The heads are large and broad and usually have prominent ridges and spines. The fins are heavily spined; the scales are large and ridged. Rockfish vary greatly in coloration, ranging from black or drab green to bright orange or crimson. Some varieties have large stripes and others are spotted.

The following rockfish are among the best for eating and the most commercially important.

1. The orange rockfish is a light olive gray color with prominent orange red coloration. This fish is distinguished by three yellow orange stripes radiating from the eyes across the head, and reddish orange streaks along the upper part of the body. It ranges from California to southwestern Alaska and is caught in deep waters. It reaches 30 inches (75 cm) in length.

2. The yellowtail rockfish is not as colorful as some others but is excellent for eating. It is usually grayish brown, mottled and streaked with dark brown, washed with dusky green, and showing yellow on the fins. It ranges from southern California to Vancouver Island, lives moderately deep, and reaches about 26 inches (65 cm) in length.

3. The bocaccio is important commercially in California. It is light green to dark brown in color, flushed with clear pale red, and often has intense black spots on the body. Bocaccio means large mouth and that aptly describes this fish. Its large mouth shows red on the protruding lower jaw with black on the tip. The bocaccio ranges from southern California to Queen Charlotte Sound. It reaches a length of about 34 inches (85 cm). The bocaccio freezes well.

4. The red rockfish is also known as red snapper, red rock, cod, or rasphead rockfish. It is deep red in color, paling to lighter red, and has whitish streaks along the lateral line of the body. In large specimens coming from deep water, the body and head are often blotched and dotted with black spots. It ranges from southern California to the Gulf of Alaska and reaches a length of 3 feet (90 cm). This very popular, good eating fish is often sold as red snapper although it is not related to the true Atlantic red snapper.

Quality and uses of rockfish. Rockfish have firm, white, fine textured flesh and a mild flavor. Most of the commercial catch is filleted and sold fresh. However, some are sold whole dressed, and some are filleted and frozen for shipment to other areas of the United States. Rockfish fillets can be used in the same way as other fish fillets, adapting readily to pan frying, deep-fat frying, broiling, and baking; it can also be used in chowders.

Sablefish

Other name. Black cod.

Appearance. The sablefish is not a true cod but a member of the skilfish family. This family is noted for a lack of ridges or spines on the head. Sablefish are streamlined fish, having rather compressed bodies with wide separation of the dorsal fins, some spines on the fins, and slender tail sections. They are a slatey black to greenish color on the top surface, shading to lighter gray on the belly.

Source. Sablefish range from the Bering Sea to California. Alaskan and Washington waters account for about two thirds of the annual catch of approximately 7 million pounds.

Availability fresh. Almost the entire catch is frozen.

Average weight. Range up to 40 pounds (18 kg) in weight, but the average size is about 8 pounds (3.6 kg).

Quality. Most of the harvest is dressed, frozen, and taken to fish-curing plants for preparation into smoked products. Smoked sablefish have long been considered a delicacy and there is an increasing demand for them. These fish are particularly suited to smoking because of their moderately high fat content and mild, delicate flavor. The smoked product is usually sold in chunks and is available at seafood markets, supermarkets or delicatessens. The fish can be steamed or used in casseroles or salads (*see* smoked haddock, page 31).

Salmon

Man can learn more from salmon than from any other species of fish. The cultural, ecological, and economic importance of this magnificent fish has been demonstrated by several governments, associations, and foundations. The programmed death mechanism of the Pacific Northwest salmon may one day help researchers to understand the aging of man. Several species of Pacific salmon go from a youthful vigor to a quick death after reaching their spawning grounds and depositing their eggs. It is known that a flood of adrenocorticotropic hormone kills the fish. Recent studies on coronary disease in Atlantic salmon have been most rewarding, giving relevant clues to human heart disease.

Many questions remain unanswered about the migration of salmon. The young parrs leave their native rivers, following a migratory route several thousand miles away from home, only to come back two or three years later to their river of birth. For many years, man has polluted and barred the rivers to salmon. Unlike other species of fish, salmon cannot tolerate pollution and seek clean, unpolluted water. The return of Atlantic salmon to several American rivers is a strong indication of environmental improvement. The day may come when the Hudson River will see the return of salmon. Several reports show that sturgeon, bass, shad, and many other fish have returned to the New York river as pollution has been controlled in some areas. As long as demand exceeds the supply, salmon will remain the most prized species of fish on the United States market.

Varieties of salmon in the United States The United States is the only country in the world with six different species of salmon available commercially (five of which are found in the Pacific). The Atlantic salmon is the only species caught in the Atlantic. The Northwest Pacific species occur mainly in Alaska, Washington, Oregon, and California. Some species are also available commercially in British Columbia, Canada.

The common names of salmon are:

1. King salmon in Alaska, chinook in British Columbia
2. Silver salmon or coho
3. Red salmon in Alaska, sockeye in British Columbia
4. Pink salmon or humpback
5. Chum salmon or keta

The six species of salmon are anadromous: the alevins remain in fresh water an average of three to six months, leave for the ocean's fertile feeding grounds, and come back at maturity (after two to seven years depending on the species). Three species are important sport fish: the Atlantic, king, and silver salmon. All the species are caught commercially, the pink yielding the highest catch, followed by the red, the king, the silver, the chum, and the Atlantic (caught mostly in Canada).

Salmon management A campaign against pollution has been undertaken in many states to improve the salmon habitat. Artificial propagation is also an important tool of salmon management. Hatcheries in Oregon and Washington release silver, chinook, and sockeye fingerlings to supplement the natural runs of adult salmon. Even Atlantic salmon are released by hatcheries into lake systems where living conditions are suitable. The mature fish become the so-called landlocked salmon.

There is yet another salmon, the small landlocked sockeye or kokanee found in the large lakes of Idaho. Commercially it is of little value.

Another fish, much like salmon, is the anadromous rainbow trout known as steelhead. It is recognized commercially by the trade. The steelhead occurs mainly in the Pacific Northwest. This excellent fish is included in the trout section.

In New England, cohos are raised in hatcheries and sold commercially when they reach a weight of 2 to 5 pounds (900 g to 2.270 kg) that is ideal for the trade. The fish are sold under the name blueback.

A general review of salmon *Producing states.* Alaska, California, Oregon, and Washington.
Availability fresh. From May to November, depending on species.
Disposition. Canned
              Frozen raw fillets and steaks
              Breaded raw steaks
              Smoked
              Caviar with roe
              Salted
              Pickled
              Mild cured

Frozen specialties: roe in rice wine mash
                        patties
                        steaks, breaded and cooked
Canned specialties: spreads and pastes

Chinook Salmon

Other names. King, blackmouth.
Appearance. The color is greenish on the back with profuse black spotting. The sides and belly are silvery, and the inside of the mouth is black or dusky.
Source. Pacific Northwest (central California to Alaska).
Availability fresh. May to October.

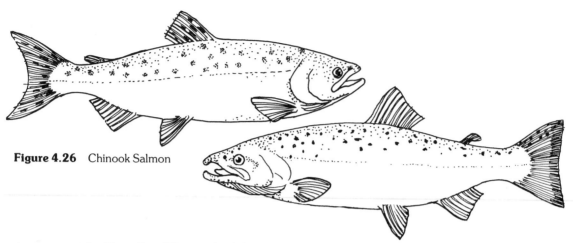

Figure 4.26 Chinook Salmon

Average weight. From 5 to 30 pounds (2.270 to 13.60 kg).

Quality. A fatty fish (10 to 13 percent) with excellent flavor. The color of the flesh ranges from deep salmon to almost white.

Note: The chinook accounts for about 20 percent of the total salmon landings in the Pacific and is one of the most commercially valuable fish in the world.

Coho Salmon

Other name. Silver salmon.

Appearance. The color is metallic blue along the back fading to silvery on the sides and belly. The silver salmon has irregular black spotting along the back. The mouth is black with a white gum or tooth line.

Source. Southern Oregon to southeastern Alaska. Coho salmon planted in the Great Lakes have shown tremendous promise. The silver salmon is also raised in New England hatcheries and sold commercially as blueback.

Availability fresh. June to September.

Average weight. From 3 to 12 pounds (1.360 to 5.4 kg). Hatchery-raised salmon usually weigh 2 to 3 pounds (900 g to 1.360 kg).

Figure 4.27 Coho Salmon

Quality. A fatty fish (10 to 12 percent) of good quality, with light to dark pink flesh.

Note: This species represents about 20 percent of the total salmon landings in the Pacific.

Sockeye Salmon

Other names. Red salmon, blueback.

Appearance. The back is greenish blue with silvery sides and belly. Sockeye salmon have no black spotting.

Source. Columbia River to Bristol Bay, Alaska.

Availability fresh. June and July.

Average weight. From 3 to 12 pounds (1.360 to 5.4 kg).

Quality. A fatty fish with an oil content of 10 to 13 percent. The excellent flavor and deep red meat are particularly suitable when richness and color are important.

Pink Salmon

Other name. Humpback.

Appearance. The pink salmon has a bluish green back and numerous black blotches on its sides. A

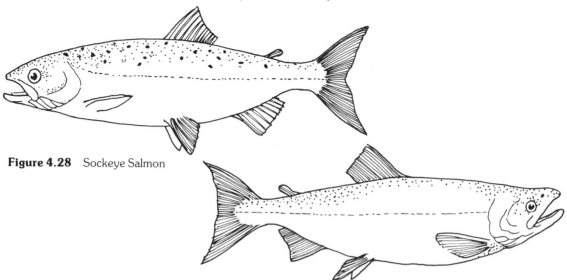

Figure 4.28   Sockeye Salmon

Figure 4.29   Chum Salmon

prominent hump appears on the backs of males at spawning time. This is the smallest of the Pacific salmon.

Source. Southern California to northwestern Alaska.

Availability fresh. June to November. Pink salmon is mostly canned.

Quality. A lean, good flavored fish with soft pink flesh.

Chum Salmon

Other names. Keta, dog.

Appearance. The back is metallic blue with a slight purplish sheen. The belly and sides are silvery. The coloring of the chum salmon is similar to that of the chinook, but it has no spots.

Source. Puget Sound to southern Alaska.

Availability fresh. August to October, but this species is mostly canned.

Average weight. From 5 to 10 pounds (2.270 to 4.5 kg).

Quality. A lean fish with poor flavor. The flesh is yellow to white.

Atlantic Salmon

Truly the king of fish and the fish of kings, the Atlantic salmon is known for its superb quality. It is universally acclaimed as the most famous freshwater gamefish, putting up a savage battle.

Unlike the Pacific salmon, the Atlantic salmon travels up river to spawn several times, returning to the ocean after each spawning. A few large salmon, with four to five years of ocean feeding, have been caught commercially and by sport fishermen.

The many attempts to establish the Atlantic salmon in tributary streams of the Pacific have met with little success. The return of the Atlantic salmon to northeastern tributaries is an indication of good management by the United States Department of Fisheries.

Although commercial landings of Atlantic salmon are negligible in the United States, in Canada in 1975 they represented a total weight of 3.6 million pounds and a total sport-fishing catch of

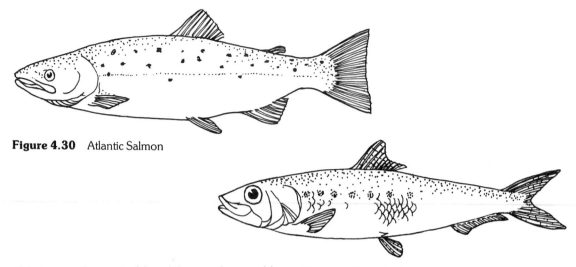

Figure 4.30   Atlantic Salmon

Figure 4.31   Sardine

480 thousand pounds. Most Atlantic salmon sold on the United States market is smoked, and demands a high price.

Sardine

Other names. Maine sardine, Atlantic herring, Pacific Sardine, Norwegian Sardine.

Appearance. Maine sardines are the immature young of the Atlantic herring. They have an elongated body and are greenish blue in color, with a silvery cast on the sides and belly. The tail is deeply forked and has a single dorsal fin directly over the small ventral. The scales are large and loosely attached, a characteristic of all fish belonging to the herring family (including shad).

Source. Atlantic herring are found from Virginia north to Labrador and Greenland. The largest number are caught north of Cape Cod, with the Maine coastline the center of the industry.

The Pacific sardine, also known as the pilchard or Pacific sea herring, occurs off the coast of California to the Bering Sea. Pacific sardines are used for fish meal, oil, or bait; a substantial amount is used as food. The Norwegian sardine is known as the brisling or sprat and is commonly available on the United States market. Sardines are so called because they were first found and caught in great abundance around the island of Sardinia, in the Mediterranean.

Availability fresh. Small quantities of sardines are marketed fresh during the winter months when there is a surplus; the major harvest is canned.

Average size. Sardines reach about 3 to 4 inches (7.5 to 10 cm) in length by the end of a year.

Quality. Sardines are recognized by nutrition experts as excellent sources of high-quality protein, minerals, vitamins, and other nutrients. The following is an excerpt from a book by Dr. Benjamen S. Frank, *No Aging Diet,* that emphasizes the importance of sardines in the diet.

To achieve the most youthful, healthy appearance along with good health itself, we need one to one and a half grams of nucleic acid per day. It does not matter much whether they come from sardines or soybeans, providing we avoid excessive cholesterol and calories. Sardines, for example, are richer in minerals than soybean and my experience shows that they have a remarkable ability to lower cholesterol. Besides they are lower on the food chain than bigger fish like tuna, and are therefore less likely to contain man-made pollutants like insecticides. Big fish eat smaller fish, smaller fish eat still smaller fish, each with some pollutants stored in its body. The smaller the fish the closer it is to the bottom of the food chain where there are less pollutants to eat.

Dr. Frank quickly points out that many people cannot stomach sardines. For those who can, he adds, "Four days a week eat a three ounce, 85 g can of small sardines. One other day a week have salmon, canned or fresh, and still another day have shrimp, lobster, squid, clam, or oysters as a main course. On the remaining day eat any other kind of fish. In other words, eat seafood seven times a week, and especially sardines to grow younger." The no aging diet conscious Americans who want to keep their youthful vigor should rely more than ever on their can openers or keys, and enjoy the unpolluted Atlantic herring, pilchard, brisling, or sprat. Chapter 15 offers a number of ways to enjoy sardines besides the common sandwich.

Sardine Canning. Large quantities of sardines are sold in cans in the United States. They are packed in olive oil, cottonseed oil, or mustard or tomato sauce. Only the very small sardines (2 to 4 inches, 5 to 10 cm) are packed in oil. The Norwegian brisling is the finest quality. Boneless and skinless Portuguese sardines are also favored. Large quantities of Maine sardines are available at lower prices and are packed in soybean or cottonseed oil. Pacific sardines, similar to the Mediterranean pilchard, have not been canned since 1968. The California State Legislature, in an effort to conserve the resource, established an indefinite moratorium on sardine fishing.

Sea Bass

Several species are caught commercially, the most common being the Northeast black sea bass and the Pacific white sea bass. The California black sea bass is also valuable commercially. The larger fish can weigh 700 pounds (317 kg) or more, and are sometimes called jewfish; they do not have the same quality as the Florida species. The California black sea bass has a white, flaky flesh with a fine flavor.

Black Sea Bass

Appearance. The black sea bass has a high back, a flat-topped head, moderately pointed snout, and one sharp spine near the uppermost point of each gill cover. The caudal fin is rounded. Like many fish that inhabit rocky bottoms, the color is variable ranging from smoky gray to dusky brown.

Source. From Cape Cod to North Carolina. Abundant in the Middle Atlantic states.

Availability fresh. All year, but mainly in the spring when the fish move inshore.

Average weight. Black sea bass are not large fish; they average 1½ pounds (680 g). Some specimens reach 5 pounds (2.270 kg).

Trade size. Pins—3 to 4 to a pound
Small—1 to 1½ pounds (450 to 680 g)
Medium—1½ to 2½ pounds (680 g to 1.140 kg)
Large—over 2½ pounds (1.140 kg)

Quality. Excellent for eating; the flesh is firm, white, and delicately flavored. The black sea bass should be handled with great care because of its stiff sharp dorsal spines. Remove the fins before attempting any preparation.

White Sea Bass

This fish is not a true sea bass; it is closely related to the West Coast corvinas and the East Coast weakfishes. It is known as white corvina in Mexico.

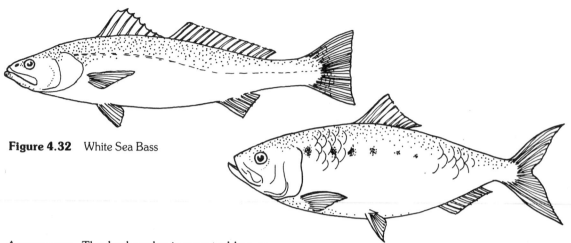

Figure 4.32   White Sea Bass

Figure 4.33   Shad

Appearance. The body color is gray to blue on the back, silvery on the sides, and white on the belly. The dorsal fins are in contact. The lateral line is spotted and slightly curved.

Source. From Alaska to Chile, but uncommon north of San Francisco.

Availability fresh. Abundant from May to September.

Average weight. Can reach 40 pounds (18 kg), but averages 10 pounds (4.5 kg).

Quality. The white sea bass is in a class with the weakfish and the sea trout.

Disposition. Fillets, fresh and frozen
                 Smoked

Sea Trout

Other names. Speckled trout, spotted sea trout.

Appearance. The spotted sea trout is so called because of numerous round black spots on its upper sides, extending on to the dorsal and caudal fins. The body coloration of the sea trout is dark gray above shading to silver below.

Source. The sea trout is primarily a southern species. Although it occurs as far north as New York, it is rarely found north of Delaware Bay. It is harvested in commercial quantities in the Gulf states where the sport catch can exceed the commercial catch. This writer has caught hundreds of pounds of sea trout on plugs and line during the winter and spring months.

Availability fresh. Mostly all year, but abundant in spring and fall.

Average weight. From 1 to 5 pounds (450 g to 2.270 kg).

Trade size. (round or drawn)

       Small—under 1½ pounds (680 g)

       Medium— 1½ to 3½ pounds (680 g to 1.590 kg)

       Large—over 3½ pounds (1.590 kg)

Quality. The flesh is fine, lean, and delicately flavored. This species of trout spoils rather quickly, and should be cleaned and stored on ice as soon as possible. When buying large quantities, carefully check the freshness of the fish. The Gulf states spotted trout can be substituted for the eastern species, and vice versa.

Shad

Other names. American shad, white shad. The shad is anadromous, spending most of its life in the ocean and returning to fresh water to spawn. The South Atlantic shad dies after spawning.

Appearance. The American shad has a greenish color with metallic luster above, and silvery sides. A dark or dusky spot above and at the rear edge of the gill cover is often followed by smaller spots. The lower jaw is enclosed by the upper when the two are pressed together. This characteristic distinguishes the shad from others of the herring family, especially the alewife and the hickory shad.

Source. Shad naturally range from the St. John's River in Florida to the St. Lawrence River in Canada. Shad from the Connecticut River and other East Coast rivers have been stocked in streams. On the West Coast, where the fish is now abundant, it ranges from the Mexican border to Cook Inlet in Alaska. American shad was introduced to the Pacific coast in 1871.

Availability fresh. Early February in the St. John's River to July in the St. Lawrence River and in Alaska. In the northeastern states, shad is most abundant in March, April, and May.

Average weight. From 3 to 4 pounds (1 kg 350 to 1 kg 800). Some specimens reach 7 pounds (3 kg 170) or more, although they are rare.

Quality. A fatty fish of exceptional quality (about 9 to 9.5 percent fat). In season, shad is in greater demand than any other fish.

Trade size. Shad: Skip—¾ to 1½ pounds (340 to 680 g)
 Cut (drawn)— 2 pounds (900 g) and over
 Buck (round)—1½ pounds (680 g) and over

Roe—3 pounds (1 kg 350) and over.
Shad roe (per pair):
 Small—under 8 ounces (225 g)
 Medium—8 to 10 ounces (225 to 285 g)
 Large—10 to 14 ounces (285 to 400 g)
 Jumbo—14 ounces (400 g) and over

It is as easy to scale a shad as it is challenging to bone it. (See chapter 5 for details on boning shad.) The annual yield of shad has decreased at an alarming rate. Problems similar to those of salmon are threatening their existence. Attempts to propagate shad in hatcheries have not been succesful. Effective management and pollution control will only stabilize the annual yield of shad.

Disposition. Over 90 percent fresh (boned)
 Canned
 Smoked Roe

Note: Boneless shad fillets can be prepared in many ways. They may be fried whole or in portions, after carefully dredging them in seasoned flour and placing them, skin side down, in a pan or skillet containing half oil and half butter. Once the fillets have firmed, they can be turned.

Broiling is probably one of the most popular ways to cook shad. The shad fillets should be broiled between hinged racks for easy handling. A marinade improves the delicate flavor of shad.

The shad roe is best when brined in salt and water for 24 hours. Shad roe has a tendency to lack taste if not carefully seasoned. The roe should be cooked at low temperature until firm.

Sheepshead

Appearance. The two unique features of the salt-water sheepshead are the 5 to 6 distinct, dark vertical bars on the sides and the broad, strong incisor teeth.

Source. The largest landings occur in the Gulf states. Sheepshead are also caught off the southern Atlantic coast in smaller quantities.

Availability fresh. April to November.

Average weight. From ¾ to 8 pounds (340 g to 3.6 kg). Best size is 3 to 4 pounds (1.360 to 1.800 kg).

Trade size. Gulf states market—1 to 5 pounds (450 g to 2.270 kg).

Quality. The meat of the sheepshead is white, flaky, well flavored, and tender.

Smelt

Other names. Icefish, frostfish, candlelight fish.

Appearance. Smelt resemble midget salmon in appearance and are distantly related to the salmon family. The smelt is a small, slender, silvery fish with olive green coloring along the back. The average size of smelt varies from 7 to 8 inches (17.5 to 20 cm). Smelt have a large mouth for their size and the lower jaw projects beyond the upper. The tip of the tongue has large, fang-like teeth that, along with the large mouth, distinguish smelt from similar small fish. Smelt have large scales that come off readily.

Source. Originally anadromous, like their relatives, smelt have adapted to fresh-water habitats, living in cold lakes and streams in many parts of the United States. The Columbia River, with its tributaries in the West, the Gulf of St. Lawrence to the Virginia Capes in the East, and the Great Lakes area in the Midwest all support smelt. Smelt were first introduced into the Great Lakes area in 1906.

Figure 4.34 Sheepshead

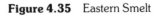

Figure 4.35 Eastern Smelt

Availability fresh. Lake-dwelling smelt are caught during the spawning runs in mid-March and April. The sea smelt are best during the winter months. The peak seasons occur in September in Maine, December in New York, June in Seattle, and June to September in California.

Average weight. Although smelt can weigh up to 1 pound (450 g), most are much smaller, ranging from 15 per pound to 4 to 7 per pound.

Trade size. Great Lakes (round)

        Medium—over 10 per pound

        No. 1—7 to 10 per pound

        Jumbo—4 to 6 per pound

Salt water, East coast (round)

        Small—15 and over per pound

        Medium—12 to 14 per pound

        No. 1—8 to 10 per pound

        Jumbo—4 to 6 per pound

Seattle (round, drawn)

        Silver—5 to 12 per pound

        Eulachon—5 to 8 per pound

Quality. Smelt have a fatty, rich mild flavor. If consumed fresh, the lake or sea smelt make the most delicious pan fish.

Sole

Sole are one of the most clearly defined and distinctive orders of fish. The order also includes such flatfish as halibut and flounder. The underside of these fish is usually white; the top is pigmented, resembling the bottom on which the flatfish lives. An interesting fact is that the eyes of these fish can be raised slightly and moved independently, thus increasing vision. In size and other characteristics flatfish vary greatly.

Description. Atlantic coast sole include two main species:

1. The gray sole is also called witch flounder. This sole, which grows up to 25 inches (62.5 cm), is noted for its fine flavor and is commercially important.

2. The lemon sole is called winter flounder or blackback when it weighs less than 3½ pounds (1.590 kg). Its usual length, when

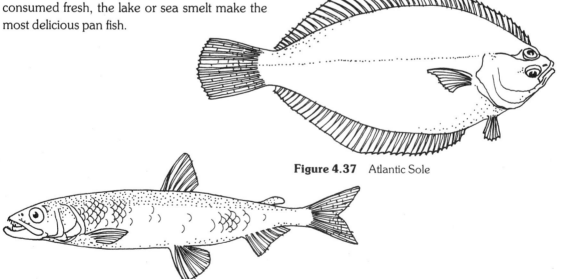

Figure 4.37   Atlantic Sole

Figure 4.36   Alaska Smelt

caught inshore, is around 18 inches (45 cm). These two Atlantic sole share characteristic small mouths, straight lateral lines on the body, and eyes on the right side.

Pacific Coast sole of commercial importance include the following:

1. The petrale sole, also known as brill sole. It averages about 17 inches (42.5 cm) in length and 2½ pounds (1.140 kg) round weight. It has a wide body, small scales, large mouth, and slightly curved lateral line, and is olive brown in color.

2. The English sole is also known as the lemon sole, but is an entirely different species than the Atlantic lemon sole. It is noted for its fine flavor. Smaller than the petrale, the English sole averages about 15 inches (37.5 cm) in length and slightly over ¾ pound (340 g) in weight. It is distinguished by a small mouth, a slender shape, and a pointed head. Other Pacific sole include the rex, California dover, and rock. The Pacific rex sole and rock sole are small flounders. The rex sole has the finest flavor. These two species are not caught in abundance and, due to their small size, are usually pan fried whole.

Source. Most sole live along the continental shelf and slope. Some come into shoal waters and are found in bays or close inshore. The lemon sole of the Atlantic range from as far north as Labrador, south as far as Georgia, with the greatest abundance off the coast of New England. The gray sole of the Atlantic live in moderately deep water from the Gulf of St. Lawrence and the Southern Grand Banks, as far south as Cape Hatteras. The Pacific petrale or brill, and the English or lemon sole, range from southern California to Alaska.

Quality. Sole are fine eating fish. The flesh is firm, lean, white, and delicate in flavor. Most sole are filleted and can be purchased either fresh or fro-

zen. Fillets vary in weight from 2 to 4 ounces (55 to 110 g) and occasionally reach 8 ounces (225 g). Some sole are dressed and sold whole for stuffing.

Dover Sole

Appearance. This species *(Microstomus Pacificus)* should not be confused with the imported Dover sole *(Solea vulgaris* or *Solea Solea)* that is imported from waters of the Channel Islands and the North Sea.

Large eyes and a small mouth characterize this righteye Pacific species. It is uniformly light to dark brown on the eyed side. The slender body has numerous small scales and is covered with a heavy slime.

Source. Southern California to northwestern Alaska.

Average weight. From 2 to 6 pounds (900 g to 2.720 kg), sometimes reaching 10 pounds (4.5 kg).

Quality. The flesh is considered delicious.

Note: European waters do not abound with such a variety of flatfish, and the term *fillet of sole* is applied strictly to the English Dover sole, so abundant in the Channel Islands and the North Sea. It is the most adaptable fish for innumerable sophisticated recipes, unsurpassed by even the salmon.

Spot

Other names. Lafayette, goody.

Appearance. A member of the croaker family, spot is a good pan fish not very well known in the trade. The spot has 12 to 15 yellowish oblique bars above the lateral line and a yellowish black spot directly behind the gills.

Source. Massachusetts to Texas, with the largest production around the Middle Atlantic states.

Availability fresh. In the Middle Atlantic states, July to October. In the South Atlantic states, mainly North Carolina, June to November.

Trade size. Small—4 to a pound (450 g)

Medium—3 to a pound (450 g)

Large—¾ to 1 pound (340 to 450 g)

Quality. Lean, flaky, and tender meat.

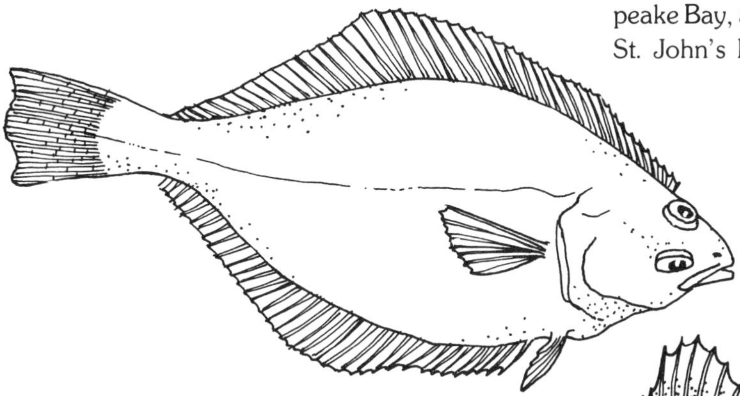

Striped Bass

Other names. Rockfish, striper.

Appearance. This fish, a member of the sea bass family, is one of the most valuable fish on the coast of North America. The striped bass is easily recognized by its 7 or 8 prominent, dark, longitudinal stripes. The body is elongated and slightly compressed.

Source. The species is most abundant in Chesapeake Bay, although it ranges from Canada to the St. John's River in Florida, and to the Gulf of

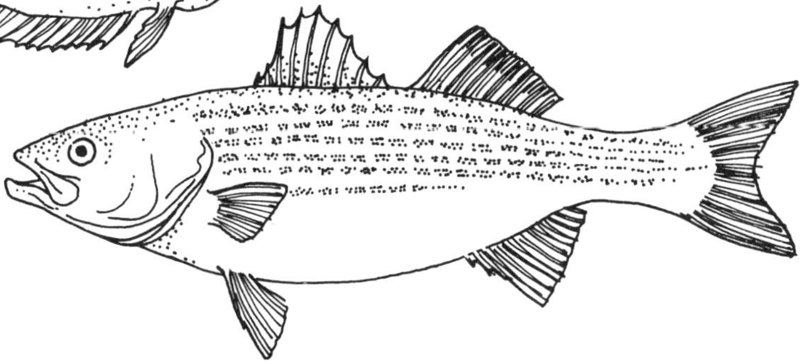

Figure 4.38 California Dover Sole

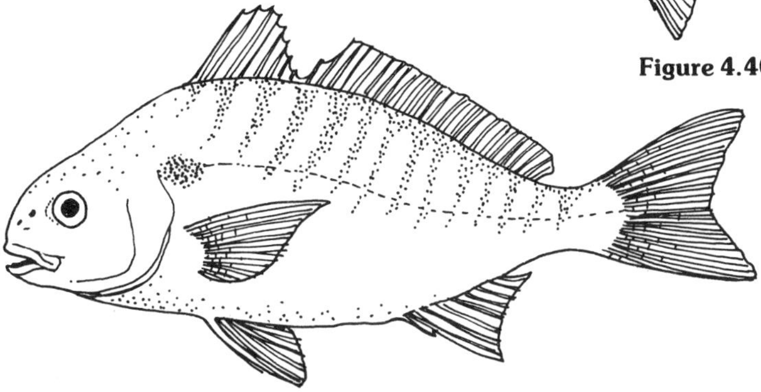

Figure 4.40 Striped Bass

Figure 4.39 Spot

Mexico, California, and Washington. The striped bass is not caught commercially on the Pacific coast but is considered a sport fish.

Availability fresh. All year, but abundant in October, November, February, March, and April.

Average weight. From 1 to 15 pounds (450 g to 6.8 kg). Some specimens reach 40 to 50 pounds (18 to 22 kg) or more, but these are rare.

Trade size. (round)

> Small—2 to 5 pounds (900 g to 2.270 kg)
>
> Medium—5 to 10 pounds (2.270 to 4.5 kg)
>
> Large—10 to 15 pounds (4.5 to 6.8 kg)
>
> Jumbo—over 15 pounds (6.8 kg)

Quality. Its excellent quality, white, flaky flesh is in high demand. Striped bass is a medium fat fish. The striped bass is adaptable to numerous culinary techniques, and its often featured on hotel and restaurant menus; 1969 was a record year for striped bass, with landings amounting to 12.4 million pounds.

Swordfish

Appearance. The swordfish is shaped like an oversized mackerel. The body is thickest in the shoulder area and tapers to the tail, which is reinforced by a keel on either side. The long upper jaw and snout form a flat, sharp, double-edged sword that can be as much as one-third of the total length of the fish. Swordfish vary in color from a dark, metallic purplish cast on the upper surfaces of the body to almost white on the sides and lower body.

Source. Swordfish are found in tropical waters around the Americas. In Pacific waters, they range from Chile to California and around the Hawaiian Islands; in Atlantic waters, from the West Indies to the Grand Banks. Swordfish tend to form schools. However, when they are plentiful, individuals are usually scattered. They seem to prefer temperatures in excess of 60°F (15°C).

Availability fresh. From June to October, with the largest landings in August.

Average weight. From 100 to 200 pounds (45 to 90 kg), with specimens reaching over 400 pounds (180 kg).

Trade size. Pups—under 110 pounds (49.8 kg)

> Large—over 110 pounds (49.8 kg and up)

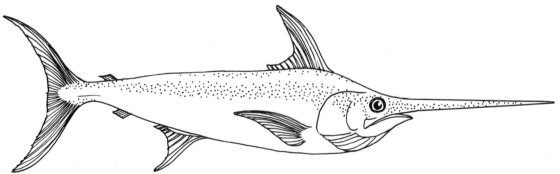

Figure 4.41 Swordfish

Quality. The meat is firm, medium fat, and of good quality. The center cuts are the best.

Disposition. Steaks, fresh and frozen

        Smoked

Americans used to consume millions of pounds of swordfish each year, with seeming insouciance and evident survival. In May 1971, the Food and Drug Administration advised the public to stop eating the fish. According to the FDA, more than 90 percent of samples tested showed more than 0.5 parts per million of mercury (the agency's safety limit). Excessive mercury intake can damage the human nervous system. Since then, swordfish imports have skyrocketed from 3.7 million pounds of whole fish and 19.3 million pounds of swordfish steaks, in 1970, to 20.7 million pounds of whole fish and 25 million pounds of steaks, in 1974. Despite arguments that the fish, by nature, probably have always contained some mercury, the FDA says that a change in the mercury ruling is not probable. To this date, no one has been known to suffer damage from swordfish consumption.

Note: The mako shark, which was once an undesirable species, is now used as a substitute for swordfish. Surprisingly, mako shark steak has a firm flesh and is palatable. Fresh swordfish steak is light pink in color; mako shark flesh has a deeper color, similar to the flesh of fresh tuna.

The blue shark is also used commercially for swordfish steak. It is clear white and has good eating qualities. But to a gourmet, the swordfish is a superior quality fish, especially when consumed fresh.

It should not come as a surprise if the FDA advises the public of excessive mercury content in fake swordfish steaks.

Tilefish

Tilefish is an excellent food fish that is relatively unknown except in the New York and New Jersey areas.

In 1882, the species almost became extinct. A temporary flood of cold water through the warm zone left several thousand square miles covered with dead tilefish. Today there is an average annual yield of 10 to 12 million pounds. They are most abundant off the New England and Middle Atlantic states.

Quality. The tilefish has firm flesh and a good flavor.

Trade size. Kitten—under 4 pounds (1.8 kg)

           Medium—4 to 7 pounds (1.8 to 3.2 kg)

           Large—7 pounds (3.2 kg) and up

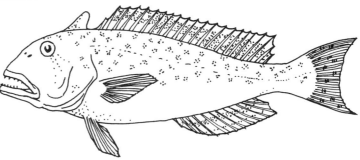

Figure 4.42   Tilefish

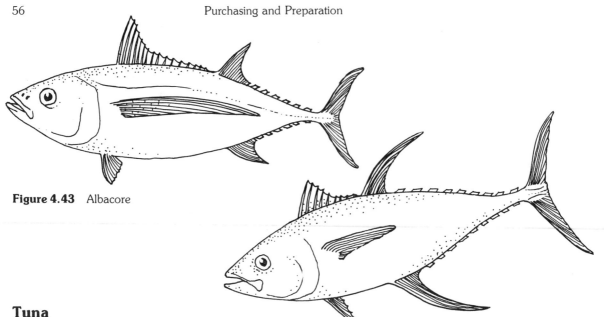

Figure 4.43   Albacore

Tuna

At the rate tuna fish were being caught in recent years, no one could have foreseen the decline of one of the most abundant species. But suddenly, the most sought after species, the bluefin, is vanishing.

For a long time we have enjoyed one of the cheapest sources of protein from our seas. We consume well over a million pounds of tuna daily in the United States. In 1976, tuna landings totaled 660 million pounds and imports exceeded 602 million pounds in the United States. American fishermen are well equipped to catch huge amounts of tuna, especially on the Pacific coast. Tuna vessels cost over $5 million and can store more than 2000 tons of tuna.

The United States and Japan process and market over 40 percent of the total world harvest. Fishermen, marine biologists, and marketers all agree that tuna, particularly the bluefin, may become extinct unless something is done in the near future. It is difficult to accept this warning. In the United States, tuna has been so pervasively advertised and marketed that nearly all of us take the supply for granted.

Figure 4.44   Yellowfin Tuna

In addition to the shortage of tuna, fishermen are facing other problems. Seiners and superseiners, operating off the East and Pacific coasts, are endangering another species. Too many friendly porpoises, the tuna's traveling companions, are killed in the giant nets. This has prompted several protection agencies to curtail tuna fishing until a compromise is reached.

Food operators who have relied on this cheap and profitable source may be compelled to turn to other economical fish. (Chapter 17 has information to help professionals and food operators acquire new tastes for underdeveloped species of fish and shellfish and, in turn, sell these species to the public.)

According to the Forecasters for Resources for the Future, (FRF), the tuna resource will have passed its maximum sustainable yield in 1980. The demand for tuna fish will continue to increase, the supply will dwindle, and the cost will skyrocket. As a result, the marketing of new, underutilized species has become a necessity. Many

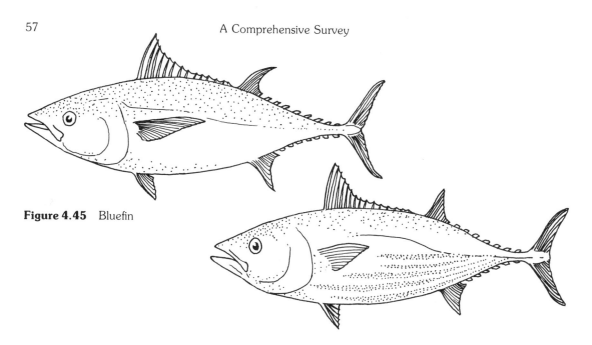

Figure 4.45 Bluefin

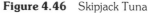

Figure 4.46 Skipjack Tuna

professionals face the challenge of developing new recipes for uncommon fish and shellfish that will satisfy the most discriminating tastes.

Eight species of tuna are hunted in the oceans. These are: albacore, yellowfin, bluefin, skipjack, bigeye, blackfin, little tuna, and bonito. The first four are of commercial importance in the United States.

Quality. Tuna supplies a rich source of protein, vitamins, and minerals. It is easily digested, and can be used straight from the can or combined with other foods. It is economical—there is no waste in the compactly packed and compressed cans.

Grades. Only the canned albacore can be labeled as "white meat." The remaining species must be labeled "light meat." Bonito, little tuna, blackfin, and bigeye cannot be labeled "tuna" since they are members of the mackerel family.

Canned tuna is labeled: Fancy—solid meat only
                             Standard—75 percent
                             solid meat
                             Grated or flaked—all
                             small pieces

Plants in the continental United States pack about 53 percent of the total. American Samoa, Hawaii, and Puerto Rico pack the remainder. In the albacore fishery, the relatively low landings and continued high prices of imports has caused prices to jump.

Processing and Canning. The following information was supplied by the marketing services of Castle and Cooke Foods, San Francisco, California.

After the tuna is caught and taken to the cannery, it is cleaned, then graded according to size and then precooked. The purpose of the pre-cook is to expel the strongly flavored natural oil of the tuna, to make it possible quickly and fully to remove the skin and dark meat of the tuna, and to separate the entire fish into four boneless loins of solid meat. After cooling, the loins go to the can-filling section on the production line. After the cans are filled by machine, measured amounts of salt and oil and/or vegetable broth are placed in the can, which then passes into the closing machines where vacuum is established in the can and it is sealed hermetically.

Only a small amount of tuna is consumed fresh in the United States. During the summer months, fresh tuna is available on the East and West Coast markets.

Processed tuna comes in 3¼ to 3½, 6½ to 7, 9¼, and 12½ to 13 ounce cans. Larger cans are sold for institutional use.

Albacore

Albacore vary from other tuna in flavor and in the whiteness of their flesh. They are also known as "longfins" and can be recognized by their long, sabre-sharp pectoral fins. They are further distinguished by the metallic, steely blue color on the top and sides of the body, a silvery color on the bottom, and by the absence of stripes. The usual weight ranges between 10 and 60 pounds (4.5 to 27.2 kg). Albacore range from southern California to mid-Mexican waters, sometimes reaching as far north as Puget Sound in the summer.

Yellowfin

Probably the favorite of the tuna fishing fleet, these tuna are light fleshed. They are considered perhaps the most commercially valuable of the top four species. Yellowfin are distinguished by elongated, yellowish dorsal and anal fins, and yellowish coloring on the sides. They vary in weight from 30 to 150 pounds (13.5 to 68 kg). The choicest for canning weigh 40 to 100 pounds (18 to 45 kg). Yellowfin tuna are found from the Gulf of California south to the waters off northern Chile.

Bluefin

This species has light flesh and varies in commercial weight from 15 to 80 pounds (6.8 to 36 kg). They are distinguished by the deep blue or green color on the top and sides of the body. Unlike most fish, the high metabolic rate of the bluefin tuna maintains its body temperature warmer than the water.

Bluefin are found from Alaska to lower California. This species is also found in the Atlantic Ocean.

Skipjack

Skipjack are also known as striped tuna. They have light flesh and are distinguished by parallel, black-to-dusky stripes on the lower sides of the body. Skipjack tuna are dark metallic blue on the top and sides, shading to a silvery color on the bottom surfaces. They are the smallest of these four tuna, weighing from 4 to 24 pounds (1.8 to 10.8 kg). Skipjack are found in the same tropical waters as the yellowfin.

Turtle

The term *turtle* is generally applied to all species, but mainly to the sea turtle. A tortoise is a land or fresh-water species. The terrapin is a variety of turtle found in the coastal swamps of the eastern seaboard and the Gulf.

The most prized turtle is the green turtle, which produces a soup of sublime quality. Green turtle soup is available mostly in cans. Turtle meat is also sold canned. Green turtle steaks resemble veal and have a fine flavor. The fresh meat is rarely sold in northeastern markets, and remains a southern specialty.

Commercial fishing for green turtles centers around South Florida, especially Key West. Green turtles are also found along the coasts of the Bahamas, Jamaica, and other islands.

The once highly prized diamond terrapin has now become very scarce.

Weakfish

Other names. Gray sea trout, squeteagues, summer trout.

Appearance. A member of the drum family, the weakfish is a slim, shapely, colorful fish with dark olive green above, and with lustrous purple, lavender, green, blue, gold, or copper tints on its back and sides. It is marked above the lateral line with many small black, dark green, or bronze spots. The lower surface is white to silvery. The large mouth is armed with two sharp canine teeth. The name weakfish refers to its delicate mouth structure.

Source. Weakfish range from the eastern coast of Florida to Massachusetts, occasionally straying northward.

Availability fresh. Abundant during the summer off the coast of New York, New Jersey, and Virginia. In the autumn, they move south to offshore waters.

Average weight. From 1 to 3 pounds (450 g to 1.360 kg), with a few reaching 5 or 6 pounds (2.270 to 2.720 kg).

Trade size. (round or dressed)

> Pin—under ½ pound (225 g)
> Small—¾ to 1¼ pounds (340 to 560 g)
> Medium—1¼ to 3½ pounds (560 g to 1.590 kg)
> Large—over 3½ pounds (1.590 kg)

Quality. Weakfish are known for their tasty, tender flesh. They are usually available whole or pan dressed because of their small size; occasionally, however, fillets from larger fish are available.

Whiting

Other names. Silver hake, silver perch.

Appearance. The whiting is a slender, soft-rayed fish with a streamlined body, two dorsal fins, and sharp teeth. The upper fins are transparent. The body is gray, turning to silver below the lateral line.

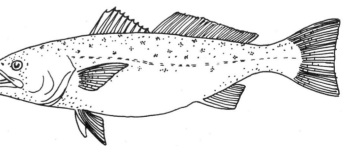

Figure 4.47   Turtle   **Figure 4.48**   Weakfish

Source. Whiting occur along the New England coast off Georges Bank, the Middle Atlantic coast, and Chesapeake Bay.

Availability fresh. In New England, north of Cape Cod, whiting appear from May until October. The peak supply is landed in July and August along the Middle Atlantic states.

Average weight. Males average ½ pound (225 g), females 3 to 5 pounds (1.360 to 2.270 kg).

Trade size. Snapper—½ to 1½ pounds (225 to 680 g)
Small—1½ to 2½ pounds (680 g to 1.140 kg)
Medium—2½ to 5 pounds (1.140 to 2.270 kg)
Large—over 5 pounds (2.270 kg)

Quality. Soft, delicate, white lean meat that flakes easily when cooked. Whiting is also sold as "deep sea fillets," along with cod and haddock. This species was not always desired as a food fish. Its popular acceptance began in the 1920s and since then annual landings increased from about 10 million pounds to a record high of 132 million pounds in 1957. Recently, annual landings have decreased considerably (47.6 million pounds in 1976).

Disposition. Fresh and frozen
Headed and dressed
Fillets—raw and breaded (raw and cooked)
Smoked

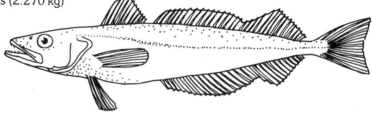

Figure 4.49   Whiting

Fresh-water Fish

Buffalofish

Other names. Bigmouth buffalo
Black buffalo, rooter, or prairie
Smallmouth buffalo or sucker-mouth

Appearance. The buffalo has a large deep body, laterally compressed. Because of its terminal mouth, body shape and color, and long dorsal fin, buffalo easily might be confused with carp. In fact, buffalofish is used interchangeably in all carp recipes. The color is a dull brown to olive on the upper sides and white on the ventral side.

Source. Large quantities are caught in the Mississippi River and tributaries, mainly in Louisiana. The fish also inhabits the Great Lakes.

Availability fresh. February through August.

Average weight. Best size is 8 to 10 pounds (3.6 to 4.5 kg).

Trade size. Medium—2 to 4 pounds (907 g to 1.8 kg)
No. 1—4 to 8 pounds (1.8 to 3.6 kg)
Jumbo—8 pounds (3.6 kg) and over

Quality. The smallmouth buffalo is considered superior in flavor. This medium fat, firm fish is preferred to carp and has fewer troublesome bones.

Disposition. Fresh and frozen fillets, and smoked.

Carp

Other names. European carp, German carp, mirror carp, leather carp.

Appearance. The carp has an elongated body with two pairs of barbels on the upper lip. Its color is olive green on the back and yellowish on the belly.

Source. The Great Lakes, mainly Michigan, Huron, and Erie. Carp fishing in the Mississippi is also important.

Availability fresh. In Chicago markets, April is the biggest month, although large quantities are sold in December, February, March, May, and June.

Average weight. From 2 to 8 pounds (907 g to 3.6 kg). Carp grow to a weight of 30 pounds (13.6 kg) or more, but the best size range is 3 to 5 pounds (1.360 to 2.270 kg). This size has a better flavor during the cold months.

Trade size. (round)

> Medium—2 to 4 pounds (907 g to 1.800 kg)
>
> No. 1—4 to 8 pounds (1.800 to 3.6 kg)
>
> Jumbo— over 8 pounds (3.6 kg)

Large quantities are shipped and sold alive, or frozen as fillets. Smoked carp is also available.

Quality. Carp is a lean, firm fish, palatable when raised in clean waters. The carp is not highly esteemed due to its muddy taste. Carp raised under controlled conditions, however, have a good flavor and can be cooked in various ways.

Channel Catfish

There is a wide variety of catfish, including the gafftopsail and sea catfish that live in the ocean (they are not considered food fish although the flesh is said to be edible). Fresh-water catfish abound, but the channel catfish is regarded by many to be the best eating.

Appearance. All catfish have long barbels about the mouth that are used to locate food. Catfish are scaleless, and have heavy, sharp pectoral and dorsal spines. Channel catfish are easily distinguished from other catfish by their deeply forked tails, relatively small heads, and small irregular spots on the sides.

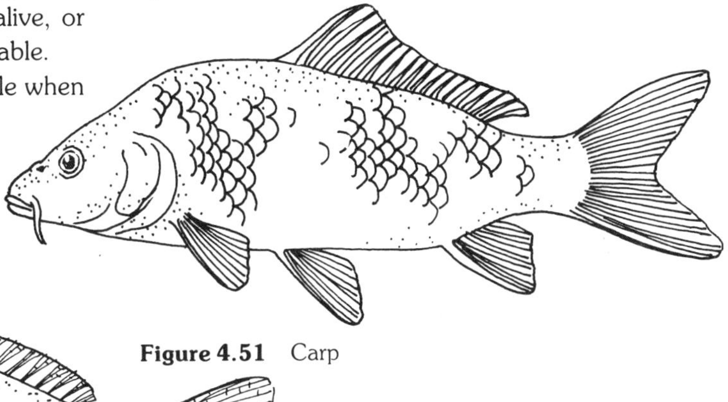

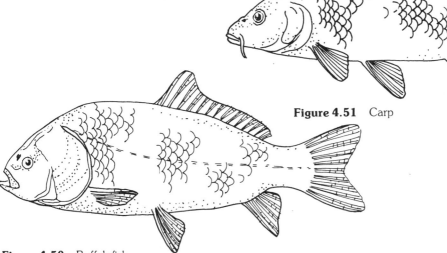

Figure 4.51 Carp

Figure 4.50 Buffalofish

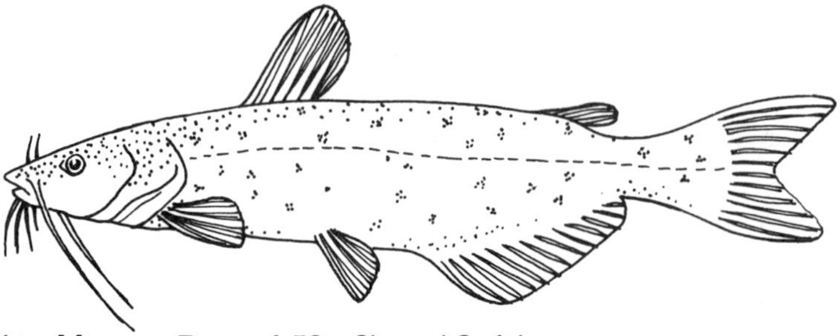

Figure 4.52   Channel Catfish

Source. Mississippi valley, Minnesota, Ohio, Missouri, and southward into Mexico.

Availability fresh. Channel catfish is usually frozen, dressed and skinned.

Average weight. From 5 to 10 pounds (2.270 to 4.5 kg).

Quality. Channel catfish is an excellent food fish. The tender, white, nutritious flesh can be prepared in a variety of ways.

Catfish farming is a thriving enterprise in ten states, ranging west from Florida into Texas and extending as far north as Kansas and Missouri.

A marketing panel of the Missouri Catfish Association has indicated that 14 percent of 900 restaurants surveyed in the United States had catfish on the menu; however only 3 percent of the 126 actually advertised that they had catfish. Strong advertising and merchandising are needed to raise the catfish image in the United States.

Over 20 million pounds of catfish are consumed annually in the United States. The fish is not readily available along the East Coast where numerous varieties of fish are available.

Skinning a catfish. Cut through the skin in a circle just behind the fish head, and pull the skin away from the body. Grasp skin with pliers and pull to remove the entire skin. Clean catfish like any other fish. (The same process is used to skin eel.)

Disposition. Fresh and frozen—dressed, skinned
      Fillets—raw and breaded raw
      Steaks
      Specialties—breaded (raw and cooked)
      Smoked

Caviar

Genuine caviar is the roe of the sturgeon, but the roe of whitefish, lumpfish, salmon, herring, pike, perch, and other fish is also known as caviar. In the wholesale trade, caviar is qualified by the name of the fish from which the roe has been processed; purists recognize only sturgeon caviar. Although the word *caviar* brings Russia to mind, it does not appear in the Russian language; in Russia it is known as *Ikra*.

Caviar is derived from the Turkish word *Khavyah*. The precious roe was brought to Italy by knights of the Holy Army. In Italy it was named *Caviala*. From Italy, caviar was introduced to all the European countries. Shakespeare mentioned it in *Hamlet*, saying, "T'was Caviare to the General!" Savarin's *Dictionaire de Commerce*, written around 1711, makes it clear that it was not despised at the highest tables of France.

What is Caviar?   What is this novelty that has such irresistible appeal for gourmets throughout the world? It is the salted roe of a species of fish called sturgeon. Sturgeon are caught in the Caspian and Black Seas, as well as in other locations. Until industry and pollution came along, the sturgeon was found in rivers running into the Atlantic and Baltic, the Rhine, and in North American lakes. Today all caviar comes from Iran, Russia, and Rumania.

Most fish containing roe are caught during the

spawning season. The anadromous sturgeons leave the deep ocean waters and seek shallow river beds in order to spawn. At this time, the roe is oily, unpalatable, and unsuited for consumption. Fish caught during this period are placed in submerged floating cages. Unable to find food, they use up the reserve of fat that is stored in the roe, thus making the roe less oily. When roe is right for salting, it is extracted from the live fish. The sturgeon is then released.

Of the varieties of sturgeon that produce caviar, the beluga is the largest, sometimes reaching 2500 pounds (1132.5 kg) and producing up to 130 pounds (58.9 kg) of roe. The next largest is the ocictrova, or osetra, weighing around 400 pounds (180 kg) and producing 40 pounds (18 kg) of roe. The smallest of the sturgeon family is the sevruga, which weighs 60 pounds (27.2 kg) and from which only 8 pounds of roe can be harvested.

The size of the roe, even from the same species, does not denote quality. The roe is taken from the fish, carefully sieved, all tissues and membranes are removed, and it is then steeped in a salt solution. The strength of the solution is carefully controlled since the extent of salting determines the quality of the caviar. The amount of salt used depends on the grade of the sturgeon roe being prepared, the weather, the condition of the roe, and the market for which it is destined. Only after the salt has been added to the sturgeon roe does it become caviar; therefore, there is no such thing as unsalted caviar. For the United States market, only salt is used as a preservative; in European countries, salt and borax may be used. Caviar prepared with salt and borax tastes sweeter; the Food and Drug Administration does not accept borax as a food additive.

Top quality caviar is known as malosol. This word does not denote a type of caviar, it means "little salt" and it is used in conjunction with the words beluga, osetra, or sevruga. The best caviar is prepared from sturgeon caught between March and April, when the water is cool and the fish roe are firm and fresh. Fall fishing does not produce as fine a quality caviar because the hotter weather causes the roe to lose its firmness.

Caviar prepared in Russia or Iran, and qualified for the malosol grade, is packed in puds weighing 41 pounds (18.5 kg) and sent to the consumer in refrigerated containers. Nonrefrigerated caviar, for example processed caviar, has a shelf life of about 3 months, and is usually vacuum-packed in 1-to-5-ounce glass jars. After 3 months, white specks may appear; the spots are fat and crystallized salt and are absolutely harmless although not always eye appealing.

Caviar made by one special process is known as paiusnaya or "pressed" caviar. After cleaning the eggs (roe) in the usual way, the caviar is packed in linen bags and hung to drain. This destroys the natural shape of the roe, as they are crushed together. The caviar is then packed in puds holding 50 to 100 pounds (22.7 to 45 kg). Pressed caviar has a much saltier taste than malosol caviar and it looks very much like a solid mass. It is a great favorite in Russia and is greatly prized among connoisseurs.

The color of caviar ranges between gray and black. Color is no indication of quality, although some eggs are more attractive than others.

All fresh caviar keeps best at a temperature between 28°F and 32°F (−2°C and 0°C) for several weeks. Caviar that has been exposed to the air should be eaten within a few days as it will deteriorate rapidly. Any container that has been opened should be covered and kept under refrigeration.

The nutritional value of caviar has been debated for years. It has been reported that caviar contains over 40 nutrients, one of which, a vitamin called actylcholine, has been identified as one of the major brain chemicals. Tests have shown that actylcholine produces a greater tolerance to alcoholic beverages, with no hangover. Could this explain why caviar-eating Russians show a remarkable capacity for alcohol? Some people claim that caviar is an aphrodisiac just as others make that claim for oysters eaten raw on the half shells. There is no evidence to prove it.

As the world supply of caviar dwindles at an alarming rate, the price goes up and up. Caviar is now the costliest food on our planet. The scarce sturgeon roe has become the epicurean status symbol. Most caviar consumed in the United States comes from Iran; much of the caviar consumed in Russia also comes from Iran because of the polluted Volga. "Today, a sturgeon in the Volga is like a Czar in the Winter Palace" said a reporter. One fact is clear. We will have to treat caviar with a growing reverence. At $250 to $300 a pound who would not. Soviet scientists think they have the answer to the caviar crunch. They won't clean their rivers so, after years of experimentation, they are ready to launch artificial caviar. This fake caviar is made of milk albumin, casein, fish oil, salt, and water. By adding food dyes, red, black, or gray caviar can be produced. The United States market, already oversaturated with fake food products, may acquire a new one. "Gelatinated cod liver oil with the consistency of potato paste is what our future caviar may be" is *Pravda*'s opinion. American food technologists should be able to come up with something more palatable. But will there be a market for such a product?

Chub

Other names. Bluefin, blackfin, tullibee.
Appearance. The chub is a member of the whitefish family. It has a larger head than the whitefish and a more slender body.

Source. Lakes Superior and Michigan.
Availability fresh. From June to December, with the peak harvest in November and December. Almost the entire catch is smoked as a substitute for whitefish. Only one species, the blackfin, is highly esteemed as a fresh fish.
Average weight. From ⅓ to 2½ pounds (150 g to 1.140 kg).
Trade size. Small—over 7 per pound (450 g)
           Medium—5 to 7 per pound
           Large—3 to 4 per pound
Quality. The chub has a very soft flesh; it is excellent when smoked.

Frogs' Legs

Two types of frogs are consumed in the United States—the wild, common uncultivated frog and the cultivated bull frog. Wild common frogs are plentiful in the southern United States. They are not sold commercially. The bull frog, a cultivated product, is the best grade with white tender meat.
Source. Middle West, Florida, Louisiana, Mississippi, and California.
Availability fresh. April to October.
Trade size. Small—9 to 12 pairs to a pound
           Medium— 6 to 8 pairs to a pound
           Large—4 to 5 pairs to a pound
           Extra large—2 to 3 pairs to a pound
Quality. A white, delicately flavored, tender lean meat.

Lake Herring

Other names. Cisco of Lake Erie, blueback.
Appearance. Several species of lake herring occur mainly in the Great Lakes. Superficially, lake herring resemble sea herring in appearance. They have large scales and the overall coloration is silvery with a pink-to-purple iridescence.

Source. Lakes Superior, Michigan, Huron, and Ontario.

Availability fresh. All year, with the peak harvest in November and December.

Average weight. From ½ to 1 pound (225 to 450 g).

Trade size. Regular—4 per pound
          Large—3 per pound.

Quality. Lake herring are fatty fish of excellent quality. The large specimens are often sold as whitefish. Smoked lake herring, also called ciscoes, are usually sold as smoked whitefish.

Disposition. Smoked, fresh, or frozen.

Lake herring production has been declining rapidly in the Greak Lakes for many years. The only remaining viable stocks are in the Canadian portion of Lake Superior. In 1976, United States production was less than 500,000 pounds, and the Canadian production approximately 1.2 million pounds. Fifteen years ago, the combined production of Canada and the United States was over 10 million pounds.

Northern Pike

Other names. Lake pickerel, grass pike.

Once this fish was featured in many gourmet dishes created by the greatest European chefs. Quenelles de brochet, known as pike dumplings, are considered a sublime recipe in French cooking. But like many species of high quality, the supply of pike has been depleted. In the United States it has been removed from the commercial species list in many states and reserved exclusively for sport fishermen. In 1976, less than 20,-000 pounds were produced in the United States, and less than 400,000 pounds in Canada.

Appearance. Pike have a long body, laterally compressed. The mouth, shaped into a moderately broad and rounded snout, is armed with sharp canine teeth. The dorsal and anal fins are placed far back on the body near the tail. The basic color arrangement of the northern pike is a pattern of light spots on a dark ground, in contrast to their cousins, the muskellunge, which have a pattern of dark markings on a lighter background.

Trade size. (round)
          Regular—½ to 1½ pounds (225 to 680 g)
          Jumbo—1½ pounds (680 g) and over

Quality. The meat is lean, firm, and flaky, and of excellent quality.

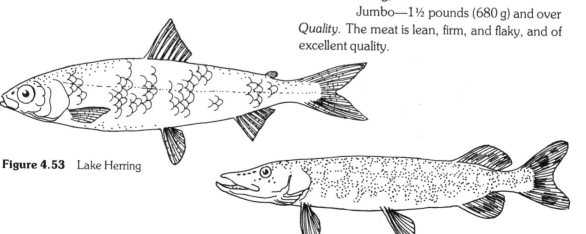

Figure 4.53 Lake Herring

Figure 4.54 Northern Pike

Sheepshead

Other names. Fresh-water drum, white perch, gasperou, gray bass.

Appearance. The fresh-water sheepshead is a relative of the marine drum, producing audible sounds of varying amplitude by twanging muscles against its air bladder. Like the salt-water drum, the fresh-water species has a strongly arched back. The lower jaw is shorter than the upper. The fish is silvery, somewhat darker above than below.

Source. The fresh-water drum is widely distributed. The species is abundant from the Great Lakes, except Lake Superior, to the Gulf and eastern Mexico, with large numbers found in the Mississippi and Red rivers. The largest landings occur mainly in the Great Lakes (Lakes Erie, Huron, and Ontario).

Availability fresh. April, May, and June.

Trade size. Small—¾ to 1½ pounds (340 to 680 g)

Medium—1½ to 5 pounds (680 g to 2.270 kg)

Large—over 5 pounds (2.270 kg)

Quality. The meat is white and lean, with large coarse flakes. In quality, the fish is similar to the marine species known as black drum. The smaller species, ¾ to 3 pounds (340 g to 1.360 kg), have the finest flavor. The larger ones have a coarse texture.

Steelhead

The migratory rainbow trout is known as a steelhead. It resembles the lake-dwelling form in color when it comes from the sea, but as it proceeds up river and nears spawning time, it becomes dark and spotted. The red band appears, and the fish looks like the mature nonmigratory form, although its body is generally slimmer. It grows to 36 pounds (16.3 kg).

Source. Oregon, Washington, and California.

Lake Sturgeon

Other names. Shortnose sturgeon, common sturgeon, Atlantic sturgeon.

Appearance. Sturgeon originate far back in geologic history and are as primitive as paddlefish. Grayish green in color, it has a sharpened but flattened head, covered with bony plates, and a long pointed snout. Along its back and down its sides are raised scutes; otherwise the fish is scaleless. The heavy, torpedo-shaped body ends with a tail resembling that of a shark, curving upward in an arch that rises well above the hump of its back.

Source. On the West Coast, white and green sturgeon are caught mainly from the Columbia River. On the East Coast, a few sturgeon occur in Georgia, South Carolina, and Louisiana, and are sold mostly at the New York Fulton Market.

Best size. Small sturgeon, ranging from 8 to 10 pounds (3.6 to 4.5 kg), are best.

Quality. The flesh has a good quality, very firm and delicately flavored. The lake sturgeon is considered endangered in many areas of the United States and Canada. In 1976, only a few pounds (less than a 1,000) were reported in the United States, and less than 30,000 pounds were produced in Canada.

Disposition. The major retail market in North America is for the smoked product. The white sturgeon is sometimes available in fresh steaks and fillets.

Lake Trout

Other names. Mackinaw, togue, longue, Great Lake trout.

Appearance. The lake trout, a member of the salmon family, is the largest trout in American waters. Lake trout vary widely in color with shades of gray and olive predominating. There are variations in the color of the flesh ranging from pale ivory to deep pink. These color differences probably are determined by environment as well as heredity. Much of the body is mottled with grayish white or white spots, and these profuse markings extend over the head and the deeply forked tail.

Several subspecies of lake trout appear to exist: one is found at moderate depths in the Great Lakes and inland lakes, and another, the siscowet, frequents the deeper waters of Lakes Superior and Michigan. The siscowet, generally considered too oily for ordinary use, is mostly smoked for market.

Source. Commercial fishing for lake trout occurs in the Great Lakes, except for Lake Erie. The catastrophic collapse of lake trout caused by the invasion of sea lamprey was brought under control after extensive research by state agencies of the United States and Canada, and with the cooperation of the Great Lakes Fishery Commission. Lake trout are being restocked in fresh-water lakes with young fish raised in fish hatcheries. Interest also centers on the hybrid splake, a cross between a female lake trout and a male brook trout, which has potential for the future of lake fishery.

Availability fresh. About 80 to 85 percent are caught from May to October.

Average weight. From 2 to 8 pounds (900 g to 3.6 kg).

Trade size. No. 1—2 to 4 pounds (900 g to 1.8 kg)

Medium—4 to 8 pounds (1.8 to 3.6 kg)

Large—8 to 10 pounds (3.6 to 4.5 kg)

The 4 to 8 pound, pink fleshed trout are preferred, but the 2 to 4 pound size usually brings the top premium prices.

Quality. Lake trout rank with whitefish as a choice fish. Lake trout have a firm textured flesh that is rich in flavor. The white to pinkish flesh is high in protein and rather fatty.

Rainbow Trout

Appearance. This native American trout is high on the world's list of game fish. Rainbow trout are easily identified by the broad reddish band or "rainbow" that runs along the side of the fish from head to tail. The reddish band blends into a dark olive green on the back, and pure white or silver on the belly. Rainbows sometimes migrate to the ocean where they spend several years. By the time they return to their stream to spawn, they have acquired a grayish tinge from the salt water and are called steelheads.

Source. The rainbow is a native of the Pacific slope of the Sierras from California to Alaska. It has since been transported to nearly every state in the Union. Trout prefer clear, cool, unpolluted water, and usually are not found in waters lacking these qualities.

Availability fresh. We don't have to rely on the whims of nature to enjoy trout. Modern trout farms raise these tempting fish for our tables. Using modern scientific equipment, trout farms create the best environment and feeding conditions for fast growing, healthy trout. Selective breeding has produced strains of rainbow trout that grow bigger and faster than their wild counterparts. A farmed trout can be fed to yield a pink flesh. A substance derived from carotene, provitamine A, which has no influence on the taste of trout, can be added to the fish diet.

Average sizes. To meet the needs of professionals and consumers, trout are sold whole, weighing 5, 6, 8, or 10 ounces (140, 170, 225, or 280 g).

Trade forms. Because of modern freezing and shipping techniques, frozen rainbow trout are available nationwide almost anytime of the year. All trout are sold with the head and tail attached. Frozen trout are sold fresh frozen, boned, and boned and breaded. Boned trout have the backbone and ribs removed. Boned and breaded trout have the fins, backbone, and ribs removed. Frozen trout are usually sold in 8-ounce (225-g) packages. Each package contains two 4-ounce (110-g) trout. Fresh whole trout are also available on the market.

Quality. The flavor is excellent and the flesh delicate. Trout are highly prized all over the United States, and satisfy the taste of a high percentage of consumers. A survey conducted by Quick Frozen Foods indicates that 90 percent of frozen trout go to the institutional market.

Whitefish

Other names. Lake whitefish, eastern whitefish, inland whitefish.

Appearance. The species, easily recognized by the small short head, is a member of the salmon and trout family. The whitefish is one of the most acclaimed fresh-water fish in the United States. The silver, thick flexible body can be curved gracefully and poached for cold presentation. The roes of females are the same quality as shad roe.

Source. The largest landings occur in the Great Lakes. Canadian imports of whitefish are also valuable.

Availability fresh. The largest catches occur from May to August.

Average weight. From 2 to 6 pounds (900 g to 2.720 kg). Best weight is 4 pounds (1.8 kg).

Trade size. (mostly drawn)

       No. 1—1½ to 3 pounds (680 g to 1.360 kg)

       Medium—3 pounds (1.360 kg)

       Large—3½ to 4 pounds (1.590 to 1.8 kg)

       Jumbo—4 pounds (1.8 kg) and over

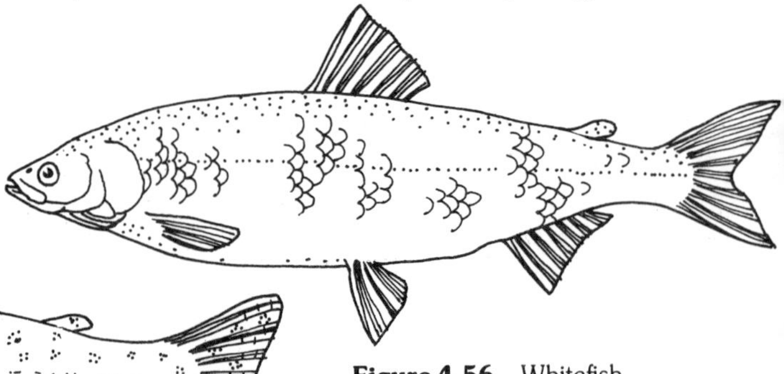

Figure 4.56   Whitefish

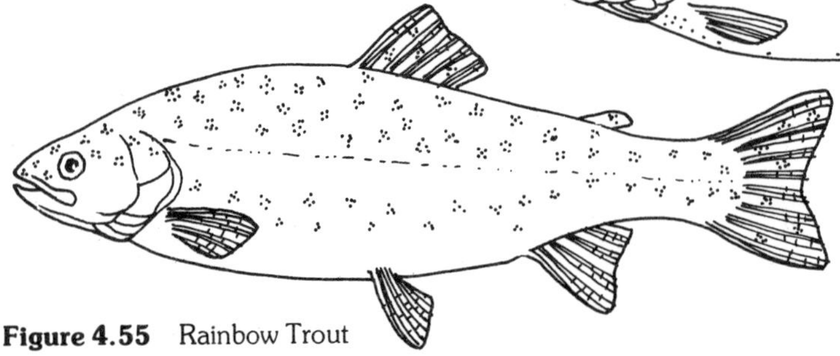

Figure 4.55   Rainbow Trout

Quality. Whitefish is one of the best fresh-water fish in the United States. The meat is fatty, white, and flaky, and has a fine flavor. Smoked whitefish, a gourmet delight, is available commercially. Smoked ciscoes, chubs, and tullibees are also sold under the name whitefish, but are of lower quality.

Yellow Perch

Other names. Lake perch, ringed perch, striped perch, coon perch.

Appearance. Yellow perch is generally classified as a pan fish. It is one of 19 species of perch, including the walleys, saugers, and darters. The perch has a moderately elongated body that is slightly compressed with a humpback appearance. The coloration is a golden yellow on the sides and white on the belly. Six to eight dark bands extend from the back to below the lateral line.

Source. Lakes Erie and Michigan produce the major crop, although the yellow perch is widely distributed in lakes and streams from Nova Scotia to South Carolina and in the lakes of the western states.

Availability fresh. Most abundant from April to November.

Average weight. Seldom reach over 1 pound (450 g); usually, the weight varies from ¼ to ¾ pounds (110 to 340 g).

Trade size. Small—over 4 per pound (450 g)
            Medium—4 per pound
            Large—3 per pound
            Jumbo—½ to ¾ pound (225 to 340 g)

Quality. Yellow perch is a lean, excellently flavored fish, with firm white meat.

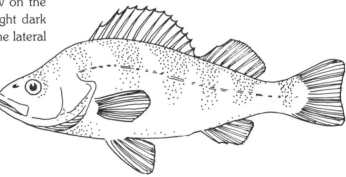

Figure 4.57 Yellow Perch

Shellfish

American Lobster

One half of the popular American dish, "Surf and Turf," may be doomed to extinction. The beef is here to stay, but the outlook for the great American lobster is bleak. This lobster is one of the largest of all marine crustaceans; it may also be the meanest. Unquestionably, it is the most valuable, which is the reason it is being overfished to the point of diminishing return.

Although many of the 14,000 New England lobstermen flatly dismiss any suggestion that *Homarus Americanus* is in trouble, the lobster harvest has declined significantly. As a result, the value of lobsters keeps rising dramatically. The National Marine Fisheries Service in Massachusetts lists the lobster as an endangered species.

Lobsters are measured from the eye socket to

the end of the carapace, rather than by overall length, because of the difficulty of straightening the tail for measurements. The legal size for lobster varies from $3^1/_6$ inches in Rhode Island, to $3^3/_6$ inches in Maine, New York, and Massachusetts. Ninety percent of the lobsters caught today fall within this size range.

The American lobster, also called the Maine lobster, which ranges from the Maritime Provinces of Canada to the coast of North Carolina, is most abundant in the waters of Maine and Newfoundland. The average weight is 1 to 5 pounds (450 g to 2.270 kg). Some species grow to 20 pounds (9.1 kg) or more, and may be 50 years old. They make remarkable buffet show pieces. Seawater temperatures and available food affect the growth rate of lobsters tremendously.

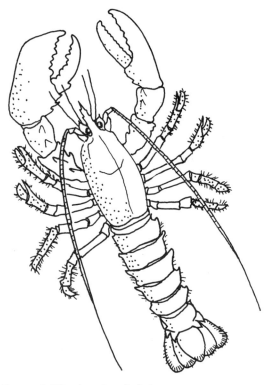

Figure 4.58 American Lobster

Trade size. Select or quarter—1¼ to 3 pounds (560 g to 1.360 kg)
Large—1½ to 2½ pounds (680 g to 1.140 kg)
Jumbo—over 3 pounds (1.360 kg)
Culls—lobsters with only one claw
Disposition. Fresh and frozen
Cooked—meat or whole
Specialties—breaded, raw and cooked; canned (deviled, dips, newburg, bisques, soups, spreads, meats, etc.)

The item marketed as lobster tail usually is a spiny lobster (for more details on spiny lobster, see page 79).

Lobster: An Eye-catching Merchandise in Tanks

An effective way to sell lobsters, guaranteed to be live, is to keep them in tanks. Specially constructed tanks are available in various sizes and shapes. Displaying the live seafood in a conspicuous place may create an immediate desire for a fresh lobster dinner. There is something exciting and intriguing about seeing fresh lobsters "swimming" in a tank. The patron selects a particular lobster and has a sense of personal participation in the preparation of dinner. An interesting fact about live lobsters in a tank is that they purify themselves after being in the tank for a few hours.

Questions asked most about lobsters

1. What is tomalley?
   Tomalley is the lobster's liver. It turns green when cooked and is considered a delicacy.
2. What is the coral?
   Coral is the underdeveloped egg mass of a female lobster. It is the best part of the lobster. Cooking colors the tiny eggs a deep coral or red.

3. How old is a one-pound lobster?

No one knows exactly, but aquarium studies suggest 5 to 7 years.

4. Can a lobster be kept alive in fresh water with ice?

No. Fresh water is lethal. A lobster has salty blood and tissue, which require a seawater environment to maintain life.

5. How long can a lobster live out of water?

Several days if kept in a cool, moist environment. The lobster is a gill breather, and moisture is essential for survival.

6. How many one-pound lobsters are needed for a pound of lobster meat?

Five, on the average.

7. How does a lobster grow?

It sheds its hard shell and grows a new, larger one. Since the skeleton is on the outside, this molting is essential for growth.

8. How many times must a lobster molt before it reaches market size?

Between 20 and 30 molts take place before a lobster reaches market size.

9. Have people been poisoned by eating lobsters that were allowed to die before being cooked? Is it true that a dead lobster deteriorates very rapidly?

Lobsters are not poisonous if they die before cooking, but cooking should not be delayed. Lobsters that have been dead for several hours (usually 6 to 8) are easy to detect when cooked; the tail shrinks to less than half, and it is mushy and unpalatable. If the lobster is "beheaded" before or soon after death, the body meat will stay fresh much longer. Freezing slows deterioration and harmful chemical actions that follow death.

10. How can one tell if a boiled lobster was alive when cooked?

The tail of a dead lobster loses its elasticity and ability to curl under the body. When plunged into boiling water, a live lobster curls under its tail. It remains in that position during and after cooking.

Display Lobsters   Although large specimens are not common, they are available commercially and can be used for exclusive buffet displays. Consider, for example, a 27-pound (12.2 kg) lobster. The amount of meat that can be expected from its tail is about 1 pound, 6 ounces (620 g); the claws yield 4 pounds (1.8 kg) of meat. The result is a 19 percent yield of meat.

Crabs

Among the salt-water fin fishes, salmon, tuna, flounder, and sole dominate the markets. They are abundant and well accepted by the public.

But the bounty from the sea is surely the edible crab family. The blue crab is naturally number one. The tremendous king crab, once considered as junk fish, is also an American favorite. The Florida stone crab is often compared to the sweet, innocent, and delicious meat of the northern lobster.

And then there is the East Coast blue crab's counterpart, the Pacific dungeness, highly prized on the West Coast.

Edible crabs are evenly distributed around the United States. But we have eaten so many of these overfished delicacies that fishermen have had to invade the untouched deep oceans, only to discover that new species abound. Some examples are the snow crab or Tanner crab from Alaska and the Bering Sea, and the Jonah crab, cancer crab, and red crab. These underutilized species are discussed in chapter 17.

Any of the crabs mentioned previously can be used interchangeably in recipes, unless otherwise specified.

The following crabs are commercially important in the United States:

blue crab, including the hard crab and soft-shell
 crab
dungeness crab
king crab
stone crab
snow crab
green crab
Jonah crab
red crab
cancer crab

Blue Crab

This is one of the crabs harvested in large quantities in the United States. The edible blue crab is one of the most abundant crustaceans in the shore waters of the Atlantic, from New Jersey to Florida, and along the Gulf Coast to Texas. Blue crabs have been introduced to Europe where occasional specimens are found from France to Denmark, along the coast of Israel, and in the Nile River Delta. Chesapeake Bay is the major source, producing millions of pounds of hard, soft, and peeler crabs annually. Maryland and Virginia provide almost all the United States supply of soft-shell crabs.

A soft-shell crab is a blue crab that has just emerged from the old shell and has a new, soft, pliable shell. In Maryland, the minimum legal size for soft-shell crab is 3½ inches (8.75 cm) across the shell.

A peeler crab is a hard crab that has a fully formed soft shell beneath the hard outer shell. The recent development of obtaining soft crabs by shedding peelers in land tanks is becoming more widespread. It permits a more efficient handling of crabs.

A buckram is a blue crab with the soft shell that has toughened. A hard crab is a blue crab with a hard shell. There is also the green crab that has very recently shed its shell. Its meat is soft and watery, and it can not be kept legally.

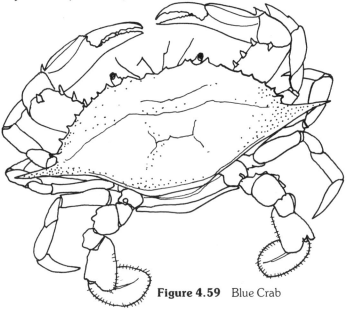

Figure 4.59 Blue Crab

Soft-shell crabs trade sizes.

Spiders (minimum legal size)—3½ inches (8.75 cm) point to point

Hotel prime—4 to 4½ inches (10 to 11.25 cm) point to point

Prime—5 to 5½ inches (12.5 to 13.75 cm) point to point

Jumbo—6 to 7 inches (15 to 17.5 cm) point to point

Marketing of blue crabs. Blue crabs are caught and marketed in both the hard-shelled and soft-shelled stages. Soft-shell crabs are considered a delicacy and bring higher prices. The entire body of a soft-shell crab can be eaten after cooking. For details on cleaning soft-shell crabs, refer to chapter 5.

Hard-shell crabs are either sold alive, or they are steamed and the meat picked from the shell, packed into containers, refrigerated, and sold as fresh crabmeat. Blue crabmeat is marketed as: lump meat—whole lumps from the large body muscles that operate the swimming legs; flake meat—small pieces of white meat from the body; flake and lump—a combination of the first two; and claw meat—a brownish tinted meat from the claws.

Pasteurization of blue crabmeat is another method of preparation for marketing. With pasteurization, the crabs are steamed, and the meat picked from the shell and packed immediately into cans. The cans are hermetically sealed and immersed in a hot-water bath. This method does not alter the taste or texture of the meat, and it is fresh and table ready. Pasteurized crabmeat must be refrigerated until ready to use. Blue crabmeat is seldom frozen or canned. All crabmeat provides excellent high-quality protein, vitamins, and minerals.

Alaskan King Crab

King crabs are the object of intense fishing by the United States in the northern Pacific Ocean and Bering Sea. King crabs are not true crabs like the dungeness crab of the Pacific coast, but are more closely related to hermit crabs. The legs of king crabs are jointed to fold behind the body, not jointed forward like the legs of true crabs. The legs and carapace are spiny, providing protection from predaceous fish.

King crabs grow as large as 24 pounds (10.8 kg) in 15 years, but commercially caught males average 7 pounds (3.180 kg) and are 8 or 9 years

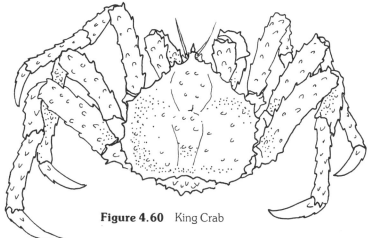

Figure 4.60 King Crab

old. Crabs of this size measure about 3 feet (90 cm) with legs extended.

Source. King crabs are located in the eastern Bering Sea and along the entire Pacific coast of Alaska, including the Aleutian Islands. Major Alaskan fisheries are centered at lower Cook Inlet, Kodiak Island, and the eastern Bering Sea.

Marketing of king crabmeat. The prime meat of the king crab is in the claws, legs, and shoulders, and this is the only part that is used. These parts are separated, washed, cooked in boiling water, chilled, and washed again before being trimmed, processed, inspected, packaged, and quick frozen, ready for marketing. State law prohibits shipping live king crab out of Alaska. Crab legs may be partially split and sold frozen as "fancy ready split legs." Whole legs are frozen, trimmed, glazed, and marketed as "fancy whole legs." King crabmeat is also available freshly packed, frozen, or canned in 5, 6½, and 13 ounce sizes. The white, sweet, coarse meat is tender and delicate.

Green Crab

This crab has little commercial value. It grows to about 3 inches (7.5 cm) and is found on the East Coast from Maine to New Jersey. The body is dark green or green with yellow mottlings. In Europe, where green crabs are abundant, they are a popular food. In the United States, they are used mostly as bait and considered a nuisance by commercial fishermen since they destroy large quantities of soft-shell clams along the New England coast.

Dungeness Crab

This popular shellfish is found on the Pacific coast. The dungeness supports both a major commercial fishery and a considerable sport fishery.

Appearance. The dungeness crab has a flattened body that is covered by a hard, chitinous, reddish brown spotted shell and two of its ten legs have large pincers. This species is distinguished from other commercially important crabs by legs that are smaller and shorter than its body.

Source. It inhabits sandy and grassy bottoms below the tidal range, from as far north as Cook Inlet and Prince William Sound south to Magdalena Bay, Mexico.

Availability fresh. Supply starts in April, increases in May, and peaks in June.

Average size. Commercial fishing regulations vary in different areas. But there is one specific regulation—only male crabs can be taken. The legal widths of the shells are set by states, and vary from 5¾ to 6½ inches (14.3 to 16¼ cm). The crabs reach legal size in 3 to 4 years and live about 8 years.

How is dungeness crabmeat marketed. Dungeness crabmeat is available by the pound, already

Figure 4.61   Dungeness Crab

cooked, with the picked meat from body and claws sold as one grade. Whole, cooked dungeness crab is also available, either fresh or frozen. Some of the crabmeat is canned, usually in 6½-ounce (200-g) cans. Dungeness crabmeat is an excellent source of easily digestable protein and vitamins (especially thiamine, niacin, and riboflavin), but low in fat and calories.

Snow Crab

Until recently, the crab fisheries of the Pacific coast and Alaska were based almost entirely on dungeness and king crabs. Now another crabmeat resource is being harvested—the snow crab.

Other names. Tanner crab, queen crab. The Food and Drug Administration has officially designated these species as snow crab for marketing and labeling purposes. Until recently, snow crabs were an underutilized resource, although their potential may be as great as that of the king crab.

Appearance. Snow crabs belong to the family of spider crabs, so called because their legs are long and slender in proportion to their rounded bodies. Like other crustaceans, snow crabs have hard shells and five pairs of jointed legs. The first pair of legs is always equipped with pincers, varying in size according to the species.

Source. Two species of snow crabs are important to the crab fishery of Alaska. They range throughout the central and southeastern waters off Alaska and down to Washington. Other species occur in waters off Washington and Oregon, and down to northern Mexico.

Availability fresh. Snow crab is only available fully cooked, either frozen or canned.

Trade size. Marketing is much the same as for the king crab. Frozen blocks of snow crabmeat are designated for the trade as:

Supreme—all leg meat
Premium—65 percent leg and 35 percent body meat
Regular 35 percent leg and 65 percent body meat
Salad—all body meat

Quality. Snow crabmeat has a delicate flavor, is tender and succulent, and low in calories. The meat from the legs is white with vivid red coloring on the surface; the body meat is white.

Disposition. The biggest proportion of snow crabmeat is packed in 7½-ounce (225-g) cans for consumer use.

Stone Crab

This member of the mud crab family is a very popular commercial crab on the west coast of Florida, especially Marathon and Key West.

Appearance. The stone crab has an oval-shaped, flattened shell with a purplish to brown or reddish brown color, and brownish mottlings. The large claws have a very hard shell with black tips.

Source. North and South Carolina and the east coast of Florida. Stone crabs reach their peak of abundance and size in Key West and the west coast of Florida. Commercial fishermen are allowed to keep only one claw of the crabs; then they must release their catch. Stone crabs will grow another claw within days, usually on the full moon or new moon. This method avoids the complete depletion of the limited stone crab fishery.

Availability. In Florida, where 90 percent of the stone crabs are harvested, the season starts on October 15 and ends on April 15.

Quality. The flesh of the stone crab is rich and very delicate, similar to the claws of northern lobster. It is the most prized of all crabs. Stone crab claws are sold frozen and cooked.

How is Crabmeat Marketed?   Crabmeat extracted from different species, mainly rock and hard-shell blue crabs, is sold cooked, chilled, or pasteurized, and by the pound, according to its body location.

Lumpmeat comes from the large muscles that operate the back fins. It is white and is considered the best grade.
Flakemeat comes from the remaining portion of the body. It is also white.
Claw meat comes from the crab claws. It is dark in color. Claw fingers are also available and are used primarily as appetizers for cocktails.
Body and leg meat, from the dungeness or Pacific crabs, is taken from both body and legs. It is a good grade of meat.

Canned crabmeat grades are: fancy, choice, passed A, and fair. Fresh hard-shell crabs sold commercially must be alive or they are unfit for consumption and should be discarded.

Norway or Icelandic Lobster
or Lobsterette

This imported species is remotely related to the American lobster. The Norway or Icelandic lobster has a long tail, large protuberant eyes, and elongated claws with sharp teeth. Its color varies from brick red to salmon red. The color does not change with cooking. This species is much smaller than the lobster and very rarely exceeds 9 inches (22.5 cm) in length when fully grown.

The Norway or Icelandic lobster is a delicacy and is known for its sweet flavor and tender texture. Only small amounts are sold on the United States markets. The frozen tails vary in size and are adaptable to a myriad of recipes.

Shrimp

"If there is anything out of the ocean with more virtues than shrimp, I'd be hard put to name it," said Craig Claiborne of the *New York Times*. Shrimp is the most valuable United States fishery, with an impressive harvest of over 411 million pounds (heads on) in 1976 that was worth a record $346,431 million. We consume over 1.5 million pounds of shrimp daily in the United States. One would think, based on these stunning figures, that the United States shrimp fishing industry would be self-sufficient. However, Americans love shrimp and 411 million pounds were not enough. Record imports of 230 million pounds of shrimp, mostly frozen and canned, came from 68 countries.

Appearance. The shrimp is a ten-legged crustacean that acquired its name because of its size. The word *shrimp* was derived from the Middle English word *shrimpe*, meaning "puny person," and the Swedish *skrympa*, meaning "to shrink." Like other crustaceans, the shrimp's skeleton is on the outside of the body and, in order to grow, it casts off its shell and replaces it with a new one.

There are three species of southern shrimp that are commercially important; all three are members of the family, *Penaeidae.* They are:

1. the common shrimp or white shrimp
2. the brown shrimp
3. the pink or white spotted shrimp

The tiny, North Pacific shrimp and the northern shrimp are the same species. Another species, also called North Pacific shrimp, is caught in Washington, Oregon, and California. Of the three varieties, southern shrimp are usually the largest and North Pacific shrimp are the smallest.

Two other underutilized species are landed in

significant quantities; the royal red shrimp in the deep waters of the continental shelf, and in the Gulf and South Atlantic region, and the rock shrimp, easily distinguished by its hard, rough sculptured shell.

Color is not a very reliable means of distinquishing the species of shrimp. White shrimp are generally grayish white and are variously tinged about the tail. Brown shrimp are usually reddish brown in color, with tinges of blue or purple on the tail section. Pink or brown spotted shrimp vary greatly in coloration according to locality. Along the Atlantic coast, they are usually lighter in color than brown shrimp; on the Tortugas grounds, they are pink; and along the northern Gulf Coast, they are often lemon yellow. The brown spot on the side of the abdomen or tail is usually present. Royal shrimp are usually deep red all over, but sometimes are only grayish pink. *Source.* The northern shrimp is found in the offshore waters of Maine and Massachusetts. The tiny, North Pacific shrimp is found along the coastlines of California, Oregon, Washington, and Alaska. The southern shrimp is taken from waters of the Gulf and South Atlantic states.

The Gulf states, principally Texas and Louisiana, account for over 80 percent of the total landings of shrimp. On the Pacific coast, Alaska and Oregon are the leading states.

Availability fresh. Shrimp are in season all year but are most expensive from January to April. During this season, they are in prime condition because the shells are harder and the flesh firmer. Peak landings occur in the Gulf states, from August to October; in the Middle Atlantic states, from May to August; in New England, from June to September; and on the West Coast, from July to September. The major harvest is frozen and beheaded.

Trade size. Shrimp are sold by weight and number per pound (count), and are usually frozen headless. The commercial count (number per pound) and descriptive size names, if used, conform to one of the following categories:

Commercial count (number of shrimp per pound)	*Descriptive size name*
under 10	extra colossal
10–15	colossal
16–20	extra jumbo
21–25	jumbo
26–30	extra large
31–35	large
36–42	medium large
43–50	medium
51–60	small
61–70	extra small
over 70	tiny

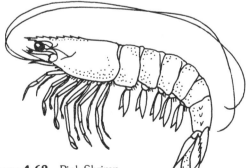

Figure 4.62   Pink Shrimp

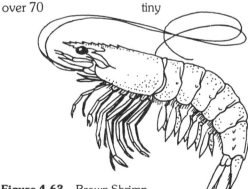

Figure 4.63   Brown Shrimp

Quality. Shrimp are an excellent source of high-quality protein, vitamins, and minerals. They are low in fat and calories and are easily digested. The edible part of the shrimp is the tail section. Raw shrimp are often referred to as "green shrimp" at the retail level. Although raw shrimp vary in color, the cooked product is pink-white, and the flavor and nutritional values are the same. Regardless of size and variety, shrimp can be used interchangeably in most recipes.

Disposition. Commercially, shrimp are processed and sold in different forms:

Raw headless

Peeled and deveined, cooked or raw

Breaded raw or breaded cooked

Cooked whole

Cooked specialties—soups, sauces, gumbos, stuffed, croquettes, canned

Smoked and sun dried

Shrimp farming. See aquaculture in chapter 17.

The Elusive Rock Shrimp   The rock shrimp is an indisputable member of the shrimp family, although its tough, rigid exoskeleton is not dainty like the thin shell of its cousin, the common or pink shrimp. In addition to the hard shell, the texture of the meat of the rock shrimp is like that of a lobster. The flavor is somewhere between lobster and shrimp.

This species of shrimp often escapes the attention of the average consumer in southwest Florida, where it is available in markets during the winter months. Rock shrimp are brought up in shrimper's nets along with regular shrimp. But rock shrimp are far more perishable than either the Florida spiny lobster or its southern shrimp relatives. Therefore, they are marketed frozen raw, as either whole or split tails.

The largest size available is usually 21 to 25 per pound. Rock shrimp are delicious broiled in the shell. However, the cleaning instructions are different when this method of cooking is used. To clean the whole rock shrimp tails for broiling, place the tails on a cutting board with the swimmerettes exposed. With a sharp knife, cut between the swimmerettes through the meat to the hard shell. Spread the shell until it lies flat, and wash thoroughly in cold water to remove all the sand vein.

Cooking rock shrimp. Rock shrimp cook faster than other shrimp and require very close attention to avoid overcooking. When overcooked, the meat becomes rubbery. To cook approximately 1½ pounds (680 g) of raw, peeled, deveined rock shrimp, add 2 tablespoons salt to 1 quart (1 l) of boiling water, and simmer for about a minute. Drain and rinse in cold water for two minutes. Remove any particles of sand vein. Serve with melted butter, with a sauce, or use in any shrimp recipe in chapter 14.

According to the National Marine Fisheries Service in Washington, evaluations of exploratory data on Florida's east coast indicate a resource of 5.7 million pounds of rock shrimp. The exploration of deeper waters in the west central Atlantic reveals the presence of many other shrimp in commercial concentrations. The royal red shrimp are the most abundant in depths of 200 to 250 fathoms (1 fathom equals 6 feet), and the estimated crop is over 1.5 million pounds. But existing gears are ineffective in depths over 150 fathoms.

Another deep-water shrimp, the small speckled shrimp, is probably more abundant than the red shrimp with which it is associated in distribution. As yet, its small size has attracted no commercial interest. In Europe, a similar tiny shrimp has been sold commercially for many years. It is called *bou-*

quet in France. The shrimp are cooked and served whole.

Imports from Spain and North Africa have introduced the giant scarlet prawn to the United States consumer. The day may come when United States shrimp trawlers will catch this species off the Gulf of Mexico and the Caribbean at depths of 350 to 500 fathoms. The deep red imported shrimp, also called shrimp royale, are sold frozen, headless raw. Their sizes vary from jumbo (7 shrimp per pound) to 24 extra small per pound. Spanish shrimp have a delicious taste and a firm white meat. The scarlet shell of this shrimp lends itself to colorful buffet presentations.

The tedious work of manually peeling shrimp is over. The peeling machine processes over one thousand pounds of shrimp an hour, and has revolutionized both the canning and freezing industry. Automated cooking and flash freezing has also greatly improved the transfer of shrimp to food operations and consumers throughout the country.

The difference between Prawns, Crayfish, and Shrimp. Often, common names are used loosely and inconsistently with the shrimp family. The prawn of Great Britain and other countries is essentially the same as the shrimp of the United States. In this country, shrimp includes all crustaceans of the *Natantia* group, regardless of size. Crayfish or crawfish are names given to both a fresh-water crustacean and the salt-water lobster.

Spiny Lobster

Other names. Crawfish, crayfish, sea crawfish, rock lobster.

Appearance. The spiny lobster is related to crabs, shrimp and crayfish. Unlike the American lobster, it lacks claws. In the western Atlantic, there are six species of spiny lobsters. It is beautifully marked with brown, yellow, orange, green, and blue mottled over the upper part and underside of the tail. Unfortunately, whole live spiny lobsters are uncommon; but they make remarkable buffet displays when presented whole.

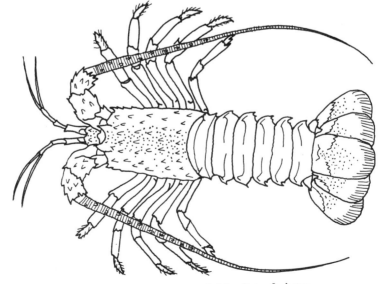

Figure 4.64 Spiny Lobster

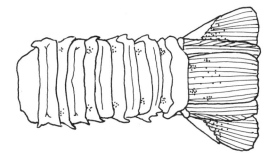

Figure 4.65   Western Australian Spiny Lobster Tail

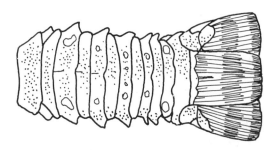

Figure 4.66   Florida or Cuban Spiny Lobster Tail

Source. Commercially, important relatives of spiny lobsters occur in California, the Mediterranean, South Africa, and Australia. In the United States, they are abundant in the Caribbean Sea, in South Florida, as far as the Bahamas, Cuba, and British Honduras, and off the coast of California.

Availability fresh. The peak season occurs from December to May.

Average weight. The live spiny lobster averages 2 to 5 pounds (900 g to 2.270 kg).

Trade size. (tails)

> Small—6 to 9 ounce (170 to 255 g)
> Medium—9 to 12 ounce (255 to 340 g)
> Large—12 to 16 ounce (340 to 450 g)
> Jumbo—over 1 pound (450 g)

Quality. The spiny lobster offers a high-quality protein, with snow-white, lean meat. Large quantities of spiny lobsters are imported into the United States annually. The South African or Australian lobsters are considered best, followed by the California and Cuban species. Florida spiny lobster is considered fair.

Crayfish

Crayfish, crawfish, Dixie lobster, and mini-lobster are some of the names given to these creatures.

This delicious fresh-water crustacean is highly prized in Louisiana, where over 90 percent of the nation's yield is produced and 85 percent is consumed. Crayfish are also found in West Coast markets, in Oregon and Washington. Minnesota, Wisconsin, and West Virginia also practice crayfish culture.

Researchers at Louisiana State University have been working for several years to strengthen this industry. The wild crayfish crop has always been erratic, with bumper crops occurring only about two years in five. The red swamp crayfish, which makes up 90 percent of the commercial catch, is very adaptable to environmental conditions. About two dozen species are scattered over several states. For many years, crayfish culture has been practiced in southern Louisiana, yielding good returns ranging from 200 to 800 pounds (91 to 362 kg) per acre. Today, crayfish farm acreage numbers more than 40,000 acres. Rice fields for crayfish farming represent a multiple use of acreage.

According to LSU's researchers, there is very little market for crayfish outside Louisiana. Surprisingly, in some sections of Hawaii and Australia, the crayfish is regarded as a crop pest. In 1970, Louisiana's prized red swamp crayfish were exported to Japan as food for bullfrogs, which that country ironically exports in large numbers to the United States.

Although marketing specialists are studying existing channels of commerce for crayfish, they are rarely found in eastern markets. There the demand is greater in gourmet restaurants. Dr. James Rutledge of the Department of Food Science at LSU is studying the storage life of crayfish, particularly as it is affected by the rancidity of fat.

In years ahead, commercial crayfish farming probably will be intensified due to increased demand, especially for Louisiana crayfish. In Europe, the supply cannot meet the demand. Europeans have many ways of preparing crayfish, and can transform them into culinary marvels.

Abalone

Abalone are marine gastropods or snails, and are related to chitons, clams, oysters, squid, octopuses, and other mollusks. The abalone is one of the most primitive in form and structure, and inhabits the temperate and tropical seas of the world. The greatest variety of species occurs off the coast of Australia. In the United States, abalone are found on the Pacific coast, mainly in California.

Appearance. This univalve (with the generic name *haliotis* from the Greek meaning "sea ear") has an ear-shaped shell that protects its body. The muscle adheres to rocks and in crevices where it feeds on algae.

Abalone have been exploited throughout the world for their shells and the eating quality of the muscles. The flavor of the muscle is unique. So is its texture—tough and rubbery. The meat must be tenderized and pounded with a wooden mallet. Abalone steaks are sliced across, parallel to the bottom of the foot, with each steak about ⅜ inch (½ cm) thick. Under no circumstances

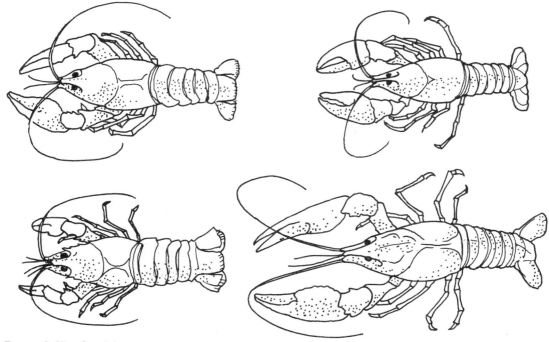

Figure 4.67 Crayfish

should abalone steaks be overcooked; they become rubbery and lose their culinary value. A thin abalone steak, sauteed in butter, is cooked about 30 seconds on each side, over intense heat. Connoisseurs often favor abalone in its raw state, cut into cubes and marinated.

Eight species of abalone appear on the West Coast: red, black, green, pink, thread, white, flat, and pinto.

Red abalone. The largest of all abalone, it reaches over 11 inches (27.5 cm) in diameter. The outside color of the shell is dull brick red. It ranges from Sunset Bay, Oregon, to Baja, California. This is the most important commercial abalone. Almost the entire catch is sold fresh frozen to restaurants. Those sold fresh in fish markets command the highest prices.

Green abalone. Once very abundant around the Channel Islands, they are taken by skindivers and sportsmen in southern California. They frequently harbor a parasitic worm that is unsightly and tends to discourage the commercial market for them.

Black abalone. This species is of little importance to commercial fishermen because of its dark meat and small size.

Flat abalone. They range in size from 3 to 5 inches (7.5 to 12.5 cm). They are taken by commercial divers and, due to their small size, sell for high prices.

White abalone. Found in depths up to 150 feet, they are commercially included with the pink abalone. They occur off the coast of California. The body is typically colored yellow to orange, and the meat is quite tender.

Threaded and pink abalone and Pinto. They are the least common species and seldom appear in the commercial catch.

The best quality abalone are the red, white, and pink species.

California law prohibits the canning of abalone and shipping of fresh and frozen abalone out-of-state. In 1975, one million pounds of fresh and frozen abalone were imported to the United States from Mexico, and 3 million pounds were canned. Minced and cubed canned abalone are also imported from Japan.

Clams

Along the Atlantic coast, the three species of clams that rank highest in commercial importance are: hard clams, surf clams, and soft-shell clams. The Pacific coast clams include: razor clams, butter clams, littleneck clams, Atlantic soft-shell clams (transplanted), and the geoducks.

Appearance. The bivalve shells that encase the clam's body are joined together at the back by a

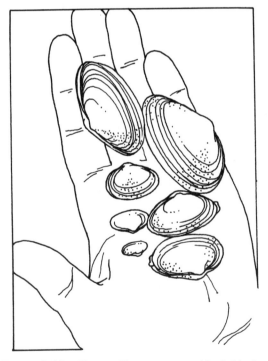

Figure 4.68   Clams - Cherrystones and Little Necks

hinge ligament that is usually visible from the outside. The shells, while varying in shape, are composed of three layers. The outer layer is often varnishlike; the thick middle layer is somewhat chalky; and the inner layer, which is usually hard, is often iridescent or lustrous. Concentric rings are laid down on the shells as the clam grows. Shell colors vary because they are affected by the habitat.

The two most prominent features of the clam's body are the foot, or adductor muscle, and the siphon or neck. The muscular foot aids the clam in digging in the soft sand or mud and in opening and closing the valves. The retractable siphon is a tubelike extension that conducts water in and out of the clam.

Hard Clams

Other names. Quahog, quohog, quauhaug.

The hard clam is distributed along the Atlantic coast, from Florida to the Gulf of St. Lawrence. It is also found along the Gulf of Mexico to the Yucatan Peninsula. New York leads in production, accounting for approximately 45 percent. The next highest producer is New Jersey, followed by Virginia, Rhode Island, and Massachusetts.

Marketing. Hard clams are sold under three names corresponding to their size. The largest and cheapest clams are marketed as "chowders," and are used mostly for chowders, clam fritters, stuffed clams, et cetera. "Cherrystones," the medium sized and medium priced clams, are used to some extent in the half-shell trade. This size is used exclusively for baked clams and the popular New England clam bake. "Little necks" are the smallest and most expensive of the legal sized hard clams. They are used in the half shells and as steamed clams, the same way the blue mussel and the soft-shell clam are cooked.

Depending on traditional practices in a given locale, hard clams are marketed not only by size, but by the "piece," by count per volume, by weight per volume, or by weight or volume alone. This causes considerable confusion when the clams are shipped interstate. The Marine Fisheries Commission has recommended the adoption of a uniform minimum legal size and the standardization of clam count and/or weight of clams marketed in any given volume.

As with any fish or shellfish, pollution presents the greatest threat to the hard clam resource. The transplanting of clams to certified clean waters and depuration would undoubtedly increase the price of clams. The ultimate solution would be the control of pollution.

Soft-shell Clams

Soft-shell clams are found from Labrador to North Carolina and in a number of scattered locations on the West Coast. New England states are the main producers. Unlike the hard and surf clams, these popular clams have elongated shells that are very thin and brittle. The soft-shell clams cannot close tightly because their long necks extend beyond the shells.

Surf Clams

The surf clams are also known as skimmer, beach, giant, sea, hen, or bar clams. This species makes up the largest volume caught along the Atlantic shores, but it is not as valuable as the hard or soft-shell clams. Practically all canned clams are surf clams.

Quality. Clams, one of our most delicious shellfish, have a nutritional value similar to mussels and oysters. They are high in protein and low in calories. They contain iodine, iron, and other minerals. A half-dozen cherrystones provides an excellent supply of protein, only 70 calories, and a level of iron comparable to that in a serving of beef liver.

Buying clams. Clams can be bought in three forms: in the shell, shucked, and canned. Clams in the shell should be alive when purchased. Hard clams with gaping shells that do not close when handled are dead clams and should be discarded. With other varieties, there will be some constriction of the siphon or neck when the clam is touched. Fresh clams in the shell, stored in the refrigerator at about 40°F (4.5°C) will live for several days.

Shucked clams are the clam meats that have been removed from the shells. They are generally sold by the pint or quart. Shucked clams should be plump, with a clear liquor, and free from shell particles. Fresh shucked clams should be refrigerated or packed in ice. When properly handled, they will stay fresh for 7 to 10 days. Shucked clams are also packaged and quick frozen, making them available all year. Frozen clams should not be thawed until ready to use. Once thawed, they should not be refrozen.

Canned clams are packed in various can sizes, whole, minced, or as chowder. Clam juice, broth, and nectar are also available canned or bottled.

Clam specialties available commercially are: breaded (raw or cooked), strips, cakes and patties, stuffed, burgers, croquettes, sticks, cocktails, and chowders.

Note: For instructions on shucking clams, see chapter 5.

The Geoduck Clam

Other names. King clam, gweduc, gooey-duck.
Appearance. The geoduck is mostly neck. Even the mantle bulges out of the shell, which is always too small to contain the entire clam. Geoducks are the most impressive clams in United States waters, and are believed to be second in size only to the giant clam found in the East Indies. The largest geoduck ever found weighed 13 pounds (5.9 kg). The average clam weighs 3 pounds (1.360 kg), and yields 1½ pounds (680 g) of meat.

Source. Geoducks are found all along the West Coast, but they are most abundant in Washington's Puget Sound. These giant clams live from 18 inches (45 cm) to 6 feet (1.80 meters) below the surface of the beach, or underwater, beneath the surface of the bottom.

Harvesting. Commercial harvesting is strictly by diving, using hand-operated equipment. Divers work at depths of 10 to 60 feet, with hoses that deliver water under pressure to them. This water jet is directed into the soil to dislodge the geoducks. Each diver collects 300 to 500 geoducks per day. According to a survey made by the State of Washington, millions of geoducks live beneath the sands in fairly deep water and could be harvested without endangering future supplies.

Uses. Geoduck meat is juicy and rich, and has a fine flavor. Enthusiasts say that geoduck steak compares in taste and texture to abalone, but is sweeter. These clams are marketed in numerous forms, including frozen breast and neck steaks, frozen and canned minced meats, frozen and canned chunks, and canned smoked chunks. They are also available fresh on request.

The steaks can be served pan fried or grilled; the minced clams are used in dips or chowder; and the canned chunks and smoked canned chunks are party snacks.

If the clams are purchased fresh, dipping them in hot water will open the shell and loosen the skin. The skin and stomach are discarded, and the clams are then washed thoroughly and rinsed in cold water. It is possible to cut 3 steaks from one geoduck—one from the breast and two from the neck. These are best breaded and fried. The remaining meat can be ground and used for clam fritters or chowder.

Sunray Venus Clam

Appearance. The shell of the sunray venus clam is elongated, compressed, and glossy-smooth with a thin, varnishlike, protective covering. Its color is dull pink to bluish purple with broken radial bands of darker color. The interior of the shell is a flat white with a blush of red over the central area.

Source. The sunray venus clam ranges from South Carolina to Florida and the Gulf states. Its attractive shell is popular with shell collectors and tourists. Commercial harvesting began in 1967; presently, the largest producing bed in Florida is off Port St. Joseph.

Average weight. Mature sunrays, from 4 to 5 years old, measure 5 to 7 inches (12.5 to 17.5 cm) in length.

Because of a plentiful supply of clams in general, processors of the sunray venus have encountered difficulty in marketing their higher priced, higher quality clam. Processors are conducting a consumer education program to convince shoppers that sunray venus clams are worth the extra pennies, partly because they come from sandy bottoms (no mud) and partly because they are hand-shucked and hand-packed and carry no grit. They are also sweeter and more tender than most other clams.

Uses. Sunray venus clams are currently available only in 5- and 10-pound (2.270- and 4.5-kg) frozen minced blocks. These raw meats are of high quality and useful for chowder, fritters, patties, dips, and clam loaf.

Ocean Quahog

Other names. Mahogany quahog, mahogany clam, black quahog.

Appearance. The ocean quahog has a black or chestnut shell that distinguishes it from all other mollusks of similar size and shape. Fresh ocean quahog meats, raw and cooked, vary in color from brown to gray.

Source. The ocean quahog was considered strictly a European species. But today, thanks to NMFS resource research, it is known to range from the Arctic Ocean to Cape Hatteras, North Carolina. Though ocean quahogs are found in depths of about 6 to 90 fathoms (1 fathom equals 6 feet or 180 cm), the best catches are made at depths of 18 to 24 fathoms. The clams are harvested year round with a hydraulic sea clam dredge.

Average size. Ocean quahogs average ½ pound (225 g) in weight, and 3½ to 4 inches (8.75 to 10 cm) in length.

Processing ocean quahog. For a long time, one disadvantage of ocean quahogs was the great amount of time and effort required for hand shucking, and the high costs that resulted. The ocean quahog has an extremely hard shell that is completely closed, with no easily accessible opening for a knife to penetrate. Even opening this clam with steam under pressure (a technique used commercially to open other species of clams) is unsatisfactory because of unpleasant effects on the meat. Now the clams are being opened with microwave energy. Experiments have shown that microwave opening of clams is feasible. This breakthrough should result ultimately in lower prices for the consumer.

Uses. Ocean quahogs are darker in color and have a stronger flavor and aroma than other clams. They are particularly suitable for Manhattan or New England chowders, and they can also be used successfully in poultry stuffing, patties, deviled clams, sausage, et cetera.

Mussels

To date, mussels do not enjoy the popularity they rightfully deserve. European cuisines have accepted the blue mussel for its true value. Only recently has it found a significant market in the United States, but it is still not generally accepted as a gourmet food.

Appearance. The mussel is a bivalve mollusk. The only edible species is the blue mussel. The shell is dark blue in color and the inside has shades of violet and white.

Source. Mussels are abundant on the New England coast. They are often found in clusters, attached to rocks, gravels, and sea walls by threads or beards that the mollusks secrete.

Availability fresh. The peak season occurs during fall, winter, and spring. Mollusks spawn during late spring and early summer, at which time they are whitish and watery.

Quality. The mussel is high in protein and low in fat (2 percent). It is rich in vitamins and minerals, iron, calcium, and phosphorous.

Consumers should be wary when buying fresh mussels; uncounted millions of mussels from the intertidal areas of the New England coast are not worth harvesting. They are slow growing, lack sufficient meat, and often contain a large number of crude pearls that make them unsuitable for marketing, either fresh or canned.

Any commercial fishery for mussels is affected to a considerable extent by the change that occurs in the meat after spawning. Field observations have shown that the yield in solid meat (drained weight), per bushel of mussels, increases from less than 9 pounds (4.05 kg) in the first week of August to almost 15 pounds (6.75 kg) by the middle of September. The yield probably continues to increase through the late fall and winter and up to the spawning season.

Octopus

In the United States, octopus will probably be one of the last marine creatures to gain acceptance as food. Actually, they are in a class with squid and very much appreciated in Spain, Portugal, and the Orient, where large amounts are consumed.

Appearance. Octopuses are mollusks and, like squid, have an ink sack that they discharge when attacked. The globular body is extended by eight long arms covered with suction cups. Octopuses are well armed to capture shellfish like clams, abalone, and scallops that are part of their diets. No wonder octopus meat is sweet and has excellent food value.

Source. The common octopus is abundant on the West Coast from Alaska to Baja, California. A different species occurs on the East Coast, where it ranges from New England to the Gulf of Mexico.

Marketing. Octopus is marketed fresh or frozen. It is usually gutted and dressed.

There are many European and Oriental recipes. The ink sack is sometimes used to season and flavor the dishes. Cooking methods used for squid are often applied to octopus.

Oysters

The American oyster is a bivalve mollusk belonging to the genus *crassostrea*, which has other members in various parts of the world. In the United States, the West Coast oyster, imported from Japan, is a representative of the genus; the eastern or Atlantic oyster is another.

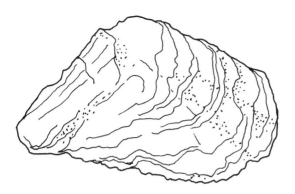
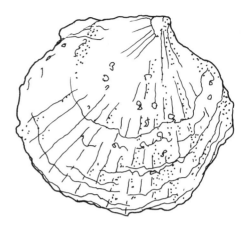
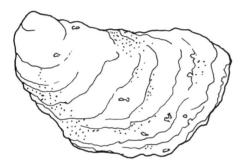

Figure 4.69 Oysters

The four species of commercially important oysters are:

1. the Japanese or Pacific oyster
2. the European oyster
3. the eastern or Atlantic oyster
4. the olympia oyster

Appearance. True oysters are distinguished by dissimilar lower and upper shells. These shells, or valves, are hinged together by a complex elastic ligament. The upper valve is normally flat, while the lower is concave, providing space for the body of the oyster. The two valves create a water-tight seal when the oyster closes, providing the shell is not damaged or broken. Near the center of the oyster's body is an adductor muscle, attached to both valves, which controls the opening and closing of the shell.

Japanese or Pacific oyster. This oyster grows in coastal waters from Alaska to northern California. The biggest production area is in the Puget Sound, Gray's Harbor, and Willapa Harbor areas of Washington. This oyster is grown from seed imported from Japan. The Pacific oyster is now the principal commercial species on the West Coast.

European oyster. The European or common oyster is established in Maine, and is grown experimentally on the West Coast.

Eastern oyster. Also known as the Chesapeake Bay oyster and Virginia oyster, it is the principal commercial oyster of the East Coast.

Olympia oyster. Also known as the western oyster, it is native to the Pacific coast. The yield of this species has declined because of predators, water pollution, and increased production costs. Some olympias are still available and it is hoped that conservation methods will increase the cultivation of this species.

Oyster harvesting. A number of methods are used in harvesting oysters. In some areas, where there are natural oyster beds, no mechanical methods are allowed and the oysters are harvested by handpicking during low water or by manual tongs. If the oysters are plentiful, a tonger may take 25 to 30 bushels a day. In other areas, such as the public grounds of Chesapeake Bay and Connecticut, only hand-operated dredges are permitted. Privately owned or leased oyster beds are harvested by large machine-hoisted dredges, or by suction dredges that operate like a vacuum cleaner. Suction dredges are very efficient in carrying oysters and other materials up from the bottom to the conveyor on the deck of the dredge boat. In addition to harvesting oysters, the suction dredge helps to clear the beds of starfish, mussels, and other enemies of oysters. The escalator or scooptype harvester is effective in shallow waters.

Oyster farming has been practiced for several years in Delaware Bay and Chesapeake Bay to avoid the parasites that destroy oysters (the most destructive is the MSX). Today, oysters are produced under controlled conditions in commercial hatcheries. It is reasonable to anticipate that healthy oysters eventually will be abundant on the United States market, although the production has been declining.

Marine waters producing oysters must have the same high quality as fresh drinking water; in all poor quality waters, the taking of oysters is prohibited. Several million acres of water are controlled by the Atlantic States Marine Fisheries Commission to insure the production of healthy oysters.

The day is coming when a fast-growing oyster of uniform size and shape will be mass produced. It will be a great achievement! After all, is there anything better than a healthy, freshly opened oyster served on the half shell?

Availability. Oysters are edible all year although they are at their peak from October to May. Spawning occurs during the warm summer months and, to most people, they are unpalatable at that time.

Trade size. (Eastern or Atlantic oyster, in shell)

Small (bluepoints)—320 to 400 per bushel

Half shell—280 to 320 per bushel

Medium—200 to 240 per bushel

Large (counts or box)—120 to 160 per bushel

Never allow oysters to reach room temperature. The best temperature is 39°F (4°C). Keep them away from sunlight. If properly handled, they will keep 7 to 10 days. Never allow oysters to freeze. Do not refrigerate in water. Discard any open oyster or any bad-smelling oyster. Such oysters are dead and are poisonous. Do not open oysters more than 5 minutes before serving on the half shell.

Northern oysters with broad, thin, tough shells are superior to the southern oysters, which have thick, spongy shells and an inferior flavor.

Quality. Nutritionally, the oyster is a gold mine, comparable to the food value of the truffle. The underground fungus and the oyster have a similar composition: 72 percent water, 8 to 10 per cent protein, 4 percent fat, 12 to 14 per cent carbohydrates, and 3 to 5 percent mineral substances.

Oysters contain large amounts of iodine, phosphorus, calcium, and iron essential to a balanced diet. Oysters are highly recommended by doctors to patients with anemia.

Disposition. Fresh and frozen

> Eastern—shucked, steamed, and specialties (breaded, raw and cooked, and pies, stews, stuffed, etc.)
> Pacific—shucked and specialties (breaded, raw and cooked, and stews)
> Western—shucked
> Canned—regular (eastern and Pacific)
> Specialties—smoked, stews, and stew bases

Scallops

Appearance. The scallop is a mollusk so named because of its fluted and scalloped shell. The shells of young scallops are particularly beautiful; the outside is delicately colored, sometimes having pink, white, or darker color variations.

Scallops, like clams and oysters, are mollusks having two shells. They differ, however, in that they are active swimmers. The scallop swims freely through the waters and over the ocean floor by snapping its shells together. This action results in the development of an oversized muscle called the "eye," and this sweetly flavored muscle is the only part of the scallop eaten by Americans. Europeans, in contrast, eat the muscle and the delicious pink roe attached to it. The creamy white muscle combined with the pink roe is as colorful as it is tasty.

Varieties of scallops. The New England sea scallop is the most commercially important scallop in the United States. It has a saucer-shaped shell and grows as large as 8 inches (20 cm) in diameter; the muscle or eye sometimes reaches 2 inches (5 cm) across.

The bay scallop is much less plentiful but greatly desired by scallop fanciers. It reaches a maximum size of about 4 inches (10 cm) in diameter with a muscle about ½ inch across. The bay scallop shell is similar to that of the sea scallop but is smaller and more grooved, and the edges are more serrated.

A new fishery has been developed for the calico scallop, located off Florida and in the Gulf of Mexico. The calico scallop is closely related to the bay scallop, although slightly larger. It gets its name from the mottled or calico appearance of the shells.

The discovery of a new and potentially important source of sea scallops in the cold waters surrounding Alaska is particularly interesting. This species, found as far south as Oregon, is different than the sea scallop found in New England waters.

Source. On the East Coast, the largest source comes from the North and Middle Atlantic states. Most of the catch is landed in New Bedford, Massachusetts. Bay scallops are found from New England to the Gulf of Mexico. Scallops cannot close their shells tightly and die soon after being taken from the water. Because of their perishability, scallops are shucked aboard ship as soon as caught, and the meats are iced.

Availability fresh. All year, but best from April to October.

Average sizes. Bay scallops yield 5 to 6 pounds (2.270 to 2.720 kg) shucked per bushel; sea scallops yield 3 to 4 pounds (1.360 to 1.800 kg) shucked per bushel, or 9 pounds (4 kg) per gallon.

Quality. The tender, succulent meats of bay, sea, or calico scallops have no waste and can be used

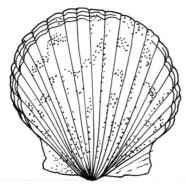

Figure 4.70 Scallop

interchangeably. All scallop meats are excellent sources of protein, vitamins, and minerals, and are low in fat (0.1 percent).

Several commercial distributors often put scallops through a soaking process, placing the muscles in fresh water for several hours and thus depleting their delicate flavor. This process increases the bulk of the muscles by one-third and turns the creamy color very white. But from a culinary standpoint, the flavor is inferior. Always buy scallops from a reputable distributor who guarantees their freshness. The cream colored muscles are an indication of unquestionable freshness. Fresh scallops have a sweet nutty odor, reminiscent of fresh lobster. Many epicureans consider bay scallops the finest, although fresh, deep sea scallops are equally good.

In 1976, the relative volumes of landings were: 19,840 million pounds (weight of meat) of sea scallops; 2,261 million pounds of calico; and 2,131 million pounds of bay scallops.

Sometimes skate is sold in lieu of scallops, but it lacks the sweet odor of scallops. Mr. Smalleys, owner of Smalleys Seafood in Dunnellen, New Jersey, has encountered this practice only once in 40 years of business. His comment was, "Skate are too scarce to be stamped out into scallops, and they make a poor imitation."

Snails

The most commonly known snails are not the marine mollusks but the terrestrial variety. Most snails eaten in the United States are imported from France; they are canned and the empty shells are sold with the mollusks. Fresh snails found in the continental United States are as good as any others, providing they are prepared and cooked properly.

Periwinkles

Periwinkles are small, black or gray, snaillike marine mollusks, found fastened to rocks and seawalls in New England coastal waters. The tiny, live, unshelled mollusks are cooked in salted boiling water for 5 to 10 minutes, or until the black cap, used as a lid by the mollusk, can be lifted and removed easily.

Periwinkles are extracted with a needle or a sharp toothpick, and the sweet morsels are dipped in lemon butter and eaten "au naturel." They can be served as appetizers, on buffets, or with cold seafood trays.

Underutilized Fish and Shellfish

Anglerfish

Other names. Monkfish, goosefish, baudroie. One of the ugliest fish in the sea, it is usually discarded by most of our fishermen. But lately the fish, highly esteemed in Europe, has appeared on the United States markets.

Appearance. The anglerfish is all mouth, with a large number of teeth. The body is flat with a thin slippery skin. Its most unusual feature is the first dorsal spine, which is terminated by a small flap of skin. The anglerfish moves this spine back and forth to attract small fish on which it feeds insatiably. The flipperlike pectoral fins are another characteristic. The fish occurs mainly off New England and is caught principally by cod hunters.

Marketing. Anglerfish is marketed headless and skinned. The flesh is white and very firm. On the market it is known as "bellyfish." Anglerfish can be baked, broiled, or deep fried in fingers.

Jonah Crab

Appearance. The Jonah crab has a broad, coarse, oval carapace that is brick red to purplish in color on top and yellowish underneath. The larger crabs are about six inches (15 cm) wide and weigh an average of 1 pound (450 g); some specimens reach 1¾ pounds (800 g). The crushing claws of the Jonah crab are moderately large. It is a walking crab, not a swimmer, so it lacks the lump meat of swimming crabs. Instead, the claws of the Jonah are more developed and contain the biggest pieces of meat.

Source. Jonah crabs appear to be extremely abundant, with an estimated resource of about 500 million pounds between Georges Bank, Massachusetts, and Cape Hatteras, North Carolina. They are commonly caught along with lobsters in lobster pots, but since crabs are of less value than lobsters, Jonah crab fishery is neglected.

A new system of meat extraction has been developed, eliminating much of the time-consuming hand labor.

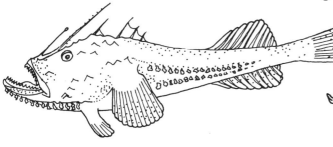

Figure 4.71   Anglerfish

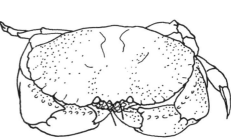

Figure 4.72   Jonah Crab

Uses. Jonah crabmeat is presently packaged in 6- and 7-ounce (170- and 200-g) jars, with the chunky leg meat on top and the smaller pieces of body meat on the bottom. Potential market forms would be similar to those of other crustaceans. They could be sold live or whole-cooked, either fresh or frozen. The large claws, cooked and attractively packaged, could be sold fresh or frozen. The picked meat could be marketed fresh or frozen, or processed into specialty products.

Red Crab

Appearance. The body of the red crab (or deep sea crab) is rather square, with long, slender walking legs. Shell color ranges between red and deep orange. The meat is white with a pinkish tinge. The maximum weight is 3 pounds (1.360 kg) for males and 1¼ pounds (560 g) for females.

Source. The red crab is abundant along the eastern and Middle Atlantic states. This species has not been fished heavily due to a lack of processing capabilities, inaccessibility (deep water), and an unestablished market. But because of the good flavor of the meat, consumer demand, and new methods of processing, red crab, like Jonah crab, may soon become as popular as king crab, dungeness, or blue crab.

A new system for extracting crabmeat has been developed in plants located in New Bedford, Massachusetts, and Point Judith, Rhode Island. For individual consumers, red crabs are available in 6-ounce (170-g) containers of frozen picked meat. For institutional purchase, the crabs are marketed in: packages of 100 percent body meat; 5-pound (2.270-kg) packages of mixed body meat and leg meat; and cocktail claws, 25 to a pound (450 g), cooked and frozen, ready to thaw and serve. The red crabmeat can be used as a substitute for other varieties of crab in suitable

recipes. Red crab is expected to be used more widely as the market becomes better established.

Krill

The krill, a small antarctic crustacean, is a new item on the long list of fishery products. Now that whalers have reduced the whale population of the antarctic by 90 percent, scientists speculate that the krill, on which the whales fed, are enjoying a population boom. The most conservative estimates put the total krill stock at 500 million to 1 billion metric tons. In view of the world's declining harvest of fish and shellfish, several nations have already joined the krill hunt, and it is conceivable that krill could alleviate some of the world's hunger.

The krill is a crustacean, about 2 to 2½ inches (5 to 6½ cm) long. It has two antennae and five pairs of legs for swimming. Its color is red orange on top and bright green underneath. Krill live in very dense concentrations, feeding near the surface.

In the early seventies, Russia began to take these creatures seriously and marketed krill paste, mixed with cheese and butter, as a spread. The krill paste, which is high in protein, is said to have a delicate taste, somewhat typical of shrimp meat. Many people, however, do not share the same opinion, calling krill paste less than tasty.

The Japanese are puzzled regarding the marketing and acceptability of krill. Their fishing companies are testing krill in frozen fish cakes, dumplings, liquid protein, soups, and other specialties. So far, the world influence of krill has not been great. Besides, krill hunters have encountered many problems at sea; it is necessary to process the catch quickly. Krill must be cooked or frozen within one to two hours, or the deterioration caused by enzymes in the krill organs spoils the catch. The short fishing season, during the No-vember-March antarctic summer, adds to the high cost of expeditions.

American fishermen are wary about the antarc-tic hunt. So far, Americans have not played a ma-jor role in krill processing. But one fact is certain: the new source of protein from the antarctic has not been exploited fully. In view of the consider-able efforts of several countries, however, krill may become the soybean of our seas.

In 1976, The Institute of Biochemistry and Technology in Hamburg, West Germany, orga-nized a krill test meal for members of the research study group on fish at the Federal Research Insti-tute for Fishery, also in Hamburg. The basis of the dishes prepared at the Institute was cooked krill paste, produced during the 1975–1976 antarctic expedition. A hotel kitchen supplemented the menu with some dishes using whole uncooked krill.

To demonstrate the potential of cooked krill paste, the menu offered only dishes using this substance as the main ingredient. Initially, a thick soup was served; this was followed by appetizers composed of eggs, cucumbers, and cream puffs filled with krill paste, and toast spread with krill paste. The main dishes were puff pastry vol-au-vent and krill sticks covered with pancake batter, both served with a cold, herbed krill sauce. The hotel kitchen supplied one clear and one thick soup, as well as a hot pastry vol-au-vent. A housewife offered a salad based on a recipe that originally called for shrimp. For some of the reci-pes prepared at the Institute, see chapter 17.

The results, after all the dishes were tasted, showed that 50 percent of the dishes were well received, and were considered very good or pal-atable. Twenty percent were given the notation, "would eat again," and 30 percent were judged as poor. Overall, the dishes prepared with krill

paste were appreciated more than those with krill meat.

It must be mentioned that krill meat, like shrimp meat, is very susceptible to heat. It is imperative that you avoid long cooking or baking times when preparing hot dishes involving krill meat. In gen-eral, this test meal demonstrated that krill proba-bly can be used to prepare tasty dishes.

Shark

Commercial shark fishing used to be a booming business when the demand for natural vitamin A was high. Shark liver is a good source of vitamin A, but since the synthetic form was discovered, the demand for the natural vitamin has dimin-ished.

Now, more and more people are discovering what Europeans already know—shark meat is a highly acceptable food product. Many fish that are considered industrial fish could be marketed as food fish, and this applies to several species of sharks. The species include: the sand shark, com-monly known as dogfish, and the dusky, sharp-nose, bonnethead, and blacktip sharks. These sharks have been used in taste tests with hundreds of people as part of a research experi-ment to determine the acceptability of shark by the average consumer. Results are conclusive—shark meat proved to be palatable to American tastes.

Several European nations have effectively ex-ploited shark, especially the dogfish or spiny dog-fish, as food fish. It is used for all types of hors d'oeuvres and for fish and chips. In the United States, the spiny dogfish, known on the market as the grayfish, is the most common shark. The spe-cies is found along the coasts and over the conti-nental shelves of the North Atlantic and the North

Pacific oceans. It is one of the most abundant fish in the North Atlantic.

The fully grown spiny dogfish is about 3½ feet (42 cm) long and weighs between 7 and 10 pounds (3 and 4.5 kg). Its slender, streamlined body is slate colored with rows of small white spots on the sides.

The Department of Fisheries of several states commercialize the dogfish as food fish. The economical, highly nutritious Jaw's Burger could become America's favorite meal (see chapter 17). Undoubtedly, new ideas for the use of shark will be developed, and public acceptance and awareness will increase.

How to prepare shark meat   Some appealing features of shark meat are its lack of bones, firm texture, economical price, and versatility of preparation. Like any fish, shark meat is best when purchased fresh. If it is to be stored longer than 24 hours, it should be wrapped in airtight wrappers and stored in the freezer.

Shark meat can be prepared much like any other fish. It lends itself well to kebabs as the flesh is firm and will not fall off the skewers. Chunks of fresh shark meat can be enjoyed in gumbos, soups, or creoles. Shark can also be broiled, baked, fried, poached, grilled, or smoked, and served with a sauce. The cooked fish can be combined with other ingredients to create salads or au gratin seafood dishes.

On the European market, the standards for judging dogfish quality are smell and color. There should be no ammonia smell and the flesh should be bright red in color. The characteristic and unpleasant smell associated with dogfish is linked to the production of ammonia in large quantities during the autolytic spoilage process. To avoid this danger, the fish must be particularly fresh when processed, and it should be frozen and stored at very low temperatures, particularly if the product is held for long periods of time in cold storage.

The color of the dogfish carcasses caught in European waters results from the fact that they are not normally eviscerated or bled on capture. This seems to contradict all the conventional processing and handling procedures normally employed with other fish at sea that ensure a white meat. Dogfish on the United States market is usually eviscerated and bled.

American consumers are reluctant to eat shark. But this is how one typical American consumer learned. At the end of the summer, as this writer was lunching on Billingsgate Fish and Chips with members of his family and some American friends of English descent, the conversation turned to great vacation fishing spots on the East Coast. "Cape Hatteras was our best fishing ground this summer. We fished off the beach and

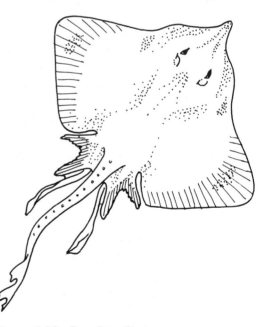

Figure 4.73   Barn Door Skate

caught all kinds of fish in a day. Most of them were junk fish, with the exception of croaker, which we dressed and broiled. They were delicious. The winged ugly sea robbins are not good to eat, so we threw them back. We also caught many persistent sand sharks that we threw back because of ecological reasons; besides, we would not eat them anyhow," said one guest. As he started to eat his fish and chips, he remarked, "This is very good! What kind of fish is it?" At the end of the meal, light was shed on the identity of the fish, much to everyone's surprise.

Educated consumers will soon learn that fresh dogfish or sand shark has a taste and food value equal to many other common food fish.

Skate

Ironically, skates, which are considered almost universally as junk fish, are sometimes disguised as a substitute for scallops, proving that their succulence is on a par with the United States sea scallop. Skates, gliding through water with sweeping motions of their wings, look strange enough to be regarded suspiciously as human food. Their relatives, the stingrays, are armed with one or two long, venemous spines on the tail, and can be

very dangerous. They should not be confused with skates.

Skate wings have an excellent food value, like scallops, and are considered a delicacy in Europe. Pieces of skate wings, pan fried or deep fried, and cut like scallops, are a gourmet delight.

Skates can be caught profitably by our fishermen. Since consumers already have a taste for scallops, skate may appear on the United States markets if the demand arises.

In quality, a skate is similar to a dogfish; it has poor keeping qualities. The fish should be frozen or marketed fresh as soon as possible after capture. If the fish has any ammonia smell when thawed, it is unacceptable.

Squid

Other names. Inkfish, cuttlefish, calamari.
Appearance. The squid and octopus belong to the same family. Squid have ten arms and usually a long, cigar-shaped body with fins at the end; octopuses have eight arms and more of a stubby body. Squid have no back bone but rather a pen that is located beneath the mantle of the body. Two fins, located near the terminal end, are about half as long as the mantle and are slightly lobed in

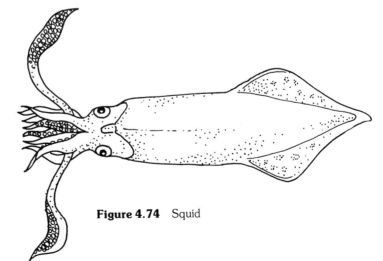

Figure 4.74 Squid

front. Squid are ordinarily a milky, translucent color, but when aroused, intense and varied colors ripple over the body, turning rapidly to red, pink, brown, blue, and yellow, even several hours after they are caught.

Squid are able to control their coloration in order to hide from prey and predators alike. An ink-like fluid is contained in a sack in the mantle and ejected at will. The siphon or funnel that ejects the ink is also instrumental in the squid's rapid movements.

Source. Squid occur on both the Atlantic and Pacific coasts and in the Gulf of Mexico. The ones most sought by commercial fishermen are found along the Pacific coast and the usual range is from Puget Sound to San Diego. Their year-round habitat is the deeper offshore water, except when spawning.

Availability fresh. February to June in the Monterey Bay area; November through February in southern California.

Quality. Squid is considered a gourmet or specialty item and has long been popular with Mediterranean, Oriental, and Mexican cooks. It is high in protein and phosphorus, and contains traces of calcium, thiamine, and riboflavin. The white meat is very lean. Squid, the poor man's lobster, may well become the rich man's delight. The inexpensive squid is readily available on the markets. Many consumers may be startled at the thought of eating squid, but after the initial bite, prejudice dissolves.

Filled with spinach and rice, or in cold salads, paella, fish soups, and chowders, or fried or simmered with tomatoes, squid is a highly nutritious seafood certain to gain popularity in the United States.

Wolf Fish

Another underutilized species of fish available commercially is the wolf fish. Their big jaws, armed with numerous sharp teeth, give these fish a fierce appearance. But the flesh is of excellent quality, firm and palatable, and can be used for chowders or soups like bouillabaisse. Commercially, the fish are available in fillets and can be adapted to the most common cooking techniques.

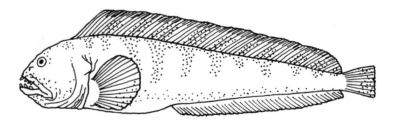

Figure 4.75   Wolf Fish

CHAPTER 5

The Basic Preparation of Fish and Shellfish

This chapter deals with basic preparatory techniques for fish and shellfish. It includes the following:

1. How to bone a shad.
2. How to bone a summer flounder or fluke.
3. How to clean blue mussels.
4. How to dress soft-shell crabs.
5. How to fillet a flounder.
6. How to fillet a whole dressed fish.
7. How to fillet imported Dover sole.
8. How to poach a whole fish for cold presentation.
9. How to shell, devein, and butterfly large shrimp.
10. How to prepare lobster for cold preparation.
11. How to shuck hard-shell clams.
12. How to shuck oysters.
13. How to clean squid.

How to Bone a Shad

The secret of boning shad has been guarded carefully and the technique has been handed down through generations in a few families. Boning a shad is a tedious process that very few professionals have mastered. It is estimated that over 95 percent of all chefs in the United States have no idea how to bone a shad. Surprisingly, in Europe, shad is very seldom boned. The French have partially solved the problem. When this author asked an eminent French chef why the alose (shad) was cooked whole, he replied that the sorrel softens the bones of the fish. In France, most shad are cooked whole (à l'oseille), with sorrel that is available fresh, frozen, or in cans or jars.

Still, in the United States, we are willing to pay high prices for boneless shad. Anyone can master the boning of shad using the following procedure. With practice, one should be able to bone a shad in ten minutes or less. Consider the fact that a 4-pound, 12-ounce (2.2 kg 150-g) whole round shad with roe yields two 6-ounce (170-g) roe and two 12-ounce (340-g) boneless fillets, about a 50 percent yield. In 1977, the average seasonal wholesale price, per pound, of whole shad with roe was $.80; boneless, the price was $2.25 to $2.50 per pound. Allowing for 50 percent waste, $1.60 would be the cost per pound for boneless shad if the consumer did the boning. This represents a saving of $.65 to $.90 per pound, depending on the market price of the boneless fish. At this price, it is worth knowing how to bone your shad.

1. Clip off all fins with shears except for the caudal (tail) fin.

2. Scale the fish even if it was purchased scaled. The scales are removed easily but stick stubbornly to any surface. Wash the shad under cold water.

3. Cut through the flesh between and under the gill covers. Use a very sharp boning knife during the entire boning process.

4. Insert the knife point between the roe, if it is a female, and the body wall. Carefully cut away from the roe and toward the vent on the left side of the belly ridge. If the shad is a male, the process is the same even though the fish does not contain roe.

(The first four steps are preliminary and need not be illustrated for our purposes here.)

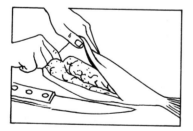

5. If you have been careful in cutting through the lower body wall (belly flap), the roe should be intact. The many small bones that are cut through

the belly will be eliminated in the final trimming.

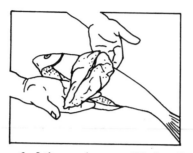

6. Lift out the roe. Wash off and soak in brine for several hours before cooking.

7. Cut off the head close behind the base of the pectoral (side) fins.

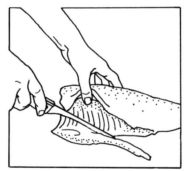

8. Cut off the belly ridge. You will feel the knife pass through the small bones that extend from the belly ridge up into the body wall.

9. Cut along the left side of the back bone and base of the dorsal fin; the cut must be made close and over the bones. (This procedure is followed when boning any other fin fish.) As

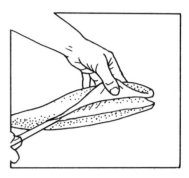

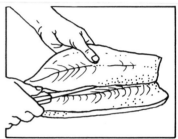

the knife passes along the vertical bones it will meet and cut through two rows of lateral bones that connect to the vertical bones. Then slide the knife along the rib cage and lift the fillet. Do not cut through the rib cage bones.

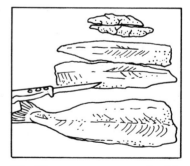

10. The same process is followed on the other side of the fish. The result is two fillets

ready for boning and a bony carcass to be discarded.

11. Select a small board about 1 inch (2.5 cm) longer and wider than the fillet.

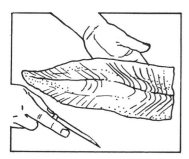

12. Start with the fillet from the right side of the fish. Blot the fillet dry with paper towels; place on the board. You will notice a row of bones that come to the surface along the lateral line of the center of the fillet.

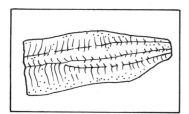

13. Step 13 shows a diagrammatic representation of the right fillet ready for boning. The back is at the top of the picture, and the belly at the bottom. The head is to the left. Note the outcropping of the ends of three rows of bones that are exposed on the fleshy side of the fillet. The bones project down into

the fillet and then curve and lay next to the skin. Examine this diagram in relation to your fillet. In some of the following steps, the fillet is turned so that the back (dorsal) side is at the lower side of the illustration. When this occurs, the terms *above*, *below, back* (dorsal) *side,* and *belly* (ventral) *side* refer to the right fillet as shown in this diagram. As you proceed in boning the fillet, refer occasionally to this diagram to orient yourself.

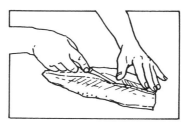

14. Place the fillet in the same relative position as the one illustrated. Start cutting on the belly (ventral) side of the center side (lateral) bones, to the skin but not through it. You will have to cut through some bones at the head end of the fillet (see diagram). Make another cut toward the back of the lateral bones. Again cut to the skin but not through it. These two cuts, one on each side of the lateral bones, are to be made the length of the fillet.

15. Pull out the lateral bones using a knife to loosen the strip

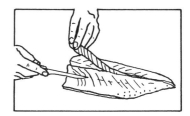

from the skin if the cuts are not perfect.

16. Now feel the row of bones that poke out the length of this fillet on the back (dorsal) part, above the strip of lateral bones that already have been removed. This row of bones begins at the head end of the fillet, curves upward slightly, then straightens out and continues to the tail end of the fillet. Begin your cut about 1/16-inch (2mm) below this row of bones (toward the lateral strip). Cut straight down to (but not through) the skin from the head end of the fillet to about half way to the tail where you will feel your knife meet some bones. Do not cut through these bones.

17. At about half the distance toward the tail, the bones you have been following start curving under the flesh close to the

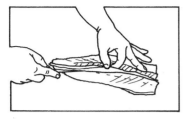

skin toward the lateral strip. Let your knife ride over the bones by turning your blade toward the lateral strip. Cut in this manner to the tail end. The boneless strip of flesh you have just cut away from the bones will be connected to the skin almost the entire length. Fold it back toward the center of the fillet.

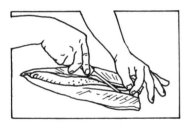

18. The next cut begins at the head end of the fillet, about 1/16-inch (2 mm) above (dorsal to) the row of bones on which you have been working. Cut down deeply to where the bones curve outward and under the knife. Do not cut through them. As you cut toward the tail, the bones become shallower. Continue this cut about one-half the length of the fillet, toward the tail.

19. After cutting half the distance to the tail, the bones begin to curve out closer to the fleshy

surface of the fillet. Turn the knife blade outward and let it ride over the bones. Cut over the bones, not through them. Feel the bones with your fingers since they are difficult to see.

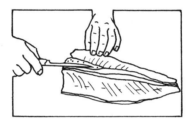

20. Turn the boning board and fillet so that the head end is closer to you. Lay back the fleshy part closest to you and carefully cut it away from the bones. Let the knife ride over the bones. Cut out to, but not past, the end of the bones. Leave the edge of the flap of flesh attached to the skin beyond the end of these bones. Lay the fleshy portion out and away from the center of the fillet.

21. The back part of the fillet now has two boneless fleshy portions; between them is a section full of bones that must be removed next. As illustrated,

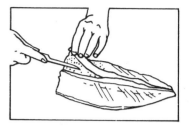

cut at the head end outward from the center. Your knife must pass under the bones and between the bones and the skin. Be careful not to cut through the skin.

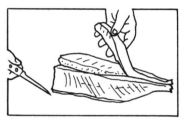

22. Continue separating the bones from the skin, working toward the tail end. After cutting two-thirds of the distance to the tail end, remove the entire bony portion with a quick tug. If this does not work, separate the bony strip with your knife until completely removed.

23. Turn the boning board and fillet so the tail end is closest to you. One more row of bones projects out of the fleshy part of the fillet. It begins about one-quarter of the distance from the head end of the fillet to the tail end, on the line where the lateral (middle side) strip was removed. This row of bones

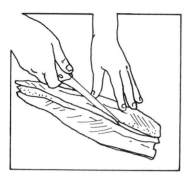

curves outward and becomes parallel to the lateral line as it approaches the tail. (See diagram.) Run your finger along these bones to locate them. Begin your cut above (dorsal to) the bones at the lateral line as illustrated. As the knife passes toward the tail, the bones curve toward the lateral line and become shallower. Do not cut through them.

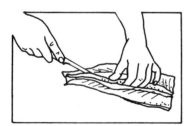

24. Let the knife ride over the bones. Fold back the flap of flesh as it is freed from the bones. Look closely, as the bones become finer as they approach the lateral line; the ends are actually fibers. Cut through the fibers toward the skin, leaving the fleshy section attached to the skin.

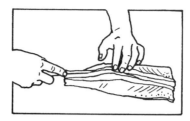

25. Begin the next cut at the head end about ⅛ inch toward the belly from the cut where the lateral strip was removed. Cut down into the fillet until you feel the bones with your knife; do not cut through them. Cut toward the tail to a point where you began the last cut. Continue the cut about ⅛ inch from your last cut on the other side of this row of bones. As the knife reaches about one-half the distance to the tail, turn the edge of the blade outward toward the edge of the fillet. Let the knife ride over the bones without cutting through them.

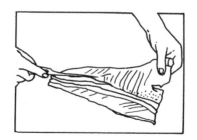

26. Continue to cut the fleshy section from the underlying bones, leaving it attached to the skin at the outer edge of the fillet, just beyond the ends of the bones. Lay the fleshy strip away from the bony portion.

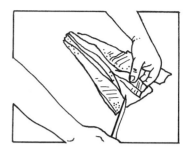

27. Turn the boning board and the fillet to the position shown in the illustration. Beginning at the head end, near the center of the fillet, start cutting under the bones, separating the bones from the skin.

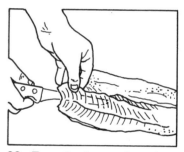

28. Turn the boning board so that the belly (ventral part) of the fillet is away from you, and slide your knife between the bones and the skin. Continue cutting in this manner until the bony strip can be removed.

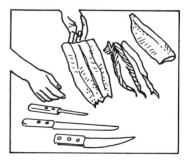

29. With the last bony section removed and with all the fleshy boneless flaps laid back, your fillet should look like the one illustrated. To the right are the three strips of bones taken from the fillet. At this point, fold the fleshy flaps back in place, trim the edge of the fillet evenly, and cut off the last ¼ inch (½ cm) to ½ inch (1 cm) at the tail section.

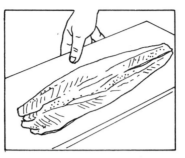

30. When the fillet is trimmed, it can be stored in a cold dry place, after being folded in wax paper. Do not let the fillet come in contact with water or ice. This will discolor the flesh, causing it to deteriorate.

Now you are ready to begin the same process with the left fillet. Don't give up—it takes practice to do the job well.

How to Bone a Summer Flounder or Fluke

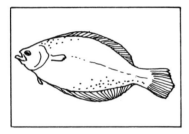

1. The illustration shows the dark side (as opposed to the white side) of a 5 pound (2.270 kg) summer flounder, also known as fluke.

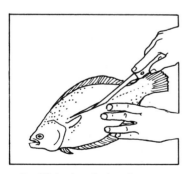

2. With the dark side up, use a sharp flexible knife to make an

incision along the spine bone of the flounder, from the gills to the tail.

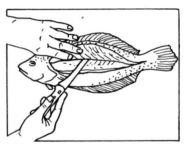

3. Slide the blade of the knife between the backbone and the flesh of the fish, lifting one fillet, but making sure it remains attached to the bones.

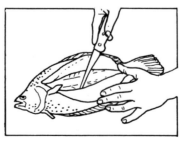

4. Cut the other fillet in the same manner. The fillets from the dark side of a fluke are approximately double the size of the white side fillets.

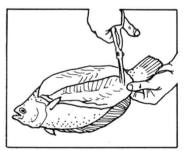

5. Cut the bone, with scissors, at the base of the tail.

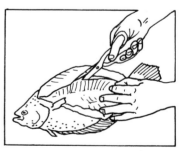

6. Cut the bone all around at the base of the fins, but not through the flesh.

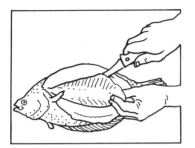

7. Slide the blade of the knife under the bone, starting from the tail end, and cut the flesh off the bone.

8. Cut off the bone at the base of the head. Clean and eviscerate the flounder.

9. Shown is a boneless flounder.

10. The fish can be stuffed with fish mousse, crabmeat, mushrooms, or other suitable stuffing.

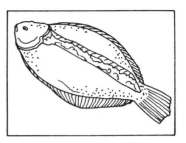

11. Fold the uncut fillets over the stuffing.

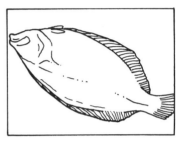

12. Turn the fish over, showing the white side, and place on a buttered baking pan. See the recipe Stuffed Flounder Nicolas for complete instructions.

How to Clean Blue Mussels

1. Live mussels usually keep their shells tightly closed; discard those with open shells.

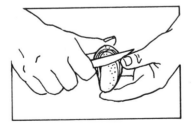

2. Scrub each shell thoroughly to remove mud and grass.

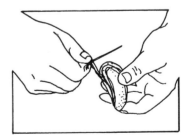

3. Pull the beards that are attached between the shells. Wash mussels in cold water and use according to the recipe.

How to Dress Soft-shell Crabs

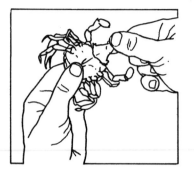

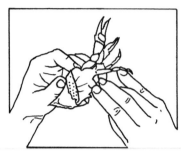

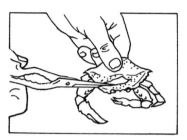

1. Remove the apron, that is, the segmented abdominal part of the body underneath the carapace.

2. Lift each of the pointed ends of the carapace to remove the spongy parts.

3. Cut off the face of the crab about ½ inch (1.25 cm) behind the eyes. This part contains the sensory and respiratory organs and the digestive system, all unsuitable for consumption.

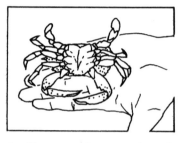

4. Shown is the muscular edible portion with the legs.

How to Fillet a Flounder

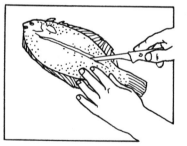

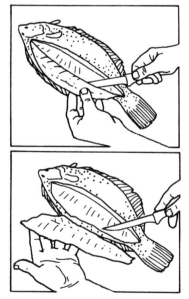

1. Shown are both the dark and white sides of the flounder.

2. Place flounder, dark side up, on a cutting board. Using a flexible boning knife, make an incision along the spine of the flounder, from the gills to the tail.

3. Slide the blade of the knife between the backbone and the flesh of the fillet, cutting the fillet away from the bone.

4. Remove the first fillet. Re-move the second fillet in the same manner.

5. To skin the fillet, place the fillet skin side down. Grasping it by the tail end, cut the meat free by working in a seesaw motion as close to the skin as possible.

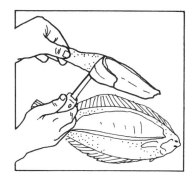

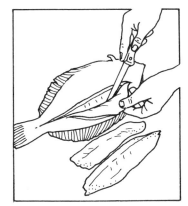

6. Turn the flounder over and repeat the process to remove

the last two fillets. Save bones for preparation of fish fumet.

How to Fillet a Whole Dressed Fish

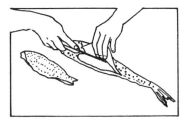

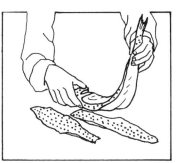

1. Slide a boning knife along the backbone, from head to tail, to remove first fillet.

2. Repeat process to remove second fillet.

3. Trim fillets, cutting off any bony edges and fins. Save backbone and head for fumet.

How to Fillet Imported Dover Sole

1. Imported sole from the Channel Islands and the North Sea is a species of flatfish in great demand in Europe. It is available frozen in the United States. The skin is light to dark gray on one side and white on the other side. Contrary to most species of domestic flounder and sole, the skin of imported

Dover sole is removed before filleting.

2. Cut off the fins with a pair of scissors. Place the fish with the white skin down on the working surface. Snip off the tail fin. Scrape off the skin starting at the tail end. Lift the skin and rip

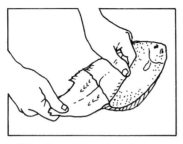

off with a tearing movement while holding the fish flat.

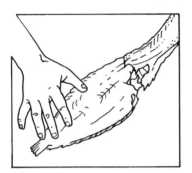

3. Following the same procedure, peel off the skin on the other side of the sole.

4. Cut off the head of the sole. Make an incision along the backbone. Slide the blade of a

flexible knife between the backbone and the fillet. Remove the first fillet.

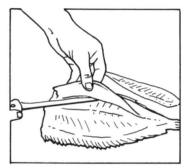

5. Remove the second fillet in the same manner. Turn the sole over and remove the third and fourth fillets. Save the bone for fumet.

6. Fillets of sole can be arranged and cooked in various manners, depending on the recipe and the presentation. Illustrated are some of the styles in

which fillets may be portioned. *Top left:* the straight fillets are slightly flattened with a meat pounder to prevent curling while cooking. *Top right:* a butterflied sole ready for cooking. The fillets remain attached to the bones. The bottom fillets are uncut. Notice that the bone is cut in three places for easy removal when cooked. Sole in this style is usually breaded and fried. *Center:* paupiettes of sole are flattened fillets seasoned and rolled up. A quenelle forcemeat can be spread over the fillets before rolling. *Bottom left:* the fillets are cut into so-called gougeonnettes and are usually breaded and fried. *Bottom center:* fillets are folded in half and can be stuffed with a forcemeat. *Bottom right:* another way of folding fillets for poaching.

How to Poach a Whole Fish for Cold Presentation

The presentation of a cold decorated fish in an upright position is an elegant, easy method of displaying a whole "swimming" fish, in contrast to the common "nature morte" (lying on the side). The fish can be slightly curved before poaching to add another dimension to the final presentation.

For best results, fish weighing 6 pounds (2.7 kg) or more should be poached, or at times baked, in the upright position.

The illustrations show a Lake Huron whitefish ready for poaching. The soft texture of whitefish permits easy curving. (See page 296 for Cold Whitefish, Sauce Andalouse.)

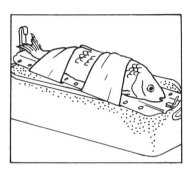

1. Clean, scale, and wash the fish. Place in an upright position on the rack of a fish poacher.

2. To hold the fish safely, wrap cheese cloth around the rack and the fish. Tie the cloth loosely.

Immerse the fish in court bouillon, making sure it is completely covered. Cook according to poaching directions in chapter 6.

How to Shell, Devein, and Butterfly Large Shrimp

1. With a sharp knife, make a ¼-inch incision along the back, from head to tail.

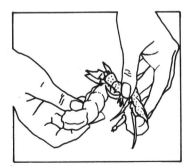

2. Wash under cold running water to remove sand track (devein). Strip off shells and legs, leaving the tail intact. You now have a fantail shrimp.

The tail is a convenient, decorative part of the shrimp. It is easily grasped by the cook for dipping in batter before frying, or by the diner for eating. Do not coat the tail with batter or breading.

When butterflying shrimp, use a large or jumbo shrimp. Shell and devein, leaving the tail intact as shown. With a sharp knife, cut along the back but not all the way through. Separate halves and spread open. The illustration shows, from top to bottom, headless unpeeled shrimp, fantail shrimp, and butterflied shrimp.

How to Prepare Lobster for Cold Preparation

1. Select a live lobster from 3 pounds (1.360 kg) up to 20 pounds (9 kgs), depending on the type of display desired.

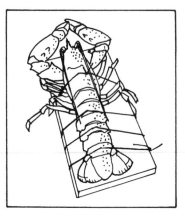

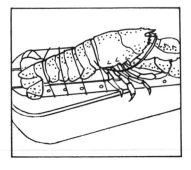

2. Lay the crustacean flat on a rectangular board or on the rack of a fish poacher (poissonniere). Tie string around the lobster to prevent the tail from curling up while cooking. Secure the attennae. Boil in court bouillon no. 3, timing it 10 minutes per pound. (Lobsters exceeding 8 to 10 pounds should simmer for the same amount of time.) When cooked, remove from bouillon and cool at room temperature, then refrigerate.

How to Shuck Hard-shell Clams

Clams on The Half Shell

1. Wash the shell clams thoroughly, discarding any broken shells or dead clams.

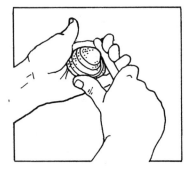

2. Hold the clam in the palm of the left hand. Place the sharp edge of a clam knife against the outside edge between shells. Exert a firm pressure with the left hand and fingers against the dull or heavy side of the knife blade, forcing the blade between the shells and severing the first muscle.

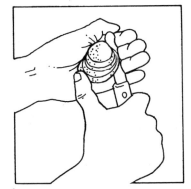

3. To pry open the shell, run knife around edge of the shell to cut the second muscle, located opposite the first. Do not damage the flesh of the clam.

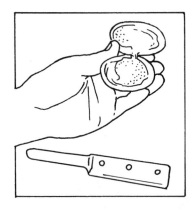

4. Open clam and discard upper shell. Loosen clam from lower shell and examine for shell fragments.

5. Serve as shown. Cocktail sauce usually accompanies raw clams on half shells.

Other Uses

1. To open a large amount of hard-shell clams rapidly, rinse and clean the shells, and arrange in one layer on a tray or sheet pan; place in a 420°F (220°C) oven for 5 minutes. The clams will open partially. *The flesh should not be cooked.*

2. Cut the muscles, remove the meat, and save the juice.

How to Shuck Oysters

1. Wash the shell oysters thoroughly.

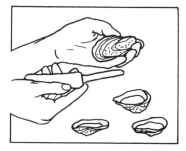

2. Hold the oyster in the palm of your hand.

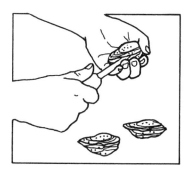

3. Place the edge of an oyster knife against the outside edge

between the shells. With the fingers, exert firm pressure against the knife blade, forcing it between the shells.

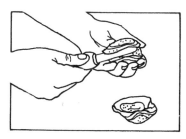

4. To pry open the shell, run the knife around the edge of the shell to cut the muscle holding the valves together.

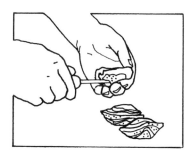

5. Loosen the oyster from the lower shell; examine for shell fragments.

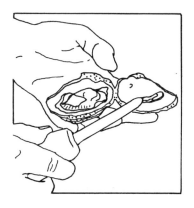

6. Shown is an oyster on a half shell, ready to be served.

How to Clean Squid

See diagram.

For Stuffing and Rings

1. Thaw squid if frozen.

2. Hold mantle with one hand. With other hand, grasp head and arms, and pinch quill at opening to separate from mantle.

3. While holding on to chitinous pen and head, remove pen, head, and intestines with pulling motion.

4. Starting with tail end, pinch fins, pulling fins and outer membrane from mantle. Peel off remaining membrane.

5. Wash mantle thoroughly under cold water. Keep whole for stuffing or cut into rings.

Preparing Tentacles and Arms

1. Squid have two tentacles and eight arms. Cut across head in front of *eyes* to retain arms.

2. Squeeze out round sack containing cartilage or beak.

3. Skin may be removed from arms more easily if they are first placed in boiling water for 2 to 3 minutes.

Preparing Squid for Strips and Pieces

1. From opening in mantle of squid, cut mantle with knife lengthwise. Spread inside of mantle open flat.

2. Pressing mantle with one hand, grasp head and arms and pull off intestines at the same time. Take out chitinous pen. With a knife, scrape away visceral remains adhering to the inside of mantle wall.

3. Turn mantle to other side and pull fins and outer membrane from mantle.

4. Wash squid under cold water. Cut mantle into strips or desired size pieces.

CHAPTER 6

Techniques for Cooking Fish

The shape, color, texture, and structure of fish and shellfish are so varied that they afford a multitude of cooking techniques, which are interesting and appealing to professionals, amateurs, and consumers.

One important point is that any cooking method applied to fish or shellfish requires low heat. The nutritive value of seafoods is destroyed by intense heat and overcooking.

There are fourteen cooking techniques detailed in this chapter:

au bleu
au gratin
baking and braising
broiling
deep frying
en papillotte
glazing
marinating and pickling
pan frying and oven frying
poaching or simmering
sauteing (meuniere)
smoking
steaming
stewing

These general techniques provide valuable information with which the reader should be acquainted before entering the wonderful world of seafood cooking. The composition of each fish helps determine the best cooking method, particularly if the reader tackles recipes not included in this book. Several fish accept almost any cooking method; salmon, trout, sole, and shrimp are among the most versatile species. One can create at will with these fish.

The cooking techniques described in this section are of utmost importance to the layperson. They provide a basic understanding of and a foundation for seafood cooking.

Au Bleu

This exclusive cooking technique of European origin is used mainly for trout and occasionally for pickerel. Fish cooked au bleu (in the blue style) must be live shortly before cooking.

The fish is dispatched with a blow on the head and gutted through the gills. Avoid overhandling of the skin. The viscous matter covering the fish takes on a bluish tint when it comes in contact with the hot vinegar that is poured over the fish before poaching in court bouillon. The hot liquid causes the flesh to curl up and sometimes split. If the fish are to be presented in an ordered manner, and this applies particularly to cold trout, it is preferable to tie the head and the tail of each fish before cooking so that they join together. A free fish that contacts boiling liquid will curl in different directions, resulting in a poor presentation. Fish au bleu, curled up from head to tail, can be decorated elegantly and served hot or cold.

How to Cook Trout Au Bleu

The best procedure is to immerse the trout, cleaned and tied, in a strong solution of vinegar and water to get a blue skin. Then the cooking process is continued in a court bouillon. Bring to a boil 2 quarts (2 l) of water and 2 cups (5 dl) of wine vinegar. In the meantime, prepare court bouillon no. 2 (see page 133). Gently lower the trout into the boiling water and vinegar until the skin becomes blue. Then transfer to the court bouillon and poach at 185°F (85°C) for 10 to 15 minutes.

Arrange on a serving platter and decorate with parsley and lemon baskets. Serve hot or cold.

Au Gratin

This method embraces many possibilities, since almost any fish is suitable for the golden brown dish called au gratin. The process consists of coating the prepared fish with cheese or breadcrumbs, or a rich fish sauce. The fish is then placed in the oven or under the broiler to brown.

The au gratin technique is classified into two types. One utilizes fresh uncooked seafood; the other has cooked or leftover seafoods as the main ingredient. The first cooking process requires perfect timing as the fish must cook and brown simultaneously. The clean whole fish or fillet is placed in a suitable buttered baking dish and covered with a small layer of duxelle (chopped mushrooms and chopped shallots). The addition of dry white wine is desirable for a large whole fish or fillets. A rich fish sauce coats the fish and the bottom of the baking dish. Allow extra sauce for a large fish (5 lbs. or over) as the longer cooking time causes a greater reduction of the sauce. Sprinkle fresh breadcrumbs over the top of the fish and bake until the fish is fully cooked and browned. To obtain the best possible results, a large fish or fillet cooks best at 350°F (180°C); a small fish portion or fillet should be cooked at 375°F (190°C) to brown the sauce quickly and prevent overcooking of the fish. To speed up the au gratin process, the fish can be browned under a hot broiler for a few seconds. This is also advisable if the fish is cooked but not yet brown.

The second cooking method is commonly used for leftover seafood or freshly poached fish and shellfish. It is a fast technique that gives remarkable results, providing the garnishes and ingredients used are of good quality. The sauce, crowning touch to a dish au gratin, must be prepared and seasoned with great care. The cooked fish is boned, skinned, and flaked and then placed in a buttered baking dish. A fine duxelle is usually combined with the flaked fish. Heat the fish in the oven for a while and pour a hot sauce over it. Sprinkle with grated cheese or breadcrumbs, and melted butter, and brown in a 375° to 400°F (190° to 205°C) oven.

Recipes of fish au gratin are easily created. Today, many canned fish have found an important role in the au gratin cooking technique. Among those fish, tuna and salmon are great favorites. Shellfish, such as crab, shrimp, and scallops, also suit our sophisticated tastes. Seafood Au Gratin a l'Americaine, Oysters Rockefeller Au Gratin, and Stone Crab Au Gratin are examples of the multitude of possibilities available with this technique.

Au gratin fish dishes have been designed recently to suit our hurried kitchen schedules. Fish recipes are increasingly turned into full meals; vegetables, potatoes, noodles, and cream soups for sauces are included in the recipes. These new dishes reflect the state of our society—everything must be done quickly and efficiently, with minimum cost, waste, and effort. Leftover fish florentine (with spinach) with cheese sauce, cooked salmon with eggplant and tomato sauce, or tuna with egg noodles, broccoli, and canned mushroom soup are just a few examples of high protein dishes, important to our diet and easy to prepare in a short time. Thrifty cooks can create many fish dishes au gratin from basic casseroles.

Baking and Braising

Baking and braising applies to whole fish, lean or fat. Baking is a form of dry heat cooking used for fish with a high fat content; the braising method, which combines dry and moist heat, is commonly used for whole lean and fat fish (salmon, large lake trout, bass, bluefish, etc.).

Depending on the recipe, the fish can be stuffed or filleted, and the cooking liquid can differ with each recipe. Usually, a rich fumet combined with a dry white wine is poured over the fish, to cover half or less, before baking or braising. A fatty fish can be baked without any liquid. In this case, it is preferable to cover the fish with strips of bacon to prevent drying. Bake at a moderate temperature and baste frequently.

Broiling

The broiling method is particularly suitable for fish with a high fat content, although lean fish are also broiled. Whole small fish, fish fillets, and fish steaks are ideal individual portions for broiling.

A lean fragile fillet of fish, like lemon sole, brook trout, sea trout, or flounder, is coated with flour and dipped in oil before broiling, to prevent drying while cooking. Even a fish with high fat content should be lightly oiled prior to broiling. Since butter has a tendency to burn under intense heat, a combination of half oil and half butter is recommended.

To facilitate the handling of fish, hand racks are commonly used. They eliminate breakage but permit turning of the fish that is held between the racks. Shellfish, particularly sea scallops and shrimp, can be broiled on skewers.

Broiled seafood should be served as soon as cooked. It is customary to garnish broiled fish and shellfish with lemon wedges or lemon baskets and a bunch of fresh parsley. A partially broiled fish, baked just before serving time, retains more moisture than a fish fully cooked on the broiler.

Maitre d'hotel butter, anchovy butter, or ravigotte butter (see chapter 11) are excellent accompaniments to broiled seafoods.

Note: The broiling method is done on a grill (charcoal, electric, gas, or other) with the source of heat coming from above or below. Today, many cooks divert from this method by cooking fish and shellfish on a sheet pan under a top broiler; the method is improperly called broiling. To be broiled, foods must be cooked on a grill.

Deep Frying

In the United States, the consumption of deep-fried fish and shellfish is greater than for seafood cooked by any other method. Deep-fat frying is a popular cooking process suitable for small whole fish, fish fillets or steaks, shellfish, or frozen breaded fish products. It is a speedy method much appreciated by food operators. Seafoods to be fried are invariably coated, breaded, or dipped in batter. To accentuate the flavor in many recipes, fish is marinated prior to breading. Frozen breaded fish and shellfish can be purchased all year round and are profitable menu items sold under various titles.

Most often, fried fish is served with tartar sauce, although many other cold sauces are favored by seafood lovers. Simple, unsophisticated, tasty cold sauces meet the approval of many gourmets, and tartar sauce is only one among many. For more details on cold sauces, see chapter 11.

Any fish or shellfish to be fried should be processed, cleaned, seasoned, sometimes marinated, and then breaded or dipped in batter. Usually, boneless fish fillets or sticks are dipped in a semi-liquid batter and cooked immediately in hot fat. Fish and shellfish to be breaded are coated in flour, dipped in beaten eggs, and rolled in preferably fresh bread crumbs. Commercially prepared crumb mixtures are also available in different forms.

Fish fried in batter does not have as crispy a surface as breaded fish. However, fast food chains are presently selling a popular fish and chips dish with a cooked batter that has a remarkably lasting crust. Perhaps culinary secrets still exist.

The fish frying method offers many advantages, providing a few factors are considered:

1. The quality of the frying medium, vegetable oil or shortening, should be without reproach; a decomposed fat increases the frying time of fish and causes a greater absortion of fat. Clean, strained fat is important for proper frying.

2. The temperature of the deep fryer should be between 350° and 375°F. It is generally recognized that the shorter the cooking time the higher the temperature. For example, freshly breaded soft-shell crabs or bay scallops cook best at 375°F for 3 to 4 minutes; the outside crust browns rapidly and the inside remains moist and tender. If the cooking time is longer, the deep-frying temperature should be lower. A thick fillet of gray sole, dipped in batter, should fry best at 350°F, until golden brown and cooked in the center. At higher temperatures, the outside surface burns, damaging the fish and preventing the penetration of heat. The result is uncooked burned fish.

3. The cooking time varies with the size and volume of the fish, the temperature of the deep fryer, the temperature of the fish, and finally the condition of the fat. These factors are of great importance when determining the proper cooking time for frying seafoods.

4. Do not overload the deep fryer, particularly when frying frozen breaded fish. A fast temperature recovery deep fryer with a thermostat is strongly recommended to keep a constant temperature when frying frozen seafood. This also applies to any large amount of fresh fish to be fried.

When using a conventional deep fryer, always determine the temperature of the fat with a thermometer, if the fryer is not equipped with one. A drop of water will not tell the temperature, and guessing can be deceiving.

5. Change the fat as soon as it shows any sign of poor frying: an abnormal absorption of fat into the fish, a dark burnt color, and unpleasant odors are indications that fat should be replaced. Fat kept in excellent condition will always give a quality fried fish with minimum effort.

Caution: reusing cooking oil may be economical, but it also exposes humans to possible health hazards. A fifteen-year study of fats and oils used in frying has shown that once the products decompose, harmful chemical changes occur. Professor Chang of Rutgers University in New Jersey said, "Using fresh fats and oils for frying is perfectly safe, but the longer cooking oil is kept at high heat and exposed to oxygen of the air, the more dangerous it becomes." A word of caution: be wary when oil appears to flow more slowly in a pan, or becomes darker.

Oil Absorption in Deep Fat Frying

We often hear that deep-fried foods are too greasy, too fattening, or unhealthy because of the high absorption of oil. An experiment conducted by this author shows that an 8-ounce (226-g) deep-fried serving of fish or shellfish absorbs less oil than a portion of salad seasoned with an oil and vinegar dressing or other oil-based dressing. The experiment was carried out under normal conditions, with 2 gallons (8 l) of fresh oil. Five pounds of freshly breaded, headless medium shrimp were deep fried at 370°F (188°C), frying 1 pound (450 g) at a time to avoid an overload. The cooking time for each load was 3½ minutes.

After the oil cooled and was strained, a measurement showed that only 5 fluid ounces (2 dl) of oil were absorbed by the fried shrimp. Considering an 8-ounce (226-g) serving of shrimp, this represents a mere tablespoon of oil per serving.

Consequently, providing all five measures described for deep frying are taken into consideration, deep-fried fish and shellfish definitely are not hazardous to our health. The absorption of oil is minimal if the fish or shellfish are breaded with care and cooked under the proper conditions.

The Breading of Fish and Shellfish

The primary objective of breading is to provide a crispy protective covering to fried seafoods. The products used in breading are flour, eggs, and breading agents that include bread crumbs, cracker meal, corn meal, and other commercially prepared products. The breading procedure is done in three steps:

1. Coat the seasoned fish or shellfish thoroughly in flour.
2. Immerse in beaten eggs, or mixture of eggs and water or milk, to cover the entire surface.
3. Drain and cover with crumbs or any other breading agent. Finally, shake off any excess breading and fry without delay. Clams and oysters contain a high degree of moisture and must be fried immediately after breading or they become soggy and sticky. In general,

moist seafood should not be breaded too far in advance.

En Papillotte

This is a clever way to seal a combination of flavors in a bag! The technique is quite simple and is applied to small whole fish or fillets. The raw or precooked fish is enclosed in a heart-shaped sheet of parchment paper. Garnishes, herbs, and seasonings are added to contribute to the development of an incomparably subtle flavor.

The dimension of the heart-shaped parchment paper should correspond to the size of the whole fish or fillet(s) to be cooked. The portion of fish is placed on one side of the heart, with butter, lemon juice, seasonings, herbs, garnishes, and any other ingredients listed in the recipe. The other side of the heart is folded over from the center, covering the fish; the edges are then sealed tightly. The parchment is greased on the outside to prevent burning, and placed in a 400°F (205°C) oven.

As the fish cooks, some steam will puff the bag and the parchment paper will brown. As soon as the fish is cooked, slide the bag onto a plate and serve immediately. At the table, supply a sharp knife to cut the paper. The opening of the bag will release a delicious aroma and the fullest flavors any recipe can possibly give. This cooking method adds drama to conventional recipes and is quite appropriate for noble fish such as pompano, salmon, and king crab.

Fish and shellfish can also be enclosed in puff pastry or other dough. The excellent recipe Mousseline of Salmon Royale is a typical example of fish en feuillete, instead of en papillotte. The golden brown, crusty pastry seals in the flavor of fish and adds a new dimension to fish and shell-fish cooking (see chapter 7).

Glazing

The most intriguing technique adaptable to sea-food is glazing. For glazing, whole fish, fillets, or shellfish are baked with fish fumet and white wine. Small fillets can be folded and stuffed with a color-contrasting mousse (fillet of sole with salmon mousse or jumbo pink shrimp stuffed with pike mousse). Other garnishes, especially chopped shallots, mushrooms, tomatoes, and chopped parsley, are often included in the recipes to add flavor.

The cooked fish is transferred to a warm serving platter and the strained cooking liquid is reduced to ½ to ⅔ of its volume in a heavy saucepan. Heavy cream is added and the reduction continues until the sauce thickens. At this time, a cream sauce and fresh butter are stirred into the sauce. The addition of hollandaise sauce contributes to the glazing ability of the sauce.

This marvelous sauce is poured over the fish and, when placed under a hot broiler, glazes instantly. Many chefs do not add a cream sauce to the reduced stock, but just use the essence of the reduced fumet with heavy cream. Continuous boiling reduces the sauce to the desired thickness. Bits of fresh butter are stirred into the sauce and a small amount of hollandaise sauce increases the glazing power of the fish sauce. Under a hot broiler the sauce will glaze in 5 to 10 seconds. This glazing technique is unique to fish and is found in several recipes in this book. The concentration of fish flavors in the sauce transforms any glazed fish into a culinary marvel.

Marinating and Pickling

Several species of fish profit from marinating or pickling. The objective of this technique is to preserve the fish and add an aromatic flavor that varies with the type of herbs and species used. Herring, mackerel, salmon, and other fish acquire a new taste and flavor when marinated or pickled. Generally, fish with a high fat content are best for marinating or pickling.

A short marinade for any fish or shellfish consists of chopped onions, chopped shallots, parsley, crushed thyme, bay leaves, lemon juice, and soy sauce. Small fish fillets, fingers, or shellfish are marinated for an hour or two before cooking. The marinade is blended thoroughly with the seafood. To accentuate the flavor of marinated fish and shellfish, monosodium glutamate is sometimes added to the marinade.

Marinades consisting of white wine, salt, pepper, and herbs are called cooked marinades, as whole fish or fillets are cooked in it. Such fish include herring, mackerel, trout, and others. For further details, refer to the chapters covering these fish.

The major ingredient for pickling fish is vinegar. A large variety of fresh- and salt-water fish can be pickled. The pickling method has the advantage of conserving fish for a great length of time. Canada, Iceland, and the Scandinavian countries produce large amounts of pickled fish. Haddock, herring, and cod are native to the cold waters of these countries and preserve better in a brine or pickling solution than in a freezer. These fish are usually prepared onboard ships and can be purchased commercially.

Fish acquire a new dimension especially when treated according to specific recipes. Such is the gravlax, a Swedish salmon delicacy that is easily prepared by marinating fillets of salmon with dill, onion, salt, sugar, spices, and lemon juice. The fish is marinated for several days (2 to 3) and served, thinly sliced, as an appetizer with brown bread and a mustard sauce. Gravlax is always part of a Swedish smorgasbord (see recipe in chapter 12).

Mackerel cooked with white wine, carrots, onions, and spices improves considerably in flavor. The recipe for mackerel in white wine is given in chapter 12.

A typical recipe of South American origin is seviche. This is a marinating method of preserving fish for a short period of time, usually from 3 to 4 days. The fish is literally "cooked" by the citric acid of fruit (lemon or lime). For a complete recipe for seviche, see page 221.

Pan Frying and Oven Frying

The pan-frying method is used for small whole fish, fish fillets, steaks, and shellfish. The surface of the seafood is seasoned and coated with flour or crumbs to provide a crisp golden brown color. The three-step breading method used for deep frying can also be used for pan-fried seafood.

Pan-fried fish or shellfish are cooked in a heavy frying pan or skillet containing a small amount of butter. Cook at low temperature to brown one side; turn to complete cooking and browning. Another pan-frying method, very popular in France, is called A l'Anglaise. This is a variation of the standard pan-frying technique that is used primarily for fish fillets. A flavored mixture (l'Anglaise) is prepared by beating whole eggs with salt, ground white pepper, and a small quantity of oil. Cover the fish fillets with flour; shake to remove any excess. Dip the fillets into the egg mixture. Drain well, then roll in breadcrumbs,

patting the fillets with the palm of the hand to make the breadcrumbs stick. With the blunt edge of a knife, mark out squares on one side of the fish fillets. Melt some butter in a heavy skillet and pan fry the fillets with the marked sides down. Cook gently to brown, turn over carefully, and cook until the fish is flaky.

Pan-fried fish and shellfish are served with lemon wedges, butter mixtures, or hot sauces.

Oven frying produces a product similar to pan frying. Place fish fillets on a shallow, well-greased baking pan. Pour melted butter or fat over the fish and bake in a 450°F (230°C) oven until fish flakes easily when tested with a fork. Fish cooked in this way do not require turning or basting, and the cooking time is short. (See Table 6.1) This method is ideal when serving fish to large groups.

Poaching or Simmering

Poaching or simmering, improperly called boiling, is a cooking technique widely used for fish. The selection of the cooking liquid, called court bouillon (see chapter 8), is determined by the type of fish to be poached. A fresh-water fish, lacking flavor, is poached in a court bouillon containing a generous amount of seasoning and herbs; the salt-water fish requires a milder court bouillon.

A poissonniere, an oblong fish poacher with a rack, allows easy handling of a whole fish when poaching (see Figure 6.1). The most common fish poached in a poissonniere are salmon, northern pike, sea trout, red snapper, weakfish, sea bass, grouper, and striped bass. Any of these fish can be poached whole, in steaks, in pieces, or in fillets. The diamond-shaped poacher with a rack, called a turbotiere, is used to poach the imported turbot and the brill (see Figure 6.2). These two flat fish

Table 6.1   Chart for poaching fish

| Whole Dressed | | Steaks, Fillets, Pieces | |
Served hot	Served cold	Served hot	Served cold
5 minutes per pound of clean fish. Take out of court bouillon. Serve hot.	3 minutes per pound of clean fish. Cool in court bouillon. Serve cold.	10 minutes per inch (2.5 cm) thickness. Take out of court bouillon. Serve hot.	5 minutes per inch (2.5 cm) thickness. Cool in court bouillon. Serve cold.

Notes: Weigh clean dressed fish, steaks, fillets or pieces or measure at the thickest point.

Start poaching in cold court bouillon.

Time fish when court bouillon reaches 180°F to 185°F (82°C to 85°C).

If served hot, take out of court bouillon after cooking time is elapsed.

If served cold, allow to cool in court bouillon.

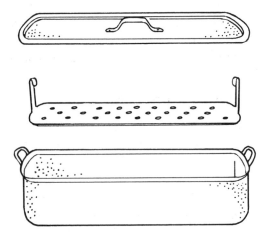

Figure 6.1   Poissonniere

are no longer in much demand in the United States.

The following points should be remembered when poaching fish:

1. All fish should be poached starting with cold court bouillon to preserve the full nutritional value.
2. The cooking time for whole fish to be served cold is 3 minutes per pound of clean drawn fish. In this case, allow the fish to cool in the

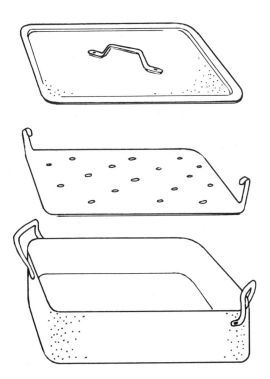

Figure 6.2   Turbotiere

court bouillon; it will retain more moisture and flavor. The cooking time starts at the simmering point, 180°–185°F (82°–85°C). To keep an accurate temperature, use a thermometer.

If the fish is to be served hot, allow 5 minutes per pound of clean drawn fish and remove from the court bouillon when the time has elapsed. A 10-pound, clean striped bass takes 50 minutes to poach if served hot. The cooking time would be 30 minutes if the fish were served cold.

3. To time the poaching of small pieces of fish, like steaks or center cut pieces and fillets, a different approach is necessary. Measure the thickness of the fish pieces at their thickest point and allow 10 minutes per inch (2.5 cm) thickness if served hot (5 minutes if served cold). The timing starts after the court bouillon has reached 180°F to 185°F (82°C to 85°C). For example, immerse a one-inch thick salmon steak in cold court bouillon. Bring the temperature of the court bouillon to 180°F to 185°F and poach 10 minutes. Remove from the cooking liquid and serve hot. If the salmon steak is to be served cold, cut the time by half and let the fish cool in the court bouillon.

When served cold, poached fish can be decorated elaborately (see chapter 16). Cold fish is accompanied by one or several cold sauces (see chapter 11). Hot poached fish is invariably served with a hot sauce and usually with parsleyed boiled or steamed potatoes.

Sauteing (Meuniere)

This excellent cooking technique is used for small fish, shellfish, fish fillets, and fish steaks. The fish are seasoned, floured, and pan fried in a small amount of clarified butter. For whole fish that take longer to cook than fillets or steaks, use half clarified butter and half oil to prevent burning. Brown the fish on one side, then turn to complete the cooking process. Transfer the fish to a warm serving platter. Sprinkle some chopped parsley on the fish. In a clean frying pan, melt some butter and pour in a small quantity of lemon juice. When the butter is brown and bubbly, pour over the fish and serve immediately.

The hazelnut flavor of the bubbling butter gives a delicious flavor to any sauteed fish. The cooking technique is simple and quick, and highly favored by many fish experts.

To complement the flavor of fish meuniere, recipes sometimes call for almonds, hazelnuts, and pine nuts. These add a new twist to this fine cooking method.

Smoking

The smoking method is probably as old as fire. The preservation of fish by smoking is a process that transforms such fish as salmon, trout, sturgeon, eel, mullet, and other species into delicacies. The salt and smoke impart a delectable flavor even to unpopular species of fish. The fatter the fish, the better for smoking. The oily sea herring is preferable to lake herring. Salmon is one of the best smoked fish, commanding high prices on the market, due to the high oil content of some species (10 to 15 percent).

Since salt-smoke cure is a drying and flavoring process, it is not recommended for lean fish; they tend to dry up and lose their flavor.

Basic Cures for Smoking

Dry salt:
2 cups (450 g) coarse pickling salt
1 cup (210 g) brown sugar
2 tbsp. cracked black pepper
½ oz. (15 g) sodium nitrate

Combine the salt, sugar, seasonings, and sodium nitrate. Rub well into the exposed surfaces of the fish. Small fish or fillets are left up to 6 hours in the curing mixture; large whole fish or fillets are generally cured for up to 12 hours. Other spices may be added to develop a particular flavor, such as cayenne, curry, caraway or cumin seeds, dill, fennel, or tarragon.

Brine:

1 gal. (4 l) water
1 cup (225 g) coarse or iodized salt
1 tbsp. cracked peppercorns
1 bay leaf

Dissolve salt in water. Add spices and immerse fish in the brine according to the instructions specified in the smoking process that follows.

Preparing Fish for Smoking

Clean fish, scale, and wash well. Wipe dry. Whole dressed fish, fillets, and butterfly pieces with the skin on are the most suitable cuts for smoking.

Smoking Procedures

There are two typical smoking methods, hot smoking and cold smoking. Both methods require curing in brine and smoking.

How to hot smoke fish   Fish processed by hot smoking are fully cooked and should be consumed within a few days, refrigerated, or frozen.

To hot smoke fish, split them into fillets, wash in cold fresh water, and soak in the brine for 30 minutes. Drain and transfer the fish to a curing mixture consisting of: 4 cups (910 g) salt; 2 cups (450 g) light brown sugar; 2 tbsp. crushed black peppercorns; 1 tbsp. crushed bay leaves; and 1 gal. (4 l) water. Allow the fish to steep in the brine for 2 to 4 hours, depending on the size, thickness,

amount of fat, and degree of curing desired. Rinse the fish in fresh water and hang in a cool breezy place to dry for 2 to 3 hours. Place fish in smoke house; build up a dense smoke keeping the temperature from 160°F (54°C) to 180°F (65°C) for up to four hours. The fish is now completely smoked.

How to cold smoke fish   The cold smoking of fish is primarily a commercial process for treating a large amount of fish. The fish are not cooked but cured in a brine and thoroughly dried at a temperature of 85°F (30°C) to 90°F (33°C) for a prolonged period. The preservation of smoked fish depends on the length of time the product is smoked and the amount of salt used. To cold smoke fish, you can use the dry salt method or the brine method.

With the dry salt method fish are cleaned, filleted (if large), and placed in brine for 30 minutes. The fish are then removed from the brine and rinsed in cold water. Drain off excess moisture. Next, place each fish or fillet in a shallow wooden box containing iodized salt. Dredge the pieces of fish and pick up as much salt as will cling to them. Place in even layers in another suitable wooden box. Leave the fish in salt for 6 hours, if split, or 12 hours, if whole, in a dry cool place. Rinse the fish in cold water and dry in a shady place until a fine shiny skin has formed on the surface. Under average conditions this will take 3 hours. Use an electric fan if necessary. The fish should not be smoked while moist; the smoke will steam the fish, impairing its color. Place the fish in a smokehouse not exceeding a temperature of 90°F (33°C). Use a thermometer to check the temperature of the smokehouse. For quality smoked fish, smoking should be done progressively, starting with light smoking and continuing more intensively. The smoking time should be proportionate to the size and shape of fish. A 10-to-12 pound (4.5 to-5.3-kg) salmon, split into fillets, will take about 48 hours of smoking; whole Idaho trout, about 12 hours. Fish exceeding 15 pounds (6.7 kg) need about 3 days of smoking. A few trial runs are helpful to determine the best timing.

The brine method for cold smoked fish differs from the dry salt process in so far as the fish are only placed for 12 hours in the curing salt mixture, then transferred to brine for 30 minutes. Before smoking, do not wash the fish but dry thoroughly as described for the cold smoking dry salt method. Follow the same cooking procedure.

Each country has curing and smoking processes similar to those described here. The species of fish may differ; the wood used for smoking is usually a hardwood native to the country (maple, hickory, oak, and apple). Scandinavians are experts in turning the silver baltic herring into a golden delicacy. What smoked herring is to Scandinavians, hamburgers are to Americans. These fish are treated with great reverence in Denmark, Norway, and Sweden. For many years, the Scots have had their particular way to smoke the champion of fish—Atlantic salmon. Here is a superb recipe for smoking salmon in the Scottish way.

Scottish Smoked Salmon

For a 10-to-12-pound (4.5-to-5.3-kg) salmon.

salt cure:
2 cups (450 g) coarse or iodized salt
2 cups (425 g) dark brown sugar
2 tbsp. cognac or brandy

Any fatty fish of good size can be smoked according to this method, but the colorful fatty flesh of salmon yields spectacular results. Anadromous fish like shad, striped bass, steelhead, or lake

whitefish are excellent substitutes. The fish should be fresh and whole.

Scrape or scale the fish. Split through the back into butterfly style to clean. Cut off the head and remove the bones. Salmon smoked according to the old Scottish method is not washed. The blood particles may or may not be washed out. Dry the fillets carefully if washed. Pour the brandy or cognac over the fillets. Rub well all over with the salt cure. Lay the fish skin down in a suitable wooden box. Rub the cure mixture into the raw flesh and fold the fish with the cure inside. Place a board on the fish with a 25-to-30-pound (11.3-to-13.5-kg) weight. According to Warren Gilker, a Director of the Atlantic Salmon Association (A.S.A.), Scottish fishermen would place a "killick" (an anchor weighing 28 lbs., 12.68 kg) over the salmon fillets to leach the moisture from the fish tissue and replace it with salt, thus inhibiting the spoiling action of bacteria. This method is still used today. Mr. Gilker, a salmon smoking expert, has shown that the Scottish method gives unsurpassable results.

Hang the fish in a dry, cool shaded place, spreading it with sticks to permit even drying, until a filmy skin or pellicle forms. Cold smoke for approximately 48 hours.

How to Preserve Smoked Fish

Smoked fish does not last indefinitely even under proper refrigeration. Smoked fish prepared without the addition of sodium nitrate to the curing mixture should be consumed within a week or stored in a freezer. Most commercially prepared smoked fish have one or more preservatives and can be kept under refrigeration for two weeks or sometimes longer. Some experts contend that smoked fish have a tendency to lose their flavor if frozen for a long period of time. Smoked fish are at their best when freshly smoked; refrigeration or freezing impairs the flavor.

Steaming

Contrary to the poaching process, in which the cooking liquid is usually discarded after the fish is poached, the steaming method utilizes a small amount of liquid, usually fish fumet and wine, that is used to prepare the sauce served with the fish. Place the fish in a suitable buttered pan, season with salt and pepper, and barely moisten with a strong fish fumet and white wine. Cover tightly with aluminum foil and cook in a moderate oven. When cooked, transfer the fish to a serving dish. The cooking liquid is reduced and used in the preparation of the sauce.

A new approach is gradually being introduced through the *nouvelle cuisine*. The fish to be steamed is placed on a bed of seaweed that provides a novel flavor to the fish while cooking. The Japanese use seaweed extensively and new culinary techniques are certain to develop using seaweed, adding a new dimension to fish cookery.

Another approach to steaming consists of cooking the fish in a tightly covered pan, with the fish resting on a steaming rack out of contact with the cooking liquid. The steam generated from the boiling liquid cooks the fish, which retains its natural juices and flavors. Allow 5 to 10 minutes per inch thickness measured at the thickest point.

Stewing

Of the many seafoods available on the market, a great number can be transformed totally by the stewing method. Specialty dishes like bouillabaisse [pronounced boo-yah-bays] and matelotes [mah-teh-lot] are seasoned with red or white wine, herbs, and spices. Bouillabaisse, the controvertial French specialty, is surely an individual dish. Despite the tremendous variety of edible seafoods available in the United States, it is hard to copy the genuine Marseille bouillabaisse. Our waters do not offer the ugly John Dory with its delicate flesh, or the bony gurnet, or the hogfish, all native to Mediterranean waters. Those fish and many others are part of the elaborate concoction that is bouillabaisse. In the United States, several substitutes are available to make a bouillabaisse Marseillaise. Depending on the region, such seafoods as red snapper or mutton snapper, American lobster, crawfish, sea bass, striped bass, redfish, other firm lean salt-water fish, mussels, and clams are often used.

Matelotes are not great American favorites. The typical French specialties no longer hold the edge in France either, although good restaurants feature matelotes of eel, perch, bream, sole, and other firm fleshed fish. In the United States, many recipes relying on the stewing technique can be turned into excellent dishes: chowders made with clams, oyster stew, codfish stew, and others. Unlike the French type of fish stews, especially matelotes that invariably contain red or white wine, American fish stews do not contain any wine. The thickening agents are mostly flour and butter, a mixture called beurre manie, or potatoes.

The following chart is a guide for cooking fish. Fish products require little time to cook. When the flesh loses it translucent appearance, becomes opaque, and flakes easily when pierced with a fork, the fish is cooked. Always test the thickest part—it takes the longest to cook.

Table 6.2   Cooking Guide for Fish

Method of cooking	Market form	Amount for 6	Cooking temperature	Approxi-mate cooking time in minutes
Baking	Dressed	3 lbs. (1 kg 360)	350°F (180°C)	45 to 60
	Pan-dressed	3 lbs. (1 kg 360)	350°F (180°C)	25 to 30
	Fillets or steaks	2 lbs. (900 g)	350°F (180°C)	20 to 25
	Frozen fried portions	12 por. 3 oz. (85 g) each	400°F (205°C)	15 to 20
	Frozen fried sticks	24 sticks 1¼ oz.(30 g) each	400°F (205° C)	15 to 20
Broiling	Pan-dressed	3 lbs. (1 kg 360)		10 to 15
	Fillets or steaks	2 lbs. (900 g).		10 to 15
	Frozen fried portions	12 por. 3 oz. (85 g) each		10 to 15
	Frozen fried sticks	24 sticks 1¼ oz.(30 g) each		10 to 15
Charcoal broiling	Pan-dressed	3 lbs. (1 kg 360)	Moderate	10 to 15
	Fillets or steaks	2 lbs. (900 g)	Moderate	10 to 15
	Frozen fried portions	12 por. 3 oz. (85 g) each	Moderate	8 to 10
	Frozen fried sticks	24 sticks 1¼ oz.(30 g) each	Moderate	8 to 10
Deep-fat frying	Pan-dressed	3 lbs. (1 kg 360)	360°F (182°C)	3 to 5
	Fillets or steaks	2 lbs. (900 g)	360°F (182° C)	3 to 5
	Frozen raw breaded portions	12 por. 3 oz. (85 g) each	360°F (182°C)	3 to 5
Oven frying	Pan-dressed	3 lbs. (1 kg 360)	450°F (230° C)	15 to 20
	Fillets or steaks	2 lbs. (900 g)	450°F (230° C)	10 to 15
Pan frying	Pan-dressed	3 lbs. (1 kg 360)	Moderate	8 to 10
	Fillets or steaks	2 lbs. (900 g)	Moderate	8 to 10
	Frozen raw breaded or frozen fried portions	12 por. 3 oz. (85 g) each	Moderate	8 to 10
	Frozen fried sticks	24 sticks 1¼ oz.(30 g) each	Moderate	8 to 10
Poaching	Dressed	3 lbs. (1 kg 360)	Simmer	See poaching technique
	Fillets or steaks	2 lbs. (900 g)	Simmer	
Steaming	Fillets or steaks	2 lbs. (900 g)	Boil	5 to 10

11. Cookery

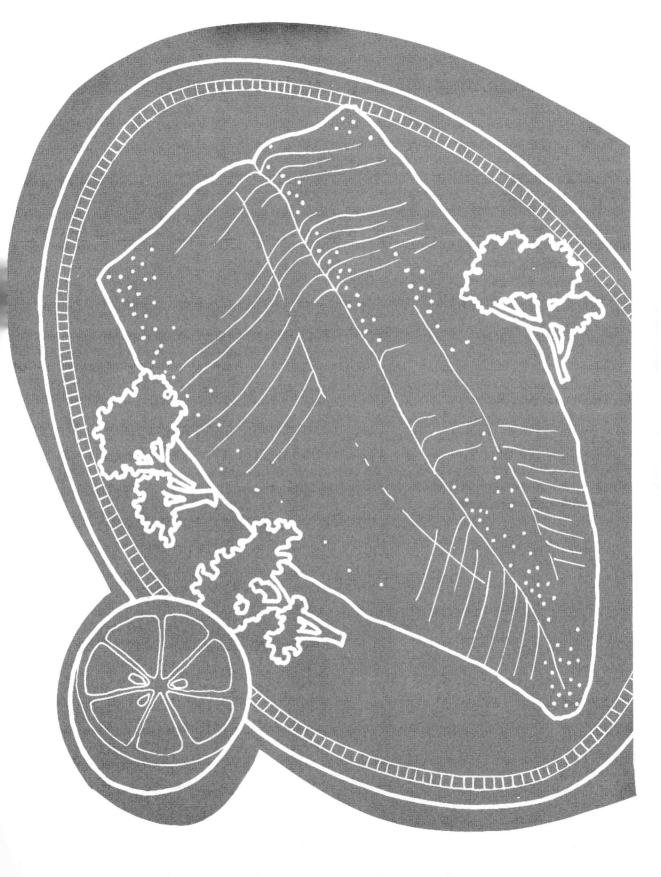

CHAPTER 7

The Marriage of Batters and Pastries in Seafood Cooking

New delights are realized by combining seafoods with light pastries or batter coverings. The results are always visually pleasing and tempt the palate if prepared with care. There are a myriad of elegant ways to serve fish and shellfish using batters and various pastries. These basic preparations are indispensable to cooking.

Batters seal in the flavors of deep-fried fish and shellfish. Puff pastries are ideal containers for seafood with sauces; vol-au-vent and bouchees are particularly suitable. Other pastry delicacies, like fleurons, are irresistibly French. Turnovers, tart shells, ravioli, pastry shells, and patty shells are some of the many interesting variations to combine with seafood.

Deep-fried fish products acquire a Japanese flavor in tempura batter. Seafood pizzas and crusty pastries bring Italy to mind. The very adaptable barquettes and tartlets make wonderful appetizers with almost any seafood. Beer batter adds another dimension to deep frying, and pie crusts are perfect for specialties like seafood quiches and tarts. Above all, these basic preparations, most of which are made with starch, blend so well in so many seafood dishes that they deserve a chapter of their own.

Batters

Batters are mixtures of light to heavy consistency, made with flour and varying amounts of such liquids as water, milk, beer, or carbonated water. Beaten egg whites add lightness to some batters. Beer adds little flavor to seafoods fried in batter, but the bubbles contribute a light and crisp texture to the cooked batter. Batter-fried seafood is not feasible for large servings. If the cooked product cannot be served within five minutes of frying, the crisp outer crust becomes soft and the steam from the cooked seafood turns the batter soggy.

Tempura Batter

Ingredients	U.S.	Metric
Flour, all purpose or bread	1 cup	120 g
Cornstarch	1 cup	120 g
Baking Powder	1 tsp.	1 tsp.
Sesame or Cottonseed Oil	2 tbsp.	2 tbsp.
White Vinegar	1 tbsp.	1 tbsp.
Whole Egg	1	1
Cold Water	1¼ cup	3½ dl

Combine all dry ingredients. Add liquid ingredients and whisk until batter is smooth. Chill before using.

Dip the prepared seafoods in the cold batter, coating the pieces completely. Drop in a deep fryer at 360°F (180°C) and fry for 2 to 5 minutes, according to size and shape.

Usage: Fried seafood tempura, vegetables tempura
Gougeonnettes of fish (small fish sticks)
Thin fillets of fish, scallops, et cetera.

Beer Batter

Ingredients	U.S.	Metric
Flour	9 oz.	250 g
Salt	1 tsp.	1 tsp.
Oil	2 oz.	0.6 dl
Whole Egg	1	1
Beer	¾ cup	2 dl
Water	1 cup	2½ dl
Egg Whites	2	2

Combine all ingredients except the egg whites. Beat well until batter is smooth. Whip egg whites medium stiff, and fold into the batter. Use without delay.

Crepes

Crepe making has become almost a cult in the United States. Many versions of crepe pans exist, but the old fashioned, well-treated inexpensive crepe pan or the new, non-stick regular pan are still highly regarded by many consumers and professionals as well. As long as the pan does not stick and is buttered as needed, and providing the batter is of proper consistency (neither too thick nor too thin), making perfect crepes can be easy.

The uses of crepes are varied. These thin french pancakes appear in glorious recipes like Crepes Farcies Aux Fruits De Mer, Stuffed Crepes with Seafood, Crepes with Lobster (Sauce Nantua) or Deep-fried Fish Fillets, wrapped in crepes and breading.

Crepe Batter

Ingredients	U.S.	Metric
Flour	4 oz. (1 cup)	120 g
Egg	1	1
Salt	½ tsp.	½ tsp.
Milk	1 cup	2½ dl
Butter, melted	2 tbsp.	25 g

Combine flour, egg, and salt in a mixing bowl. Stir in the milk until batter is smooth. Add the melted butter and prepare crepes in the usual manner.

Doughs

Brioche Dough

Ingredients	U.S.	Metric
Active Dry Yeast	1 envelope	1 envelope
Sugar	1 tsp.	1 tsp.
Lukewarm Water	2 oz.	0.6 dl
Flour	½ cup	60 g
Flour	9 oz.	250 g
Whole Eggs, lightly beaten	3	3
Salt	¾ tsp.	¾ tsp.
Butter, softened	6 oz.	180 g

Dissolve yeast and sugar in the water. Add flour and blend well. Cover with a towel and allow to double in size in a warm place. Meanwhile, beat half of the remaining flour with the eggs and salt. Add the yeast mixture and butter and knead in the remaining flour. Let rise at room temperature for 3 hours. Punch the dough and refrigerate for 12 hours, covered with a wet towel.

Usage: Coulibiac (see under salmon).

Cream Puff Dough

Ingredients	U.S.	Metric
Water	1 cup	2½ dl
Butter	4 oz.	110 g
Salt	½ tsp.	½ tsp.
Flour	1 cup	120 g
Whole Eggs, beaten	4	4

Combine water, butter, and salt in a saucepan. Bring to a boil. Add the flour and stir well until it forms a smooth paste. Remove from heat and stir in the beaten eggs, one at a time. Pipe the dough on a baking sheet, and bake at 400°F (205°C). The cooking time varies according to size and shape.

Usage: Profiteroles (tiny cream puffs) as appetizers, filled with seafood
Small eclairs, as appetizers.

Puff Pastry

This magic pastry is probably the most intriguing and spectacular of all pastries. Puff pastry is created by a series of rollings, foldings, and chillings, and finally baking. Excellent puff pastry dough is available commercially, in 15-pound (6.8-kg) portions; at the consumer level, patty shells and 1-pound (½-kg) blocks of puff pastry can be purchased.

Puff pastry is a mixture of flour, salt, and water rolled several times between layers of butter or shortening, making it puff when baked. The dough is rolled and chilled several times, which makes it a time-consuming process.

The use of butter can present problems, even to the experienced baker. Butter can become too hard or too soft, resulting in an unpuffed pastry of poor quality. Shortening specially processed for use in puff pastry is highly recommended; it does not have the fine flavor or taste of butter, but it certainly eases the preparation, blends well into layers when rolled in the dough, and results in a feathery light, cooked pastry.

Puff Pastry

Ingredients	U.S.	Metric
Bread Flour	2 lb.	900 g
Salt	1 tsp.	1 tsp.
Cold Water	2 cups	5 dl
Puff Pastry Shortening or Butter	1½ lb.	680 g

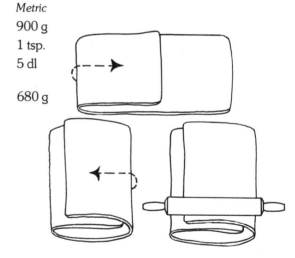

Figure 7.1

Mix flour, salt, and enough water to make a firm dough. Roll out the dough, 12 to 14 inches (30 to 35 cm) wide and about three times as long. Shred the chilled butter or shortening over one half of the dough, leaving a 1-inch (2½-cm) border. Fold the other half over. Seal edges with rolling pin.

Carefully roll out dough into a rectangle 12 by 36 inches (30 by 90 cm). Fold in thirds. (See Figure 7.1.) Cover dough and refrigerate for 15 to 20 minutes. Repeat the same process five times, allowing the dough to rest 20 minutes between each rolling.

Usage: Vol-au-vent—large puff pastry shells to serve 6 to 8 persons (See Figure 7.2.)
Patty shells—individual puff pastry shells

Fleurons—crescent-shaped puff pastry used as garnish with fish
Bouchees—appetizer puff pastry shells
Turnovers—for quenelles (see Mousselines of Salmon)

Pie Crust Dough

Basic Dough

Ingredients	U.S.	Metric
Flour	1 lb.	450 g
Butter	8 oz.	225 g
Whole egg	1	1
Water, cold	1 oz.	0.3 dl
Salt	½ tsp.	½ tsp.

Combine all ingredients in a mixing bowl. Mix well until dough is smooth and can be formed into a ball.

Usage: Barquettes—small boat-shaped crusts

Tart shells for quiches

Tartlets—individual small round tarts

Flaky Pie Crust Dough

Ingredients	U.S.	Metric
Flour	1 lb.	450 g
Shortening	8 oz.	225 g
Water	5 oz.	1½ dl
Salt	1 tsp.	1 tsp.

Combine all ingredients and blend until dough is mixed well and can be shaped into a ball.

Usage: For seafood quiches and turnovers.

Figure 7.2

Pizza Dough
(Makes two 12-inch (30-cm) pizzas)

Ingredients	U.S.	Metric
Yeast, dry active	1 package	1 package
Sugar	1 tsp.	1 tsp.
Lukewarm Water	1 cup	2.5 dl
Flour	2½ cups	280 g
Salt	1 tsp.	1 tsp.
Olive or Vegetable Oil	¼ cup	.6 dl

In an electric mixer bowl, dissolve the yeast in water and sugar. Add the flour, salt, and oil, and work the dough for ten minutes. Cover with a cloth, and allow to rise in a warm place until double in bulk.

Usage: Seafood pizzas and pissaladieres (see under Anchovy).

CHAPTER 8

Court Bouillons and Fumets

Auguste Escoffier, the wizard of French culinary art, was correct when he said, "Stock is everything in good and well-flavored cooking. If one's stock is of good flavor, what remains of the work is easy; if on the other hand, flavor is lacking, or merely mediocre, it is quite hopeless to expect anything approaching a satisfactory result."

Stocks are often the basis of sauce preparation; their reductions are called fumets. The essence of quality dishes comes from the flavors of stocks or fumets and their abundance of protein. Fatty fish, such as salmon, mackerel, and shad, have a distinctive flavor and usually do not require the addition of foreign flavors to improve their taste. On the other hand, bland fish like sole, flounder, and most ground fish, which are usually lean, are best when spiked with rich sauces containing wines and cooked with well-flavored court bouillons. Fresh-water fish, which by nature lack character,

cannot be seasoned lightly if the results are to reach professional standards.

The pH scale of most fish is close to 7 (representing neutrality between acidity and alkalinity), which offers a wealth of culinary possibilities. For the same reason, wines play a predominant role in fish cookery. Some of the most glorious seafood recipes contain wine combined with stock or fumets. Since lean fish do not hold up well on their own, rich stocks, fumets, and wine sauces must come to their rescue. Cooks and chefs have learned to take advantage of the neutrality of lean, bland fish. Sole and flounder, America's favorite fish, have been transformed into many different specialties, some of which could be called marvels. Above all, stocks, court bouillons, or fumets can contribute greatly to the success of any seafood dish.

Court Bouillon

Fish and shellfish poached in plain water acquire no flavor unless enhanced by the addition of vegetables, herbs, and seasonings. This is the purpose of court bouillon (short broths).

In most cases, court bouillon is prepared in advance to develop its flavor, especially if the fish must be cooked in half an hour or less. There is no single standard recipe for court bouillon, as fish differ in flavor, size, and color. Marine species,

which usually have more flavor than fresh-water species, are poached in mildly seasoned court bouillons that contain a small proportion of vegetables, seasonings, and herbs. Fresh-water fish need a flavorful court bouillon to improve their taste. This applies particularly to lake-dwellers like whitefish, lake trout, or rainbow or so-called brook trout. In comparison with the migrating steelhead, which spends most of its life in salt water, the fresh-water cultured rainbow trout has much to gain from a strongly flavored court bouillon. Both fish belong to the same family, but the steelhead is comparable to salmon with its pink color and rich flavor. The court bouillon used to poach farmed rainbow trout would impair its taste.

Occasionally, it is unnecessary to alter the taste of fish. In this case, salted water should be used to poach fish and shellfish. For example, fresh cod steaks can be poached in this manner. The plain fish is not very palatable, but served with a contrasting, flawless rich sauce, the cod is delightful to taste. Lobster is also at its best when cooked in salted boiling water; lemon butter accentuates the sweet rich taste of this prized crustacean. Details for poaching fish and shellfish are described in chapter 6.

Court Bouillon No. 1
(Yields 5 quarts, 5 l.)

Ingredients	U.S.	Metric
Water	5 qt.	5 l
White Vinegar	1 cup	2½ dl
Salt	2 oz.	50 g
Carrots, peeled and sliced	1 lb.	450 g
Onions, peeled and sliced	1 lb.	450 g
Thyme	½ tsp.	½ tsp.
Bay Leaves	2	2
Parsley Stems	2 oz.	50 g
Black Peppercorns	1 oz.	25 g

Combine all ingredients in a suitable pot. Bring to a boil and simmer for 45 minutes to an hour. Strain and cool. Refrigerate if not used within a few hours.

Usage: For poaching salmon, steelhead, striped bass, and basically all marine fish having a fat content over 5 to 6 percent.

Court Bouillon No. 2
(Yields 5 quarts, 5 l.)

Ingredients	U.S.	Metric
Water	4 qt.	4 l
Dry White Wine	1 qt.	1 l
Green Parts of Leeks	1 lb.	450 g
Sliced Onions	2 lb.	1 kg
Parsley Stems	2 oz.	50 g
Thyme	1 tsp.	1 tsp.
Bay Leaves	2	2
Peppercorns	½ oz.	12 g
Salt	2 oz.	50 g

Combine all ingredients except wine. Simmer for 30 minutes. Strain, then add the wine. Cool and refrigerate if not used within a few hours.

Usage: For poaching pike, lake trout, whitefish, and most freshwater fish suitable for poaching.

Court Bouillon No. 3
(Yields 5 quarts, 5 l.)

Ingredients	U.S.	Metric
Water	5 qt.	5 l
Salt (coarse sea salt if available)	2½ oz.	75 g

Combine water and salt. Heat to dissolve salt.

Usage: To boil lobsters, spiny lobsters, lobsterettes, and other shellfish. To poach fish without altering flavor.

Court Bouillon No. 4
(Yields 5 quarts, 5 l.)

Ingredients	U.S.	Metric
Water	4 qt.	4 l
Milk	1 qt.	1 l
Salt	2 oz.	50 g
Lemon Slices	2	2

Combine all ingredients in a suitable pot.

Usage: To poach smoked fish (finnan haddie, smoked hake, etc.) and other fresh fish without altering the flavor.

Fish Stocks and Fumets

Court bouillons are used strictly to poach fish and shellfish. They do not constitute a base for other preparations like sauces or soups. Stocks and fumets, however, offer a wide range of possibilities for sauces and soups, and are basic indispensable elements in many recipes.

Fish Stock
(Yields 2 quarts, 2 l.)

Ingredients	U.S.	Metric
Butter	2 oz.	50 g
Bones from lean fish. Use head, if available, with gills removed.	3 lb.	1.3 kg
Water	3 qt.	3 l
Bay Leaves	2	2
Dried Thyme	1 tsp.	1 tsp.
Large Onions, sliced	2	2
Ribs of Celery, cut in pieces ...	2	2
Carrots, sliced	1 lb.	450 g
Peppercorns	1 tsp.	1 tsp.
Salt	2 tsp.	2 tsp.

Melt butter in a kettle. Stir in the cleaned bones and head. Add the remaining ingredients and simmer for 30 minutes. Strain through a fine china cap.

Fish fumet is obtained by reducing a stock to achieve a richer flavor. Depending on the use of the fumet, the addition of wine is sometimes desirable. The reduction of fish stock is not necessary if a large quantity of fish bones are included in the stock. The bones provide a richer stock that approximates a fumet. If the fish stock gells under refrigeration, it can be called fumet.

In culinary language, fish stock and fish fumet are synonymous—they both serve the same purpose. In fact, in French the only term used is fumet, regardless of the richness of flavor.

A fish fumet reduced to a glaze is called *essence of fish*. Like meat glaze (glace de viande), the essence of fish is always appropriate when fumet is not available.

CHAPTER 9

Quenelles and Mousses

Many highly respected fish recipes stem from great achievements in finesse and are the ultimate in fish cookery. These recipes often start with basic elements known as *quenelles* and *mousses*. These are ground forcemeats from clean, boneless, and skinless raw or cooked fish or shellfish, combined with cream, eggs, jelly, and other ingredients, and seasoned to perfection.

Formerly, the making of quenelles and mousses was a tedious preparation due to the lack of modern equipment. Fish was forced through fine sieves, separating sinews and bones from the flesh. Today, food processors are the robots in our kitchens, whether we are professionals or amateurs. These miraculous food machines can turn a piece of fish into a velvety mousse in record time. The prepared forcemeat is put through a food mill to eliminate any sinews or bones.

Basic Recipes for Quenelles and Mousses

Pike, a lean, white, and firm fish, is one of the most suitable fish for forcemeat, known in French as farce. This fish is now scarce in the United States, but others like whiting, salmon, sole, trout, shrimp, and lobster are excellent candidates for mousses and quenelles.

Basic Recipe for Quenelles and Mousses

Ingredients	6 portions		24 portions	
	U.S.	Metric	U.S.	Metric
Raw Fish Flesh, boned and skinned, or Shellfish, shelled and deveined	9 oz.	250 g	2¼ lb.	1 kg
Egg Whites	2	2	8	8
Heavy Cream	1 cup	2½ dl	1 qt.	1 l
Salt	¾ tsp.	¾ tsp.	1 tbsp.	1 tbsp.
White Pepper, ground	¼ tsp.	¼ tsp.	1 tsp.	1 tsp.
Cayenne Pepper	⅛ tsp.	⅛ tsp.	½ tsp.	½ tsp.

Cut the fish or shellfish into cubes. Grind in a meat grinder or preferably in a food processor. Slowly add the egg whites and heavy cream, while mixing continuously. Season with salt, pepper, and cayenne. To remove any sinews or bones that might be present in the forcemeat, run the mixture through a food mill.

This recipe can be used for mousses, quenelles, and souffles, and for stuffing large fish that are to be braised whole.

Another version of this recipe features the addition of a panada. By adding a panada to fish forcemeat, you increase the volume of the cooked fish product and improve the texture and lightness. However, the delicate flavor of the seafood is often impaired. For this reason, quenelles, mousses, or souffles made with a fish forcemeat containing panada are accompanied by sauces prepared with rich fumets, preferably containing the same flavor and taste as the main ingredient. For example, salmon bones make the best fumet and sauce for a mousse or quenelle of salmon.

Quenelles and Mousse Forcemeat with Panada

Ingredients	8 portions		24 portions	
	U.S.	Metric	U.S.	Metric
Raw Fish Flesh, boned and skinned, or Shellfish, shelled and deveined	9 oz.	250 g	1¾ lb.	750 g
Egg Whites	1	1	3	3
Heavy Cream	1½ cups	3.75 dl	4½ cups	1.10 l
Salt	¾ tsp.	¾ tsp.	2¼ tsp.	2¼ tsp.
White Pepper	¼ tsp.	¼ tsp.	¾ tsp.	¾ tsp.
Cayenne Pepper	⅛ tsp.	⅛ tsp.	½ tsp.	½ tsp.
Panada				
Milk	½ cup	1¼ dl	1½ cups	4 dl
Butter	2 oz.	60 g	6 oz.	170 g
Flour	5 oz.	140 g	15 oz.	420 g
Egg Yolks (use whites for above)	2	2	6	6
Whole Eggs	1	1	3	3

Follow the same method of preparation described in Basic Recipe for Quenelles and Mousses.

Panada   Boil the milk with the butter in a medium saucepan. Add the flour and mix well with a wooden spoon to obtain a smooth paste. Dry the panada over low heat. Away from the heat, mix in the egg yolks and the whole eggs, one at a time. Cool the panada and mix well with the forcemeat. This recipe is used for mousses, quenelles, mousselines, or fish pates, and to fill the cavity of whole fish to be cooked.

Specialty recipes like Quenelles of Pike Sauce Normande, Mousse of Salmon, Sauce Americaine, and Mousseline of Trout Royale, are variations of the standard recipes. Their preparation is tailored to acquire new flavors, and sometimes new presentations are used. These recipes allow cooks and specialty chefs to demonstrate their talents and savoir-faire.

Quenelles

Quenelles, poorly translated as dumplings, are oval-shaped fish or shellfish forcemeats poached in water or fumets, or simply steamed. Mousseline is another term used for quenelles. They are served with a sauce as garnish, with other fish, or even in soups. Their size varies depending on their use.

How to shape quenelles Oval-shaped scoops, similar to ice cream scoops, are ideal for shaping fish forcemeat into quenelles. But the most common method consists of dipping a large soup spoon in hot water and scooping up a heaping amount of the forcemeat. Using another spoon, round the mixture to make a neat, egg-shaped quenelle. Cook according to directions in the specific recipe.

Test and sample any quenelle to determine its taste and texture, as all fish are different. Results can also vary if the raw seafood has been frozen. An adjustment in seasoning may be required; and sometimes the addition of egg whites will improve the texture of the product.

Mousses

Seafood mousses are classified into two categories: hot and cold mousses. Mousses to be served hot are cooked in various molds—ring, fish-shaped, or individual portion molds. They are prepared from the basic recipe for fish forcemeat, with or without panada. The cooked dish is always served hot with an appropriate sauce. Many variations of mousse recipes exist, with the addition of such garnishes as truffles, pistachio nuts, and mushrooms. The same recipe is used to make fish pate, but it is served cold. For more details, see the recipe for Pate of Salmon.

Cold seafood mousses offer another dimension in fish cooking. Freshly poached fish, shellfish, and smoked fish can be mixed into a fine smooth paste. Fish jelly and whipped cream are invariably added to the recipe.

As these preparations are always served cold, the seasonings must be balanced carefully; cold mousses often require more seasoning than hot mousses, both in variety and quantity. A poorly seasoned cold mousse is unpalatable and deceiving. Resourceful cooks and chefs know many ways to improve the taste of a cold mousse. A good quality fish jelly is definitely of great help. Mayonnaise, white wine, cold cream sauces or veloutes, lemon juice, and herbs are choice ingredients to overcome the neutrality of cooked fish.

Basic Recipe for Cold Fish or Shellfish Mousse

Ingredients	6 portions		24 portions	
	U.S.	Metric	U.S.	Metric
Cooked Poached Fish (salmon, trout, sole, pike, halibut, shrimp, lobster, etc.)	1 lb.	450 g	4 lb.	1.8 kg
Unflavored Gelatin	1 tbsp.	1 tbsp.	4 tbsp.	4 tbsp.
Liquid Fish Jelly	1 cup	2½ dl	1 qt.	1 l
Salt	1 tsp.	1 tsp.	4 tsp.	4 tsp.
White Pepper, ground	¼ tsp.	¼ tsp.	1 tsp.	1 tsp.
Worcestershire Sauce	¼ tsp.	¼ tsp.	1 tsp.	1 tsp.
Dill, chopped	1 tsp.	1 tsp.	4 tsp.	4 tsp.
Mayonnaise	½ cup	1¼ dl	1 pt.	½ l
Dry White Wine	¼ cup	6 dl	1 cup	2½ dl
Heavy Cream, whipped	½ cup	1¼ dl	1 pt.	½ l

Carefully remove all bones and skin from fish. Dissolve gelatin in the fish jelly. Mix fish in a food processor, adding the jelly gradually. Add the seasonings and blend the mixture to the consistency of paste.

Transfer the fish mixture to a mixing bowl. Add mayonnaise and wine, and combine well with a spatula. Then cool on ice. When mixture has partially set, fold in the whipped cream.

Fish mousse can be poured in various molds and decorated to suit any occasion. Fish mousse can also be used as a filling in various garnishes for cold seafood dishes. Barquettes (small boat-shaped pie crust shells), tomatoes, cucumbers, artichoke bottoms, and mushroom caps stuffed with fish mousse are perfect accompaniments with cold fish and shellfish.

Interesting variations can be prepared by mixing several kinds of fish and shellfish to make mousses in combinations; for example, ½ trout mousse (using weakfish, sea trout, or lake trout) and ½ salmon mousse (chinook or sockeye). The color contrast is eye catching. Other combinations, such as ⅓ salmon mousse, ⅓ sole, and ⅓ crabmeat mousse, are possible. And remember that any leftovers of cooked shellfish or poached fish can be transformed into splendid decorative creations.

Smoked fish mousses are also delicacies. For a standard recipe for smoked fish mousse, refer to Smoked Salmon Mousse.

Cold fish souffles are unusual presentations easily accomplished in souffle molds (like cold dessert souffles). Simply surround a suitable souffle mold with a paper collar extending at least 1 inch (2½ cm) above the rim of the mold. Chill until set and remove the paper. Decorate the top with radish slices, olives, et cetera.

CHAPTER 10

Fish Soups, Stews, and Matelotes

Combinations of seafood, vegetables, herbs, stocks, and wines are many and varied. All over the world, fish soups, stews, or matelotes, are typical specialties of imaginative cooks and chefs—bouillabaisse in France, clam chowder on the Eastern coast of the United States, conch chowder in the Southern states, and cioppino on the Pacific coast are examples. These creations often depend on the regional availability of fresh fish and shellfish, and the ingredients in the recipes may vary during the year.

A chowder, fish soup, or stew, prepared with strictly fresh fish and shellfish, easily can make the reputation of an establishment, if prepared with the utmost care. Those who live near water learn to explore the nature of fish, and inevitably take advantage of their quality and freshness. Some of the best fish soups are found in seafood dining places near shores where fish abound and freshness is guaranteed.

Lobster Bisque

Ingredients	6 portions		24 portions	
	U.S.	Metric	U.S.	Metric
Live Lobster	1½ lb.	680 g.	6 lb.	2.7 kg
Butter	3½ oz.	100 g	14 oz.	400 g
Mirepoix	7 oz.	200 g	1¾ lb.	800 g
Cognac	2 oz.	0.6 dl	1 cup	2.5 dl
Dry White Wine	3 oz.	1 dl	1½ cups	4 dl
Tomato Paste	1 tbsp.	1 tbsp.	4 tbsp.	4 tbsp.
Thyme	½ tsp.	½ tsp.	2 tsp.	2 tsp.
Bay Leaves	1	1	4	4
Parsley Stems	4	4	16	16
Rice	2½ oz.	70 g	10 oz.	280 g
Heavy Cream	½ cup	1.2 dl	2 cups	5 dl
Fish Stock	1½ qt.	1.5 l	6 qt.	6 l
Salt and Pepper, to taste				
Cayenne Pepper	¼ tsp.	¼ tsp.	1 tsp.	1 tsp.

Cut the lobster tails into sections at joints. Remove the claws and crack for easy extraction of the meat. Split the heads in half lengthwise. Remove stomach, then cut crosswise into quarters. Separate legs.

In a heavy, wide pot, melt the butter, add the mirepoix, and cook over low heat without browning. Stir in the lobster pieces and cook until they turn red. Pour in the cognac and ignite for a few seconds.

Add the wine, half of the fish stock, the tomato paste, and herbs, and cook covered for 15 to 18 minutes. Cook the rice separately in remaining stock. Take out the lobster pieces. Remove the meat from the shell.

In a food processor or blender, puree the cooked rice with the stock. Combine with the lobster cooking liquid and strain through a fine china cap. Add the cream. Bring to a boil and simmer for 5 minutes. Add the cayenne pepper and the diced lobster pieces. Serve hot.

A shrimp bisque can be prepared in the same manner.

Oyster Bisque Florentine

Ingredients	6 portions		24 portions	
	U.S.	Metric	U.S.	Metric
Oysters, shucked with liquid . . .	1 pt.	5 dl	2 qt.	2 l
Butter	3 oz.	85 g	12 oz.	340 g
Onion, chopped	2 oz.	50 g	8 oz.	225 g
Flour	4 oz.	110 g	1 lb.	450 g
Fish Fumet	1 pt.	5 dl	2 qt.	2 l
Dry White Wine	1 cup	2.5 dl	1 qt.	1 l
Fresh Spinach, chopped, or . . .	1 lb.	450 g	4 lb.	1.8 g
Frozen Spinach, chopped	10 oz.	280 g	2½ lb.	1.1 g
Heavy Cream	1 cup	2.5 dl	1 qt.	1 l
Sour Cream	½ cup	1.2 dl	2 cups	5 dl

Remove any bits of shell in oysters. Melt the butter. Add the onion and cook over low heat for 5 minutes. Stir in the flour and blend. Cook over low heat for 10 minutes.

Pour the fumet over and whip until the soup comes to a boil. Add the wine and simmer for 15 minutes. Add the clean spinach and the oysters with their juice, and simmer for 5 minutes.

Add the cream and bring to a boil. Season to taste with salt and pepper. Mix in the sour cream and serve hot.

Shrimp Bisque

Ingredients	6 portions		24 portions	
	U.S.	Metric	U.S.	Metric
Butter	2 oz.	50 g	8 oz.	225 g
Onion, chopped	1 oz.	25 g	4 oz.	100 g
Carrots, chopped	1 oz.	25 g	4 oz.	100 g
Celery, chopped	1 oz.	25 g	4 oz.	100 g
Shrimp, in the shells	1¼ lb.	600 g	5 lb.	2.4 kg
Cognac	2 oz.	0.6 dl	1 cup	2.5 dl
Dry White Wine	3 oz.	1 dl	1½ cups	4 dl
Thyme	¼ tsp.	¼ tsp.	1 tsp.	1 tsp.
Bay Leaf	1	1	4	4
Parsley Stems	6	6	2 doz.	2 doz.
Fish Stock	1 qt.	1 l	1 gal.	4 l
Rice	2 oz.	60 g	8 oz.	240 g
Cream	¾ cup	2 dl	3 cups	8 dl
Shrimp Butter	2 oz.	50 g	8 oz.	225 g
Salt and Pepper, to taste				

Melt the butter in a large saucepan. Add the onion, carrots, and celery and cook over low heat for 5 minutes. Stir occasionally.

Rinse the shrimp and add to the vegetables. Saute over high heat until the shells turn pink. Flambe with the Cognac. De-glaze with the white wine and add the parsley stems, bay leaf, and thyme. Reduce by one half.

Pour in the stock, add the rice, and cook for 20 minutes. Shell and devein the cooked shrimp; save some for garnish. Puree the bisque in a food processor or blender and strain through a fine china cap. Press to extract all juices. Add the cream and heat. Season to taste with salt and pepper.

Stir in the shrimp butter. Garnish the bisque with the reserved shrimp. Serve hot.

Bouillabaisse Marseillaise

It is as impossible to duplicate cioppino in Marseille as it is to make bouillabaisse in San Francisco. The Mediterranean Sea produces such fish as vive (weever), Saint Pierre (John Dory), baudroie (monkfish), grondin (sea robin), rascasse (scorpion fish), and rouget (goatfish), all necessary for the genuine bouillabaisse.

In the United States, it would be hard to find all these species. They are available, but our fishermen consider most of them "junk fish," unwanted by consumers and many professionals. But everyone should be able to improvise a perfect bouillabaisse, providing the right varieties of fish are combined for the stew.

In the North East and Middle Atlantic states, the following fish and shellfish are good substitutes: croaker, whiting, ocean perch, flounder, cod or cusk, striped bass, hake, tilefish, and lobster, mussels, clams, and conger eel. In the Southern and Gulf states, use pompano, red fish, red snapper, grouper and spanish mackerel, seatrout, sheepshead, stone crab, and spiny lobster. On the West Coast, use white seabass, salmon, sole, halibut, Pacific cod and rockfish, goeducks, and razor clams. Fresh-water fish are not suitable for bouillabaisse.

Whatever the varieties of seafood used, they must be fresh. Combine 75 percent lean fish with 25 percent fatty fish. Shellfish are also recommended.

Bouillabaisse

As made in the New England and Middle Atlantic states.

Ingredients	10 to 12 portions		20 to 24 portions	
	U.S.	Metric	U.S.	Metric
Striped Bass, dressed	1 lb.	450 g	2 lb.	900 g
Flounder, dressed	1 lb.	450 g	2 lb.	900 g
Cod, dressed	1 lb.	450 g	2 lb.	900 g
Whiting	1 lb.	450 g	2 lb.	900 g
Anglerfish or Tilefish, dressed .	1 lb.	450 g	2 lb.	900 g
Conger Eel	1 lb.	450 g	2 lb.	900 g
Mussels or Cherry Stone Clams	12	12	24	24
Live Lobster	2 lb.	900 g	4 lb.	1.8 kg
Olive Oil	1 cup	2.5 dl	2 cups	5 dl
Onion, chopped	1 lb.	450 g	2 lb.	900 g
White of Leek, chopped	2 oz.	50 g	4 oz.	100 g
Garlic Cloves, minced	1 oz.	25 g	2 oz.	50 g
Parsley, chopped	2 tbsp.	2 tbsp.	4 tbsp.	4 tbsp.
Tomatoes, peeled, seeded, and chopped	1½ lb.	680 g	3 lb.	1.4 kg
Bouquet Garni	1	1	2	2
Fennel Julienne	4 oz.	110 g	8 oz.	225 g
Salt	1½ tsp.	1½ tsp.	1 tbsp.	1 tbsp.
White Pepper	½ tsp.	½ tsp.	1 tsp.	1 tsp.
Saffron Threads	½ tsp.	½ tsp.	1 tsp.	1 tsp.
French Bread	1	1	2	2
Garlic Cloves	1	1	2	2

(cont.)

Wash and cut the fish into small portions. Scrub and wash the mussels or clams. Cut the lobster across into 10 to 12 pieces. Crack the claws.

In a deep, wide kettle or heavy pot, heat the oil. Add the onion and leeks, and cook over low heat for 15 minutes. Add the garlic, parsley, tomatoes, bouquet garni, and fennel. Simmer for 10 to 15 minutes.

Layer the fish and shellfish on top of the vegetables, except for the whiting, which has a tender flesh and cooks faster. Add boiling water to cover. Season with salt and pepper. Stir in the saffron. Simmer the stew for 15 minutes. Add the whiting and simmer for another 5 to 7 minutes. Remove from heat. Arrange fish and shellfish in a shallow earthenware dish.

Reduce the cooking liquid by one third. Strain into a soup tureen.

Cut the bread into round slices and toast lightly under a broiler. Rub each slice with garlic.

When serving, each guest takes a helping of the fish and croutons, pours the liquid over, and tops this with Sauce Rouille (recipe follows).

Sauce Rouille

Ingredients	6 portions		24 portions	
	U.S.	Metric	U.S.	Metric
Red Bell Pepper	1	1	2	2
Garlic Cloves, chopped	4	4	8	8
Boiled Potatoes, mashed	½ cup	1.2 dl	1 cup	2.5 dl
Olive Oil	¼ cup	0.6 dl	½ cup	1.2 dl

Broil the peppers until the skin is blackened. Rub off the skin, trim off the bottom, and remove seeds. In a food processor or blender, puree the garlic and pepper, and add the potatoes and oil to make a thick paste. Add one cup of the strained liquid from the bouillabaisse.

Cod Bouillabaisse

Ingredients	6 portions		24 portions	
	U.S.	Metric	U.S.	Metric
Salted Cod	1¾ lb.	800 g	7 lb.	3.2 kg
Oil	¼ cup	0.6 dl	1 cup	2.5 dl
Onion, chopped	3½ oz.	100 g	14 oz.	400 g
White of Leeks, chopped	2 oz.	50 g	8 oz.	200 g
Garlic Cloves, minced	3	3	12	12
Water	1½ qt.	1.5 l	5 qt.	5 l
Thyme	½ tsp.	½ tsp.	2 tsp.	2 tsp.
Bay Leaves	2	2	8	8
Saffron	½ tsp.	½ tsp.	2 tsp.	2 tsp.
Potatoes, diced	6 oz.	170 g	1½ lb.	680 g
Parsley, chopped	1 tbsp.	1 tbsp.	4 tbsp.	4 tbsp.
French Bread				
Garlic Cloves				

Soak the cod in cold water for 12 hours.

Heat the oil in a heavy wide pot. Add the onion, leeks, and garlic and cook over low heat for 10 minutes. Pour in the water and add the saffron, thyme, and bay leaves. Bring to a boil and add the potatoes. Cook for 10 to 12 minutes, then add the cod cut into small pieces. Simmer until cod is flaky and potatoes are done. Stir in the parsley.

Serve with bread croutons rubbed with garlic.

San Francisco Cioppino

Ingredients	6 portions		24 portions	
	U.S.	Metric	U.S.	Metric
Vegetable Oil	½ cup	1.2 dl	2 cups	5 dl
Onion, chopped	4 oz.	110 g	1 lb.	450 g
Garlic, finely chopped	1 tsp.	1 tsp.	1 tbsp.	1 tbsp.
Parsley, chopped	1 tbsp.	1 tbsp.	4 tbsp.	4 tbsp.
Italian Style Canned Tomatoes	1½ lb.	680 g	6 lb.	2800 g
Tomato Paste	1 tbsp.	1 tbsp.	4 tbsp.	4 tbsp.
Dry White Wine	1½ cups	4 dl	1½ qt.	1.5 l
Salt	1 tsp.	1 tsp.	1 tbsp.	1 tbsp.
Ground Pepper	¼ tsp.	¼ tsp.	1 tsp.	1 tsp.
Dungeness Crab, or	1	1	4	4
Small Blue Crab, or	4	4	16	16
Lobster, 1¼ lb. each	1	1	4	4
Rockfish Fillets, or other lean fish	1½ lb.	680 g	6 lb.	2800 g
Shrimp, shelled and deveined	12	12	4 doz.	4 doz.
Clams, small hard shell	12	12	4 doz.	4 doz.
Mussels, in shells, cleaned, and scrubbed	12	12	4 doz.	4 doz.

In a heavy casserole or large pot, heat the oil. Add the onion, garlic, and parsley. Stir over moderate heat. Do not brown. Add the chopped, seeded tomatoes and tomato paste, wine, salt, and pepper. Simmer for 15 minutes. Cut the lobster or crab into serving pieces. Combine with first ingredients and cover to steam for 10 minutes. Add the fish and cook for 5 minutes. Add the shrimp and cook until pink and firm.

Steam clams and mussels in a covered casserole with a little water. As soon as they are open, strain the liquid into the shellfish stew, and add the clams and mussels in their shells.

Heat and serve with garlic bread.

Matelote Illhaeusern

Ingredients	6 portions		24 portions	
	U.S.	Metric	U.S.	Metric
Fish, cleaned and drawn (perch, pickerel, trout, eel, bass, drum, sheepshead) . . .	3½ lb.	1.5 kg	14 lb.	6 kg
Butter	2 oz.	50 g	8 oz.	200 g
Shallots, chopped	2 oz.	50 g	8 oz.	200 g
Rhine Wine	1 cup	2.5 dl	1 qt.	1 l
Fish Fumet	1 qt.	1 l	1 gal.	4 l
Salt	½ tsp.	½ tsp.	2 tsp.	2 tsp.
Ground Pepper	¼ tsp.	¼ tsp.	1 tsp.	1 tsp.
Thyme Leaves	¼ tsp.	¼ tsp.	1 tsp.	1 tsp.
Nutmeg	⅛ tsp.	⅛ tsp.	½ tsp.	½ tsp.
Butter	2 oz.	50 g	8 oz.	200 g
Flour	2 oz.	50 g	8 oz.	200 g
Lemon Juice	2 tbsp.	2 tbsp.	4 oz.	1.2 dl
Mushrooms, diced	1 cup	100 g	14 oz.	400 g
Egg Yolks	2	2	8	8
Heavy Cream	½ cup	1.2 dl	2 cups	5 dl

For this recipe, use eel and two or three of the other fish. Cut the fish into steaks.

Melt the butter. Add the shallots and simmer for 5 minutes. Add the wine, fish fumet, salt, pepper, thyme, and nutmeg. Place the pieces of eel into the stock first and simmer for 15 to 20 minutes. Add the other pieces of fish, ending with the most tender.

Prepare a roux with the flour and butter. Transfer the pieces of fish to a shallow serving dish. Pour the cooking stock over the roux and stir until smooth. Simmer for 10 minutes. Add the lemon juice and mushrooms. At serving time, add the liaison of egg yolks and cream. Pour the sauce over the fish and serve immediately.

Matelote of Salmon

Ingredients	6 portions		24 portions	
	U.S.	Metric	U.S.	Metric
Oil	2 oz.	0.6 dl	1 cup	2.5 dl
Salmon Steaks, 1-inch thick . . .	6	6	24	24
Salt	½ tsp.	½ tsp.	2 tsp.	2 tsp.
White Pepper, ground	¼ tsp.	¼ tsp.	1 tsp.	1 tsp.
Onion, chopped	4 oz.	110 g	1 lb.	450 g
Shallots, chopped	1 tbsp.	1 tbsp.	4 tbsp.	4 tbsp.
Red Wine	1 cup	2.5 dl	1 qt.	1 l

(cont.)

Ingredients	6 portions		24 portions	
	U.S.	Metric	U.S.	Metric
Fish Stock	2 cups	5 dl	2 qt.	2 l
Garlic Cloves, chopped	1	1	4	4
Butter, softened	1 tbsp.	1 tbsp.	2 oz.	50 g
Flour	1 tbsp.	1 tbsp.	4 tbsp.	4 tbsp.
Pearl Onions, peeled and blanched	8 oz.	225 g	2 lb.	900 g
Mushroom Caps, cleaned	8 oz.	225 g	2 lb.	900 g

Heat the oil in a frying pan. Brown the salmon steaks on both sides. Remove excess oil. Season the salmon steaks with salt and pepper. Add the onion and shallots and cook over low heat for 2 to 3 minutes.

Pour in the red wine and fish stock. Bring to a boil, then add the garlic. Simmer for 6 to 8 minutes. Transfer the salmon steaks to a warm serving platter, after removing bones and skin.

Reduce the cooking liquid to one half. Mix the butter and flour and whip into the liquid to thicken. Strain over the salmon steaks and garnish with the cooked, glazed (golden browned in butter) pearl onions and the sauteed mushroom caps.

Spanish Fish Stew

Ingredients	6 portions		24 portions	
	U.S.	Metric	U.S.	Metric
Cod Fillets	1 lb.	450 g	4 lb.	1.8 kg
Haddock or Cusk	1 lb.	450 g	4 lb.	1.8 kg
Spiny Lobster Tails, cut in fours	2	2	8	8
Lobsterette Tails	6	6	24	24
Squid Rings	8 oz.	225 g	2 lb.	900 g
Mussels, in shells	6	6	24	24
Shrimp, shelled and deveined	6	6	24	24
Spanish Onion, chopped	1 lb.	450 g	4 lb.	1.8 kg
Olive Oil	¼ cup	0.6 dl	1 cup	2.5 dl
Tomatoes, seeded and chopped	2 lb.	900 g	8 lb.	3.5 kg
Garlic Cloves, chopped	3	3	12	12
Saffron	¼ tsp.	¼ tsp.	1 tsp.	1 tsp.
Fish Stock	3 cups	8 dl	3 qt.	3 l

Cut fish into serving portions. In a heavy casserole or large pot, cook the onion in olive oil. Add the chopped tomatoes, garlic, saffron, and fish stock. Simmer for 15 minutes.

In the bottom of an oven-proof serving dish, arrange the squid, fish, shrimp, lobster tails, lobsterettes, and the clean, scrubbed mussels. Pour the sauce over.

Bake at 375°F (190°C) for 15 minutes, basting the fish occasionally.

Abalone Chowder

Use the same recipe as for clam chowder but substitute canned abalone for clams.

Codfish Chowder

	6 portions		24 portions	
Ingredients	U.S.	Metric	U.S.	Metric
Cod Fillets	2 lb.	900 g	8 lb.	3.6 kg
Water	2 cups	5 dl	2 qt.	2 l
Fish Fumet	2 cups	5 dl	2 qt.	2 l
Potatoes, peeled and diced ...	8 oz.	225 g	2 lb.	900 g
Salt Pork, cubed	2 oz.	50 g	8 oz.	225 g
Onions, diced	4 oz.	110 g	1 lb.	450 g
Milk	3 cups	7.5 dl	3 qt.	3 l
Salt and Pepper, to taste				

Poach the fish in water and fumet until flaky but firm. Remove fish from liquid and add potatoes. Cook until done.

Brown the salt pork in a soup pot. Add the onions and cook over low heat until transparent. Stir in the potatoes with liquid, flaked fish, milk, and a small amount of butter. Bring to a boil. Season with salt and pepper. Serve hot.

Cod and Potato Chowder

	6 portions		24 portions	
Ingredients	U.S.	Metric	U.S.	Metric
Salt Pork, ground	3 oz.	85 g	12 oz.	340 g
Onion, chopped	8 oz.	225 g	2 lb.	900 g
Garlic Clove, minced	1	1	4	4
Bay Leaves	1	1	4	4
Thyme	¼ tsp.	¼ tsp.	1 tsp.	1 tsp.
Parsley Stems	2	2	8	8
Saffron Threads, crushed	½ tsp.	½ tsp.	2 tsp.	2 tsp.
Potatoes, diced	1 lb.	450 g	4 lb.	1800 g
Fish Stock	1 qt.	1 l	1 gal.	4 l
Salt and Pepper, to taste				
Milk, heated	2 cups	5 dl	2 qt.	2 l
Parsley, chopped	1 tbsp.	1 tbsp.	4 tbsp.	4 tbsp.
Cod, skinless and boneless	1½ lb.	680 g	6 lb.	2800 g

In a large soup pot, cook the salt pork until slightly brown. Stir in the onions and cook until wilted. Add the garlic, bay leaves, thyme, parsley stems, and saffron, stirring for 5 minutes.

Add the potatoes and fish stock. Season with salt and pepper. Bring to a boil and simmer for 30 minutes.

Five minutes before serving, add the fish cut into cubes. Simmer for 5 minutes, then add the milk and sprinkle with chopped parsley.

Conch Chowder

Use the same recipe as for clam chowder but substitute ground conch for clams.

Manhattan Clam Chowder

Ingredients	6 portions		24 portions	
	U.S.	Metric	U.S.	Metric
Potatoes, diced	2 oz.	50 g	8 oz.	225 g
Bacon, diced	4 oz.	110 g	1 lb.	450 g
Carrots, diced small	4 oz.	110 g	1 lb.	450 g
White of Leeks, diced small . . .	1 oz.	25 g	4 oz.	110 g
Onion, chopped	4 oz.	110 g	1 lb.	450 g
Celery, chopped	2 oz.	50 g	8 oz.	225 g
Garlic, minced	¼ tsp.	¼ tsp.	1 tsp.	1 tsp.
Tomatoes, peeled, seeded, and chopped	4 oz.	1.2 dl	2 cups	5 dl
Chopped Calms and Juice	6 oz.	170 g	1½ lb.	680 g
Water	2½ cups	6 dl	2½ qt.	2.5 l
Salt	½ tsp.	½ tsp.	2 tsp.	2 tsp.
Pepper, ground	¼ tsp.	¼ tsp.	1 tsp.	1 tsp.
Thyme	¼ tsp.	¼ tsp.	1 tsp.	1 tsp.
Bay Leaves	1	1	4	4

In a heavy soup pot, render the bacon; add the carrots, leeks, onion, and celery. Simmer over low heat for 5 to 10 minutes. Add the garlic and tomatoes and cook for a few minutes. Cook the potatoes separately with enough water to cover.

Bring the clams, clam juice, and water to a boil. Strain into the vegetables. Save clams.

Add the salt, pepper, thyme, and bay leaves. Simmer the soup for 30 minutes. Add the potatoes and clams.

Note: This recipe is also called Philadelphia Chowder.

New England Clam Chowder

Ingredients	6 portions		24 portions	
	U.S.	Metric	U.S.	Metric
Water	2 cups	5 dl	2 qt.	2 l
Raw Clams, shucked and chopped	6 oz.	170 g	1½ lb.	680 g
Potatoes, small diced	6 oz.	170 g	1½ lb.	680 g
Salt Pork, ground	2 oz.	50 g	8 oz.	225 g
Onion, diced	4 oz.	100 g	1 lb.	450 g
Flour	1 oz.	25 g	4 oz.	110 g
Milk	1 cup	2.5 dl	1 qt.	1 l
Light Cream	½ cup	1.2 dl	1 pt.	½ l
Salt and pepper	¾ tsp.	¾ tsp.	1½ tsp.	1½ tsp.
Worcestershire Sauce	½ tsp.	½ tsp.	2 tsp.	2 tsp.

Combine water and clams. Bring to a boil. Remove clams from stock with a skimmer and strain stock through a cheese cloth to eliminate sand. Cover the potatoes with stock and simmer until done. Strain and save stock.

Melt salt pork in a heavy soup pot. Add the onion and cook over low heat for 10 minutes. Stir in the flour to make a roux. Cook for 5 minutes. Pour in the clam stock from potatoes and mix well until smooth.

Add the clams, milk, cream, and potatoes. Season with salt, pepper, and Worcestershire sauce, and simmer for 5 to 10 minutes.

Boula Boula

Ingredients	6 portions		24 portions	
	U.S.	Metric	U.S.	Metric
Fresh or Frozen Peas	4 oz.	110 g	1 lb.	450 g
Beef Stock	1 qt.	1 l	1 gal.	4 l
Clear Turtle Soup	1 cup	2.5 dl	1 qt.	1 l
Turtle Meat	6 oz.	170 g	1½ lb.	680 g
Sherry Wine	2 oz.	0.6 dl	1 cup	2.5 dl
Whipped Cream	½ cup	1.2 dl	2 cups	5 dl

If frozen, thaw the peas. Puree the peas in a blender. In a soup pot, combine the peas, stock, and turtle soup. Bring to a boil and simmer for 20 to 30 minutes. Strain, then add the wine and the turtle meat.

Pour into individual earthenware soup tureens. Spoon whipped cream on top of soup.

Brown under broiler and serve hot.

Note: Any leftover pea soup and turtle soup can be used to prepare this recipe.

Consomme Belle Vue

Ingredients	6 portions		24 portions	
	U.S.	Metric	U.S.	Metric
Soft Shell Clams	4 lb.	1800 g	16 lb.	7.250 kg
Celery Stalks, cut in halves	3	3	12	12
Chicken Broth	1½ qt.	1.5 l	6 qt.	6 l
Salt and White Pepper, to taste				
Heavy Cream, whipped	½ cup	1.2 dl	2 cups	5 dl

Wash the clams. Place the celery in the bottom of a heavy soup pot. Add the clams and stock. Bring to a boil. Simmer for 5 minutes. Remove from fire. Let stand for 10 minutes. Strain the broth through a fine china cap. Season to taste. Top each serving with whipped cream. Serve the clams separately.

Curried Clam Soup

Ingredients	6 portions		24 portions	
	U.S.	Metric	U.S.	Metric
Clams, chopped	2 cups	5 dl	2 qt.	2 l
Clam Juice	2 cups	5 dl	2 qt.	2 l
Shallots, chopped	1 tsp.	1 tsp.	4 tsp.	4 tsp.
Parsley Sprigs	2	2	8	8
Dry White Wine	1 cup	2.5 dl	1 qt.	1 l
Curry Powder	2 tsp.	2 tsp.	2½ tbsp.	2½ tbsp.
Heavy Cream	2 cups	5 dl	2 qt.	2 l
Egg Yolks	3	3	12	12
Salt and Pepper, to taste				

Combine the first six ingredients and simmer for 10 minutes. Make a liaison with the cream and the egg yolks. Stir into the soup. Season. Bring to the boiling point but do not boil. Hold over a waterbath. Serve hot.

Key West Turtle Soup

Ingredients	6 portions		24 portions	
	U.S.	Metric	U.S.	Metric
Beef Consomme	1 qt.	1 l	1 gal.	4 l
Thyme	pinch	pinch	¼ tsp.	¼ tsp.
Basil	pinch	pinch	¼ tsp.	¼ tsp.
Rosemary	pinch	pinch	¼ tsp.	¼ tsp.
Fennel Seeds	pinch	pinch	¼ tsp.	¼ tsp.
Canned Green Turtle Meat . . .	6½ oz.	170 g	1½ lb.	680 g
Cornstarch or Arrowroot	1½ tbsp.	1½ tbsp.	6 tbsp.	6 tbsp.
Dry Sherry Wine	1½ oz.	0.5 dl	6 oz.	2 dl
Salt and Pepper, to taste				

Combine the consomme and herbs in a soup pot. Simmer for 10 minutes. Strain. Dice the turtle meat. Add to consomme and simmer for 20 minutes.

Dissolve cornstarch or arrowroot in the wine. Stir into the hot soup, season, and simmer for 2 to 3 minutes. Serve hot.

Mussel Soup Trois Gros*

Ingredients	6 portions		24 portions	
	U.S.	Metric	U.S.	Metric
Fresh Mussels	4½ lb.	2 kg	17½ lb.	8 kg
Dry White Wine	3 oz.	1 dl	1½ cups	4 dl
Shallots, chopped	1 tbsp.	1 tbsp.	4 tbsp.	4 tbsp.
Olive Oil	¼ cup	0.6 dl	1 cup	2.5 dl
Carrots, diced	5 oz.	150 g	1¼ lb.	600 g
Onion, chopped	5 oz.	150 g	1¼ lb.	600 g
White of Leeks, chopped	2	2	8	8
Garlic Cloves, minced	2	2	8	8
Tomatoes, chopped	4 oz.	110 g	1 lb.	450 g
Saffron Threads, crushed	½ tsp.	½ tsp.	2 tsp.	2 tsp.
Fish Fumet	1 qt.	1 l	1 gal.	4 l
Heavy Cream	3 oz.	1 dl	1½ cups	4 dl
Thyme Leaves	½ tsp.	½ tsp.	2 tsp.	2 tsp.
Salt and Pepper, to taste				

*A specialty from the Trois Gros restaurant in Roanne, France.

Wash and scrub the mussels, remove beards, and discard dead open mussels.

In a heavy, deep pot, combine the wine and shallots. Bring to a boil. Add the mussels, cover the pot, and steam until all mussels are open, tossing occasionally. Strain cooking liquid. Take mussels out of their shells.

In the same soup pot, heat the oil and add the mirepoix (carrots, onion, leeks). Simmer for 5 minutes. Add the garlic, chopped tomatoes, and saffron. Pour in the fish fumet and mussel cooking liquid. Bring to a boil and simmer for 30 to 40 minutes.

Before serving, stir the cream, mussels, and thyme into the soup. Season to taste with salt and pepper.

Provencale Fish Soup

Ingredients	6 portions U.S.	Metric	24 portions U.S.	Metric
Olive Oil	2 oz.	0.6 dl	1 cup	2.5 dl
Leeks, chopped	4 oz.	110 g	1 lb.	450 g
Onion, chopped	4 oz.	110 g	1 lb.	450 g
Celery, chopped	2 oz.	55 g	8 oz.	225 g
Garlic Cloves, minced	3	3	12	12
Paprika	1 tsp.	1 tsp.	4 tsp.	4 tsp.
Saffron Threads	1 tsp.	1 tsp.	4 tsp.	4 tsp.
Lean Fish Bones (bass, snapper, cod)	2½ lb.	1100 g	10 lb.	4.5 kg
Fish Fumet	1 qt.	1 l	1 gal.	4 l
Tomato Paste	2 oz.	55 g	8 oz.	225 g
Bay Leaf	1	1	4	4
Dry Thyme	½ tsp.	½ tsp.	2 tsp.	2 tsp.
Dry White Wine	1 cup	2.5 dl	1 qt.	1 l
Boneless Fish Flesh, cut into cubes (cod, halibut, bass) . . .	1½ lb.	680 g	6 lb.	2.7 kg
Aioli Sauce				

Heat the oil. Add the leeks, onion, celery, and garlic, and cook over low heat for 10 minutes. Stir in the paprika, saffron, and fish bones. Add the fumet, tomato paste, bay leaf, thyme, and wine. Bring to a boil and simmer for 20 minutes.

Strain the soup through a fine china cap. Press the bones to extract all juices. Add the pieces of fish to the soup. Bring to a boil and cook briefly.

Serve hot with aioli sauce on the side. (For Aioli Sauce, see page 172.)

Variation: The same recipe can be prepared with shrimp and oysters to make Shrimp and Oyster Creole Soup.

CHAPTER 11

Fish Sauces and Butter Mixes

Classical sauces remain the indestructible foundation of culinary art. Although international cooking has been altered and adapted to meet the new tastes of an everchanging society, the preparation of sauces remains, by professional standards, the same as at the beginning of this century. The fact is, no one dares weaken the very foundation of one of the oldest arts.

Fish sauces must be prepared with great care and seasoned to perfection. These criteria apply to any sauce, but particularly to fish and shellfish hot sauces. For the benefit of the reader, the use of herb mixes, monosodium glutamate, Season All, numerous aromats, and seasoning mixes available commercially can instantly improve the taste of a dull sauce. The reduction of a weak sauce, without character, will invariably improve its taste and flavor. One often hears that the sauce makes the dish; undoubtedly, hot and cold sauces contribute immensely to the success of any fish dish. A large number of cooking techniques applied to fish and shellfish require the complement of a quality sauce. Fish stocks and fumets are often the base of these sauces.

Hot Sauces

Sauce Allemande

Ingredients	6 portions		24 portions	
	U.S.	Metric	U.S.	Metric
Egg Yolks	1	1	5	5
Heavy Cream	2 oz.	0.6 dl	1 cup	2.5 dl
Veloute Sauce, heated	1½ cups	4 dl	1½ qt.	1.5 l
Lemon Juice	1 tbsp.	1 tbsp.	2 oz.	0.6 dl
Nutmeg	pinch	pinch	⅛ tsp.	⅛ tsp.
White Pepper, ground	pinch	pinch	⅛ tsp.	⅛ tsp.

Prepare a liaison with the egg yolks and heavy cream. Stir in the hot veloute sauce and bring to a boil quickly. Add the lemon juice. Season with nutmeg and pepper. Strain through a fine china cap.

154

Sauce Americaine

Ingredients	6 portions		24 portions	
	U.S.	*Metric*	*U.S.*	*Metric*
Lobsters, 1½ lb. (675 g) each.	1	1	4	4
Butter	2½ oz.	75 g	10 oz.	300 g
Olive Oil	2 oz.	.5 dl	7 oz.	2 dl
Cognac	2 oz.	.5 dl	7 oz.	2 dl
White Wine	3 oz.	1 dl	1½ cups	4 dl
Fish Fumet	3 oz.	1 dl	1½ cups	4 dl
Garlic Cloves, crushed	1	1	2	2
Shallots, chopped	½ oz.	15 g	2 oz.	60 g
Tomato Paste	2 tsp.	2 tsp.	2 tbsp.	2 tbsp.
Parsley, chopped	1 tsp.	1 tsp.	2 tbsp.	2 tbsp.
Tarragon, chopped	1 tsp.	1 tsp.	2 tbsp.	2 tbsp.
Cayenne Pepper	1 pinch	1 pinch	¼ tsp.	¼ tsp.

Cut the tails of the live lobsters into sections at the joints. Break off the claws and crack for easy extraction of the meat. Split the head in half lengthwise. Remove the stomach. Take out the coral (if female) and other creamy parts. Mix with about 2/3 of the butter and set aside.

In a heavy pan, heat the oil and remaining butter. Add the lobster pieces and saute over a brisk fire until the shells turn red. Pour in the cognac and ignite. Deglaze with white wine and fish fumet. Add the garlic, shallots, and tomato paste. Cover and simmer for 15 minutes.

Take out the lobster pieces and extract all the meat. Reduce the sauce to 3 oz. (1 dl) for 6 portions, or 1½ cups (4 dl) for 24 portions, and strain through a china cap. Add the fish veloute and simmer for 10 more minutes. Whip in the mixture of coral and butter, add the chopped tarragon and parsley, cayenne pepper, and the diced lobster meat. Adjust seasoning to taste.

Anchovy Sauce

Ingredients	6 portions		24 portions	
	U.S.	*Metric*	*U.S.*	*Metric*
Sauce Normande	1½ cups	4 dl	1½ qt.	1.5 l
Anchovy Butter	1¼ oz.	35 g	5 oz.	150 g
Anchovy Paste	½ oz.	12 g	2 oz.	50 g

Bring the sauce to a boil. Remove from the fire and stir in the anchovy butter and anchovy paste. Keep sauce in a double boiler.

Sauce Aurore

Ingredients	6 portions		24 portions	
	U.S.	Metric	U.S.	Metric
Fish Veloute	1½ cups	4 dl	1½ qt.	1.5 l
Tomato Paste	2 oz.	0.6 dl	7 oz.	2 dl

Mix the tomato paste into the hot fish veloute.

Sauce Bearnaise

Ingredients	6 portions		24 portions	
	U.S.	Metric	U.S.	Metric
Shallots, chopped	1¼ oz.	35 g	5 oz.	150 g
Peppercorns, cracked	1 tsp.	1 tsp.	4 tsp.	4 tsp.
Tarragon Vinegar	¼ cup	0.6 dl	¾ cup	2 dl
Tarragon, chopped	1½ tbsp.	1½ tbsp.	6 tbsp.	6 tbsp.
Egg Yolks	4	4	16	16
Clarified Butter, warmed	10 oz.	250 g	2½ lb.	1150 g
Parsley, chopped	1½ tsp.	1½ tsp.	2 tbsp.	2 tbsp.
Cayenne Pepper	pinch	pinch	¼ tsp.	¼ tsp.

Place the shallots, peppercorns, vinegar, and half of the chopped tarragon in a saucepan. Reduce by three quarters. Cool the reduction. Add the egg yolks with 1 tsp. (1 tbsp.) of water. Transfer to a stainless steel bowl. Place the bowl over boiling water. Do not allow the bowl to touch the water as it would overcook the egg yolks. Slow, progressive heating is best when making bearnaise sauce. Whip the egg yolk mixture until it reaches a creamy consistency. Remove from heat.

Add the warm clarified butter and strain through a fine china cap. Garnish with remaining chopped tarragon and parsley. Season with cayenne pepper.

Sauces derived from Bearnaise Sauce

Ingredients	6 portions		24 portions	
	U.S.	Metric	U.S.	Metric
Sauce Choron				
Tomato Paste	1½ tsp.	1½ tsp.	2 tbsp.	2 tbsp.
Sauce Arlesienne				
Tomato Paste	1½ tsp.	1½ tsp.	2 tbsp.	2 tbsp.
Anchovy Paste	¾ tsp.	¾ tsp.	1 tbsp.	1 tbsp.
Sauce Veron				
Puree of Cooked Spinach	1¼ oz.	35 g	5 oz.	150 g
Anchovy Paste	¾ tsp.	¾ tsp.	1 tbsp.	1 tbsp.

Bechamel Sauce

Ingredients	6 portions		24 portions	
	U.S.	Metric	U.S.	Metric
Roux for *light* sauce:				
Butter	1½ tbsp.	1½ tbsp.	3 oz.	85 g
Flour	¾ oz.	25 g	3 oz.	85 g
Roux for *medium* sauce:				
Butter	2 tbsp.	2 tbsp.	4 oz.	120 g
Flour	1 oz.	30 g	4 oz.	120 g
Roux for *heavy* sauce:				
Butter	1½ oz.	45 g	6 oz.	170 g
Flour	1½ oz.	45 g	6 oz.	170 g
Other ingredients for all 3 sauces:				
Milk	2 cups	5 dl	2 qt.	2 l
Salt	½ tsp.	½ tsp.	2 tsp.	2 tsp.
White Pepper	pinch	pinch	¼ tsp.	¼ tsp.
Nutmeg	pinch	pinch	⅛ tsp.	⅛ tsp.

Melt the butter in a sauce pot. Stir in the flour and cook over low heat for 10 minutes, stirring occasionally. Do not brown. Cool the roux.

Heat the milk and pour over the roux. Mix with a wire whip until smooth. Simmer for 5 minutes. Season with salt, pepper, and nutmeg.

Bechamel sauce can be stored in a bowl for future use. Lightly coat the top of the sauce with melted butter to prevent skin formation.

Sauce Bercy

Ingredients	6 portions		24 portions	
	U.S.	Metric	U.S.	Metric
Butter	1 oz.	30 g	4½ oz.	125 g
Shallots, chopped	½ oz.	15 g	2 oz.	60 g
White Wine	½ cup	1 dl	1½ cups	4 dl
Fish Fumet	½ cup	1 dl	1½ cups	4 dl
Fish Veloute	1½ cups	4 dl	6 cups	1.5 l
Parsley, chopped	1 tsp.	1 tsp.	2 tbsp.	2 tbsp.

In a heavy skillet, melt half of the butter, stir in the shallots, and cook over low heat for 5 minutes. Add the wine and fumet. Reduce by one half, then add the veloute. Simmer the sauce for 30 minutes or until it has reached the proper consistency (medium thick).

Away from the heat, drop pieces of the remaining butter into the sauce, stirring until melted. Adjust the seasoning and add the chopped parsley.

Bordeaux Wine Sauce

Ingredients	6 portions		24 portions	
	U.S.	Metric	U.S.	Metric
Shallots, chopped	1 tbsp.	1 tbsp.	3 tbsp.	3 tbsp.
Bordeaux Red Wine	7 oz.	2 dl	3¼ cups	8 dl
Thyme	pinch	pinch	½ tsp.	½ tsp.
Peppercorns, crushed	pinch	pinch	½ tsp.	½ tsp.
Fish Veloute	1½ cups	4 dl	1½ qt.	1.5 l
Fresh Tarragon, chopped	1 tsp.	1 tsp.	1 tbsp.	1 tbsp.

In a saucepan, combine the chopped shallots, red wine, thyme, and peppercorns. Reduce by one half. Mix in the fish veloute. Simmer for 10 minutes. Strain through a fine china cap. Stir in the chopped tarragon.

Bretonne Sauce

Ingredients	6 portions		24 portions	
	U.S.	Metric	U.S.	Metric
White of Leeks	1 oz.	30 g	3½ oz.	100 g
Celery Hearts	1 oz.	30 g	3½ oz.	100 g
Onion	1 oz.	30 g	3½ oz.	100 g
Mushrooms	1 oz.	30 g	3½ oz.	100 g
Butter	1 oz.	30 g	3½ oz.	100 g
Fish Veloute	1½ cups	4 dl	1½ qt.	1.5 l
Heavy Cream	1 oz.	2 tbsp.	½ cup	1.2 dl

Cut the vegetables julienne style. Melt the butter in a heavy pan. Add the vegetables and simmer over low heat without coloring. Stir frequently, adding a small amount of water to prevent burning. Mix in the fish veloute. Bring to a boil. Stir in the cream. Simmer for 5 to 6 minutes.

Beurre Blanc
(White Butter Sauce)

Ingredients	6 portions		24 portions	
	U.S.	Metric	U.S.	Metric
Shallots, chopped	2 oz.	50 g	8 oz.	225 g
Wine Vinegar	2 oz.	0.6 dl	1 cup	2.5 dl
Dry White Wine	3 oz.	1 dl	1½ cups	4 dl
Butter	8 oz.	225 g	2 lb.	900 g
Salt and Pepper, to taste				

In a saucepan, combine the shallots, vinegar, and white wine. Reduce to two thirds. Cool and stir in small pieces of butter with a whisk, making sure the butter does not get too hot. Season with salt and pepper.

Sauce Cardinal

Ingredients	6 portions		24 portions	
	U.S.	Metric	U.S.	Metric
Bechamel Sauce	1½ cups	4 dl	1½ qt.	1.5 l
Fish Fumet	½ cup	1 dl	1¾ cups	4 dl
Heavy Cream	½ cup	1 dl	1¾ cups	4 dl
Lobster Butter	1½ oz.	50 g	7 oz.	200 g

Combine the bechamel sauce with the fish fumet and the heavy cream. Reduce by one quarter. Remove from the fire and gradually add the lobster butter, stirring constantly.

Caper Sauce

Ingredients	6 portions		24 portions	
	U.S.	Metric	U.S.	Metric
Fish Veloute	1½ cups	4 dl	1½ qt.	1.5 l
Capers, tiny	1½ tbsp.	1½ tbsp.	6 tbsp.	6 tbsp.

At serving time, stir the capers into the hot veloute sauce.

Cream Sauce

Ingredients	6 portions		24 portions	
	U.S.	Metric	U.S.	Metric
Bechamel Sauce	1½ cups	4 dl	1½ qt.	1.5 l
Light Cream	7 oz.	2 dl	3 cups	8 dl
Lemon Juice	1 tbsp.	1 tbsp.	2 oz.	0.6 dl

Combine the bechamel sauce and light cream. Simmer to reduce by one quarter. Strain through a china cap. Mix in the lemon juice.

Curry Sauce

Ingredients	6 portions		24 portions	
	U.S.	Metric	U.S.	Metric
Butter	2 tbsp.	2 tbsp.	3½ oz.	100 g
Onion, chopped	2 oz.	60 g	9 oz.	250 g
Curry Powder	1 tsp.	1 tsp.	4 tsp.	4 tsp.
Mace	pinch	pinch	¼ tsp.	¼ tsp.
Cooking Apple, diced	½	½	2	2
Small Banana, diced	¼	¼	1	1
Fish Veloute	1½ cups	4 dl	1½ qt.	1.5 l
Heavy Cream	2 oz.	0.6 dl	1 cup	2.5 dl

Melt the butter. Add the onion and cook over low heat for 10 minutes. Mix in the curry powder, mace, diced apple, and banana. Cook for 5 more minutes. Stir in the veloute and then the heavy cream. Simmer for 20 minutes. Strain the sauce through a china cap. Adjust the seasoning, adding lemon juice if necessary.

Dill Sauce

Ingredients	6 portions		24 portions	
	U.S.	Metric	U.S.	Metric
White Wine Sauce	1½ cups	4 dl	1½ qt.	1.5 l
Heavy Cream	2 oz.	0.6 dl	1 cup	2.5 dl
Fresh Dill, chopped or	1 tsp.	1 tsp.	2 tbsp.	2 tbsp.
Dry Dill	½ tsp.	½ tsp.	1 tbsp.	1 tbsp.

Combine the white wine sauce with the heavy cream. Bring to a boil and simmer to reduce by one quarter. Strain through a china cap and mix in the dill.

Diplomate Sauce

Ingredients	6 portions		24 portions	
	U.S.	Metric	U.S.	Metric
Sauce Normande	1½ cups	4 dl	1½ qt.	1.5 l
Lobster Butter	1 oz.	30 g	4 oz.	120 g
Lobster Meat, diced	1 oz.	30 g	4 oz.	120 g
Small Truffles, diced	1 tsp.	1 tsp.	1 oz.	30 g

Heat the sauce normande. Whip in the lobster butter. Add the lobster meat and truffles. Adjust seasoning if necessary.

Fine Herb Sauce

Ingredients	6 portions		24 portions	
	U.S.	Metric	U.S.	Metric
White Wine Sauce	1½ cups	4 dl	1½ qt.	1.5 l
Shallot Butter	¾ oz.	25 g	3½ oz.	100 g
Parsley, chopped	2 tsp.	2 tsp.	2 tbsp.	2 tbsp.
Fresh Tarragon	½ tsp.	½ tsp.	1 tbsp.	1 tbsp.
Fresh Basil, chopped	½ tsp.	½ tsp.	1 tbsp.	1 tbsp.

Note: If using dried herbs, use half of the amount. Combine all ingredients and simmer the sauce for 5 minutes.

Sauce Genevoise

Ingredients	6 portions		24 portions	
	U.S.	Metric	U.S.	Metric
Butter	2 oz.	50 g	8 oz.	200 g
Carrots, chopped	1	1	3	3
Onions, chopped	1	1	3	3
Thyme	¼ tsp.	¼ tsp.	1 tsp.	1 tsp.
Bay Leaves	1	1	3	3
Parsley Stems	4	4	12	12
Fish Bones	8 oz.	225 g	2 lb.	900 g
Peppercorns, crushed	1½ tsp.	1½ tsp.	2 tbsp.	2 tbsp.
Red Wine	¾ cup	2 dl	3 cups	8 dl
Fish Fumet	1 cup	2½ dl	4 cups	1 l
Demi-glaze Sauce	2 oz.	0.6 dl	1 cup	2.5 dl
Anchovy Paste	½ tsp.	½ tsp.	2 tsp.	2 tsp.

Melt the butter. Add the carrots and onions and cook over low heat for 5 minutes. Add the thyme, bay leaves, parsley stems, fish bones, and peppercorns. Cover and steam for 10 minutes. Pour off excess butter.

Add the wine and fish fumet. Reduce over medium heat for 10 minutes. Add the demi-glaze. Bring the sauce to a boil and simmer for 5 minutes. Strain, pressing the bones to extract all the sauce. Stir in the anchovy paste.

Glazing Wine Sauce

Ingredients	6 portions		24 portions	
	U.S.	Metric	U.S.	Metric
Fish Veloute	1½ cups	4 dl	1½ qt.	1.5 l
Fish Fumet	3 oz.	1 dl	1½ cups	4 dl
White Wine	1½ oz.	.5 dl	¾ cup	2 dl
Hollandaise Sauce	2 oz.	0.6 dl	1 cup	2.5 dl

Combine the fish veloute, fish fumet, and white wine. Reduce by one quarter. Adjust seasoning. Remove from the fire and stir in the hollandaise sauce.

Hollandaise Sauce

Ingredients	6 portions		24 portions	
	U.S.	Metric	U.S.	Metric
Egg Yolks	4	4	16	16
Cold Water	1½ tbsp.	1½ tbsp.	3 oz.	1 dl
Cayenne Pepper	pinch	pinch	⅛ tsp.	⅛ tsp.
Salt	⅛ tsp.	⅛ tsp.	½ tsp.	½ tsp.
Clarified Butter	10 oz.	280 g	2½ lb.	1150 g
Lemon Juice	1 tbsp.	1 tbsp.	2 oz.	0.6 dl

Whip egg yolks and water together in a stainless steel bowl. Place the bowl over boiling water. Do not allow the bowl to touch the water as it will overcook the egg yolks. Slow, progressive heating is best when making hollandaise sauce.

Whip the yolks until they reach a creamy consistency. Add seasonings. Remove from heat. Slowly pour warm butter into the yolks, whipping continuously to blend.

Note: Add the lemon juice at serving time to prevent fermentation of the sauce.

Sauces derived from Hollandaise Sauce

Ingredients	6 portions		24 portions	
	U.S.	Metric	U.S.	Metric
Sauce Mousseline				
Whipped Cream, fold in	2 oz.	0.6 dl	1 cup	2.5 dl
Sauce Maltaise				
Juice and Grated Peel of Orange, mix in	½	½	2	2
Sauce Moutarde				
Imported Mustard, mix in	1 tsp.	1 tsp.	1 tbsp.	1 tbsp.
Hazelnut Sauce				
Ground Hazelnuts, mix in	4 tbsp.	4 tbsp.	1 cup	110 g
Macadamia Sauce				
Chopped Macadamia Nuts, mix in	4 tbsp.	4 tbsp.	1 cup	110 g
Maximilian Sauce				
Anchovy Paste, whip in	¾ tsp.	¾ tsp.	1 tbsp.	1 tbsp.

Sauce Joinville

Ingredients	6 portions		24 portions	
	U.S.	Metric	U.S.	Metric
Sauce Normande	1½ cup	4 dl	1½ qt.	1.5 l
Shrimp Butter	1 oz.	25 g	3½ oz.	100 g
Truffle, chopped (optional) ...	1 tsp.	1 tsp.	1 oz.	25 g

Bring the sauce normande to a boil and whip in the shrimp butter. Add the truffles.

Lobster Sauce

Ingredients	6 portions		24 portions	
	U.S.	Metric	U.S.	Metric
Fish Veloute	1½ cups	4 dl	1½ qt.	1.5 l
Heavy Cream	¼ cup	0.6 dl	1 cup	2.5 dl
Lobster Butter	1 oz.	30 g	4 oz.	120 g

Bring the veloute to a boil. Add the cream and simmer for 10 minutes. Remove from the fire and stir in the lobster butter.

Sauce Mornay

Ingredients	6 portions		24 portions	
	U.S.	Metric	U.S.	Metric
Sauce Bechamel	1½ cups	4 dl	1½ qt.	1.5 l
Fish Fumet	3 oz.	1 dl	1½ cups	4 dl
Parmesan Cheese, grated	1 oz.	30 g	4 oz.	120 g
Egg Yolks	1	1	4	4

Combine the bechamel sauce and fish fumet. Reduce by one quarter. Mix the cheese with the egg yolks. Stir into the sauce and bring to the boiling point.

Mushroom Sauce

Ingredients	6 portions		24 portions	
	U.S.	Metric	U.S.	Metric
Sauce Allemande	2 cups	.5 l	2 qt.	2 l
Mushroom Cooking Liquid . . .	5 oz.	1.5 dl	2½ cups	6 dl
Boiled Mushroom Buttons	2 oz.	50 g	7 oz.	200 g

Combine the mushroom cooking liquid with the allemande sauce. Reduce by one quarter and add the mushroom buttons.

Mussel Sauce

Ingredients	6 portions		24 portions	
	U.S.	Metric	U.S.	Metric
Mussel Cooking Liquid	2 tbsp.	2 tbsp.	½ cup	1.2 dl
Sauce Bercy	1½ cups	4 dl	1½ qt.	1.5 l
Egg Yolks	2	2	6	6

Mix the mussel cooking liquid with the egg yolks. Stir in the boiling bercy sauce. Keep the sauce hot over a waterbath.

Mustard Sauce

Ingredients	6 portions		24 portions	
	U.S.	Metric	U.S.	Metric
Butter	1½ tsp.	1½ tsp.	2 tbsp.	2 tbsp.
Shallots, chopped	1½ tsp.	1½ tsp.	2 tbsp.	2 tbsp.
White Wine	3 oz.	1 dl	1½ cups	4 dl
White Wine Sauce	1½ cups	4 dl	1½ qt.	1.5 l
Imported Mustard (Dijon, Dusseldorf)	1 tbsp.	1 tbsp.	4 tbsp.	4 tbsp.

Brown the shallots in butter. Deglaze with white wine. Reduce by one half. Add the white wine sauce. Bring to a boil. Simmer for 10 to 15 minutes. Before serving, stir in the mustard.

Sauce Nantua

Ingredients	6 portions		24 portions	
	U.S.	Metric	U.S.	Metric
Bechamel Sauce	1½ cups	4 dl	1½ qt.	1.5 l
Heavy Cream	½ cup	1.2 dl	2 cups	5 dl
Lobster, Shrimp, or Crayfish Butter	¾ oz.	25 g	3½ oz.	100 g
Lobster, Shrimp, or Crayfish Meat, diced	2 oz.	50 g	7 oz.	200 g

Combine the bechamel sauce and heavy cream. Reduce by one quarter. Remove from the heat and stir in the butter mix and the meat.

Newburg Sauce

Ingredients	6 portions		24 portions	
	U.S.	Metric	U.S.	Metric
Cream Sauce	1½ cups	4 dl	1½ qt.	1.5 l
Lobster Butter	1¼ oz.	35 g	5 oz.	150 g
Sherry Wine	2 oz.	0.6 dl	¾ cup	2 dl
Paprika	1 tsp.	1 tsp.	1 tbsp.	1 tbsp.
Salt and Pepper, to taste				

Bring the cream sauce to a boil. Stir in the remaining ingredients. Adjust the seasoning.

Sauce Normande

Ingredients	6 portions		24 portions	
	U.S.	Metric	U.S.	Metric
Veloute Sauce	1½ cups	4 dl	1½ qt.	1.5 l
Oyster Cooking Stock	¼ cup	0.6 dl	1 cup	2.5 dl
Mushroom Stock	¼ cup	0.6 dl	1 cup	2.5 dl
Heavy Cream	½ cup	1 dl	1½ cups	4 dl
Egg Yolks	3	3	12	12
Lemon Juice	1 tsp.	1 tsp.	1 oz.	0.3 dl
Butter	1¼ oz.	35 g	5 oz.	150 g

Combine the first three ingredients and reduce by one quarter. Make a liaison with the egg yolks and the heavy cream. Slowly pour over the veloute. Bring the sauce to a boil quickly. Strain. Season to taste, add the lemon juice, and stir in the butter pieces.

Sauce Orientale

Ingredients	6 portions		24 portions	
	U.S.	Metric	U.S.	Metric
Sauce Americaine	1½ cups	4 dl	1½ qt.	1.5 l
Curry Powder	2 tsp.	2 tsp.	2 tbsp.	2 tbsp.
Heavy Cream	¼ cup	0.6 dl	1 cup	2.5 dl

Combine all ingredients and reduce by one quarter.

Oyster Sauce

Ingredients	6 portions		24 portions	
	U.S.	Metric	U.S.	Metric
Sauce Normande	1½ cups	4 dl	1½ qt.	1.5 l
Oyster Cooking Liquid	1 oz.	2 tbsp.	3 oz.	1 dl
Cooked Oysters, diced	6	6	24	24

Combine the sauce normande with the oyster cooking liquid. Simmer for 5 minutes or to the desired consistency. At serving time, mix in the cooked oysters.

Sauce Poulette

Ingredients	6 portions		24 portions	
	U.S.	Metric	U.S.	Metric
Sauce Veloute	1½ cups	4 dl	1½ qt.	1.5 l
Mushroom Stock	¼ cup	0.6 dl	1 cup	2.5 dl
Egg Yolks	2	2	8	8
Heavy Cream	¼ cup	0.6 dl	1 cup	2.5 dl
Lemon Juice	1 tbsp.	1 tbsp.	2 oz.	0.6 dl
Sweet Butter	1 oz.	25 g	3½ oz.	100 g
Parsley, chopped	1 tbsp.	1 tbsp.	4 tbsp.	4 tbsp.

Combine the veloute and mushroom stock. Simmer for 5 minutes. Slowly add to the liaison of egg yolks and heavy cream. Bring to a boil quickly and strain. Season to taste. Add the lemon juice, sweet butter, and chopped parsley.

Sauce Ravigotte

Ingredients	6 portions		24 portions	
	U.S.	Metric	U.S.	Metric
Wine Vinegar	2 oz.	0.6 dl	¾ cup	2 dl
White Wine	½ cup	1 dl	1½ cups	4 dl
Fish Veloute	1½ cups	4 dl	1½ qt.	1.5 l
Shallot Butter	1¼ oz.	35 g	5 oz.	150 g
Chives, chopped	1 tsp.	1 tsp.	1 tbsp.	1 tbsp.
Tarragon, chopped	1 tsp.	1 tsp.	1 tbsp.	1 tbsp.
Parsley, chopped	1 tsp.	1 tsp.	1 tbsp.	1 tbsp.

Combine the white wine and vinegar. Reduce by two thirds. Add the veloute sauce. Bring to a boil and simmer for 10 minutes. Remove from the heat and stir in the shallot butter and the herbs.

Sauce Soubise

	6 portions		24 portions	
Ingredients	U.S.	Metric	U.S.	Metric
Onions, chopped	7 oz.	200 g	1¾ lb.	800 g
Butter	2 oz.	50 g	7 oz.	200 g
Bechamel Sauce, medium	1½ cups	4 dl	1½ qt.	1.5 l
Heavy Cream	2 oz.	0.6 dl	1 cup	2.5 dl

Blanch the onions. Drain. Melt the butter. Add the onions and cook over low heat for 10 minutes. Mix in the bechamel sauce and the cream. Simmer for 10 minutes and strain through a fine china cap.

Sauce Souchet

	6 portions		24 portions	
Ingredients	U.S.	Metric	U.S.	Metric
Carrots	1¾ oz.	50 g	7 oz.	200 g
Celery	1¾ oz.	50 g	7 oz.	200 g
Butter	1¼ oz.	35 g	5 oz.	150 g
White Wine	½ cup	1 dl	1½ cups	4 dl
Fish Fumet	½ cup	1 dl	1½ cups	4 dl
White Wine Sauce	1½ cups	4 dl	1½ qt.	1.5 l

Cut the vegetables julienne style and stew in the butter. Add the wine and fish fumet. Reduce by one half. Mix in the white wine sauce. Bring to a boil. Adjust seasoning if necessary.

Shrimp Sauce

	6 portions		24 portions	
Ingredients	U.S.	Metric	U.S.	Metric
Fish Veloute	1½ cups	4 dl	1½ qt.	1.5 l
Fish Fumet	3 oz.	1 dl	1½ cups	4 dl
Heavy Cream	3 oz.	1 dl	1½ cups	4 dl
Tomato Paste	1 tsp.	1 tsp.	1 tbsp.	1 tbsp.
Cooked Shrimp, diced	2 oz.	50 g	7 oz.	200 g

Combine the fish veloute, fish fumet, and heavy cream. Reduce by one quarter. Strain through a china cap. Adjust the seasoning. Hold the sauce in a waterbath. At serving time, stir in the tomato paste and diced shrimp.

Sauce St. Malo

Ingredients	6 portions		24 portions	
	U.S.	Metric	U.S.	Metric
White Wine Sauce	1½ cups	4 dl	1½ qt.	1.5 l
Imported Mustard	1½ tsp.	1½ tsp.	2 tbsp.	2 tbsp.
Anchovy Butter	¾ oz.	25 g	3½ oz.	100 g
Anchovy Paste	1½ tsp.	1½ tsp.	2 tbsp.	2 tbsp.

Bring the white wine sauce to a boil. Remove from the fire and stir in the remaining ingredients.

Sweet and Sour Sauce

Ingredients	6 portions		24 portions	
	U.S.	Metric	U.S.	Metric
Water	¾ cup	2 dl	3 cups	8 dl
Sugar	½ cup	1 dl	1½ cups	4 dl
Cider Vinegar	½ cup	1 dl	1½ cups	4 dl
Cornstarch	1 tbsp.	1 tbsp.	4 tbsp.	4 tbsp.
Soy Sauce	1 tbsp.	1 tbsp.	4 tbsp.	4 tbsp.
Water	¼ cup	0.6 dl	1 cup	2.5 dl

Bring the water to a boil. Add the sugar and stir until dissolved. Stir in the vinegar.

Blend the cornstarch, soy sauce, and remaining water. Stir in the boiling liquid to thicken.

Note: The addition of one or several of the following ingredients is common:

cooked green pepper
pineapple chunks
grated ginger root
tomatoes
pickles
bamboo shoots
crab apples

Tarragon Sauce

Ingredients	6 portions		24 portions	
	U.S.	Metric	U.S.	Metric
Fresh Tarragon, coarsely chopped	2 tbsp.	2 tbsp.	2 oz.	50 g
Fish Veloute	1½ cups	4 dl	1½ qt.	1.5 l
Tarragon, finely chopped	1 tsp.	1 tsp.	2 tbsp.	2 tbsp.

Combine the coarsely chopped tarragon with a small amount of hot veloute. Puree in a blender. Combine with the remaining hot sauce. Strain through a fine china cap. Garnish with finely chopped fresh tarragon.

Tomato Sauce

Ingredients	6 portions		24 portions	
	U.S.	Metric	U.S.	Metric
Fish Veloute	1½ cups	4 dl	1½ qt.	1.5 l
Tomato Puree or	1¾ oz.	50 g	7 oz.	200 g
Fresh Tomatoes, peeled and quartered	7 oz.	200 g	1¾ lb.	800 g
Garlic Cloves, crushed	1	1	4	4
Butter	1 oz.	25 g	3½ oz.	100 g

Add the tomato puree, or the fresh tomatoes, and garlic cloves to the veloute. Bring to a boil and simmer for 10 minutes. Strain through a china cap and adjust the seasoning. Stir in the butter, in pieces, at serving time.

Veloute Sauce

Ingredients	6 portions		24 portions	
	U.S.	Metric	U.S.	Metric
Butter	3 tbsp.	40 g	5 oz.	140 g
Flour	1½ oz.	40 g	5 oz.	140 g
Fish Fumet	1 pt.	.5 l	2 qt.	2 l
Salt	¼ tsp.	¼ tsp.	1 tsp.	1 tsp.
White Pepper, ground	pinch	pinch	¼ tsp.	¼ tsp.

Melt the butter, add the flour, and cook over low heat until the roux is slightly brown. Gradually pour in the fish fumet, whipping until smooth. Bring to a boil, stirring occasionally, until the sauce thickens. Simmer 10 minutes and season to taste.

Sauce Venitienne

Ingredients	6 portions		24 portions	
	U.S.	Metric	U.S.	Metric
Tarragon Vinegar	½ cup	1 dl	1½ cups	4 dl
Shallots, chopped	1 tsp.	1 tsp.	2 tbsp.	2 tbsp.
Parsley, with stems, chopped . .	1 tbsp.	1 tbsp.	1 oz.	25 g
White Wine Sauce	1½ cups	4 dl	1½ qt.	1.5 l
Green Butter	1 oz.	30 g	4 oz.	120 g
Fresh Tarragon, chopped	1 tsp.	1 tsp.	2 tbsp.	2 tbsp.
Fresh Parsley, chopped	2 tsp.	2 tsp.	2 tbsp.	2 tbsp.

Combine the vinegar and shallots and reduce by two thirds. Add the parsley and white wine sauce. Bring to a boil and simmer for 10 minutes. Strain through a fine china cap. Remove from the fire and stir in the green butter and the chopped parsley and tarragon.

White Wine Sauce

Ingredients	6 portions		24 portions	
	U.S.	Metric	U.S.	Metric
Veloute Sauce	1½ cups	4 dl	1½ qt.	1.5 l
Fish Fumet	½ cup	1 dl	1½ cups	4 dl
White Wine	2 oz.	0.6 dl	¾ cup	2 dl
Egg Yolks	1	1	4	4
Fresh Butter	1¼ oz.	35 g	5 oz.	150 g

Combine the veloute sauce, fish fumet, and white wine. Simmer to reduce by one quarter. Slowly pour over the creamed egg yolk(s) and bring to a boil quickly. Strain and stir in the butter.

Cold Sauces

Aioli Sauce

Ingredients	6 portions		24 portions	
	U.S.	Metric	U.S.	Metric
Garlic Cloves	4	4	16	16
Egg Yolks	2	2	8	8
Salt	⅛ tsp.	⅛ tsp.	½ tsp.	½ tsp.
Potato, boiled and diced	1	1	4	4
Olive Oil	1 cup	2.5 dl	1 qt.	1 l
Lemon Juice	1 tsp.	1 tsp.	4 tsp.	4 tsp.

Prepare the sauce like a mayonnaise, mixing the first four ingredients and beating the oil in very slowly. Add lemon juice.

Sauce Albigeoise

Ingredients	6 portions		24 portions	
	U.S.	Metric	U.S.	Metric
Capers	2 tsp.	2 tsp.	3 tbsp.	3 tbsp.
Small Dill Pickles, chopped ...	1 tbsp.	1 tbsp.	4 tbsp.	4 tbsp.
Hard-boiled Eggs	2	2	8	8
Parsley, chopped	2 tsp.	2 tsp.	2 tbsp.	2 tbsp.
Garlic Cloves	1	1	3	3
Salad Oil	1½ cups	4 dl	1½ qt.	1.5 l
Wine Vinegar	½ cup	1 dl	1½ cups	4 dl
Salt	¼ tsp.	¼ tsp.	1 tsp.	1 tsp.
Pepper, ground	⅛ tsp.	⅛ tsp.	½ tsp.	½ tsp.
Anchovy Fillets, minced	3	3	12	12

Puree the capers, pickles, eggs, parsley, and garlic together. Mix in the oil and vinegar as for a mayonnaise. Season with salt and pepper. Stir in the anchovies.

Sauce Andalouse

Ingredients	6 portions		24 portions	
	U.S.	Metric	U.S.	Metric
Mayonnaise Sauce	1½ cups	4 dl	1½ qt.	1.5 l
Tomato Paste	2 tsp.	2 tsp.	3 tbsp.	3 tbsp.
Pimentos, diced	1 tbsp.	1 tbsp.	4 tbsp.	4 tbsp.
Lemon Juice	¾ tsp.	¾ tsp.	1 tbsp.	1 tbsp.
Worcestershire Sauce	¼ tsp.	¼ tsp.	1 tsp.	1 tsp.

Combine all ingredients.

Sauce Antiboise

Ingredients	6 portions		24 portions	
	U.S.	Metric	U.S.	Metric
Mayonnaise Sauce	1½ cups	4 dl	1½ qt.	1.5 l
Anchovy Paste	1 tsp.	1 tsp.	1 tbsp.	1 tbsp.
Tomato Paste	2 tsp.	2 tsp.	3 tbsp.	3 tbsp.
Fresh Tarragon, chopped	¾ tsp.	¾ tsp.	1 tbsp.	1 tbsp.

Combine all ingredients.

Chantilly Sauce

Ingredients	6 portions		24 portions	
	U.S.	Metric	U.S.	Metric
Mayonnaise Sauce	1½ cups	4 dl	1½ qt.	1.5 l
Whipped Cream	1 oz.	0.3 dl	½ cup	1.2 dl

Prepare the mayonnaise sauce with lemon juice instead of vinegar. Fold in the whipped cream.

Cocktail Sauce

Ingredients	6 portions		24 portions	
	U.S.	Metric	U.S.	Metric
Mayonnaise Sauce	1½ cups	4 dl	1½ qt.	1.5 l
Chili Sauce	½ cup	1.2 dl	2 cups	5 dl
Ketchup	2 oz.	0.6 dl	1 cup	2.5 dl
Worcestershire Sauce	2 tsp.	2 tsp.	2 tbsp.	2 tbsp.
Lemon Juice	1 tbsp.	1 tbsp.	2 oz.	0.6 dl
Brandy	1 tbsp.	1 tbsp.	2 oz.	0.6 dl
Seasoned Salt	¼ tsp.	¼ tsp.	1 tsp.	1 tsp.
Paprika	¼ tsp.	¼ tsp.	1 tsp.	1 tsp.
Whipping Cream	½ cup	1.2 dl	2 cups	5 dl

Blend all ingredients until smooth. Whip the cream until medium thick and fold in sauce.

Sauce Cypriote

Ingredients	6 portions		24 portions	
	U.S.	Metric	U.S.	Metric
Mayonnaise Sauce	1½ cups	4 dl	1½ qt.	1.5 l
Hard-boiled Egg Yolks, chopped	3	3	12	12
Tomato Puree	1 tbsp.	1 tbsp.	4 tbsp.	4 tbsp.
Anchovy Paste	½ tsp.	½ tsp.	2 tbsp.	2 tbsp.
Fresh Fennel, chopped	2 tsp.	2 tsp.	3 tbsp.	3 tbsp.

Blend all ingredients together.

Frozen Horseradish Sauce

Ingredients	6 portions		24 portions	
	U.S.	Metric	U.S.	Metric
Whipped Cream	1 cup	2½ dl	1 qt.	1 l
Horseradish, grated	1½ tbsp.	1½ tbsp.	6 tbsp.	6 tbsp.
White Vinegar	2 tsp.	2 tsp.	2 tbsp.	2 tbsp.
Salt	¼ tsp.	¼ tsp.	1 tsp.	1 tsp.
Sugar	pinch	pinch	½ tsp.	½ tsp.
Black Pepper, ground	pinch	pinch	½ tsp.	½ tsp.

Combine the whipped cream with horseradish and vinegar. Gently mix with all other ingredients. Roll in greased parchment paper and freeze until set.

At serving time, cut into ¼-inch (½-cm) thick slices.

Sauce Gribiche

Ingredients	6 portions		24 portions	
	U.S.	Metric	U.S.	Metric
Hard-boiled Egg Yolks	3	3	12	12
Prepared Mustard	1½ tsp.	1½ tsp.	2 tbsp.	2 tbsp.
Salt	¼ tsp.	¼ tsp.	1 tsp.	1 tsp.
White Pepper	⅛ tsp.	⅛ tsp.	½ tsp.	½ tsp.
Tarragon Vinegar	2 oz.	0.6 dl	1 cup	2.5 dl
Oil	¾ cup	2 dl	3 cups	8 dl
Small Dill Pickles, chopped . . .	2 tbsp.	2 tbsp.	6 oz.	150 g
Capers, chopped	1 tbsp.	1 tbsp.	4 oz.	100 g
Hard-boiled Egg Whites	1	1	4	4
Parsley, chopped	1½ tsp.	1½ tsp.	2 tbsp.	2 tbsp.

In a food processor or blender, make a paste with the egg yolks. Add the mustard, salt, pepper, and vinegar. Continue mixing, adding the oil progressively as for a mayonnaise.

Transfer to a mixing bowl. Blend in the chopped pickles and capers, and the egg whites cut julienne style, and the chopped parsley.

Mayonnaise Sauce

Ingredients	6 portions		24 portions	
	U.S.	Metric	U.S.	Metric
Egg Yolks	2	2	8	8
Salt	½ tsp.	½ tsp.	2 tsp.	2 tsp.
Cayenne Pepper	pinch	pinch	¼ tsp.	¼ tsp.
Prepared Mustard	1 tsp.	1 tsp.	1 tbsp.	1 tbsp.
Oil	1½ cups	4 dl	1½ qt.	1.5 l
Vinegar or Lemon Juice	¾ tsp.	¾ tsp.	1 tbsp.	1 tbsp.

Note: To ensure perfect emulsification, all ingredients should be at room temperature.

In a mixing bowl, mix the egg yolks, salt, pepper, and mustard. Pour the oil in a slow stream, stirring continuously with a whip. When the sauce thickens, alternate oil and vinegar or lemon juice until used.

If the sauce is too thick after all the ingredients have been combined, add a small amount of lukewarm water.

How to Restore a Broken Mayonnaise In a clean bowl, place 1 tbsp. of cold water, regardless of the amount of sauce to be restored. Slowly whip 1 tbsp. of sauce into the cold water. As soon as the mayonnaise thickens, larger amounts can be added until all the sauce is used.

Mustard Sauce

Ingredients	6 portions		24 portions	
	U.S.	Metric	U.S.	Metric
White Wine	½ cup	1.2 dl	2 cups	5 dl
Shallots, chopped	1 tsp.	1 tsp.	2 tbsp.	2 tbsp.
Mustard Seeds	1 tsp.	1 tsp.	2 tbsp.	2 tbsp.
Mayonnaise Sauce	1½ cups	4 dl	1½ qt.	1.5 l
Dijon or Dusseldorf Mustard . .	1 tsp.	1 tsp.	2 tbsp.	2 tbsp.

Combine the wine, shallots, and mustard seeds and bring to a boil. Reduce by three quarters and cool.

Mix in the mayonnaise and mustard. Strain through a fine china cap or cheese cloth.

Picadilly Sauce

Ingredients	6 portions		24 portions	
	U.S.	Metric	U.S.	Metric
Mayonnaise Sauce	1½ cups	4 dl	1½ qt.	1.5 l
Sour Cream	¼ cup	0.6 dl	1 cup	2.5 dl
Worcestershire Sauce	¼ tsp.	¼ tsp.	1 tsp.	1 tsp.
Lemon Juice	1 tsp.	1 tsp.	1 tbsp.	1 tbsp.
Fresh Fennel, chopped	¾ oz.	20 g	3 oz.	85 g

Blend all the ingredients to obtain a smooth sauce.

Ravigotte Sauce

Ingredients	6 portions		24 portions	
	U.S.	Metric	U.S.	Metric
Vinaigrette Sauce	½ cup	1.2 dl	2 cups	5 dl
Fresh Parsley	1 tsp.	1 tsp.	1 tbsp.	1 tbsp.
Fresh Chervil	1 tsp.	1 tsp.	1 tbsp.	1 tbsp.
Fresh Tarragon	1 tsp.	1 tsp.	1 tbsp.	1 tbsp.
Fresh Chives	1 tsp.	1 tsp.	1 tbsp.	1 tbsp.
Onion, chopped	1 tbsp.	15 g	2½ oz.	50 g
Capers	1 tbsp.	1 tbsp.	3 tbsp.	3 tbsp.

Finely chop the herbs, onion, and capers. Mix into the vinaigrette sauce.

Remoulade Sauce

Ingredients	6 portions		24 portions	
	U.S.	Metric	U.S.	Metric
Mayonnaise Sauce	1½ cups	4 dl	1½ qt.	1.5 l
Capers	1 tbsp.	1 tbsp.	4 tbsp.	4 tbsp.
Tiny Sour Pickles, chopped ...	1 tbsp.	1 tbsp.	4 tbsp.	4 tbsp.
Fillet of Anchovy	1	1	4	4
Tarragon, chopped	1 tsp.	1 tsp.	1 tbsp.	1 tbsp.
Shallots, chopped	1 tsp.	1 tsp.	1 tbsp.	1 tbsp.
Parsley, chopped	2 tsp.	2 tsp.	2 tbsp.	2 tbsp.
Prepared Mustard	1 tsp.	1 tsp.	1 tbsp.	1 tbsp.

Blend all ingredients together.

Russian Sauce

Ingredients	6 portions		24 portions	
	U.S.	Metric	U.S.	Metric
Mayonnaise Sauce	1½ cups	4 dl	1½ qt.	1.5 l
Pressed Caviar	2 oz.	50 g	8 oz.	200 g
Worcestershire Sauce	½ tsp.	½ tsp.	2 tsp.	2 tsp.

Combine all ingredients.

Serbian Garlic Sauce

Ingredients	6 portions		24 portions	
	U.S.	Metric	U.S.	Metric
Garlic Cloves	3	3	12	12
Salt	½ tsp.	½ tsp.	2 tsp.	2 tsp.
Egg Yolks	3	3	12	12
White Pepper, ground	⅛ tsp.	⅛ tsp.	½ tsp.	½ tsp.
Oil	1 cup	2.5 dl	1 qt.	1 l
Lemon Juice	1 tsp.	1 tsp.	1 tbsp.	1 tbsp.

Mash the garlic with the salt. Add the egg yolks and pepper. Mix in the oil as for a mayonnaise. Stir in the lemon juice.

Tartare Sauce

Ingredients	6 portions		24 portions	
	U.S.	Metric	U.S.	Metric
Hard-boiled Eggs	2	2	8	8
Mayonnaise Sauce	1½ cups	4 dl	1½ qt.	1.5 l
Chives, chopped	2 tsp.	2 tsp.	2 tbsp.	2 tbsp.
Shallots, chopped	1 tsp.	1 tsp.	4 tsp.	4 tsp.
Tarragon, chopped	1 tsp.	1 tsp.	1 tbsp.	1 tbsp.
Chervil, chopped	1 tsp.	1 tsp.	1 tbsp.	1 tbsp.
Parsley, chopped	1 tsp.	1 tsp.	1 tbsp.	1 tbsp.

Chop the eggs in a food processor or put through a food mill. Combine with the remaining ingredients. Adjust seasoning to taste.

Tuna—Anchovy Sauce

Ingredients	6 portions		24 portions	
	U.S.	Metric	U.S.	Metric
Olive Oil	½ cup	1.2 dl	2 cups	5 dl
Hard-boiled Egg Yolks, crushed	6	6	24	24
Tuna, flaked	1 tbsp.	1 tbsp.	4 tbsp.	4 tbsp.
Parsley, chopped	1 tbsp.	1 tbsp.	4 tbsp.	4 tbsp.
Anchovy Paste	1 tbsp.	1 tbsp.	4 tbsp.	4 tbsp.
Small Dill Pickles, chopped . . .	6	6	24	24
Wine Vinegar	3 oz.	1 dl	1½ cups	4 dl
Salt	½ tsp.	½ tsp.	2 tsp.	2 tsp.
Pepper, ground	⅛ tsp.	⅛ tsp.	½ tsp.	½ tsp.

Whip the oil with the egg yolks until smooth. Add the tuna, chopped parsley, anchovy paste, and pickles. Pour in the vinegar, season with salt and pepper, and stir the sauce well.

Sauce Verte

Ingredients	6 portions		24 portions	
	U.S.	Metric	U.S.	Metric
Fresh Spinach	½ oz.	15 g	2 oz.	50 g
Watercress	½ oz.	15 g	2 oz.	50 g
Parsley	½ oz.	15 g	2 oz.	50 g
Fresh Tarragon	½ oz.	15 g	2 oz.	50 g
Garlic Powder	⅛ tsp.	⅛ tsp.	½ tsp.	½ tsp.
Lemon Juice	2 tsp.	2 tsp.	3 tbsp.	3 tbsp.
Mayonnaise Sauce	1½ cups	4 dl	1½ qt.	1.5 l

Blanch and drain the spinach and herbs. Squeeze out the water. Puree in a blender with the garlic and lemon juice. Stir into the mayonnaise.

Vinaigrette Sauce

Ingredients	6 portions		24 portions	
	U.S.	Metric	U.S.	Metric
Salt	¼ tsp.	¼ tsp.	1 tsp.	1 tsp.
Prepared Mustard	½ tsp.	½ tsp.	2 tsp.	2 tsp.
Wine Vinegar	2 oz.	0.6 dl	1 cup	2.5 dl
Oil	¾ cup	2 dl	3 cups	8 dl
Onion Powder	⅛ tsp.	⅛ tsp.	½ tsp.	½ tsp.
Black Pepper, ground	⅛ tsp.	⅛ tsp.	½ tsp.	½ tsp.

Dissolve the salt and mustard in the vinegar. Add the oil and remaining ingredients and blend well.

Vincent Sauce

Ingredients	6 portions		24 portions	
	U.S.	Metric	U.S.	Metric
Tarragon, chopped	1½ tsp.	1½ tsp.	2 tbsp.	2 tbsp.
Parsley, chopped	1½ tsp.	1½ tsp.	2 tbsp.	2 tbsp.
Chives, chopped	1½ tsp.	1½ tsp.	2 tbsp.	2 tbsp.
Chervil, chopped	1½ tsp.	1½ tsp.	2 tbsp.	2 tbsp.
Spinach, chopped	½ oz.	12 g	2 oz.	50 g
Watercress, chopped	½ oz.	12 g	2 oz.	50 g
Hard-boiled Eggs, finely chopped	2	2	8	8
Mayonnaise Sauce	1½ cups	4 dl	1½ qt.	1.5 l
Worcestershire Sauce	¼ tsp.	½ tsp.	1 tsp.	1 tsp.

Combine all ingredients.

Butter and Cheese Mixtures

Butter and cheese are combined with many ingredients to make spreads used in a large variety of canapes. These spreads enhance the flavor and taste of the canapes. The following list of butter and cheese mixtures is by no means complete; in fact, there is no limit to the variations that can be created.

Anchovy Butter

Blend 12 anchovy fillets with 4 oz. (110 g) of sweet butter and mix into a paste.

Caviar Butter

Blend 2 oz. (50 g) of fresh caviar with 4 oz. (110 g) of butter and mix into a paste.

Crayfish Butter

Blend 2 oz. (50 g) of cooked crayfish tails with 4 oz. (110 g) of butter and mix into a paste.

Curry Butter

Cook 2 oz. (50 g) of chopped onions in butter and add 1 tsp. of curry powder. Simmer for 5 minutes. Cool and add 4 oz. (110 g) of butter. Mix into a paste.

Egg Butter

Blend 12 egg yolks with 8 oz. (225 g) of butter. Mix into a paste and season with salt and pepper.

Herring Butter

Blend 2 desalted fillets of herring with 12 oz. (340 g) of butter and mix into a paste.

Herring Roe Butter

Blend 3 oz. (85 g) of herring roe, which has been poached in white wine, with 4 oz. (110 g) of butter. Add a pinch of mustard and mix into a paste.

Horseradish Butter

Mix 2 oz. (50 g) of grated horseradish with 1 lb. (450 g) of butter.

Lobster Butter

Blend 4 oz. (110 g) of lobster coral with 8 oz. (225 g) of butter and mix into a paste.

Maitre d'Hotel Butter

Soften 8 oz. (225 g) of butter and add 1 tbsp. chopped parsley and ½ tsp. lemon juice. Salt and pepper to taste.

Moscovite Butter

Blend 8 oz. (225 g) of butter with 4 oz. (110 g) of caviar and 6 hard-cooked egg yolks. Mix all ingredients into a paste. Season with salt and cayenne pepper.

Mustard Butter

Mix 1 tsp. of prepared or English mustard with 8 oz. (225 g) of butter.

Portuguese Butter

Blend 3 hard-cooked egg yolks with 5 oz. (140 g) of butter. Add 1 tbsp. of tomato paste, and season with salt and pepper. Mix into a paste.

Smoked Salmon Butter

Blend 8 oz. (225 g) of smoked salmon with 1 lb. (450 g) of butter and mix into a paste.

Sardine Butter

Blend 12 boneless sardines with 12 oz. (340 g) of butter and mix into a paste.

Shrimp Butter

Blend 2 oz. (50 g) of cooked shrimp with 4 oz. (110 g) of butter. Add 2 oz. (50 g) of chopped parsley, season with salt and pepper, and mix into a paste.

Tarragon Butter

Blend 2 oz. (50 g) of blanched tarragon leaves with 12 oz. (340 g) of butter and put through a very fine sieve.

Tunafish Butter

Blend 2 oz. (50 g) of tunafish with 4 oz. (110 g) of butter and mix into a paste.

Lobster Cheese

Follow the procedure for Langouste Cheese.

Crab Cheese

Blend 4 oz. (110 g) of crab meat with 8 oz. (225 g) of cream cheese. Add 2 oz. (50 g) of butter. Mix into a paste and season with salt and pepper.

Langouste Cheese

Follow the procedure described for Crab Cheese, substituting 4 oz. (110 g) of spiny lobster.

Salmon Cheese

Blend 4 oz. (110 g) of cooked salmon with 4 oz. (110 g) of cream cheese and 1 oz. (25 g) of butter. Mix into a paste. Finish with a small amount of heavy cream and a little port wine.

Tunafish Cheese

Blend 8 oz. (225 g) of tunafish with 8 oz. (225 g) of cream cheese. Mix into a paste and finish with heavy cream.

CHAPTER 12

Salt-water Fish Recipes

This chapter contains recipes for the following:

Anchovy	Mackerel	Shad
Bluefish	Miscellaneous Seafood Recipes	Sheepshead
Butterfish	Mullet	Smelt
Cod	Ocean Perch	Sole
Croaker	Pollock	Spot
Cusk	Pompano	Striped Bass
Dolphin	Porgy	Swordfish
Eel	Redfish	Tilefish
Flounder	Red Snapper	Tuna
Grouper	Rockfish	Turbot
Haddock	Sablefish	Turtle
Hake	Salmon	Weakfish
Halibut	Sardine	Whiting
Herring	Sea Bass	
Lingcod	Sea Trout	

Anchovy

Anchovy and cheese pizza

	6 portions		24 portions	
Ingredients	U.S.	Metric	U.S.	Metric
Pizza Dough (see chapter 7) . . .	½ recipe	½ recipe	2 recipes	2 recipes
Anchovy Fillets	12	12	48	48
Canned Italian Tomatoes, drained	6 oz.	170 g	1½ lb.	680 g
Capers	1 oz.	25 g	4 oz.	110 g
Oregano	½ tsp.	½ tsp.	2 tsp.	2 tsp.
Mozzarella Cheese, grated	8 oz.	225 g	2 lb.	900 g

(cont.)

183

Line 1 (4) pizza pan(s) with dough, about ⅓-inch (1-cm) thick. Cut the anchovy fillets in halves and dice the tomatoes. Spread anchovies, tomatoes, and capers evenly over the dough. Sprinkle with oregano, then cheese. Season with freshly ground pepper.

Bake at 375°F (190°C) for 15 to 20 minutes or until the dough is crisp on the bottom.

Bagna Cauda

| | 6 portions | | 24 portions | |
Ingredients	U.S.	Metric	U.S.	Metric
Butter	3 oz.	85 g	12 oz.	340 g
Olive Oil	2 oz.	0.6 dl	1 cup	2.5 dl
Garlic Cloves, crushed	3	3	12	12
Anchovy Fillets, pureed	12	12	48	48
White Truffle (optional)	1	1	4	4
Salt to taste				

Bagna Cauda is a specialty of Piemont, Italy. It is used as a dip with raw vegetable pieces, such as celery hearts, fennel, cardons, and green and red sweet peppers.

In a fondue pot, place the butter, oil, garlic, and anchovies. Heat until garlic is slightly brown. Remove from heat and add the chopped white truffle. Add salt to taste.

The sauce must be kept hot. Serve small pieces of raw vegetables. Fondue forks are often used to dip the vegetable pieces.

Note: Stir in heavy cream if mixture is too thick.

Stuffed Peppers with Anchovies

| | 6 portions | | 24 portions | |
Ingredients	U.S.	Metric	U.S.	Metric
Medium Green Peppers	6	6	24	24
White Bread, without crust	2 oz.	50 g	8 oz.	225 g
Olive Oil	3 oz.	1 dl	1½ cups	4 dl
Parmesan Cheese	3 oz.	85 g	12 oz.	340 g
Ricotta Cheese	2 oz.	50 g	8 oz.	225 g
Anchovy Fillets, chopped	2 oz.	50 g	8 oz.	225 g
Black Olives, pitted	1 oz.	25 g	4 oz.	110 g
Green Olives, pitted	1 oz.	25 g	4 oz.	110 g
Eggs, beaten	2	2	8	8
Capers	1 tbsp.	1 tbsp.	4 tbsp.	4 tbsp.
Black Pepper, ground	⅛ tsp.	⅛ tsp.	½ tsp.	½ tsp.

Slice off the bottoms of peppers and remove seeds. Deep fry at 360°F (185°C) for 1 minute. Drain and peel off the skin.

Soak the bread in water. Squeeze dry and combine with ⅔ of the olive oil, and remaining ingredients. Season to taste.

Stuff the peppers. Pour remaining oil over.

Bake at 360°F (185°C) until peppers are tender and top is brown.

Anchovy Stuffed Eggs

Ingredients	6 portions		24 portions	
	U.S.	Metric	U.S.	Metric
Hard-boiled Eggs	6	6	24	24
Butter	2 oz.	50 g	8 oz.	225 g
Cream Cheese	2 oz.	50 g	8 oz.	225 g
Salt	¼ tsp.	¼ tsp.	1 tsp.	1 tsp.
Mayonnaise	1 tbsp.	1 tbsp.	¼ cup	0.6 dl
Hot Pepper Sauce	dash	dash	¼ tsp.	¼ tsp.
Anchovy Paste	2 tsp.	2 tsp.	3 tbsp.	3 tbsp.
Anchovy Fillets	6	6	24	24

Peel the eggs. Cut in halves, lengthwise. Remove yolks. Mix yolks, butter, cream cheese, salt, mayonnaise, hot pepper sauce, and anchovy paste in a food processor.

Pipe mixture into whites and top with strips of anchovy fillet.

Cover plates with shredded lettuce and arrange stuffed eggs on top.

Pissaladiere

Ingredients	6 portions		24 portions	
	U.S.	Metric	U.S.	Metric
Pizza Dough	1 recipe	1 recipe	4 recipes	4 recipes
Olive Oil	½ cup	1.2 dl	2 cups	5 dl
Onion, chopped	2 tbsp.	2 tbsp.	½ cup	110 g
Tomatoes, chopped and seeded	2 lb.	900 g	8 lb.	3.6 kg
Garlic Cloves, crushed	2	2	8	8
Salt and Pepper, to taste				
Anchovy Fillets	12	12	48	48
Nicoise or Small Black Olives . .	2 oz.	50 g	8 oz.	225 g

Line 9-inch (22.5-cm) pie dish(es) with the pizza dough. Heat the oil in a skillet. Add the onions and cook fully over low heat.

In a separate skillet, combine the tomatoes and crushed garlic and reduce over medium heat. Season with salt and pepper.

Spread the onion over the pizza dough and add the tomatoes. Crisscross the anchovy fillets on top and decorate with olives. Bake at 375°F (190°C) for 30 to 40 minutes. Serve hot.

The following are additional suggestions for anchovies, some of which appear in other chapters of this book.

Potato Salad and Anchovies

Dress potato salad on a bed of lettuce. Sprinkle with chopped egg yolk and egg white. Arrange stuffed anchovies on salad.

Scallopine of Veal Holstein

Pan-fried veal scallopine garnished with fried eggs and anchovy fillets.

Anchovy Allumettes

Roll out puff paste dough. Cut into small rectangles. Spread one half of the rectangles with anchovy butter and top with remaining rectangles. Arrange a fillet of anchovy on top of each pastry. Bake at 375°F (190°C).

See chapter 11 for:

Anchovy Butter
Anchovy Sauce
Sauce St. Malo
Sauce Albigeoise
Sauce Maximilian
Sauce Antiboise
Sauce Veron
Sauce Cypriote
Tuna-Anchovy Sauce

Bluefish (Blue Runner)

Bluefish Fillets Espagnole

Ingredients	6 portions		24 portions	
	U.S.	Metric	U.S.	Metric
Oil	2 oz.	0.6 dl	1 cup	2.5 dl
Onions, sliced	4 oz.	110 g	1 lb.	450 g
Tomatoes, peeled and seeded	2 lb.	900 g	8 lb.	3.6 kg
Garlic Cloves, chopped	2	2	8	8
Salt	½ tsp.	½ tsp.	2 tsp.	2 tsp.
Black Pepper	¼ tsp.	¼ tsp.	1 tsp.	1 tsp.
Bluefish Fillets	2 lb.	900 g	8 lb.	3.6 kg
Lemon Juice	1 tsp.	1 tsp.	1 tbsp.	1 tbsp.
Parsley, chopped	1 tbsp.	1 tbsp.	4 tbsp.	4 tbsp.

Heat oil in heavy skillet. Add onions and cook over low heat for 10 minutes. Stir in tomatoes, garlic, salt, and pepper. Cook over low heat for 10 to 15 minutes. Arrange bluefish portions in buttered baking pan. Sprinkle with lemon juice. Spoon sauce over fish. Bake at 400°F (205°C) for 10 to 15 minutes. Transfer to heated serving platter(s). Sprinkle with chopped parsley. Serve hot.

Bluefish Meuniere

Skin fillets; remove dark meat strip. Saute as for Dover Sole Meuniere and sprinkle with chopped fresh dill.

Note: The fatty bluefish are best broiled in fillets. Remove skin and dark middle meat with a sharp boning knife. This dark strip of meat is very fatty and has a fishy odor, especially if the fish is not very fresh.

Bluefish Stuffed with Crab

Ingredients	6 portions		24 portions	
	U.S.	Metric	U.S.	Metric
Bluefish, whole, cleaned 4 lbs. (1.8 kg)	1	1	4	4
Salt	½ tsp.	½ tsp.	2 tsp.	2 tsp.
Pepper, ground	¼ tsp.	¼ tsp.	1 tsp.	1 tsp.
Crabmeat..................	1 lb.	450 g	4 lb.	1.8 kg
Cream Sauce	½ cup	1.2 dl	2 cups	5 dl
Olive Oil	2 oz.	0.6 dl	1 cup	2.5 dl
Lemon Juice	1 oz.	0.3 dl	½ cup	1.2 dl

Place cleaned fish on large baking pan(s). Season the cavity with salt and pepper. Combine the crabmeat with cream sauce and stuff the cavity of the fish. Secure stuffing by inserting small skewers into belly flaps. a quarter turn to obtain a checkered effect. Turn the fish over and repeat the process until fully cooked. Arrange the pieces on preheated platters. Sprinkle with lemon juice, capers, and parsley.

Note: This dish can also be served with anchovy butter.

Grilled Fillets of Bluefish with Capers

Ingredients	6 portions		24 portions	
	U.S.	Metric	U.S.	Metric
Bluefish Fillets	2 lb.	900 g	8 lb.	3.6 kg
Salt	½ tsp.	½ tsp.	2 tsp.	2 tsp.
Pepper, ground	¼ tsp.	¼ tsp.	1 tsp.	1 tsp.
Oil	½ cup	1.2 dl	2 cups	5 dl
Lemon juice...............	2 oz.	0.6 dl	1 cup	2.5 dl
Capers	1 tbsp.	1 tbsp.	4 tbsp.	4 tbsp.
Parsley, chopped	1 tbsp.	1 tbsp.	4 tbsp.	4 tbsp.

Cut the fillets into 5 oz. (140 g) portions. Season with salt and pepper and brush with oil. Cook the fish on a hot grill or charcoal broiler. Give the pieces Brush fish with oil and lemon juice. Bake at 375°F(190°C) for 40 to 45 minutes. Serve on preheated serving platter(s).

Butterfish (Dollar Fish, Harvest Fish)

Butterfish a la Provencale

Ingredients	6 portions		24 portions	
	U.S.	Metric	U.S.	Metric
Whole Butterfish, dressed	6	6	24	24
Salt	½ tsp.	½ tsp.	2 tsp.	2 tsp.
Pepper, ground	¼ tsp.	¼ tsp.	1 tsp.	1 tsp.
Flour	2 oz.	50 g	8 oz.	200 g
Olive Oil	½ cup	1.2 dl	2 cups	5 dl
Garlic Cloves, chopped	2	2	8	8
Tomatoes, grilled	6	6	24	24
Anchovy Fillets	6	6	24	24
Ripe Olives	12	12	48	48

Season the fillets with salt and pepper. Coat with flour. Fry in olive oil, turning the fish once. Add the garlic to flavor the fish. Arrange the butterfish on a warm serving platter. Garnish with grilled tomatoes, anchovy fillets, and ripe olives.

Butterfish en Papillote

Ingredients	6 portions		24 portions	
	U.S.	Metric	U.S.	Metric
Anchovy Butter	9 oz.	250 g	2¼ lb.	1 kg.
Whole Butterfish, dressed	6	6	24	24
Canadian Bacon Slices	6	6	24	24
Salt	½ tsp.	½ tsp.	2 tsp.	2 tsp.
Black Pepper, ground	¼ tsp.	¼ tsp.	1 tsp.	1 tsp.
Tomato Paste	6 oz.	170 g	1½ lb.	680 g
Parsley, chopped	1 tbsp.	1 tbsp.	4 tbsp.	4 tbsp.

Cut heart-shaped pieces of parchment paper, large enough to hold the fish. (For more details, see the cooking technique, en papillotte, in chapter 6.) Spread anchovy butter on the edge of each paper. Top with butterfish and Canadian bacon slices. Season with salt and pepper. Spoon 1 oz. (25 g) of tomato paste on the top of each fish and sprinkle with chopped parsley. Fold the other side of parchment paper over the fish and seal the edges of paper. Bake at 425°F (220°C) for 15 to 20 minutes.

Broiled Butterfish, Sauce Bercy

See Grilled Fillets of Bluefish. Serve with sauce bercy (chapter 11).

Butterfish Meuniere with Almonds

See Dover Sole Meuniere.

Smoked Butterfish

Smoked butterfish are available commercially and have a delicate flavor. Bone them and serve with frozen horseradish sauce, lemon wedges, and capers.

Cod

Cod, like sole and salmon, is so versatile that the recipes are seemingly endless. Cod can be used in any cooking technique, but a fresh piece of poached cod is a pure marvel when served with hollandaise sauce. The following recipes are excellent presentations of cod.

Cod Basque

Ingredients	6 portions		24 portions	
	U.S.	Metric	U.S.	Metric
Cod Fillets or Steaks	3 lb.	1.3 kg	12 lb.	5.4 kg
Flour	4 oz.	110 g	1 lb.	450 g
Salt	1 tsp.	1 tsp.	4 tsp.	4 tsp.
Pepper, ground	¼ tsp.	¼ tsp.	1 tsp.	1 tsp.
Olive Oil	5 oz.	1.5 dl	2½ cups	6 dl
Mushrooms, sliced	7 oz.	200 g	¾ lb.	800 g
Tomatoes, chopped and seedless	10 oz.	300 g	2½ lb.	1.2 kg
Garlic Clove, minced	1	1	4	4
Dry White Wine	5 oz.	1.5 dl	2½ cups	6 dl

Cut the cod into steaks or fillet portions. Mix the flour with salt and pepper. Flour the cod and sear on both sides in the hot oil. Transfer the fish to an ovenproof serving dish.

Saute the mushrooms in the oil. Add the tomatoes and garlic. Stir together and pour in the wine. Spoon the sauce over the fish and bake at 350°F (180°C) for 10 to 15 minutes.

Codfish Steaks Dantin

Ingredients	6 portions		24 portions	
	U.S.	Metric	U.S.	Metric
Shallots, chopped	1 oz.	25 g	3½ oz.	100 g
Tomatoes, chopped and seedless	4 oz.	110 g	1 lb.	450 g
Parsley, chopped	1 tbsp.	1 tbsp.	4 tbsp.	4 tbsp.
Mushrooms, sliced	2½ oz.	70 g	10 oz.	280 g
Codfish Steaks	6—5 oz.	6—150 g	24—5 oz.	24—150 g
Salt and Pepper, to taste				
Dry White Wine	3 oz.	1 dl	1½ cup	4 dl
Fish Fumet	¼ cup	0.6 dl	1 cup	2.5 dl
Butter	2 oz.	50 g	7 oz.	200 g
Flour	1 oz.	25 g	4 oz.	110 g

Butter suitable baking sheet pan(s). Sprinkle shallots, tomatoes, some parsley, and mushrooms over the whole surface of the pan. Arrange the fish steaks over the vegetables. Season with salt and pepper and moisten with wine and fumet. Bake at 400°F (205°C) for 15 minutes.

Transfer to serving platter after removing skin and bones. Garnish the fish steaks with the vegetables. Strain the cooking liquid. Reduce the cooking liquid for 5 to 10 minutes. Thicken with beurre manie (mixture of butter and flour). Bring to a boil and cook for 10 minutes over low heat. Pour over the fish, sprinkle with chopped parsley, and serve hot.

Deep-fried Codfish Patties

Ingredients	6 portions		24 portions	
	U.S.	Metric	U.S.	Metric
Salted Cod	1 lb.	450 g	4 lb.	1.8 kg
Potatoes, mashed	1 lb.	450 g	4 lb.	1.8 kg
Parsley, chopped	1 tbsp.	1 tbsp.	4 tbsp.	4 tbsp.
Dry Mustard	1 tsp.	1 tsp.	1 tbsp.	1 tbsp.
White Pepper, ground	¼ tsp.	¼ tsp.	1 tsp.	1 tsp.
Eggs, beaten	2	2	8	8
Oil, for frying				

Soak the cod in cold water for 12 hours. Drain and poach, starting with fresh cold water. Simmer for 15 minutes or until fish flakes when tested.

Drain and flake the fish. Combine with the remaining ingredients. Shape into patties, allowing two per person. Deep fry at 375°F (190°C) until brown.

Arrange on a serving platter and serve hot.

Note: Any leftover codfish, fresh or salted, can be used.

Batter-fried Pacific Cod

Ingredients	6 portions		24 portions	
	U.S.	Metric	U.S.	Metric
Pacific Cod, fresh or frozen fillets	2 lb.	900 g	8 lb.	3.6 kg
Salt	½ tsp.	½ tsp.	2 tsp.	2 tsp.
Flour	4 oz.	110 g	1 lb.	450 g
Whole Eggs	2	2	8	8
Beer	6 oz.	2 dl	3 cups	8 dl
Salt	½ tsp.	½ tsp.	2 tsp.	2 tsp.
Ginger, ground	¼ tsp.	¼ tsp.	1 tsp.	1 tsp.
Oil, for frying				
Lemon Wedges	6	6	24	24
Parsley, for garnish				

Thaw the fish, if frozen. Bone and skin. Cut into 5-oz (140-g) portions. Season with salt and pepper. Combine the flour, eggs, beer, salt, and ginger. Mix until the batter is smooth and re-frigerate for 30 minutes.

Dip fish into the batter. Deep fry at 375°F (190°C) for 3 to 5 minutes. Serve on a warm plat-ter. Garnish with parsley and lemon wedges.

Cod Boulangere

Ingredients	6 portions		24 portions	
	U.S.	Metric	U.S.	Metric
Butter	6 oz.	170 g	1½ lb.	680 g
Potatoes, thinly sliced	1 lb.	450 g	4 lb.	1.8 kg
Onions, sliced	4 oz.	110 g	1 lb.	450 g
Salt and Pepper, to taste				
Cod Steaks	2 lb.	900 g	8 lb.	3.6 kg
Garlic Cloves, chopped	1	1	4	4
Parsley, chopped	2 tbsp.	2 tbsp.	½ cup	45 g
Fresh Bread Crumbs	1 oz.	25 g	4 oz.	225 g

Butter oven-proof serving dish(es). Blanch the potatoes in boiling water and drain. Ar-range in the bottom of the dish with the onion slices. Season with salt and pepper. Place the cod on top. Dot with remaining butter.

Bake at 360°F (185°C) until potatoes are done and the fish is flaky. Baste occasionally. Com-bine the garlic, parsley, and breadcrumbs. Sprinkle over the fish and bake until brown.

Fillets of Cod Florentine

| | 6 portions | | 24 portions | |
Ingredients	U.S.	Metric	U.S.	Metric
Cod fillets, fresh or frozen	2 lb.	900 g	8 lb.	3.6 kg
Salt	1 tsp.	1 tsp.	1 tbsp.	1 tbsp.
Pepper	¼ tsp.	¼ tsp.	1 tsp.	1 tsp.
White Wine	½ cup	1.2 dl	2 cups	5 dl
Spinach, fresh cleaned	1½ lb.	680 g	6 lb.	2.7 kg
Mornay Sauce	2 cups	5 dl	2 qt.	2 l
Swiss Cheese, grated	4 oz.	110 g	1 lb.	450 g

Cut the fresh or thawed fillets into 6 (24) equal portions. Arrange in a buttered baking pan. Season with salt and pepper. Pour the wine over, cover, and bake at 350°F (180°C) until flaky, about 8 to 10 minutes.

Blanch the spinach in salted boiling water. Drain and squeeze out excess water. Mix a small amount of sauce into spinach. Spread the bottom of an oven-proof serving dish with the spinach. Arrange the cod fil-lets on top and pour the remaining sauce over. Sprinkle with cheese and brown under a broiler.

Fillets of Cod Orientale

| | 6 portions | | 24 portions | |
Ingredients	U.S.	Metric	U.S.	Metric
Cod fillets	2½ lb.	1.2 kg	10 lb.	4.5 kg
Oil	½ cup	1.2 dl	2 cups	5 dl
Fresh Fennel	8 oz.	225 g	2 lb.	900 g
Tomatoes, chopped and seedless	10 oz.	300 g	2½ lb.	1.2 kg
Garlic Cloves, crushed	2	2	8	8
Parsley, chopped	1 tbsp.	1 tbsp.	4 tbsp.	4 tbsp.
Salt	1 tsp.	1 tsp.	1 tbsp.	1 tbsp.
Pepper, ground	¼ tsp.	¼ tsp.	1 tsp.	1 tsp.
Dry White Wine	1 cup	2½ dl	1 qt.	1 l
Saffron	1 tsp.	1 tsp.	1½ tbsp.	1½ tbsp.
Cumin	¼ tsp.	¼ tsp.	1 tsp.	1 tsp.
Coriander, ground	¼ tsp.	¼ tsp.	1 tsp.	1 tsp.
Pepper, ground	¼ tsp.	¼ tsp.	1 tsp.	1 tsp.

Cut the fillets into 7-oz. (200-g) portions. Heat the oil. Stir in the fennel and cook over low heat for 10 minutes. Add the tomatoes and garlic. Season with the saffron, cumin, and coriander. Simmer for 20 minutes.

Arrange the fish fillets on buttered sheet pans. Season with salt and pepper. Pour the wine over and cover with the sauce. Bake for 10 minutes at 400°F (205°C). Transfer the fillets onto serving platter(s). Coat with the sauce. Sprinkle with parsley and garnish with lemon wedges.

Fillets of Cod Polonaise

Ingredients	6 portions		24 portions	
	U.S.	Metric	U.S.	Metric
Cod Fillets	2½ lb.	1.2 kg	10 lb.	4.5 kg
Eggs, hard-boiled	3	3	12	12
White Sandwich Bread	4 oz.	110 g	1 lb.	450 g
Oil	½ cup	1.2 dl	2 cups	5 dl
Salt	1 tsp.	1 tsp.	1½ tbsp.	1½ tbsp.
Parsley, chopped	2 tbsp.	2 tbsp.	½ cup	45 g
Flour	1½ oz.	40 g	5 oz.	150 g
Butter	6 oz.	170 g	1½ lb.	680 g
Parsley, chopped	2 tbsp.	2 tbsp.	½ cup	½ cup
Lemon Wedges	6	6	24	24

Cut the fillets into 7-oz. (200-g) portions. Separate the egg yolks from the whites and chop each finely. Dice the bread into small pieces and fry in a small amount of oil.

Season the cod fillets with salt and pepper. Coat in flour and fry in oil on both sides. Arrange the fish on heated platter(s). Melt the butter to brown and pour over fish. Sprinkle with chopped egg, parsley, and croutons. Serve with lemon wedges.

Fried Fillets of Cod

Ingredients	6 portions		24 portions	
	U.S.	Metric	U.S.	Metric
Cod fillets	2½ lb.	1.2 kg	10 lb.	4.5 kg
Salt	1 tsp.	1 tsp.	1 tbsp.	1 tbsp.
White Pepper, ground	¼ tsp.	¼ tsp.	1 tsp.	1 tsp.
Flour	4 oz.	110 g	1 lb.	450 g
Eggs	2	2	8	8
Fresh Bread Crumbs	3 cups	170 g	12 cups	680 g
Tartare Sauce (see chapter 11)	2 cups	5 dl	2 qts.	2 l
Oil, for frying				
Parsley, to garnish				

Cut the fillets into 7-oz. (200-g) portions. Season with salt and pepper. Coat with flour. Dip in beaten eggs and roll in bread crumbs.

Deep fry at 360°F (185°C) for 3 to 4 minutes. Drain and arrange on serving platter(s). Garnish with parsley. Serve sauce separately.

Fresh Cod Mornay with Noodles

Ingredients	6 portions		24 portions	
	U.S.	Metric	U.S.	Metric
Fresh Cod	2 lb.	900 g	8 lb.	3.6 kg
Court Bouillon no. 4				
Egg Noodles	4 oz.	110 g	1 lb.	450 g
Mornay Sauce	1½ cups	4 dl	1½ qt.	1.5 l
Swiss Cheese, grated	2 oz.	50 g	8 oz.	225 g

Poach the cod in court bouillon. Cook the noodles in salted boiling water. Flake the cod fish.

Arrange the noodles in the bottom of a buttered, ovenproof serving dish. Spread the cod over the noodles and coat with mornay sauce. Sprinkle with cheese and bake at 350°F (180°C) for 15 to 20 minutes or until brown.

Planked New England Cod

Clean and bone a cod weighing 4 to 5 lbs (1.8 to 2.2 kg). Dry thoroughly. Season the inside with a mixture of salt and pepper. Brush fish with butter.

Place on oiled, preheated plank, skin side down. Bake in a hot oven, 375°F (190°C) for 30 minutes, basting frequently with melted butter. Remove plank from oven. Garnish with vegetables and serve with hollandaise sauce (chapter 11).

Salted Cod Pie

Ingredients	6 portions		24 portions	
	U.S.	Metric	U.S.	Metric
Salted Cod	2 lb.	900 g	8 lb.	3.6 kg
Egg Yolks	3	3	12	12
Bechamel Sauce	2 cups	5 dl	2 qt.	2 l
Puff Pastry Dough	1 lb.	450 g	4 lb.	1.8 kg
Egg Yolks	1	1	4	4

Soak the cod in cold water for 12 hours. Poach, starting with fresh cold water, until flaky. Mix the egg yolks with the bechamel sauce. Combine the sauce with the flaked fish.

Line pie dish(es) with the puff pastry dough. Spoon in the fish. Cover with dough. Brush with egg yolk and bake at 350°F (180°C) for 20 minutes.

Poached Cod Hollandaise

Ingredients	6 portions		24 portions	
	U.S.	Metric	U.S.	Metric
Whole Cod, dressed	1—5 lb.	1—2.3 kg	4—5 lb.	4—2.3 kg
Court Bouillon No. 4				
Hollandaise Sauce	1½ cups	4 dl	1½ qt.	1.5 l
Parsley				

Poach the whole fish, following directions described for the poaching technique in chapter 6. Transfer the cooked fish onto a serving platter. Garnish with parsley. Serve the sauce separately. This recipe can also be served cold with a cold sauce.

Salted Cod Aioli

Ingredients	6 portions		24 portions	
	U.S.	Metric	U.S.	Metric
Salted Cod	2 lb.	900 g	8 lb.	3.6 kg
Eggs, hard-boiled	3	3	12	12
Potatoes, small	1½ lb.	680 g	6 lb.	2.7 kg
Aioli Sauce	1 cup	2.5 dl	1 qt.	1 l

Soak the cod in cold water for 12 hours. Cut into 8-oz. (200-g) portions. Poach, starting in fresh cold water.

Peel and shape the potatoes. Cook in salted boiling water. Cut peeled eggs in halves. Drain the cod and arrange on a warm serving platter. Garnish with the warm eggs and potatoes. Serve the sauce separately.

Croaker
(Crocus, Hard Head, King Billy)

Croaker Meuniere
See Dover Sole Meuniere.

Broiled Croaker
See broiling cooking technique.

Pan-fried Croaker
See pan-fried cooking technique.

Golden Fried Croaker
See deep-frying cooking technique.

Cusk (Tusk, Torsk)
See cod and haddock recipes.

Dolphin (Dorado, Mahimahi)

Poached Dorado
Poach fillets of dorado in milk and coconut milk. Serve with mousseline sauce.

Poached Mahimahi, Fine Herb Sauce
Follow the cooking technique for poaching. Serve with fine herb sauce.

Seviche of Dorado
See Seviche recipe under miscellaneous seafood recipes in this chapter.

Broiled Mahimahi, Dill Sauce
Follow the cooking technique for broiling. Serve with dill sauce.

Dorado Espagnole
See Bluefish Fillets Espagnole.

Deep-fried Mahimahi Steaks
See deep-frying technique.

Pan-fried Hawaiian Dolphin
See pan-frying technique.

Eel

Anguille au Vert (Eel in Green Herbs)

Ingredients	6 portions		24 portions	
	U.S.	Metric	U.S.	Metric
Eel pieces, 3 in. (7.5 cm), skinned	3 lb.	1.4 kg	12 lb.	5.4 kg
Butter	2 oz.	50 g	8 oz.	225 g
Onion, chopped	2 oz.	50 g	8 oz.	225 g
White Wine	1 cup	2.5 dl	1 qt.	1 l
Fish Fumet	2 cups	5 dl	2 qt.	2 l
Sorrel, chopped	2 oz.	50 g	8 oz.	225 g
Mint Leaves	½ cup	5 g	2 cups	20 g
Cornstarch	1 tsp.	1 tsp.	4 tsp.	4 tsp.
Egg Yolks	4	4	16	16
Heavy Cream	½ cup	1.2 dl	2 cups	5 dl

Brown the eel pieces in butter. Add the onion and cook to brown. Add the white wine and fish fumet. Bring to a boil. Mix in the sorrel and mint leaves and cook for 10 to 12 minutes. Remove eel pieces. Keep warm.

Mix cornstarch with 1 (4) tbsp. of cold water. Pour into cooking liquid to thicken. Mix egg yolks and cream. Stir into the sauce. Do not boil. Pour sauce over eel pieces. Serve hot.

Eel Matelote

Ingredients	6 portions		24 portions	
	U.S.	Metric	U.S.	Metric
Eel Pieces, 3 in. (7.5 cm), skinned	2 lb.	900 g	8 lb.	3.6 kg
Flour	2 oz.	50 g	8 oz.	225 g
Salt	1 tsp.	1 tsp.	1 tbsp.	1 tbsp.
Pepper	¼ tsp.	¼ tsp.	1 tsp.	1 tsp.
Butter	2 oz.	50 g	8 oz.	225 g
Garlic Cloves, crushed	2	2	8	8
Onion, sliced	4 oz.	110 g	1 lb.	450 g
Cognac	2 oz.	0.6 dl	1 cup	2.5 dl
Red Wine	6 oz.	2 dl	3 cups	8 dl
Fish Stock	2 cups	5 dl	2 qt.	2 l
Thyme	¼ tsp.	¼ tsp.	1 tsp.	1 tsp.
Bay Leaf	1	1	4	4
Beurre Manie	1 oz.	25 g	4 oz.	110 g
Croutons	6	6	24	24

Roll eel pieces in flour, seasoned with salt and pepper. Brown in butter. Add the garlic and onion. Stir until lightly colored. Remove eel pieces.

Deglaze with cognac and ignite. Add the red wine, fish stock, thyme, and bay leaf. Simmer for 30 minutes. Strain the cooking liquid and thicken with beurre manie. Return eel pieces to sauce. Surround with croutons.

Fried Eel with Tarragon Sauce

Ingredients	6 portions		24 portions	
	U.S.	Metric	U.S.	Metric
Onion, chopped	2 oz.	50 g	8 oz.	225 g
Eel Pieces, 3 in. (7.5 cm), skinned	2 lb.	900 g	8 lb.	3.6 kg
Butter	2 oz.	50 g	8 oz.	225 g
Mushroom Caps	8 oz.	225 g	2 lb.	900 g
Tarragon Sauce	1½ cups	4 dl	1½ qt.	1.5 l

Brown the onion in butter. Add the eel pieces and cook to color lightly. Saute the mushrooms separately in a small amount of butter. Add to the eel pieces. Pour in the sauce and simmer for 10 to 15 minutes.

Pan-fried Eel Provencale

Ingredients	6 portions		24 portions	
	U.S.	Metric	U.S.	Metric
Eel Pieces, 3 in. (7.5 cm), skinned	3 lb.	1.4 kg	12 lb.	5.4 kg
Flour	2 oz.	50 g	8 oz.	225 g
Salt	1 tsp.	1 tsp.	1 tbsp.	1 tbsp.
Pepper	¼ tsp.	¼ tsp.	1 tsp.	1 tsp.
Olive Oil	½ cup	1.2 dl	2 cups	5 dl
Garlic Cloves, chopped	3	3	12	12

Dredge eel pieces in flour, seasoned with salt and pepper. Saute in olive oil until brown. Add the chopped garlic and parsley. Season to taste and serve on a warm platter.

Smoked Eel with Horseradish and Pumpernickel

Ingredients	6 portions		24 portions	
	U.S.	Metric	U.S.	Metric
Smoked Eel	2 lb.	900 g	8 lb.	3.6 kg.
Frozen Horseradish (see chapter 11)	1½ cups	4 dl	1½ qt.	1.5 l
Pumpernickel Bread Slices	12	12	4 doz.	4 doz.

Remove skin and bones from smoked eel. Carve into thin slices. Arrange on a serving platter. Garnish with frozen horseradish slices and pumpernickel bread.

Flounder (Blackback, Fluke, Dab or Plaice)

Summer Flounder Nicolas

Ingredients	6 portions U.S.	6 portions Metric	24 portions U.S.	24 portions Metric
Whole Summer Flounder	1—3⅓ lb.	1—1.6 kg	4—3½ lb.	4—1.6 kg
Salt and Pepper, to taste				
Crabmeat	1 lb.	450 g	4 lb.	1.8 kg
White Wine	1 cup	2.5 dl	1 qt.	1 l
Glazing White Wine Sauce	2 cups	5 dl	2 qt.	2 l
Fleurons	6	6	24	24

Bone the flounder according to directions in chapter 5. Prepare a fumet with the bones; use other bones if available. Season the cavity of the fish with salt and pepper. Fill with crabmeat. Turn fish over onto a buttered baking pan. Pour fumet and white wine over fish. Cover with a piece of foil and bake at 350°F (180°C) for 35 to 40 minutes.

Prepare a glazing white wine sauce with stock (see chapter 11). Transfer fish to a serving platter. Cover with half the sauce. Glaze using a salamander. Garnish with mushroom buttons and fleurons and serve hot. Serve leftover sauce separately.

Yellowtail Flounder with Tart Apples

Ingredients	6 portions U.S.	6 portions Metric	24 portions U.S.	24 portions Metric
Yellowtail Fillets	2 lb.	900 g	8 lb.	3.6 kg
Tart Apples	1 lb.	450 g	4 lbs	1.8 kg
Butter	6 oz.	170 g	1½ lb.	680 g
Oil	3 oz.	1 dl	1½ cups	4 dl
Flour	3½ oz.	100 g	14 oz.	400 g
Salt	½ tsp.	½ tsp.	2 tsp.	2 tsp.
White Pepper	¼ tsp.	¼ tsp.	1 tsp.	1 tsp.

Season the fillets with salt and pepper. Dredge in flour. Heat a small amount of butter and oil in a large skillet. Brown the fish fillets on both sides until crisp. Peel and slice the apples. Saute in remaining butter. Arrange the fillets on preheated serving platter(s). Top with the sauteed apples. Serve hot.

Note: Most sole recipes can be adapted for flounder as the quality of the fish is very similar.

Grouper

Gougeonnettes of Grouper

See Gougeonnettes of Sea Trout

Batter-fried grouper fillet

See Billinsgate Fish and Chips under Miscellaneous Seafood Recipes in this chapter.

Note: Grouper fillets can also be poached and served with hollandaise or other sauces, or used in chowder (for example, see Cod Chowder in chapter 10).

Haddock

Broiled Haddock Fillet, Sauce Choron

Follow the broiling cooking technique. Serve fish with sauce choron (see chapter 11).

Fillets of Haddock Breval

Ingredients	6 portions		24 portions	
	U.S.	Metric	U.S.	Metric
Shallots, chopped	2 oz.	50 g	8 oz.	225 g
Haddock Fillets	2 lb.	900 g	8 lb.	3.6 kg
Salt	½ tsp.	½ tsp.	2 tsp.	2 tsp.
Pepper	¼ tsp.	¼ tsp.	1 tsp.	1 tsp.
Fresh Mushrooms, sliced	8 oz.	225 g	2 lb.	900 g
White Wine	½ cup	1.2 dl	2 cups	5 dl
Parsley, chopped	1 tbsp.	1 tbsp.	4 tbsp.	4 tbsp.
Butter	2 oz.	50 g	8 oz.	225 g
Veloute Sauce, medium thick .	1½ cups	4 dl	1½ qt.	1.5 l
Hollandaise Sauce	½ cup	1.2 dl	2 cups	5 dl
Whipped Cream	2 tbsp.	2 tbsp.	½ cup	1.2 dl
Tomatoes, peeled and seedless	3 oz.	85 g	12 oz.	340 g

(cont.)

Spread the shallots in a well-buttered pan. Line up fish side by side, season with salt and pepper, and add mushrooms, white wine, and parsley. Cover with buttered paper. Bring to a boil on top of range, then place in 350°F (180°C) oven until fish is done.

Remove fish to serving platter. Reduce cooking liquid to syrup consistency. Add fish veloute and hollandaise sauce. Fold in whipped cream. Add tomatoes and correct seasoning. Pour sauce over fish and glaze under salamander or broiler.

Fillets of Haddock Duglere

Ingredients	6 portions		24 portions	
	U.S.	Metric	U.S.	Metric
Haddock Fillets	2 lb.	900 g	8 lb.	3.6 kg
Butter	4 oz.	110 g	1 lb.	450 g
Shallots, chopped	2 oz.	50 g	8 oz.	225 g
Onion, chopped	2 oz.	50 g	8 oz.	225 g
Tomatoes, chopped and seedless	1½ lb.	680 g	6 lb.	2.7 kg
Salt and pepper, to taste				
Dry White Wine	5 oz.	1.5 dl	2½ cups	6.2 dl
Fish Fumet	2 cups	5 dl	2 qt.	2 l
Veloute Sauce	¾ cup	2 dl	3 cups	8 dl
Parsley, chopped	1 tbsp.	1 tbsp.	4 tbsp.	4 tbsp.

Cut haddock fillets into 5-oz. (140-g) portions. Butter baking pan(s) with half of the butter. Sprinkle with shallots, onion, chopped tomatoes, salt, and pepper. Arrange the fish portions in a single layer on top. Pour the wine and fumet over fish and bring to a boil. Bake at 350°F (180°C) for 10 to 15 minutes.

Pour cooking liquid into a saucepan. Reduce by one half. Stir in the veloute sauce and remaining butter. Transfer fish portions to preheated serving platter(s). Coat with hot sauce.

Finnan Haddie and Macaroni

Ingredients	6 portions		24 portions	
	U.S.	Metric	U.S.	Metric
Smoked Haddock Fillets	1½ lb.	680 g	6 lb.	2.7 kg
Macaroni	6 oz.	170 g	1½ lb.	680 g
Light Cream Sauce	2 cups	5 dl	2 qt.	2 l
Parmesan Cheese	1 tbsp.	1 tbsp.	4 tbsp.	4 tbsp.
Butter, melted	1 tbsp.	1 tbsp.	¼ cup	0.6 dl

Poach the smoked haddock in half milk and half water. Cook macaroni in salted boiling water. Drain. Combine macaroni, flaked haddock, and cream sauce. Arrange in oven-proof serving dish(es). Sprinkle with Parmesan cheese and melted butter. Bake at 350°F (180°C) for 15 to 20 minutes, or until brown.

Finnan Haddie Basquaise

Ingredients	6 portions		24 portions	
	U.S.	Metric	U.S.	Metric
Smoked Haddock	2 lb.	900 g	8 lb.	3.6 kg
Onion, sliced	8 oz.	225 g	2 lb.	900 g
Butter	2 oz.	50 g	8 oz.	225 g
Tomatoes, chopped and seedless	1½ lb.	680 g	6 lb.	2.7 kg
Basil	½ tsp.	½ tsp.	2 tsp.	2 tsp.
Egg Noodles	8 oz.	225 g	2 lb.	900 g
Veloute Sauce	2 cups	5 dl	2 qt.	2 l

Simmer the smoked haddock in half water and half milk. Saute the onion in butter and cook over low heat for 5 to 10 minutes. Add tomatoes and basil. Simmer into a medium thick sauce.

Cook noodles in salted boiling water. Drain and stir in the veloute sauce. Transfer into casserole serving dish(es). Flake the haddock and arrange over noodles. Pour the tomato sauce over. Serve hot.

Haddock Fillets and Broccoli

Ingredients	6 portions		24 portions	
	U.S.	Metric	U.S.	Metric
Fresh Haddock Fillets	2 lb.	900 g	8 lb.	3.6 kg
Dry White Wine	½ cup	1.2 dl	2 cups	5 dl
Scallions, chopped	2	2	8	8
Lemon Juice	1 tbsp.	1 tbsp.	2 oz.	0.6 dl
Broccoli, chopped, cooked . . .	10 oz.	280 g	2½ lb.	1.2 kg
Pepper, ground	¼ tsp.	¼ tsp.	1 tsp.	1 tsp.
Salt	½ tsp.	½ tsp.	2 tsp.	2 tsp.
Heavy Cream Sauce	1 cup	2.5 dl	1 qt.	1 l
Cheddar Cheese, grated	½ cup	50 g	2 cups	200 g

Cut fish into 5-oz. (140-g) portions. Combine white wine, lemon juice, and scallions. Poach fish in the simmering liquid.

Arrange trimmed broccoli in buttered baking dish(es). Place fillets on top. Season with salt and pepper. Reduce cooking liquid to one half and add to cream sauce. Pour sauce over fish. Sprinkle with cheese and bake at 400°F (205°C) until brown.

Souffle of Haddock

Ingredients	6 portions		24 portions	
	U.S.	Metric	U.S.	Metric
Milk	1 pt.	5 dl	2 qt.	2 l
Butter	2 oz.	50 g	8 oz.	225 g
Flour	2 oz.	50 g	8 oz.	225 g
Salt	1 tsp.	1 tsp.	4 tsp.	4 tsp.
Pepper	¼ tsp.	¼ tsp.	1 tsp.	1 tsp.
Nutmeg	⅛ tsp.	⅛ tsp.	½ tsp.	½ tsp.
Poached Haddock	1 lb.	450 g	4 lb.	1.8 kg
Eggs, separated	5	5	20	20
Swiss cheese, grated	1 cup	110 g	4 cups	450 g
Tomato Sauce	1½ cups	4 dl	1½ qt.	1.5 l

Boil the milk. In a separate pan, melt the butter and stir in the flour. Cook over low heat for 5 minutes. Add the milk and mix with a whip until sauce thickens and comes to a boil. Season with salt, pepper, and nutmeg. Simmer for 8 to 10 minutes.

Strain the sauce into a mixing bowl. Stir in the flaked haddock, egg yolks, and cheese. Whip the egg whites to a medium peak. Fold into the haddock mixture.

Butter and flour 1 (4) medium souffle dish(es). Fill with the mixture to three-fourths. Bake at 350°F (180°C) for 35 to 40 minutes. Serve as soon as the souffle is ready. Pass tomato sauce separately.

Stewed Haddock in Red Wine Sauce

Ingredients	6 portions		24 portions	
	U.S.	Metric	U.S.	Metric
Haddock Fillets	2 lb.	900 g	8 lb.	3.6 kg
Thyme Leaves	½ tsp.	½ tsp.	2 tsp.	2 tsp.
Olive Oil	½ cup	1.2 dl	2 cups	5 dl
Onions, Chopped	4 oz.	110 g	1 lb.	450 g
Red Wine	1½ cups	4 dl	1½ qt.	1.5 l
Canned Tomatoes, seedless and chopped	1 lb.	450 g	4 lb.	1.8 kg
Garlic Cloves, minced	3	3	12	12
Bay Leaves	1	1	4	4
Savory	1 tsp.	1 tsp.	4 tsp.	4 tsp.
Salt	½ tsp.	½ tsp.	2 tsp.	2 tsp.
Ripe Olives	2 oz.	50 g	8 oz.	225 g
Capers	1 oz.	25 g	4 oz.	110 g
Parsley, chopped	1 tbsp.	1 tbsp.	4 tbsp.	4 tbsp.

Cut fillets into 5-oz. (140-g) portions. Sprinkle with crushed thyme leaves. Heat half of the oil in a skillet. Cook the fish for 3 minutes on each side.

Heat remaining oil in a saute pan. Stir in the onions. Add the wine and simmer for 5 minutes.

Mix in the tomatoes, garlic, bay leaves, savory, salt, and pepper. Cook for 20 minutes. Discard bay leaf. Puree the sauce in blender.

Coat the bottom of an oven-proof serving dish(es) with half of the sauce. Place the fish on top. Cover with remaining sauce. Bake for 10 minutes at 350°F (180°C). Sprinkle olives, capers, and parsley over fish. Serve hot.

Hake (Ling)

Hake can be prepared like haddock or cod. This fish is best when served poached, hot or cold, with a variety of sauces.

Halibut

Halibut can be cooked in a variety of recipes (in particular, see Sole). Halibut steaks should be broiled, poached, or grilled, and served with a hot sauce.

Herring

Broiled Herring Italian

Ingredients	6 portions		24 portions	
	U.S.	Metric	U.S.	Metric
Herring Fillets, fresh or frozen	2 lb.	900 g	8 lb.	3.6 kg
Water	1 qt.	1 l	4 qt.	4 l
Vinegar	2 cups	5 dl	2 qt.	2 l
Salt	1 tbsp.	1 tbsp.	4 tbsp.	4 tbsp.
Lemon Juice	2 tbsp.	2 tbsp.	½ cup	1.2 dl
Butter	1 oz.	25 g	4 oz.	110 g
Oil	1 oz.	0.3 dl	½ cup	1.2 dl
Water	1 tbsp.	1 tbsp.	2 oz.	0.6 dl
Parsley, chopped	1 tbsp.	1 tbsp.	4 tbsp.	4 tbsp.
Garlic Clove, crushed	1	1	4	4
Salt	½ tsp.	½ tsp.	2 tsp.	2 tsp.
Pepper	¼ tsp.	¼ tsp.	1 tsp.	1 tsp.
Lemon Wedges	6	6	24	24

Thaw frozen fillets. Remove dorsal fins. Cover fillets with water, vinegar, and salt. Refrigerate for 12 hours. Drain fillets and place in a single layer, skin side down, on greased baking pan.

Combine remaining ingredients except lemon wedges. Baste fillets with sauce. Broil for 10 to 12 minutes, basting while broiling. Arrange on serving platters and garnish with lemon wedges.

Fried Herring Bercy

Ingredients	6 portions		24 portions	
	U.S.	Metric	U.S.	Metric
Herring Fillets, fresh or frozen	2 lb.	900 g	8 lb.	3.6 kg
Lemon Juice	2 tbsp.	2 tbsp.	½ cup	1.2 dl
Salt	½ tsp.	½ tsp.	2 tsp.	2 tsp.
White Pepper	¼ tsp.	¼ tsp.	1 tsp.	1 tsp.
Capers	1 tbsp.	1 tbsp.	4 tbsp.	4tbsp.
Parsley, chopped	1 tbsp.	1 tbsp.	4 tbsp.	4 tbsp.
Bercy Sauce	1½ cups	4 dl	1½ qt.	1.5 l

Thaw frozen fillets. Remove dorsal fin. Sprinkle with lemon juice and season with salt and pepper. Roll fillets in flour. Fry in butter until brown on both sides. Transfer the fillets to a preheated serving platter. Garnish with capers and parsley, and serve with bercy sauce.

Note: This recipe can also be served with tomato sauce.

Herring Cocktail

Ingredients	6 portions		24 portions	
	U.S.	Metric	U.S.	Metric
Large Cucumbers	2	2	8	8
Smoked Herring	1 lb.	450 g	4 lb.	1.8 kg
Eggs, hard-boiled	2	2	8	8
Horseradish, grated	2 tsp.	2 tsp.	2 tbsp.	2 tbsp.
Ripe Olives	6	6	24	24

Peel cucumbers and cut in half lengthwise. Slice and blanch in boiling salted water. Bone the herring. Blend into a paste in a food processor, adding the eggs and horseradish. Alternate layers of smoked herring puree and cucumber slices in cocktail glasses. Top with a ripe olive.

Herring in Mustard Sauce
(For appetizers or buffet.)

Ingredients	20 portions	
	U.S.	Metric
Small Fresh Herrings	20	20
White Vinegar	2 qt.	2 l
Sugar	1 lb.	450 g
Dill	1 oz.	25 g
Carrots, sliced	8 oz.	225 g
Fresh Horseradish, cut into sticks	2 oz.	50 g
Onions, sliced	8 oz.	225 g
Juniper Berries	20	20
Cloves	4	4
Peppercorns	1 tbsp.	1 tbsp.
Mustard Seeds	2 tsp.	2 tsp.
Cold Mustard Sauce	2 cups	5 dl
Dill Weed	1 tsp.	1 tsp.

Combine all ingredients, except mustard sauce, herring, and dill weed, for marinade. Bring to a boil, then cool. Fillet herring and soak overnight in cold water. Place fillets in a crock and pour cold marinade over them. Marinate for 4 or 5 days.

Remove the fillets from marinade. Cut into 2-in. (5-cm) pieces. Drain well and mix with mustard sauce. Arrange in serving dish and sprinkle with dill weed.

Pickled Herring

Ingredients	3 portions		12 portions	
	U.S.	Metric	U.S.	Metric
Schmaltz Herring Fillets	3	3	12	12
White Vinegar	½ cup	1.2 dl	2 cups	5 dl
Water	¼ cup	0.6 dl	1 cup	2.5 dl
Sugar	1 tsp.	1 tsp.	1 tbsp.	1 tbsp.
Carrots, sliced	1	1	4	4
Red Onion, sliced	4 oz.	110 g	1 lb.	450 g
Pickling Spices	1 tsp.	1 tsp.	1 tbsp.	1 tbsp.
Bay Leaf	1	1	4	4
Sour Cream	½ cup	1.2 dl	2 cups	5 dl

Soak herring in water for 2 days, changing water twice. Combine vinegar, water, and sugar and boil for 2 minutes. Set aside. Slice drained herring in 2-in. (5-cm) pieces. Arrange herring, carrots, onions, pickling spices, and bay leaves in glass or earthenware bowls. Pour vinegar mixture over top. Cover and refrigerate at least 2 days before using. Stir in the sour cream before serving.

Lingcod

(Blue Cod, Buffalo Cod, Cultus Cod)

Lingcod fillets and steaks can be broiled, sauteed in butter, or poached. Whole fish can be baked or poached. An increasingly popular method of preparation is to pan-fry or deep-fry for fish and chips (see Billinsgate Fish and Chips).

Mackerel

Fillets of Mackerel Ravigotte

Ingredients	6 portions		24 portions	
	U.S.	Metric	U.S.	Metric
Mackerel Fillets	2 lb.	900 g	8 lb.	3.6 kg
Salt	½ tsp.	½ tsp.	2 tsp.	2 tsp.
White Pepper	¼ tsp.	¼ tsp.	1 tsp.	1 tsp.
Flour	3 oz.	85 g	12 oz.	340 g
Oil	3 oz.	1 dl	1½ cups	4 dl
Butter	3 oz.	85 g	12 oz.	340 g
Sauce Ravigotte	1½ cups	4 dl	1½ qt.	1.5 l

Cut mackerel fillets into 5-oz. (140-g) portions. Season with salt and pepper. Coat with flour. Fry in oil and butter until crisp. Arrange on preheated serving platter(s). Garnish with parsley. Serve sauce separately.

Marinated Mackerel in White Wine

Ingredients	6 portions		24 portions	
	U.S.	Metric	U.S.	Metric
Fresh Atlantic Mackerel	3	3	12	12
Onion, sliced	4 oz.	110 g	1 lb.	450 g
Parsley, chopped	1 tbsp.	1 tbsp.	4 tbsp.	4 tbsp.
Peppercorns	1 tsp.	1 tsp.	4 tsp.	4 tsp.
Salt	½ tsp.	½ tsp.	2 tsp.	2 tsp.
Bay Leaves	1	1	4	4
Dry White Wine	2 cups	5 dl	2 qt.	2 l
Lemon Juice	1 tbsp.	1 tbsp.	¼ cup	0.6 dl

Clean fish and discard heads. Wash fish thoroughly and dry. Place fish in baking pan(s). Sprinkle with onion, parsley, peppercorns, and salt. Add bay leaf. Pour wine and lemon juice over. Bring to a boil. Bake at 350°F (180°C) for 15 to 20 minutes. Cool at room temperature, then refrigerate several hours.

Debone mackerel and arrange on serving platter(s). Strain cooking liquid and pour over fillets. Garnish with sprigs of parsley.

Note: This recipe can be prepared using half white wine and half white vinegar.

Grilled Mackerel
Serve with curry sauce, sauce verte, or maitre d'hotel. (See Grilled Dover Sole.)

Poached Spanish Mackerel
Serve with sauce bercy.
See poaching technique.

Meuniere Mackerel
See meuniere cooking technique.

Mackerel Baked with Shallots
See baking cooking technique.

Miscellaneous Seafood Recipes

Avocado Mexicaine

Ingredients	6 portions U.S.	Metric	24 portions U.S.	Metric
Lobster Meat, cooked and diced	8 oz.	225 g	2 lb.	900 g
King Crab, diced	8 oz.	225 g	2 lb.	900 g
Romaine Lettuce, shredded	3 oz.	85 g	12 oz.	340 g
Capers	1 tbsp.	1 tbsp.	4 tbsp.	4 tbsp.
Mayonnaise	1 cup	2.5 dl	1 qt.	1 l
Lemon Juice	1 tsp.	1 tsp.	1 tbsp.	1 tbsp.
White Pepper, ground	¼ tsp.	¼ tsp.	1 tsp.	1 tsp.
Ripe Avocados	3	3	12	12
Parsley, chopped	1 tbsp.	1 tbsp.	4 tbsp.	4 tbsp.

Combine the first four ingredients. Mix in the mayonnaise, lemon juice, and pepper. Adjust seasoning if necessary. Cut avocados in half lengthwise. Remove stones. Fill with seafood. Sprinkle with chopped parsley. Arrange on a platter and serve chilled.

Baked Fish Portions or Sticks

Ingredients	6 portions U.S.	Metric	24 portions U.S.	Metric
Frozen Fish, sticks or portions, 2–3 oz. (50–85 g) each	12	12	48	48
Cold Sauce	2 cups	5 dl	2 qt.	2 l
Lemon Wedges	6	6	24	24

Place frozen fish in a single layer on baking sheet pan(s). Bake at 400°F (205°C) for 15 to 20 minutes. (Time 20 minutes per inch thickness if frozen, and 10 minutes if fresh.) Serve with a cold sauce and lemon wedges.

Billinsgate Fish and Chips

Ingredients	6 portions		24 portions	
	U.S.	Metric	U.S.	Metric
Firm, White Skinless Fish (dogfish, shark, cod, or haddock)	2 lb.	900 g	8 lb.	3.6 kg
Salt	½ tsp.	½ tsp.	2 tsp.	2 tsp.
Beer Batter (see chapter 7)	1 recipe	1 recipe	4 recipes	4 recipes
Baking Potatoes, for chips	2 lb.	900 g	8 lb.	3.6 kg
Oil, for deep frying.				

Cut the fish into 5-oz. (140-g) pieces. Wash under cold water and dry. Season with salt. Coat in cold batter. Deep fry at 360°F (190°C) for 4 to 5 minutes. Arrange in a warm dish lined with a napkin. Serve with chips and lemon pieces or the traditional malt vinegar. (The chips are actually large French fries, fried simultaneously with the fish.)

Chinese Fried Fish

Ingredients	6 portions		24 portions	
	U.S.	Metric	U.S.	Metric
Dressed Carp, Seabass, or Snapper	2 lb.	900 g	8 lb.	3.6 kg
Soy Sauce	¼ cup	0.6 dl	1 cup	2.5 dl
Rice Wine	¼ cup	0.6 dl	1 cup	2.5 dl
Salt	½ tsp.	½ tsp.	2 tsp.	2 tsp.
Fresh Ginger Root	4 slices	4 slices	16 slices	16 slices
Scallions, chopped	1	1	4	4
Chicken Stock	¼ cup	0.6 dl	1 cup	2.5 dl
Dark Brown Sugar	1 oz.	25 g	4 oz.	110 g
Peanut Oil, for frying	1 qt.	1 l	1 gal.	4 l

Fillet, bone, and skin the fish. Cut crosswise into ½-inch (1.5-cm) slices. Combine the soy sauce, rice wine, salt, ginger root, and scallions and marinate the fish for 3 to 4 hours. Drain the fish. Simmer the marinade with the stock and sugar. Fry the fish in oil at 375°F (190°C) for 5 minutes, or until crisp. Serve hot with the sauce separate.

Deep-fried Fillets or Steaks

Ingredients	6 portions		24 portions	
	U.S.	Metric	U.S.	Metric
Fish Fillets or Steaks, 8 oz. (225 g) each	6	6	24	24
Milk	¼ cup	0.6 dl	1 cup	2.5 dl
Eggs, beaten	1	1	4	4
Salt	1 tsp.	1 tsp.	1 tbsp.	1 tbsp.
White Pepper	¼ tsp.	¼ tsp.	1 tsp.	1 tsp.
Flour	3 oz.	85 g	12 oz.	340 g
Dry Bread Crumbs, Cracker Crumbs, or	1 cup	110 g	4 cups	450 g
Fresh Bread Crumbs	2 cups	110 g	8 cups	450 g
Fat, for frying				
Cold Sauce	2 cups	5 dl	2 qt.	2 l

Thaw fish if frozen. Combine milk, egg, salt, and pepper. Roll fish in flour. Dip in milk and egg, and coat with bread crumbs.

Deep fry at 350°F (180°C) for 3 to 5 minutes, or until fish is brown and flakes easily when fork tested. Serve with a cold sauce.

Fish Kebabs Teriyaki

Ingredients	6 portions		24 portions	
	U.S.	Metric	U.S.	Metric
Lean White Fish Fillets	2 lb.	900 g	8 lb.	3.6 kg
Pineapple Juice	¼ cup	0.6 dl	1 cup	2.5 dl
Soy Sauce	½ cup	1.2 dl	2 cups	5 dl
Sherry Wine	¼ cup	0.6 dl	1 cup	2.5 dl
Brown Sugar	4 oz.	110 g	1 lb.	450 g
Fresh Ginger Root, grated or . .	1 tbsp.	1 tbsp.	4 tbsp.	4 tbsp.
Ginger, ground	1 tsp.	1 tsp.	4 tsp.	4 tsp.
Dry Mustard	1 tsp.	1 tsp.	4 tsp.	4 tsp.
Garlic Clove, chopped	1	1	4	4
Pineapple Chunks	1 lb.	450 g	4 lb.	1.8 kg
Green Pepper, blanched and cut into 1-in. (2.5-cm) squares	1	1	4	4

Cut fish into 1-in. (2.5-cm) cubes. Combine pineapple juice, soy sauce, wine, sugar, ginger, mustard, and garlic. Pour over fish and marinate for 1 to 2 hours in the refrigerator. Drain fish. Thread on skewers, alternating with pineapple chunks and green peppers.

Broil for 5 minutes or until fish flakes. Brush with a little oil and marinade. Serve with rice.

Fish Souffle

Any fish souffle can be prepared using, in volume:

  ⅓ quenelle forcemeat
  ⅓ veloute or bechamel sauce

Use 1 egg per serving. Mix in the egg yolks. Season with season salt, onion powder, and MSG. Beat the egg whites until stiff. Fold into the souffle mix.

Bake in 350°F (180°C) oven. Spoon into buttered and floured souffle mold(s). Serve with a hot sauce.

Gefilte Fish

Ingredients	6 portions		24 portions	
	U.S.	Metric	U.S.	Metric
Whitefish, Carp, or Buffalo Fish Fillets	3 lb.	1.360 kg	12 lb.	5.4 kg
Onions, chopped	8 oz.	225 g	2 lb.	900 g
Eggs	2	2	8	8
Matzo Meal	1 tbsp.	1 tbsp.	4 tbsp.	4 tbsp.
Salt	1 tsp.	1 tsp.	1 tbsp.	1 tbsp.
Pepper, ground	¼ tsp.	¼ tsp.	1 tsp.	1 tsp.
Fish Stock	1 qt.	1 l	4 qt.	4 l

Skin, bone, and grind the fish fillets. Add the chopped onions, eggs, matzo meal, salt, and pepper, and mix well. Shape the mixture into dumplings using about 3 oz. (85 g) of mixture for each dumpling.

Simmer in stock for 1 to 1½ hours. Chill dumplings in the stock. Serve with grated raw carrots and lemon juice or horseradish.

Kedgeree

Ingredients	6 portions		24 portions	
	U.S.	Metric	U.S.	Metric
Rice	1 cup	225 g	4 cups	900 g
Fish Fillets	2 lb.	900 g	8 lb.	3.6 kg
Eggs, hard-boiled	3	3	12	12
Parsley, chopped	1 tbsp.	1 tbsp.	4 tbsp.	4 tbsp.
Butter	2 oz.	50 g	8 oz.	225 g
Curry Powder	½ tsp.	½ tsp.	2 tsp.	2 tsp.
Veloute Sauce	1 cup	2.5 dl	1 qt.	1 l

Cook the rice according to standard directions. Poach the fish in water or court bouillon. Chop the eggs and mix with the parsley. Flake the fish and combine with the rice, melted butter, curry, and half of the egg mixture. Heat and toss together.

Sprinkle remaining egg mixture over the fish mixture. Heat in oven before serving. Serve veloute sauce separately.

Oven-fried Fillets or Steaks

Ingredients	6 portions		24 portions	
	U.S.	Metric	U.S.	Metric
Fish Fillets or Steaks, 8 oz. (225 g) each	6	6	24	24
Milk	½ cup	1.2 dl	2 cups	5 dl
Salt	1 tsp.	1 tsp.	1 tbsp.	1 tbsp.
Flour	3 oz.	85 g	12 oz.	340 g
Dry Bread Crumbs or	1 cup	110 g	4 cups	450 g
Fresh Bread Crumbs	2 cups	110 g	8 cups	450 g
Butter, melted	4 oz.	110 g	1 lb.	450 g
Lemon Wedges	6	6	24	24
Hot Fish Sauce	2 cups	5 dl	2 qt.	2 l

Thaw fish if frozen. Combine milk and salt. Roll the fish in flour. Dip in milk and cover with bread crumbs. Place fish in a single layer, skin side down, on a well-greased baking pan. Pour melted butter over. Bake at 450°F (230°C) for 10 to 12 minutes or until fish is brown and flakes easily when fork tested. (Time 10 minutes per inch thickness of fish at the thickest point.) Arrange on a serving platter and serve hot with lemon wedges and a hot fish sauce.

Paella Valenciana
(A combination of seafoods, chicken, and rice.)

Ingredients	6 portions		24 portions	
	U.S.	Metric	U.S.	Metric
Live Lobsters	1—1½ lb.	1—675 g	4—1½ lb.	4—675 g
Tiny Shrimp, cooked	8 oz.	230 g	2 lb.	1 kg

(cont.)

Ingredients	6 portions		24 portions	
	U.S.	Metric	U.S.	Metric
Cherry Stone Clams	6	6	24	24
Live Mussels	6	6	24	24
Chorizo or Garlic Smoked Pork Sausage	8 oz.	230 g	2 lb.	1 kg
Broilers, cut into 8 pieces	1—2 lb.	1—1 kg	4—2 lb.	4—1 kg
Salt	1½ tsp.	1½ tsp.	2 tbsp.	2 tbsp.
Pepper, ground	¼ tsp.	¼ tsp.	1 tsp.	1 tsp.
Olive Oil	½ cup	1.25 dl	2 cups	5 dl
Onions, finely chopped	2 oz.	50 g	8 oz.	230 g
Garlic, finely chopped	1 tsp.	1 tsp.	1 tbsp.	1 tbsp.
Red Sweet Peppers	1 small	1 small	3 medium	3 medium
Green Sweet Peppers	1 small	1 small	3 medium	3 medium
Whole Tomatoes, seeded and chopped	12 oz.	340 g	3 lb.	1.350 kg
Long Grain Converted Rice ...	1 lb.	450 g	4 lb.	1.8 kg
Saffron Threads	¾ tsp.	¾ tsp.	1 tbsp.	1 tbsp.
Boiling Water	1 qt.	1 l	4 qt.	4 l
Sweet Green Peas, cooked ...	7 oz.	200 g	1 lb., 12 oz.	800 g
Lemon Wedges	6	6	24	24

With a large French knife, cut lobster tails in sections at joints. Remove the claws and crack for easier meat extraction. Split the heads in half lengthwise, remove stomach, then cut crosswise into quarters. Separate legs. Wash and scrub clams and mussels. Remove beards from the mussels.

Cover the sausage with cold water and simmer for 5 minutes. Drain.

Season the chicken with half of the salt and pepper. Brown on both sides in half of the olive oil in a heavy skillet. Transfer to a sheet pan. Add lobster pieces to skillet and saute over high heat for 2 to 3 minutes. Remove lobster and brown the sausage on all sides in the same skillet.

Pour fat out and replace with remaining olive oil. Add the onions, garlic, and julienned peppers. Cook over low heat for 5 minutes, then add the tomatoes. Cook over high heat to reduce liquid.

Transfer to a large, heavy braising pan. Add the rice, remaining salt and pepper, and saffron. Stir in the boiling water and arrange the chicken, lobster pieces, sliced sausage, shrimp, clams, and mussels on top of the rice.

Bake the paella, uncovered, for 25 minutes at 375°F (190°C) or until all liquid has been absorbed by the rice. Garnish with steamed peas and lemon wedges.

Note: This dish makes an ideal buffet display served as is, although the paella can be served individually, a la carte, or otherwise. The selection of seafood may vary. In Spain, squid is used in the recipe. Lobster can be omitted for cost control; just add more shrimp.

Polynesian Seafood, Hale Nanat

Ingredients	6 portions		24 portions	
	U.S.	Metric	U.S.	Metric
Fillets of Sole	1½ lb.	680 g	6 lb.	2.7 kg
Raw Shrimp, peeled and deveined	1½ lb.	680 g	6 lb.	2.7 kg
Salt	½ tsp.	½ tsp.	2 tsp.	2 tsp.
Pepper, ground	¼ tsp.	¼ tsp.	1 tsp.	1 tsp.
Lemon Juice	1 tbsp.	1 tbsp.	2 oz.	0.6 dl
Flour	4 oz.	110 g	1 lb.	450 g
Eggs	4	4	16	16
Fresh Bread Crumbs	12 oz.	340 g	3 lb.	1.4 kg
Almonds, chopped	4 oz.	110 g	1 lb.	450 g
Saffron Rice, cooked	1½ lb.	680 g	6 lb.	2.7 kg
Almonds, sliced	3 oz.	85 g	12 oz.	340 g
Pineapple, diced	4 oz.	110 g	1 lb.	450 g
Curry Sauce	2 cups	5 dl	2 qt.	2 l

Cut the fillets of sole into strips. Butterfly the shrimp (for details, see chapter 5). Season the sole and shrimp with salt and pepper, and marinate in lemon juice. Dip the seafood in flour, beaten egg, and a mixture of breadcrumbs and chopped almonds.

Deep fry at 360°F (185°C) for 3 to 4 minutes. Pack the saffron rice in a ring mold. Unmold on a round serving platter. Place the fish in the middle. Toast the sliced almonds. Saute the pineapple in butter. Sprinkle over fish. Serve hot with curry sauce separate.

Sea Burgers

Ingredients	6 portions		24 portions	
	U.S.	Metric	U.S.	Metric
Breaded Raw Fish Portions, frozen	12—2½ oz.	12—70 g	48—2½ oz.	48—70 g
American Cheese, grated	6 oz.	170 g	1½ lb.	680 g
Prepared Mustard	1 tbsp.	1 tbsp.	2 oz.	0.6 dl
Ketchup	2 tbsp.	2 tbsp.	4 oz.	110 g
Butter, softened	2 oz.	50 g	8 oz.	225 g
Hamburger Rolls, separated ..	6	6	24	24

Place frozen fish on well-greased baking pan. Bake at 450°F (230°C) for 10 to 15 minutes, or 20 minutes per inch thickness of the fish portions. Combine cheese, mustard, and ketchup. Spread butter over bottom half of rolls. Place two fish portions on each. Top with cheese mixture and cover with remaining roll halves.

Bake at 350°F (180°C) until cheese is melted. Serve with French fried potatoes.

Seafood a la King

Ingredients	6 portions U.S.	Metric	24 portions U.S.	Metric
Lobster, Scallops, or Shrimp, cooked	6 oz.	170 g	1½ lb.	680 g
Crabmeat..................	6 oz.	170 g	1½ lb.	680 g
Eggs, hard-boiled and diced ...	3	3	12	12
Fresh Mushrooms, diced	4 oz.	110 g	1 lb.	450 g
Butter.....................	2 oz.	50 g	8 oz.	225 g
Lemon Juice	2 tsp.	2 tsp.	3 tbsp.	3 tbsp.
Sweet Red Peppers, diced	2	2	8	8
Dry White Wine.............	¼ cup	0.6 dl	1 cup	2.5 dl
Medium Cream Sauce	2 cups	5 dl	2 qt.	2 l
Worcestershire Sauce	1 tsp.	1 tsp.	4 tsp.	4 tsp.
Salt	½ tsp.	½ tsp.	2 tsp.	2 tsp.
White Pepper	¼ tsp.	¼ tsp.	1 tsp.	1 tsp.

Combine the first three ingredients. Saute the mushrooms in butter and lemon juice over a brisk fire. Add the peppers and white wine. Reduce the liquid to two thirds.

Combine all the above ingredients with the cream sauce. Simmer for 10 minutes. Season with Worcestershire sauce, salt and pepper.

Seafood Brochettes

Ingredients	6 portions U.S.	Metric	24 portions U.S.	Metric
Fish Fillets	2 lb.	900 g	8 lb.	3.6 kg
Green Pepper	1	1	4	4
Oil.......................	¼ cup	0.6 dl	1 cup	2.5 dl
Lemon Juice	¼ cup	0.6 dl	1 cup	2.5 dl
Parsley, chopped	1 tbsp.	1 tbsp.	4 tbsp.	4 tbsp.
Soy Sauce	¼ cup	0.6 dl	1 cup	2.5 dl
Salt	½ tsp.	½ tsp.	2 tsp.	2 tsp.
White Pepper	¼ tsp.	¼ tsp.	1 tsp.	1 tsp.
Mushroom Buttons	8 oz.	225 g	2 lb.	900 g
Cherry Tomatoes	8 oz.	225 g	2 lb.	900 g
White Pepper	¼ tsp.	¼ tsp.	1 tsp.	1 tsp.

(cont.)

Cut the fish fillets into chunks. Cut the green pepper into 1-inch (2.5-cm) squares and blanch for 1 minute. Combine oil, lemon juice, parsley, soy sauce, salt, and pepper. Pour over fish and vegetables and let stand for 30 minutes, stirring occasionally.

Using long skewers, alternate fish, mushrooms, green peppers, and cherry tomatoes until skewers are filled. Broil about 4 inches (10 cm) from source of heat. Baste with the marinade while cooking. Turn after 5 minutes. Cook for 5 to 7 more minutes or until fish flakes. Serve hot on a warm serving platter.

Seafood Crepes

Ingredients	6 portions		24 portions	
	U.S.	Metric	U.S.	Metric
Crabmeat	5 oz.	140 g	1¼ lb.	560 g
Cooked Lobster, diced	5 oz.	140 g	1¼ lb.	560 g
Cooked Shrimp, diced	5 oz.	140 g	1¼ lb.	560 g
Medium Bechamel Sauce	2 cups	5 dl	2 qt.	2 l
Hollandaise Sauce	½ cup	1.2 dl	2 cups	5 dl
Sherry Wine	¼ cup	0.6 dl	1 cup	2.5 dl
Heavy Cream	½ cup	1.2 dl	2 cups	5 dl
Butter	3 oz.	85 g	12 oz.	340 g
Crepes	12	12	48	48

Combine the seafood with a small amount of bechamel sauce and hollandaise to bind. Stir in the wine. Fill the crepes with the seafood mixture. Arrange in buttered, oven-proof serving dish(es). Combine the remaining bechamel and hollandaise sauce with the heavy cream. Coat the crepes. Brown in oven at 350°F (180°C). Use any leftover seafood for this recipe.

Note: Veloute sauce, sauce cardinal, sauce Americaine, or other sauces can be used to prepare seafood crepes.

Seafood Fondue

Ingredients	6 portions		24 portions	
	U.S.	Metric	U.S.	Metric
Sea Scallops, breaded	8 oz.	225 g	2 lb.	900 g
Shelled Shrimp, breaded	8 oz.	225 g	2 lb.	900 g
Shucked oysters, breaded	8 oz.	225 g	2 lb.	900 g
Sole Fillets, cut into strips and breaded	1 lb.	450 g	4 lb.	1.8 kg
Sauce Remoulade	½ cup	2.5 dl	2 cups	5 dl
Sauce Vincent	½ cup	2.5 dl	2 cups	5 dl
Tartare Sauce	½ cup	2.5 dl	2 cups	5 dl
Oil, for frying	½ gal.	2 l	2 gal.	8 l
Lemon Wedges	6	6	24	24

Arrange a fondue set (pot, plates, forks) on a table with the uncooked seafood. Let the guests cook their own. Place the sauces on the table as dips. Unbreaded, raw fresh seafood can also be served and cooked at the table. Soy sauce can also accompany the seafoods.

Seafood Newburg

Ingredients	6 portions		24 portions	
	U.S.	Metric	U.S.	Metric
Butter	4 oz.	110 g	1 lb.	450 g
Flour	1 oz.	25 g	4 oz.	110 g
Paprika	½ tsp.	½ tsp.	2 tsp.	2 tsp.
Nutmeg, ground	¼ tsp.	¼ tsp.	1 tsp.	1 tsp.
Cognac	¼ cup	0.6 dl	1 cup	2.5 dl
Sherry Wine	½ cup	1.2 dl	2 cups	5 dl
Egg Yolks	4	4	16	16
Light Cream	1½ cups	4 dl	1½ qt.	1.5 l
Cooked Lobster, diced or Shrimp, Crabmeat, or a combination	2 lb.	900 g	8 lb.	3.6 kg
Salt	½ tsp.	½ tsp.	2 tsp.	2 tsp.
Pepper, ground	¼ tsp.	¼ tsp.	1 tsp.	1 tsp.

Melt the butter in a shallow saute pan. Add the seafood and the flour. Mix well and simmer for 5 minutes. Season with paprika and nutmeg. Pour in the cognac and sherry.

Make a liaison with the egg yolks and cream and, just before serving, stir into the seafood until thickened. The sauce *must not* boil. Season to taste with salt and pepper. Serve hot with rice or on toast.

Seafood Sausages

Ingredients	6 portions		24 portions	
	U.S.	Metric	U.S.	Metric
Sole Fillets, or other lean firm fish	12 oz.	340 g	3 lb.	1.4 kg
Egg Whites	1	1	4	4
Heavy Cream	¾ cup	2 dl	3 cups	8 dl
Salt	½ tsp.	½ tsp.	2 tsp.	2 tsp.
White Pepper	¼ tsp.	¼ tsp.	1 tsp.	1 tsp.
Parsley, chopped	1 tbsp.	1 tbsp.	4 tbsp.	4 tbsp.
Mushrooms, chopped	2 oz.	50 g	8 oz.	225 g
Fresh Salmon, diced	2 oz.	50 g	8 oz.	225 g
Fresh Shrimp, diced	2 oz.	50 g	8 oz.	225 g
Fresh Scallops, diced	2 oz.	50 g	8 oz.	225 g
Sausage Casing	2 feet	60 cm	8 feet	2.4 m
Veloute Sauce				

Preferably using a food processor, puree the fish fillets while gradually adding the egg whites, heavy cream, salt, and pepper. Transfer to a mixing bowl. Fold in the remaining ingredients.

Using a sausage stuffer or funnel, stuff mixture into casings. Poach the sausages in salted boiling water for 15 to 20 minutes. Brown in oil. Arrange on a serving platter and coat with the boiling veloute sauce. Serve hot.

Seafood Pizza

Ingredients	6 portions		24 portions	
	U.S.	Metric	U.S.	Metric
Pizza Dough (chapter 7)	1 recipe	1 recipe	4 recipes	4 recipes
Italian Tomato Sauce	1 lb.	450 g	4 lb.	1.8 kg
Garlic Clove, minced	1	1	4	4
Oregano	1 tsp.	1 tsp.	4 tsp.	4 tsp.
Mozzarella Cheese	8 oz.	225 g	2 lb.	900 g
Mushrooms, sliced	4 oz.	110 g	1 lb.	450 g
Crabmeat	4 oz.	110 g	1 lb.	450 g
Small Shrimp	4 oz.	110 g	1 lb.	450 g
Clams or Oysters	4 oz.	110 g	1 lb.	450 g

Roll out pizza dough to fit 14 by 17 in. (35 × 42.4 cm) baking sheet pan. Mix tomato sauce, garlic, and oregano. Spread over dough. Sprinkle cheese and mushrooms over and bake for 15 minutes. Sprinkle the seafood over and bake for 5 more minutes or until the crust is done.

Seviche

Ingredients	6 portions		24 portions	
	U.S.	Metric	U.S.	Metric
Fresh Fillets of Sole or Bay Scallops	2 lb.	900 g	8 lb.	3.6 kg
Salt	1 tsp.	1 tsp.	1 tbsp.	1 tbsp.
Lime Juice	½ cup	1.2 dl	2 cups	5 dl
Green Pepper, chopped	1	1	4	4
Parsley, chopped	1 tbsp.	1 tbsp.	4 tbsp.	4 tbsp.
French Dressing	¾ cup	2 dl	3 cups	8 dl
Scallions, chopped	2	2	8	8
Large Tomato, peeled and chopped	1	1	4	4
Chili Peppers, crushed	¼ tsp.	¼ tsp.	1 tsp.	1 tsp.
Liquid Hot Pepper Sauce, to taste				

Cut the fish into bite-size pieces and mix with salt and lime juice. Refrigerate for 12 hours. Combine remaining ingredients and store in refrigerator. Drain fish well, add to vegetable mixture, and marinate 3 to 4 hours more. Serve well chilled as an appetizer.

Steamed Fish with Ginger Sauce

Ingredients	6 portions		24 portions	
	U.S.	Metric	U.S.	Metric
Whole Fish (Summer Flounder, Sea Bass, Pike, Butterfish, Shad, or Snapper)	3 lb.	1.350 kg	12 lb.	5.5 kg
Dry Sherry	¼ cup	0.6 dl	1 cup	2.5 dl
Fresh Ginger Root, shredded . .	1 tbsp.	1 tbsp.	4 tbsp.	4 tbsp.
Peanut Oil	2 tbsp.	2 tbsp.	½ cup	1.2 dl
Soy Sauce	2 tbsp.	2 tbsp.	½ cup	1.2 dl
Sugar	½ tsp.	½ tsp.	2 tsp.	2 tsp.

Cut the clean, scaled fish into 6 or 24 pieces. Arrange on a rack that will fit in a steamer. Sprinkle the sherry on top. Bring water to a boil in a steamer. Cover tightly and steam the fish 10 minutes per inch thickness.

Cut the scallions into 2-inch (5-cm) pieces. Mix with the ginger. Heat the oil in a wok or large skillet. Add the ginger and scallions and stir fry for a few seconds over high heat. Add the soy sauce and sugar. Remove from heat. Arrange fish on a serving platter. Pour the sauce over. Serve hot.

Mullet

Grilled Mullet Bernaise
See Grilled Dover Sole Bernaise.

Smoked Mullet
This is a delicacy used in salads or diced for an appetizer.

Key Lime Florida Mullet

Ingredients	6 portions		24 portions	
	U.S.	Metric	U.S.	Metric
Fillets of Mullet	2 lb.	900 g	8 lb.	3.6 kg
Salt	½ tsp.	½ tsp.	2 tsp.	2 tsp.
White Pepper	¼ tsp.	¼ tsp.	1 tsp.	1 tsp.
Lime Juice	3 oz.	1 dl	1½ cup	4 dl
Butter	4 oz.	110 g	1 lb.	450 g
Lime Wedges	6	6	24	24

Skin the fillets and cut into serving portions. Place fish on buttered sheet pan(s). Season with salt and pepper. Pour the lime juice over and let stand for 30 minutes, turning fish once. Melt butter, combine with lime juice, and brush fillets with this mixture. Place under a broiler about 4 inches (10 cm) from the source of heat, for 8 to 10 minutes, or until done. Serve at once.

Mullets Grenobloise

Ingredients	6 portions		24 portions	
	U.S.	Metric	U.S.	Metric
Fillets of Mullet	2 lb.	900 g	8 lb.	3.6 kg
Salt	½ tsp.	½ tsp.	2 tsp.	2 tsp.
White Pepper	¼ tsp.	¼ tsp.	1 tsp.	1 tsp.
Oil	3 oz.	1 dl	12 oz.	4 dl
Butter	5 oz.	140 g	1¼ lb.	560 g
Capers	2 oz.	50 g	8 oz.	200 g
Flour	3 oz.	85 g	12 oz.	340 g
Bread Croutons	4 oz.	110 g	1 lb.	450 g
Lemons	2	2	8	8
Parsley, chopped	1 tbsp.	1 tbsp.	4 tbsp.	4 tbsp.

Skin fillets and cut into portions. Season with salt and pepper. Saute in oil and half of the butter allocation, browning fish on both sides. Arrange on a serving platter. Sprinkle with capers, croutons, and peeled lemon slices. Brown remaining butter, pour over fish, and sprinkle with chopped parsley before serving.

Stuffed Baked Mullet

Ingredients	6 portions		24 portions	
	U.S.	Metric	U.S.	Metric
Dressed Whole Mullet, 2-lb. (900 g) pieces	3	3	12	12
Bacon, diced	8 oz.	225 g	2 lb.	900 g
Onion, chopped	2 oz.	50 g	8 oz.	200 g
Celery, chopped	4 oz.	110 g	1 lb.	450 g
Fresh Bread Crumbs	2 oz. (1 cup)	50 g	8 oz.	200 g
Oregano	1 tsp.	1 tsp.	4 tsp.	4 tsp.
Salt	½ tsp.	½ tsp.	2 tsp.	2 tsp.
Pepper	¼ tsp.	¼ tsp.	1 tsp.	1 tsp.
Shrimp, cooked and diced	8 oz.	225 g	2 lb.	900 g
Whole Eggs, beaten	2	2	8	8
Tomato Sauce	1½ cup	4 dl	1½ qt.	1.5 dl

Scale, clean, and wash fish. Fry bacon over low heat. Add onions and celery and cook until tender. Stir in the bread crumbs and seasonings. Mix shrimp and egg and combine with the stuffing ingredients. Stuff the cavity of each fish with some of the mixture. Close the cavity with small skewers. Place fish on greased baking pans. Bake at 450°F (230°C) for 30 to 40 minutes, or until fish is tender and flaky. Transfer onto serving platter. Serve the tomato sauce separately.

Sea Dogs

A new product, called *sea dog,* made from Florida mullet has been tested by University of Florida food scientists. The sea dog resembles the hot dog but contains only about 140 calories (per 100 grams), whereas a typical hot dog has 248 calories and pork sausage has 470 calories. The sea dog could be produced commercially or by consumers in their kitchens.

Preparation of mullet sea dogs is simple. After the fish have been deboned and put through a grinder, liquid smoke flavoring, spices, and TPP (sodium tripolyphosphate) are added to the meat before cooking at 375°F (190°C) for 50 minutes. Liquid smoke flavoring enhances the taste characteristics of mullet and retards rancidity. TPP increases the juiciness of the product, according to Dr. J.C. Deng, assistant professor at the Institute of Food and Agricultural Sciences.

Ocean Perch

(Redfish, Rosefish)

Note: Ocean perch is best grilled, meuniere, or poached and served with hollandaise sauce.

Fillets of Perch Bearnaise

Ingredients	6 portions		24 portions	
	U.S.	Metric	U.S.	Metric
Perch Fillets	2 lb.	900 g	8 lb.	3.6 kg
Salt	½ tsp.	½ tsp.	2 tsp.	2 tsp.
Pepper	¼ tsp.	¼ tsp.	1 tsp.	1 tsp.
Flour	3 oz.	85 g	12 oz.	340 g
Butter	4 oz.	110 g	1 lb.	450 g
Tomatoes, grilled	6	6	24	24
Parsley, to garnish				
Bearnaise Sauce	1½ cups	4 dl	1½ qt.	1.5 l

Season the fillets of perch with salt and pepper. Coat with flour. Fry in butter until crisp. Arrange on preheated platter. Garnish with tomatoes and parsley. Serve bearnaise sauce separately.

Ocean Perch en Cocotte

Ingredients	6 portions		24 portions	
	U.S.	Metric	U.S.	Metric
Pan-dressed Perch, 8 oz. (225 g) each	6	6	24	24
Salt	½ tsp.	½ tsp.	2 tsp.	2 tsp.
Butter	3 oz.	85 g	12 oz.	340 g
Shallots, chopped	1 oz.	25 g	4 oz.	110 g
Parsley, chopped	1 tbsp.	1 tbsp.	4 tbsp.	4 tbsp.
Dry White Wine	¾ cup	2 dl	3 cups	8 dl
Lemon Juice	2 oz.	0.6 dl	1 cup	2.5 dl

Clean, scale, wash, and dry perch. Season with salt. Butter oven-proof serving dish(es). Sprinkle shallots and parsley over bottom of dish. Arrange perch on top. Pour wine and lemon juice over. Bake at 350°F (180°C) for 15 to 20 minutes. Serve garnished with Parisianne potatoes.

Pollock

(Boston Bluefish)
See recipes for cod and haddock.

Pompano

(Cobblerfish, Butterfish, Palmenta)

Pompano is excellent prepared meuniere and served with toasted sliced almonds or on a bed of noodles mixed with veloute sauce.

Pompano Captiva

Ingredients	6 portions		24 portions	
	U.S.	Metric	U.S.	Metric
Fillets of Pompano	2 lb.	900 g	8 lb.	3.6 kg
Salt	½ tsp.	½ tsp.	2 tsp.	2 tsp.
Pepper, ground	¼ tsp.	¼ tsp.	1 tsp.	1 tsp.
Shrimp Quenelle Forcemeat . .	10 oz.	280 g	2½ lb.	1.2 kg
Shallots, chopped	1 tbsp.	1 tbsp.	4 tbsp.	4 tbsp.
Dry White Wine	5 oz.	1½ dl	2½ cups	6 dl
Fish Fumet	5 oz.	1½ dl	2½ cups	6 dl
Mushrooms, sliced	7 oz.	200 g	1 lb 12 oz.	800 g
Beurre Manie	1 oz.	25 g	4 oz.	110 g
Heavy Cream	3 oz.	1 dl	1½ cups	4 dl
Lemon Juice	1 oz.	0.3 dl	½ cup	1.2 dl
Tomatoes, chopped, seedless, and peeled	1 lb.	450 g	4 lb.	1.8 kg
Butter	1 oz.	25 g	4 oz.	110 g

Flatten pompano fillets with a mallet. Season with salt and pepper. Spread quenelle forcemeat over half of each fillet and fold other half over.

Butter baking pan(s). Sprinkle with shallots. Arrange fillets on top in one layer. Moisten with wine and fumet. Arrange mushroom slices on top of each fillet. Cover with foil. Bake at 400°F (204°C) for 20 to 25 minutes. Transfer fillets onto serving platter(s).

Reduce cooking liquid by one third. Stir in beurre manie and cream. Reduce to a medium consistency. Add lemon juice and season to taste. Saute tomatoes in butter. Arrange around pompano. Pour sauce over fish and glaze under a broiler or salamander.

Pompano Papillottes

Ingredients	6 portions		24 portions	
	U.S.	Metric	U.S.	Metric
Whole Pompano	3—2 lb.	3—900 g	12—2 lb.	12—900 g
or Fillets of Pompano	2 lb.	900 g	8 lb.	3.6 kg
Butter	4 oz.	110 g	1 lb.	450 g
Scallions, chopped	2 tbsp.	2 tbsp.	½ cup	1.2 dl
White wine	5 oz.	1.5 dl	2½ cups	6 dl
Salt	½ tsp.	½ tsp.	2 tsp.	2 tsp.
Pepper	¼ tsp.	¼ tsp.	1 tsp.	1 tsp.
Sherry Wine	2 oz.	0.6 dl	1 cup	2.5 dl
Shrimp, cooked	6 oz.	170 g	1½ lb.	680 g
Crabmeat	6 oz.	170 g	1½ lb.	680 g
Veloute or Cream Sauce	2 cups	5 dl	2 qt.	2 l
Tabasco	dash	dash	¼ tsp.	¼ tsp.

Fillet pompano if whole. Remove skin and bones. Melt half of the butter in a saute pan. Add scallions. Place pompano fillets on top, cover, and steam for 3 to 5 minutes. Add the white wine, sherry, salt, and pepper. Cook until the pompano is firm. Transfer fish to a pan and keep warm. To the same pan, add the cooked sliced shrimp and crabmeat. Stir in the sauce. Bring to a boil. Adjust seasonings.

Following the procedure described in chapter 6, cut parchment paper into heart shapes, about 14 inches (35 cm) wide. Oil one side of paper and place oily side on working surface. In center of right side of heart, place two tablespoons of seafood sauce. Top with two pompano fillets, then spoon two more tablespoons of sauce over. To close, fold over the left half of heart, and roll edges of paper, starting from the top left inside, until the parchment paper is shaped into a well-sealed envelope. Place the bags on oiled sheet pan(s), and bake in a very hot oven to puff and brown the bags. Serve hot.

Scallopine of Pompano Neas

Ingredients	6 portions U.S.	Metric	24 portions U.S.	Metric
Onion, sliced	8 oz.	225 g	2 lb.	900 g
Oil	½ cup	1.2 dl	2 cups	5 dl
Tomatoes, chopped and seedless	1½ lb.	680 g	6 lb.	2.7 kg
Garlic Cloves, minced	2	2	8	8
Tomato Juice	1 cup	2.5 dl	1 qt.	1 l
Salt	½ tsp.	½ tsp.	2 tsp.	2 tsp.
White Pepper	¼ tsp.	¼ tsp.	1 tsp.	1 tsp.
Fillets of Pompano	2 lb.	900 g	8 lb.	3.6 kg
Egg Noodles	8 oz.	225 g	2 lb.	900 g
White Wine Sauce	1 cup	2.5 dl	1 qt.	1 l
Parsley, chopped	1 tbsp.	1 tbsp.	4 tbsp.	4 tbsp.

Saute the onion in half of the oil until tender. Add tomatoes, garlic, tomato juice, salt, and pepper. Cook over low heat for 15 minutes.

Skin and slice the pompano into scallopines. Flatten with a mallet. Season with salt, pepper, and lemon juice. Dredge pompano in flour and saute briskly in remaining oil.

Cook noodles in salted boiling water. Drain. Combine noodles with white wine sauce. Arrange on preheated serving platter. Top with pompano slices. Spoon hot tomato and onion sauce over fish. Sprinkle with parsley. Serve hot.

Porgy (Scup)
Porgies are best sauteed meuniere or pan fried.
See the chapter on cooking techniques.

Redfish
(Channel Bass, Red Drum, Red Bass)
Redfish can be baked or poached whole (see chapter 6), and served hot or cold.

Redfish Polonaise
See Cod.

Gougeonnettes of Redfish
See Sole.

Red Snapper

Baked Florida Red Snapper

Ingredients	6 portions		24 portions	
	U.S.	Metric	U.S.	Metric
Red Snapper, whole, dressed, 5 lb. (2.270 kg)	1	1	4	4
Salt	1 tsp.	1 tsp.	4 tsp.	4 tsp.
White Pepper	¼ tsp.	¼ tsp.	1 tsp.	1 tsp.
White Wine	1 cup	2.5 dl	1 qt.	1 l
Butter	4 oz.	110 g	1 lb.	450 g
Parsley, to garnish				

Season the snapper(s) with salt and pepper. Place on a well-greased baking sheet. Measure the fish at the thickest point. Pour the wine over, dot with butter, and bake at 400°F (205°C) timing 10 minutes per inch thickness. A 5-lb. (2.270-kg) red snapper can measure about 3 inches at the thickest point and will bake in 30 minutes. Baste fish while cooking. Transfer to a serving platter. Serve with the cooking liquid and an additional sauce, if desired.

Baked Red Snapper with White Wine Sauce

Ingredients	6 portions		24 portions	
	U.S.	Metric	U.S.	Metric
Red Snapper, whole, dressed 5 lb. (2.270 kg)	1	1	4	4
Salt	½ tsp.	½ tsp.	2 tsp.	2 tsp.
White Pepper	¼ tsp.	¼ tsp.	1 tsp.	1 tsp.
White Wine	1 cup	2.5 dl	1 qt.	1 l
Butter	4 oz.	110 g	1 lb.	450 g
Fish Fumet	2 cups	5 dl	2 qt.	2 l
Heavy Cream	1 cup	2.5 dl	1 qt.	1 l
Beurre Manie	2 oz.	50 g	8 oz.	200 g

Wash and scale red snapper(s). Season with salt and pepper. Place on greased baking pans. Pour wine over, with the melted butter. Bake at 350°F (180°C), timing 15 minutes per inch thickness as measured at the thickest point. Baste frequently with the pan juices. Transfer baked fish to serving platter(s). Combine pan juices with fumet. Boil for 10 minutes. Add cream and reduce one half. Thicken with beurre manie to a medium consistency. Serve fish whole, garnished with parsley. Serve sauce separately.

Poached Red Snapper

Ingredients	6 portions		24 portions	
	U.S.	Metric	U.S.	Metric
Red Snapper, whole, dressed 5 lb. (2.270 kg)	1	1	4	4
Court Bouillon no. 1 (to cover fish)				
Small Potatos, boiled	1 lb.	450 g	4 lb.	1.8 kg
Lemon Wedges	6	6	24	24
Lemon Baskets and Parsley Garnish				
Lemon Wedges	6	6	24	24
Lemon Baskets and Parsley Garnish				
Hollandaise or Mousseline Sauce	2 cups	5 dl	2 qt.	2 l

Poach the fish in court bouillon, according to the poaching technique described in chapter 6. Transfer the cooked fish onto a serving platter and garnish with boiled potatoes, lemon wedges, baskets, and parsley. Serve the hollandaise or mousseline sauce separately.

Fillet of Red Snapper Louisianne

Saute meuniere (see cooking techniques). Garnish with chopped cooked tomatoes, sliced green peppers cooked in butter, sliced cooked bananas, and top with lemon butter.

Grilled Red Snapper Maitre d'Hotel

See Sole.

Mousseline of Red Snapper Royale

See Salmon.

Rockfish (Bocaccio)

Prepare rockfish according to red snapper recipes.

Sablefish (Black Cod)

Broiled California Sable Steaks

Ingredients	6 portions		24 portions	
	U.S.	Metric	U.S.	Metric
Sablefish Fillets, fresh or frozen	2 lb.	900 g	8 lb.	3.6 kg
Oil	½ cup	1.2 dl	2 cups	5 dl
Oregano	½ tsp.	½ tsp.	2 tsp.	2 tsp.
Garlic Salt	½ tsp.	½ tsp.	2 tsp.	2 tsp.
Lemon Juice	2 oz.	0.6 dl	1 cup	2.5 dl
Dill Weed or Fresh Dill, chopped	½ tsp.	½ tsp.	2 tsp.	2 tsp.
Lemon Wedges	6	6	24	24

Thaw fish if frozen. Cut into 5-oz. (140-g) portions. Marinate the fish in oil, oregano, garlic salt, lemon juice, and dill. Broil on both sides. Arrange on a serving platter. Serve with lemon wedges and decorate with parsley.

Salmon

Numerous salmon recipes result in tasty and delectable dishes. A fresh piece of salmon, cooked according to the best culinary principles and accompanied by the right sauce, is a gastronomical triumph.

The rich flavor of some species of salmon makes them remarkably versatile in numerous preparations. Connoisseurs generally agree that the Atlantic salmon, caught mostly in Canada, the Pacific coho or silver, and the chinook or king, also caught on the West Coast, are tops on the list. The pink color of salmon, combined with the flavor, make the fish a favorite on our tables.

Sport fishermen know that catching the "rod busters" requires a great deal of knowledge, experience, and practice. The same applies to proper cooking of the fish.

How to Poach a Whole Salmon

Poaching is the most common technique for cooking salmon. Salmon can be poached in fillets, steaks, or center cuts; but a whole poached salmon remains the ultimate in fish cooking. Before poaching, the fish should be cleaned, scaled, and washed thoroughly. A frozen salmon should be fully thawed to poach it correctly without any nutritional loss.

A fish poacher with a rack is required for proper poaching and handling of the salmon. The standard fish poacher can accomodate a whole salmon weighing 10 to 12 pounds (4.5 to 5.4 kg). (See illustration on page 118) For larger fish or several whole fish, a custom-made poissonniere is necessary. Another method is to cut one half of the fish in steaks; the other half can then be poached in one piece. This writer recalls poaching a 48-pound (21.7-kg) salmon—a real trophy. The fish had to be cooked in a five-foot-long poacher containing 20 gallons (80 l) of court bouillon. After two days of elaborate decorating, the salmon was displayed at a culinary exhibition and won first prize for best presentation. (See chapter 16 for details on modern methods of seafood decoration.)

For complete details on poaching salmon, refer to the poaching technique in chapter 6.

Braised Blueback au Champagne

	6 portions		24 portions	
Ingredients	U.S.	Metric	U.S.	Metric
Blueback, 6 lb. each	1	1	4	4
Shallots, chopped	3 tbsp.	3 tbsp.	3 oz.	85 g
Butter	1 tbsp.	1 tbsp.	2 oz.	60 g
Fish Stock	2 cups	5 dl	2 qt.	2 l
Champagne	2 cups	5 dl	2 qt.	2 l
Butter	2 oz.	60 g	8 oz.	230 g
Flour	2 oz.	60 g	8 oz.	230 g
Salt and Pepper, to taste				
Mushroom Caps, sauteed in butter	6	6	24	24

Clean, scale, and place the whole fish on one side in a buttered baking dish. Sprinkle the shallots around the fish. Pour the champagne and fish stock over the fish. Cover with a sheet of foil. Bake in a 350°F (180°C) oven, allowing 10 to 12 minutes per pound for cooking time. Baste occasionally. Transfer the fish to a serving platter. Skin both sides and cover with the foil.

Strain the cooking liquid and reduce to 2 cups. Combine the soft butter with the flour for a beurre manie. Thicken the reduced stock with the beurre manie, whipping vigorously until the sauce becomes light and creamy. Season with salt and pepper to taste. Cover the fish with the sauce and top with mushroom caps.

Chinook Bellevue
(For buffet presentation only.)

	12 portions	
Ingredients	U.S.	Metric
Fresh Chinook or King Salmon, 9–10 lb. (4–4.5 kg)	1	1
Court Bouillon No. 1		
Tomatoes and Cucumbers, sliced, to garnish	12	12
Cucumbers, stuffed with smoked salmon mousse	12	12
Radish and leek, to garnish . . .		
Mayonnaise Sauce	1 qt.	1 l

Clean, scale, and wash the salmon. Cut fish in half crosswise. Keep the tail piece whole and fillet the other piece. Poach salmon piece and fillets in court bouillon, following directions described for the poaching technique. Let cool. Lift the cold fish out of court bouillon. Slice the fillets into serving portions. Skin the whole piece of salmon. Decorate with cucumber and tomato slices inserted into partly sliced fish.

Arrange salmon piece and slices on a board or mirror. Decorate each slice with radish slivers and green leek stems for a floral effect. Arrange stuffed cucumbers around fish. Serve cold with the mayonnaise sauce.

Cold Salmon Mousse
See Mousse of Salmon Trout.

Coulibiac

Ingredients	6 portions U.S.	Metric	24 portions U.S.	Metric
Salmon Fillets, thinly sliced . . .	1½ lb.	750 g	6 lb.	2.700 kg
Lemon Juice	1 tbsp.	1 tbsp.	2 oz.	0.6 dl
Salt	½ tsp.	½ tsp.	2 tsp.	2 tsp.
White Pepper, ground	⅛ tsp.	⅛ tsp.	½ tsp.	½ tsp.
Onion, chopped	1	1	4	4
Oil	1 tbsp.	1 tbsp.	2 oz.	0.6 dl
Fresh Mushrooms, chopped . .	1 oz.	30 g	4 oz.	115 g
Parsley, chopped	1 tbsp.	1 tbsp.	4 tbsp.	4 tbsp.
Couscous, Kashe, or Rice, cooked	6 oz.	180 g	1½ lb.	680 g
Hard-boiled Egg, chopped	2	2	6–7	6–7
Cooked Vesiga (sturgeon marrow), optional	6 oz.	180 g	1½ lb.	680 g
Veloute Sauce	½ cup	1.25 dl	2 cups	5 dl
Egg, for egg wash	1	1	4	4
Melted Butter	1 tbsp.	1 tbsp.	2 oz.	60 g
Brioche Dough				
Active Dry Yeast	1 envelope	1 envelope	4 envelopes	4 envelopes
Sugar	1 tsp.	1 tsp.	1 tbsp.	1 tbsp.
Lukewarm Water	2 oz.	0.6 dl	1 cup	2.5 dl
Flour	2 oz.	60 g	8 oz.	230 g
Flour	9 oz.	250 g	2¼ lb.	1 kg
Whole Eggs, lightly beaten	3	3	12	12
Salt	¾ tsp.	¾ tsp.	1 tbsp.	1 tbsp.
Soft Butter	6 oz.	180 g	1½ lb.	680 g

Season the salmon slices with salt, pepper, and lemon juice. Saute the onion in oil. Add the mushrooms and parsley. Cook over medium heat for 5 minutes.

Roll out the brioche dough (see following directions) into a rectangle, about ¼ inch thick. (For 24 portions, make 4 coulibiacs.) Place on a baking sheet. Gently mix mushrooms, onions, parsley, couscous, eggs, and vesiga together. Alternate with salmon slices, heaping over one half of the rectangle of dough, lengthwise, to within 1 inch of edges. Pour the veloute sauce over the filling.

Brush the edges of dough with water. Fold the dough over the salmon mixture and seal all edges. Roll the coulibiac over so that the long seam is underneath. Brush the whole surface of the coulibiac with egg wash (1 egg mixed with 1 tbsp. of water). Cut decorative designs out of brioche dough trimmings

(cont.)

and arrange attractively on top. Allow the brioche to rise at room temperature for 20–25 minutes.

Brush with melted butter. Cut an opening on the center top of the coulibiac to let the steam escape while cooking. Bake at 375°F (190°C) for 30–35 minutes. Serve with lemon butter and one of the hot sauces listed in chapter 11.

Note: Individual coulibiacs can be prepared following the same recipe.

Brioche Dough Dissolve the yeast and sugar in the warm water. Add ½ cup of flour (2 cups) and blend well. Cover with a wet towel and allow to double in size in a warm place.

Meanwhile, beat half of the remaining flour with the eggs and salt. Add the yeast mixture and butter, and knead in the remaining flour. Let rise at room temperature for 3 hours. Punch the dough and refrigerate overnight, covered with a wet towel.

Creamed Salmon with Mushrooms

Ingredients	6 portions		24 portions	
	U.S.	Metric	U.S.	Metric
Canned Salmon	2 lb.	900 g	8 lb.	3.6 kg
Butter	2 oz.	50 g	8 oz.	225 g
Onion, chopped	1 oz.	25 g	4 oz.	110 g
Shallots, chopped	1 tbsp.	1 tbsp.	4 tbsp.	4 tbsp.
Fresh Mushrooms, sliced	8 oz.	225 g	2 lb.	900 g
Flour	1 oz.	25 g	4 oz.	110 g
Dry White Wine	½ cup	1.2 dl	2 cups	5 dl
Heavy Cream	½ cup	1.2 dl	2 cups	5 dl
Parsley, chopped	1 tbsp.	1 tbsp.	4 tbsp.	4 tbsp.

Break up the salmon and set aside. Save liquid. Saute onion, shallots and mushrooms in butter until tender. Stir in the flour. Add the wine and salmon liquid. Stir well until thick. Add the heavy cream and parsley. Season to taste and simmer for 5 minutes. Mix in the salmon and heat through. Serve in casserole dish with rice.

Fried Salmon Steaks Bonne Femme

Ingredients	6 portions		24 portions	
	U.S.	Metric	U.S.	Metric
Salmon Steaks	6	6	24	24
Salt	½ tsp.	½ tsp.	2 tsp.	2 tsp.
White Pepper	¼ tsp.	¼ tsp.	1 tsp.	1 tsp.
Olive Oil	2 tsp.	2 tsp.	1½ oz.	.5 dl
Butter	2 tsp.	2 tsp.	1½ oz.	40 g
Shallots, chopped	2 tbsp.	2 tbsp.	2 oz.	60 g
White Wine	1½ cups	4 dl	1½ qt.	1.5 l
Heavy Cream	¾ cup	2 dl	3 cups	7.5 dl
Butter	1½ tbsp.	1½ tbsp.	3 oz.	85 g
Flour	2 tsp.	2 tsp.	3 tbsp.	3 tbsp.

Season the salmon steaks with salt and pepper. Heat the butter and oil in a frying pan. Brown the salmon steaks on both sides. Carefully remove bones and skin and transfer to a serving platter. Keep warm.

Sprinkle the shallots in the frying pan and cook over low heat for 2 minutes. Add the white wine and simmer for 10 minutes. Pour in the heavy cream and boil for 5 minutes. Drop pieces of the butter and flour mixture into the boiling liquid. Whip until the sauce is smooth and medium thick. Season with salt and pepper to taste. Cook the sauce for about 10 minutes. Pour over the salmon steaks and serve at once.

Galantine of Salmon
(For buffet service.)

Ingredients	20 portions	
	U.S.	Metric
Salmon	5–6 lb.	2.2–2.7 kg
White Bread, sliced with crusts removed	6	6
Egg Whites	5	5
Heavy Cream	2 cups	5 dl
Salt	3 tsp.	3 tsp.
White Pepper	1 tsp.	1 tsp.
Nutmeg	2 gratings	2 gratings
Pistachio Nuts	2 tbsp.	2 tbsp.
Pimentos	6 oz.	170 g

Remove head and tail of salmon. Bone salmon without damaging the skin. Remove meat, keeping both meat and skin intact. Chill meat thoroughly. Prepare stock from the fish bones. Scale the fish skin, clean, and save.

Mince the meat very fine and put through a sieve to remove muscles and bones. Keep in the refrigerator. Soak bread in

(cont.)

heavy cream and egg whites and mix well. Combine fish, bread, salt, pepper, and nutmeg. Place in food chopper. Mix until the forcemeat is smooth. Mix in the pimentos and pistachio nuts. Poach a teaspoon of mixture in boiling water; taste and adjust seasoning if necessary.

Spread a piece of cheese cloth, slightly larger than the salmon skin, on a table. Place the salmon skin on top. Spread half of the fish mixture over half of the skin. Stuff slices of smoked salmon with some forcemeat and roll up to resemble roulades. Arrange them lengthwise down the center of the galantine. Place remaining fish mixture on top. Fold the skin around the forcemeat, roll it up in the cheese cloth, and tie both ends tightly. Place 3 or 4 loose strings around the galantine. Poach in fish stock about 10 to 12 minutes per pound. Allow to cool in the stock. Remove cheese cloth and decorate before slicing. Serve with one of the cold cauces in chapter 11.

Gravlax
(Swedish Marinated Salmon)

Yields 2-oz. appetizers for 40.

Ingredients	U.S.	Metric
Salmon Fillet	5 lb.	2.3 kg
Salt	2½ oz.	70 g
Sugar	5½ oz.	150 g
Fresh Dill Stems	6	6
Onion, thinly sliced	1	1
Black Pepper, ground	1	1
Juniper Berries, crushed	1	1
Lemons	2	2

Scale, wash, and dry the fillet thoroughly. Extract all bones. Mix the salt and sugar and rub the mixture into the salmon fillet. Place dill and sliced onion on the bottom of a rectangular pan. Lay the salmon fillet on top, skin side up. Sprinkle pepper and juniper berries over the fish. Place a board on top of the fish with a weight on it. Marinate in the refrigerator for 2 to 3 days, basting the fish each day with marinade. Slice thinly and serve with rye bread.

Mousse of Salmon Joinville

Prepare a fresh salmon mousse using the basic recipe for quenelle and mousse in chapter 8. Poach in ring molds. Serve with shrimp sauce.

Note: It is possible to vary the presentation of the above recipe, alternating a mousse of salmon and a mousse of sole or trout. The contrast is quite interesting if the two-color mousses are served with two sauces: for example, a lobster sauce for the salmon mousse, and a creamed veloute sauce for the white mousse.

For a higher yield, the quenelle forcemeat can be prepared using panada (see also chapter 9).

Mousseline of Salmon Royale
(Quenelles of Salmon in Puff Pastry)

| Ingredients | 6 portions | | 24 portions | |
	U.S.	Metric	U.S.	Metric
Fresh Salmon, boneless and skinless	9 oz.	250 g	2 lb.	1 kg
Egg Whites	2	2	8	8
Heavy Cream	10 oz.	3 dl	5 cups	1.2 l
Cayenne Pepper	⅛ tsp.	⅛ tsp.	½ tsp.	½ tsp.
Salt	¾ tsp.	¾ tsp.	1 tbsp.	1 tbsp.
Truffles, minced	¾ oz.	20 g	3 oz.	85 g
Fresh Spinach	10 oz.	300 g	2 lb. 10 oz.	1.200 kg
Butter	2 tbsp.	2 tbsp.	4 oz.	110 g
Puff Paste Dough	10 oz.	300 g	2 lb. 10 oz.	1.200 kg
Egg Yolks	2	2	8	8
Sauce				
Salmon Fumet, made with bones	7 oz.	2 dl	3½ cups	8 dl
Fennel Seeds	1 tsp.	1 tsp.	4 tsp.	4 tsp.
Dry White Wine	7 oz.	2 dl	3½ cups	8 dl
Shallots, chopped	2	2	8	8
Heavy Cream	7 oz.	2 dl	3½ cups	8 dl
Butter	3½ oz.	100 g	14 oz.	400 g
Flour	2 tbsp.	2 tbsp.	2 oz.	60 g
Large Canned Tomatoes, seeded and chopped	4	4	16	16

In a food processor, mix the salmon and egg whites, and gradually add the cream. Season with salt and cayenne pepper. Stir in the truffles.

Poach 12 (48) egg-shaped mousselines in the fumet seasoned with fennel seeds. To shape the mousselines, see the recipe for Quenelles of Pike. Simmer for 10 minutes. Drain and cool.

Clean the spinach and cook with the butter and as little water as possible. Season with salt and pepper to taste. Chop.

Divide the dough into 2 pieces and roll out into rectangles ⅛" (2 mm) thick. Brush the first rectangle with water. Place about 1 tbsp. of spinach every 4 inches (10 cm) across and down the dough. You should have 12 (48) mounds. Top each with a mousseline. Spread the second sheet of dough over, pressing down firmly around the mousselines. Using a pastry wheel, cut into oval-shaped pastries.

Arrange on a baking sheet, brush with the egg yolks, and bake at 425°F (220°C) for 8 to 10 minutes.

Arrange the mousselines on a serving platter covered with a napkin. Serve the sauce separately.

(cont.)

Sauce   Reduce the fumet, white wine, and shallots by half. Add the cream and simmer for 5 minutes. Thicken the sauce with the beurre manie. Simmer over low heat. Strain the sauce and add finely chopped tomatoes.

Pate of Salmon
(Serves 8 to 10 for buffet)

Ingredients	U.S.	Metric
Pie Crust Dough		
Salmon Mousse (see pg 232) .	1 lb.	450 g
Salt	1 tsp.	1 tsp.
Nutmeg	pinch	pinch
Salmon, cut into fillets and marinated in white wine	8 oz.	225 g
Black Truffles	1 oz.	25 g

Line the bottom and sides of a pate mold with the pie crust dough. Alternate layers of the salmon mousse, seasoned with salt and nutmeg, with layers of salmon fillet and truffles. Fill mold only ¾ full as pate increases in volume while cooking. Cover with dough. Decorate with any remaining dough. Cut a chimney in the middle of the pate for the steam to escape. Bake at 350°F (180°C) for 1 hour. Serve with one of the cold sauces from chapter 11.

Poached Salmon Steaks, Cucumber Sauce

| Ingredients | 6 portions | | 24 portions | |
	U.S.	Metric	U.S.	Metric
Salmon Steaks, 7 oz. (200 g) each	6	6	24	24
Court Bouillon no. 1				
Cucumber, peeled and grated	2 cups	225 g	2 lb.	900 g
Dairy Sour Cream	1½ cups	4 dl	1½ qt.	1.5 l
Scallions, minced	1 tsp.	1 tsp.	1 tbsp.	1 tbsp.
Lemon Juice	1½ tsp.	1½ tsp.	2 tbsp.	2 tbsp.
Salt	¾ tsp.	¾ tsp.	1 tbsp.	1 tbsp.
White Pepper	¼ tsp.	¼ tsp.	1 tsp.	1 tsp.
Dill Weed	½ tsp.	½ tsp.	2 tsp.	2 tsp.

Thaw salmon steaks if frozen. Poach in court bouillon no. 1, following procedure described for the poaching technique. Chill salmon. Remove skin and bones. Arrange salmon on a serving platter.

Combine remaining ingredients, except dill, to make the sauce. Spoon over salmon. Sprinkle with chopped dill.

Quenelles of Salmon

Prepare a salmon quenelle forcemeat and shape into quenelles (see procedure in chapter 9). The quenelle can be served with a variety of hot sauces (see chapter 11).

Salmon and Shrimp Terrine

| | 6 portions | | 24 portions | |
Ingredients	U.S.	Metric	U.S.	Metric
Butter	2 oz.	50 g	8 oz.	225 g
Shallots, chopped	2 oz.	50 g	8 oz.	225 g
Medium Shrimp, peeled and deveined	8 oz.	225 g	2 lb.	900 g
Dry White Wine	1 cup	2.5 dl	1 qt.	1 l
Tomato Paste	1 tbsp.	1 tbsp.	4 tbsp.	4 tbsp.
Thyme Leaves	¼ tsp.	¼ tsp.	1 tsp.	1 tsp.
Fresh Salmon	10 oz.	280 g	2½ lb.	1.2 kg
Butter, softened	2 oz.	50 g	8 oz.	225 g
Heavy Cream	1 cup	2.5 dl	1 qt.	1 l
Eggs	2	2	8	8
Salt	½ tsp.	½ tsp.	2 tsp.	2 tsp.
White Pepper	¼ tsp.	¼ tsp.	1 tsp.	1 tsp.
Parsley, chopped	1 tbsp.	1 tbsp.	4 tbsp.	4 tbsp.
Fresh Tarragon or Dill, chopped	1 tbsp.	1 tbsp.	4 tbsp.	4 tbsp.
Beurre Blanc or	1 recipe	1 recipe	4 recipe	4 recipe
Sauce Verte	1 recipe	1 recipe	4 recipe	4 recipe

Melt butter in a skillet or saute pan. Add shallots and cook over low heat for 5 minutes. Add shrimp and wine. Bring to a boil over brisk fire. Stir in tomato paste and thyme. Keep warm.

Cut skinned and boned salmon into cubes. Puree in a food processor, adding the butter, heavy cream, eggs, salt, pepper, and herbs. Transfer to a mixing bowl and fold in the prepared shrimp. Spoon the salmon mixture into a buttered 1 qt. terrine(s), smoothing the top with a spatula.

Put the terrine in a baking pan half filled with water. Cover the terrine and bake at 300°F (155°C) for about 45–60 minutes. Test by inserting a skewer in center. If the terrine is cooked, the skewer should come out clean. Remove terrine from baking pan. Slice and serve hot with beurre blanc. This recipe can be served cold with sauce verte.

Salmon au Gratin

Ingredients	6 portions		24 portions	
	U.S.	Metric	U.S.	Metric
Cooked Salmon	2½ lb.	1.200 kg	10 lb.	4.500 kg
Cooked Duxelle	4 oz.	110 g	1 lb.	450 g
Cream Sauce or Veloute Sauce	2 cups	5 dl	2 qt.	2 l
Hollandaise Sauce	½ cup	1.25 dl	2 cups	5 dl

Bone, skin, and flake the salmon. Arrange in a buttered casserole dish. Spread the duxelle over the fish. Heat in the oven at 350°F (180°C).

Combine the cream sauce or veloute sauce with the hollandaise. Ladle over the salmon, blending the sauce with the fish. Brown under a broiler. Serve with boiled rice, a mushroom souffle, or a spinach casserole.

Salmon Brochettes
(Fried Salmon on Skewers)

Ingredients	6 portions		24 portions	
	U.S.	Metric	U.S.	Metric
Salmon Fillet, boned and skinned	2½ lb.	1.200 kg	10 lb.	4.500 kg
Salt	1 tsp.	1 tsp.	4 tsp.	4 tsp.
Pepper	¼ tsp.	¼ tsp.	1 tsp.	1 tsp.
Lemon Juice	1 tbsp.	1 tbsp.	2 oz.	0.6 dl
Butter	4 oz.	115 g	1 lb.	450 g
Medium Mushroom Caps	1 doz.	1 doz.	4 doz.	4 doz.
Fresh Bread Crumbs	2 oz.	60 g	8 oz.	230 g

Cut the salmon into 1-inch (2.5-cm) cubes. Season with the salt, pepper, and lemon juice.

Melt a piece of butter in a frying pan. Cook the mushroom caps over low heat.

Alternate salmon pieces and mushroom caps on skewers. Dip in melted butter and roll in the bread crumbs. Saute in the remaining butter for about 10 minutes or until golden brown on all sides. Serve with a hot sauce.

Salmon Cutlets Pojarsky

Ingredients	6 portions		24 portions	
	U.S.	Metric	U.S.	Metric
Fresh Salmon, skinned, cleaned, and boned	1½ lb.	675 g	6 lb.	2.7 kg
White Bread, without crust	4 oz.	110 g	1 lb.	450 g
Milk	1 cup	2.5 dl	1 qt.	1 l
Soft Butter	4 oz.	110 g	1 lb.	450 g
Salt and Pepper, to taste				
Clarified Butter	½ cup	1.2 dl	2 cups	5 dl

Chop the salmon finely in a food processor. Soak the bread in milk for 10 minutes. Squeeze out excess moisture and mix well into the salmon paste. Blend in the butter until the mixture is smooth. Season with salt and pepper to taste.

On a floured surface, shape the salmon mix into cutlets. Saute in clarified butter and serve with a hot sauce.

Salmon Florentine

Ingredients	6 portions		24 portions	
	U.S.	Metric	U.S.	Metric
Fresh Spinach	1½ lb.	680 g	6 lb.	2.7 kg
Butter	2 tsp.	2 tsp.	1½ oz.	40 g
Cooked Salmon	2½ lb.	1.2 kg	10 lb.	4.5 kg
Mornay Sauce	2 cups	5 dl	2 qt.	2 l
Swiss Cheese, grated	2 oz.	60 g	8 oz.	225 g

Cook the spinach in salted boiling water. Cool and squeeze out excess moisture. Chop coarsely and saute in butter. Spread the spinach over bottom of a buttered baking dish. Skin, bone, and flake the salmon. Cover the spinach with salmon and coat with mornay sauce. Sprinkle with cheese and add a few dots of butter on top. Bake for 10 minutes at 375°F (190°C). Brown under a broiler.

Smoked Salmon with Blinis and Red Caviar

A colorful combination of thinly sliced smoked salmon and red caviar, served with blinis. This is ideal for a brunch.

Salmon Gratine Nantua

Ingredients	6 portions		24 portions	
	U.S.	Metric	U.S.	Metric
Poached Salmon, boned and skinned	2½ lb.	1.200 kg	10 lb.	4.500 kg
Mushroom Caps	6 oz.	170 g	1½ lb.	675 g
Butter	1 oz.	30 g	3 oz.	90 g
Lemon Juice	2 tsp.	2 tsp.	1½ oz.	0.5 dl
Nantua Sauce	2 cups	5 dl	2 qt.	2 l
Parmesan or Swiss Cheese, grated	2 oz.	60 g	8 oz.	230 g

Wash and slice the mushroom caps. Melt the butter in a saucepan. Add the lemon juice and mushrooms. Cook over medium heat until mushrooms are tender.

Flake the salmon in a buttered baking dish. Spread the mushrooms over the salmon and cover with the nantua sauce. Sprinkle with the cheese and bake at 375°F (190°C) for 15 minutes, or until golden brown.

Salmon Provencale

Ingredients	6 portions		24 portions	
	U.S.	Metric	U.S.	Metric
Onion, peeled and sliced	1	1	3	3
Olive Oil	2 tsp.	2 tsp.	1½ oz.	0.5 dl
Garlic Clove, chopped	1	1	3	3
Nicoise Olives, pitted	1 doz.	1 doz.	3–4 doz.	3–4 doz.
Tomato Sauce	2 cups	5 dl	2 qt.	2 l
Cooked Salmon	2½ lb.	1.2 kg	10 lb.	4.5 kg
Fresh Bread Crumbs	1 oz.	30 g	4 oz.	110 g

Heat the oil in a frying pan and saute the onion over low heat until tender. Add the garlic and sliced olives. Simmer over medium heat for 5 minutes. Mix in the tomato sauce and simmer for 10 minutes.

Flake the salmon in a buttered baking dish. Pour the sauce over. Sprinkle with the bread crumbs and bake at 350°F (180°C) for 15 minutes.

Salmon Salad

Ingredients	6 portions		24 portions	
	U.S.	Metric	U.S.	Metric
Cooked Salmon, boned and skinned	2½ lb.	1.2 kg	10 lb.	4.5 kg
Small Cucumber	1	1	4	4
Mayonnaise	2 cups	5 dl	2 qt.	2 l
Oil and Vinegar Dressing	½ cup	1.2 dl	2 cups	5 dl
Salt	½ tsp.	½ tsp.	2 tsp.	2 tsp.
White Pepper, freshly ground .	⅛ tsp.	⅛ tsp.	½ tsp.	½ tsp.
Fresh Tomatoes	2	2	8	8
Butter	2 tbsp.	25 g	4 oz.	110 g

Flake the salmon. Combine mayonnaise, oil and vinegar dressing, salt, and pepper. Fold the mayonnaise mixture with the salmon. Arrange on a serving platter and surround with tomato wedges and sliced cucumber. Serve a cold sauce separately.

Salmon Steaks in White Wine Sauce

Ingredients	6 portions		24 portions	
	U.S.	Metric	U.S.	Metric
Salmon Steaks	6	6	24	24
Salt	½ tsp.	½ tsp.	2 tsp.	2 tsp.
White Pepper, ground	¼ tsp.	¼ tsp.	1 tsp.	1 tsp.
Fish Stock	3 cups	7.5 dl	3 qt.	3 l
Butter	1½ oz.	40 g	3 oz.	85 g
Flour	1½ oz.	40 g	3 oz.	85 g
Egg Yolks	2	2	6	6
Heavy Cream	¾ cup	2 dl	3 cups	7.5 dl

Season the salmon steaks with salt and pepper and arrange, side by side, in a baking dish. Pour the cold fish stock over, bring to a simmer, and poach for 5 minutes. Remove bones and skin. Arrange the fish on a serving platter.

Reduce the cooking liquid to 2¼ cups (5 dl) or 2¼ quarts (2 l). Melt the butter in a saucepan. Stir in the flour and cook over low heat for 5 minutes. Whip in the stock and simmer over medium heat for about 10 minutes, stirring occasionally. Beat the egg yolks lightly with the cream. Whip into the sauce but do not allow it to boil. Season to taste with salt and pepper. Strain over the salmon steaks and serve at once.

Salmon Steaks Italienne

Ingredients	6 portions		24 portions	
	U.S.	Metric	U.S.	Metric
Shallots, chopped	1½ tbsp.	1½ tbsp.	1½ oz.	45 g
Mushrooms, washed and sliced	6 oz.	170 g	1½ lb.	675 g
Salmon Steaks	6	6	24	24
Dry White Wine	1½ cups	4 dl	1½ qt.	1.5 l
Fish Stock	¾ cup	2 dl	3 cups	7.5 dl
Green Pepper, diced small	1	1	3	3
Canned Whole Tomatoes	12 oz.	340 g	3 lb.	1.3 kg
Flour	2 tsp.	2 tsp.	1½ oz.	45 g
Butter	2 tbsp.	2 tbsp.	2¼ oz.	60 g

Butter a baking pan large enough to hold the salmon steaks. Sprinkle shallots and mushrooms on bottom. Place the salmon steaks over them side by side. Pour the wine and fish stock over, and add the chopped tomatoes and green pepper. Cover with a sheet of foil. Bring to a boil over medium heat and bake at 350°F (180°C) for 10 to 12 minutes. Skin and bone the steaks and transfer to a serving platter.

Strain the cooking liquid and reserve the garnish. Boil the cooking liquid for 10 minutes. Thicken with the mixture of flour and soft butter, and whip until sauce is smooth and medium thick. Simmer for about 5 minutes. Season with salt and pepper to taste. Place some of the garnish on top of each salmon steak. Cover with the sauce and serve at once.

Reduce the cooking liquid by half. Add the heavy cream and lobster butter and continue cooking until the sauce reaches the right consistency. Mix in the hollandaise sauce. Pour over the salmon steaks. Top with mushroom caps, sauteed in butter, and serve immediately.

Salmon Steaks en Papillottee

Ingredients	6 portions		24 portions	
	U.S.	Metric	U.S.	Metric
Salmon Steaks	6	6	24	24
Salt	½ tsp.	½ tsp.	2 tsp.	2 tsp.
White Pepper, ground	⅛ tsp.	⅛ tsp.	¾ tsp.	¾ tsp.
Lemon Juice	2 tsp.	2 tsp.	2½ tbsp.	2½ tbsp.
Heart-shaped Parchment Paper	6	6	24	24
Bacon Slices	6	6	24	24
Juniper Berries	18	18	72	72
Hollandaise Sauce	1½ cups	4 dl	1½ qt.	1.5 l

Season the salmon steaks with salt, pepper, and lemon juice. Wrap a slice of bacon around each steak. Place three juniper berries on top of each steak. Place each steak on one side of a sheet of parchment pa-per. Fold the other side over and seal well. Brush the paper with melted butter to prevent burning.

Arrange the salmon steaks on a baking sheet and bake at 400°F (200°C) for 15 to 20 min-utes. The bags will then be puffed. Unwrap and transfer the steaks to a serving platter. Serve the hollandaise sauce sepa-rately.

Salmon Steaks St. Laurent

Ingredients	6 portions		24 portions	
	U.S.	Metric	U.S.	Metric
Butter	1½ oz.	40 g	6 oz.	170 g
Onion, chopped	2 tsp.	2 tsp.	3 tbsp.	3 tbsp.
Shallots, chopped	4 tsp.	4 tsp.	1½ oz.	40 g
Chives, chopped	2 tsp.	2 tsp.	3 tbsp.	3 tbsp.
Tarragon, chopped	1 tsp.	1 tsp.	1 tbsp.	1 tbsp.
Sorrel, chopped	2 tsp.	2 tsp.	2 tbsp.	2 tbsp.
Mushrooms, chopped	2 tbsp.	2 tbsp.	4 oz.	120 g
Fresh Tomatoes, peeled and chopped	2 small	2 small	6 medium	6 medium
Dry White Wine	6 oz.	2 dl	3 cups	7.5 dl
Fish Fumet	1½ cups	4 dl	6 cups	1.5 l
Brandy	2 tsp.	2 tsp.	1½ oz.	.5 dl
Salmon Steaks	6—7 oz.	6—200 g	24—7 oz.	24—200 g
Heavy Cream	6 oz.	2 dl	3 cups	7.5 dl
Lobster Butter	2 tsp.	2 tsp.	3 tbsp.	3 tbsp.
Hollandaise Sauce	1 tbsp.	1 tbsp.	2 oz.	0.6 dl
Mushroom Caps	6	6	24	24
Butter	1 tbsp.	1 tbsp.	2 oz.	50 g

Melt the butter in a saucepan. Add the onion, shallots, chives, tarragon, sorrel, and mush-rooms. Cook over low heat for 5 minutes. Add the tomatoes. Simmer for a few minutes. Pour in the white wine, fish fumet, and brandy.

Place the salmon steaks in a buttered baking pan. Pour the cooking liquid over and bake for 20 minutes at 350°F (180°C). Transfer the salmon to a serving platter, after removing bones and skin. Keep warm.

Souffle of Smoked Salmon

Ingredients	6 portions		24 portions	
	U.S.	Metric	U.S.	Metric
Butter	2 oz.	60 g	8 oz.	230 g
Flour	2 oz.	60 g	8 oz.	230 g
Milk, scalded	1½ cups	4 dl	6 cups	1.5 l
White Pepper, ground	¼ tsp.	¼ tsp.	1 tsp.	1 tsp.
Nutmeg, ground	⅛ tsp.	⅛ tsp.	½ tsp.	½ tsp.
Smoked Salmon, finely chopped	1 lb. 2 oz.	500 g	4½ lb.	2 kg
Eggs, separated	5	5	20	20

Melt the butter in a saucepan. Add the flour and cook over medium heat for 5 minutes. Cool the roux. Pour the milk into the roux. Whip and return to heat until the sauce thickens and comes to a boil. Season with pepper and nutmeg. Mix in the salmon. Cool the mixture. Add the egg yolks and blend well.

Whip the egg whites until medium stiff. Fold into the salmon mixture. Pour into 1 (4) 7-inch souffle dish(es) that has been buttered and floured. Bake in the middle of the oven for 30 minutes at 350°F (180°C). Serve immediately.

Note: A veloute sauce made with salmon bones is the ideal accompaniment for this souffle.

Sardine (Atlantic Herring)

For sardine recipes, see chapter 15, Nibbling On Seafood.

Sea Bass

Sea bass can be prepared following trout recipes.

Sea Bass Royale

See Mousseline of Salmon Royale.

White Sea Bass Mariniere

Ingredients	6 portions		24 portions	
	U.S.	Metric	U.S.	Metric
Onions	8 oz.	225 g	2 lb.	900 g
Carrots	2	2	8	8
Leeks	2	2	8	8
Celery Sticks	2	2	8	8
Bay Leaves	2	2	8	8
Olive Oil	½ cup	1.2 dl	2 cups	5 dl
Butter	2 oz.	50 g	8 oz.	225 g
Whole White Sea Bass, dressed	1—4 ½ lb.	1—2 kg	4—4½ lb.	4—2 kg
White Wine	2 cups	5 dl	2 qt.	2 l
Salt	1 tsp.	1 tsp.	1 tbsp.	1 tbsp.
Pepper, ground	¼ tsp.	¼ tsp.	1 tsp.	1 tsp.
Lemon Butter	6 oz.	170 g	1¾ lb.	700 g

Clean and slice the vegetables. Brown lightly in oil and butter. Add the bay leaves and wine. Simmer for 10 minutes. Clean and scale the sea bass. Place in buttered baking pan(s). Add the cooking liquid with the vegetables, and season with salt and pepper. Bake at 350°F (180°C) for 25 to 30 minutes.

Transfer to a serving platter. Pour cooking liquid over and garnish with the vegetables. Serve with lemon butter.

Sea Trout

Sea trout can be prepared following rainbow trout and salmon recipes.

Shad

Baked Fillets of Shad with Roe Stuffing

Ingredients	6 portions		24 portions	
	U.S.	Metric	U.S.	Metric
Fillets of Shad, boneless	2 lb.	900 g	8 lb.	3.6 kg
Shad Roe				
Butter	2 oz.	50 g	8 oz.	225 g
Fresh Bread Crumbs	4 oz.	110 g	1 lb.	450 g
Salt	½ tsp.	½ tsp.	2 tsp.	2 tsp.
Eggs, beaten	1	1	4	4
Sage, ground	¼ tsp.	¼ tsp.	1 tsp.	1 tsp.
Lemon Butter	½ cup	1.2 dl	2 cups	5 dl

Parboil the shad roe in salted boiling water for 5 to 6 minutes. Drain and allow to cool. Remove the tissue and break the small eggs apart. Add the bread crumbs, seasonings, eggs, melted butter. Spread the stuffing over each fillet. Put two fillets together, with stuffing in the middle and skin on the outside. Tie each pair with a string.

Place the trussed fillets on a greased sheet pan. Bake at 400°F (204°C) for 25 to 30 minutes, basting with lemon butter while cooking. Transfer to a warm serving dish.

Broiled Marinated Fillets of Shad

Ingredients	6 portions		24 portions	
	U.S.	Metric	U.S.	Metric
Fillets of Shad, boneless	2 lb.	900 g	8 lb.	3.6 kg
Vegetable Oil	½ cup	1.2 dl	2 cups	5 dl
Lemon Juice	1 oz.	0.3 dl	½ cup	1.2 dl
Salt	1 tsp.	1 tsp.	1 tbsp.	1 tbsp.
Parsley, chopped	1 tbsp.	1 tbsp.	4 tbsp.	4 tbsp.
Rosemary	1 tsp.	1 tsp.	4 tsp.	4 tsp.
Bay Leaf	1	1	4	4
Mayonnaise	¼ cup	0.6 dl	1 cup	2.5 dl
Scallions, chopped	1	1	4	4
French Dressing	¼ cup	0.6 dl	1 cup	2.5 dl

Place the fillets of shad, skin side down, in a shallow dish. Combine all the ingredients for the marinade. Pour over the fillets. Refrigerate overnight and allow the fillets to come to room temperature before broiling.

Place fillets, skin side down, on a preheated broiler pan,

about 3 inches (7.5 cm) from the source of heat. Baste liberally with the marinade after two minutes of broiling. Continue broiling until the fish is flaky, about 6 to 8 minutes.

The juice at the bottom of the pan can be used to prepare a sauce to accompany the fish. The shad roe can be marinated at the same time and broiled on both sides.

Delaware Planked Shad

Ingredients	6 portions		24 portions	
	U.S.	Metric	U.S.	Metric
Whole Shad, 4 lb. (1.8 kg)	1	1	4	4
Salt	¼ tsp.	¼ tsp.	1 tsp.	1 tsp.
Pepper, ground	⅛ tsp.	⅛ tsp.	½ tsp.	½ tsp.
Butter	2 oz.	50 g	8 oz.	225 g
Lemon Wedges	6	6	24	24

Scale, wash, fillet, and bone the shad, following the instructions in chapter 5. Place skin side down on a heated plank, 1 inch (2.5 cm) longer than the fish. Sprinkle with salt and pepper. Brush with melted butter. Broil 2 inches (5 cm) from source of heat for 10 to 15 minutes. Serve with lemon wedges.

Fillets of Shad Provencale

Ingredients	6 portions		24 portions	
	U.S.	Metric	U.S.	Metric
Fillets of Shad, boned	2 lb.	900 g	8 lb.	3.6 kg
Salt	½ tsp.	½ tsp.	2 tsp.	2 tsp.
Worcestershire Sauce	1 tsp.	1 tsp.	1 tbsp.	1 tbsp.
Dry White Wine	¾ cup	2 dl	3 cups	8 dl
Onion, chopped	4 oz.	110 g	1 lb.	450 g
Garlic Cloves, minced	2	2	8	8
Medium Green Peppers, diced	2	2	8	8
Tomatoes, chopped and seedless	1 lb.	450 g	4 lb.	1.8 kg
Parsley, chopped	1 tbsp.	1 tbsp.	4 tbsp.	4 tbsp.

Arrange the fillets on a greased sheet pan(s). Sprinkle with salt and worcestershire sauce. Pour the wine over. Saute the onion in hot oil, add the garlic, green peppers, and tomatoes, and cook over medium heat for 15 minutes. Spoon the sauce over the fillets of shad and bake at 350°F (180°C) for about 15 to 20 minutes. Test for doneness. Transfer to a warm serving platter. Sprinkle with chopped parsley before serving.

Shad Roe Souffle

Ingredients	6 portions U.S.	Metric	24 portions U.S.	Metric
Butter	2 oz.	50 g	8 oz.	225 g
Flour	2 oz.	50 g	8 oz.	225 g
Fish Fumet	2 cups	5 dl	2 qt.	2 l
Pair of Shad Roe	1	1	4	4
Lemon Juice	1 tbsp.	1 tbsp.	¼ cup	0.6 dl
Egg Yolks	5	5	20	20
Parsley, chopped	1 tbsp.	1 tbsp.	4 tbsp.	4 tbsp.
Egg Whites	5	5	20	20

Melt butter in a saucepan. Stir in flour and cook over low heat for 5 minutes. Add the hot fumet to make a veloute. Cook until thickened, stirring continuously. Transfer to a mixing bowl.

Cook the shad roe in salted boiling water. Remove the membrane. Stir into the veloute. Mix in the egg yolks and parsley. Season to taste with salt and pepper. Beat the egg whites until stiff. Fold into the sauce.

Butter and flour 2-qt. (2-1) souffle dish(es). Pour in the souffle mixture. Bake at 350°F (180°C) for 30 to 40 minutes. Serve immediately.

Sheepshead

Sheepshead can be prepared following fillet of sole recipes.

Smelt
(Icefish, Frostfish, Candlelight Fish)

Fried Smelt

Ingredients	6 portions U.S.	Metric	24 portions U.S.	Metric
Whole Clean Smelts	3 lb.	1.4 kg	12 lb.	5.4 kg
Flour	4 oz.	110 g	1 lb.	450 g
Parsley Sprigs	1 oz.	25 g	4 oz.	110 g
Season Salt	1 tsp.	1 tsp.	1 tbsp.	1 tbsp.
Pepper	¼ tsp.	¼ tsp.	1 tsp.	1 tsp.
Lemon Wedges	6	6	24	24
Oil, for deep frying				

Toss the smelts in the seasoned flour. Shake off excess flour. Deep fry at 375°F (190°C) until golden brown and crisp. Fry the dry parsley for 3 to 5 seconds.

Arrange smelts in a round serving platter. Garnish with lemon wedges and fried parsley. Serve hot.

Note: Smelt can also be pan fried.

Sole

Broiled Fillets of Sole, Sweet and Sour Sauce

Ingredients	6 portions		24 portions	
	U.S.	Metric	U.S.	Metric
Fillets of Sole	12	12	4 doz.	4 doz.
Salt	½ tsp.	½ tsp.	2 tsp.	2 tsp.
Pepper, ground	¼ tsp.	¼ tsp.	1 tsp.	1 tsp.
Flour	2 oz.	50 g	8 oz.	225 g
Oil	2 oz.	0.6 dl	1 cup	2.5 dl
Sweet and Sour Sauce	1 cup	2.5 dl	1 qt.	1 l
Lemon Wedges	6	6	24	24
Parsley				

Trim the fillets. Flatten. Season with salt and pepper. Dredge in flour, dip in oil, and broil on a hot grill, making a quarter turn to mark the fillets with a checkered pattern. Turn fillets over and cook until flaky. Arrange the fillets on a heated platter. Pour hot sauce over. Garnish with lemon wedges and sprigs of parsley.

Pour the cooking liquid into a saucepan. Reduce to two thirds, and add it to the heavy cream and veloute sauce. Bring to a boil and stir in the hollandaise sauce. Transfer the fillets to a warm serving platter. Cover with the sauce and glaze under a hot broiler. Serve immediately.

Dover Sole Meuniere

Ingredients	6 portions		24 portions	
	U.S.	Metric	U.S.	Metric
Dover Sole (whole)	6—7 oz.	6—200 g	24—7 oz.	24—200 g
Salt	½ tsp.	½ tsp.	2 tsp.	2 tsp.
Pepper, ground	¼ tsp.	¼ tsp.	1 tsp.	1 tsp.
Butter	6 oz.	170 g	1½ lb.	680 g
Vegetable Oil	3 oz.	1 dl	1½ cup	4 dl
Flour	3.5 oz.	100 g	14 oz.	400 g
Lemon Slices	6	6	24	24
Parsley, chopped	1 tbsp.	1 tbsp.	4 tbsp.	4 tbsp.

Skin the sole. Cut off the fins and remove the intestines. Wash under cold running water. Salt and pepper on both sides. Dredge in flour. Heat a small amount of butter and oil in a large skillet and brown the fish with the white skin side down. Turn the soles and cook until the flesh can be separated easily from the bones. Remove the bones. Arrange the whole soles on a serving platter. Melt the butter in a clean frying pan until brown. Pour the lemon juice over the fish, sprinkle on the parsley, and pour the hot foamy butter over the fish. Decorate with lemon slices and serve immediately.

Fillets of Sole Bonne Femme

Ingredients	6 portions		24 portions	
	U.S.	Metric	U.S.	Metric
Mushrooms, sliced	7 oz.	200 g	1¾ lb.	800 g
Shallots, chopped	2 oz.	50 g	8 oz.	200 g
Parsley, chopped	1 tbsp.	1 tbsp.	4 tbsp.	4 tbsp.
Fillets of Sole	12	12	48	48
Dry White Wine	¾ cup	2 dl	3 cups	8 dl
Fish Fumet	2 cups	5 dl	2 qt.	2 l
Butter	5 oz.	150 g	1¼ lb.	600 g
Heavy Cream	1 cup	2.5 dl	1 qt.	1 l
Veloute Sauce	1 cup	2.5 dl	1 qt.	1 l
Hollandaise Sauce	2 oz.	0.6 dl	1 cup	2.5 dl

Butter a baking sheet. Sprinkle with shallots, chopped parsley, and sliced mushrooms. Flatten and fold the fillets in half. Arrange on top of the mushrooms. Season with salt and pepper. Moisten with some of the white wine and fish fumet. Cover fish with parchment paper and bake at 350°F (180°C) for 10 to 15 minutes.

Fillets of Sole Dieppoise

Ingredients	6 portions		24 portions	
	U.S.	Metric	U.S.	Metric
Butter	4 oz.	110 g	1 lb.	450 g
Shallots, chopped	1 tbsp.	1 tbsp.	4 tbsp.	4 tbsp.
Fillets of Sole	12	12	48	48
White Wine	5 oz.	1.5 dl	2½ cups	6 dl
Fish Fumet	2 cups	5 dl	2 qt.	2 l
Cooked Mussels and Juice	4 oz.	110 g	1 lb.	450 g
Medium Shrimp, cooked	4 oz.	110 g	1 lb.	450 g
Whole Mushrooms, fluted	6	6	24	24
Fleurons	6	6	24	24
White Wine Sauce, see chapter 11				

Butter a baking pan and sprinkle with the chopped shallots. Fold the fillets in half and arrange in the pan. Pour over the wine, fish fumet, and mussel cooking juice. Cover with parchment paper and bring to a boil on top of the stove. Bake at 350°F (180°C) for approximately 5 to 8 minutes.

Arrange the fish fillets on a serving platter. Garnish with the mussels, shrimp, and fluted mushrooms. Prepare the white wine sauce with fish fumet. Pour over the fish. Garnish with fleurons and serve hot.

Fillets of Sole Domino

Ingredients	6 portions		24 portions	
	U.S.	Metric	U.S.	Metric
Fillets of Sole	12	12	48	48
Salt	½ tsp.	½ tsp.	2 tsp.	2 tsp.
Pepper, ground	¼ tsp.	¼ tsp.	1 tsp.	1 tsp.
Fish Fumet	2 cups	5 dl	2 qt.	2 l
Dry White Wine	1 cup	2.5 dl	1 qt.	1 l
Truffle Sheet	½ recipe	½ recipe	1 recipe	1 recipe
Mayonnaise Chaud-Froid	2 cups	5 dl	2 qt.	2 l

Trim and flatten fillets. Season with salt and pepper. Fold them in thirds. The maximum length should be 3 inches. Place fillets in a buttered baking dish. Cover with fumet and wine. Bake for 15 minutes at 400°F (205°C). Cool the fish. Trim each fillet into a rectangle, 3 by 1¼ inches (7.5 by 3 cm).

Coat with mayonnaise chaud-froid. Decorate the rectangles like dominos using the truffle sheet. Arrange on a platter and garnish with aspic jelly made with fish fumet and wine (see chapter 16).

Fillets of Sole Rosette

Ingredients	6 portions		24 portions	
	U.S.	Metric	U.S.	Metric
Fillets of Sole	12	12	48	48
Salt	½ tsp.	½ tsp.	2 tsp.	2 tsp.
Pepper, ground	¼ tsp.	¼ tsp.	1 tsp.	1 tsp.
Whole Eggs	3	3	12	12
Oil......................	2 oz.	0.6 dl	1 cup	2.5 dl
Flour....................	3 oz.	85 g	12 oz.	340 g
Fresh Bread Crumbs........	12 oz.	340 g	3 lb.	1.360 kg
Medium Eggplant	1	1	4	4
Butter	4 oz.	110 g	1 lb.	450 g
Lemon Butter	4 oz.	110 g	1 lb.	450 g

Season the fillets with salt and pepper. Mix the eggs with the oil. Dip the fillets and coat with the bread crumbs. Melt some butter in a frying pan and saute the fillets until golden brown. Peel and slice the eggplant into rings. Season and flour, and deep fry in oil. Drain on absorbent paper. Arrange the fillets of sole on a warm serving platter. Garnish with eggplant rings. Sprinkle with lemon butter.

Fillets of Sole Roubette

Ingredients	6 portions		24 portions	
	U.S.	Metric	U.S.	Metric
Smoked Salmon Mousse	½ recipe	½ recipe	2 recipes	2 recipes
Fillets of Sole	12	12	48	48
White Wine	½ cup	1.2 dl	2 cups	5 dl
Fish Fumet	½ cup	1.2 dl	2 cups	5 dl
Shallots, chopped	1 tbsp.	1 tbsp.	4 tbsp.	4 tbsp.
Sauce Americaine	2 cups	5 dl	2 qt.	2 l
Fish Veloute	½ cup	1.2 dl	2 cups	5 dl
Heavy Cream	½ cup	1.2 dl	2 cups	5 dl
Aspic Jelly	1 cup	2.5 dl	1 qt.	1 l
Cold Liquid Jelly	½ cup	1.2 dl	2 cups	5 dl
Apic Sheets (truffle and egg whites)				

Flatten each fillet with a mallet. Poach the fillets in white wine, fish fumet, and shallots.

Cool the fillets and assemble by twos with salmon mousse between the fillets.

Combine the sauce Americaine, veloute sauce, heavy cream, and aspic. Coat each fillet with the cold sauce. Glaze with cold liquid jelly. Trim and cut the fillets in half. Decorate with truffle and egg white cutouts.

The sole trimmings can be chopped finely, mixed with a small amount of sauce Americaine, and shaped into small balls. Roll in chopped truffle peelings and arrange around platter.

Fillets of Sole Tour d'Argent

Ingredients	6 portions		24 portions	
	U.S.	Metric	U.S.	Metric
Fillets of Sole	12	12	48	48
Salt	½ tsp.	½ tsp.	2 tsp.	2 tsp.
Pepper, ground	¼ tsp.	¼ tsp.	1 tsp.	1 tsp.
Strong Fish Fumet	2 cups	5 dl	2 qt.	2 l
Dry Vermouth	1 cup	2.5 dl	1 qt.	1 l
Tomatoes, peeled, seeded, and chopped	1 lb.	450 g	4 lb.	1.8 kg
Hollandaise Sauce	3 oz.	1 dl	1½ cups	4 dl

Trim and flatten the fillets. Season with salt and pepper. Poach in the fumet, vermouth, and tomatoes. Drain the fillets and keep warm on a serving platter.

Reduce the cooking liquid until thickened. Stir in the hollandaise sauce. Adjust seasoning. Strain over the fillets and serve at once.

Fillets of Sole Venitienne

Ingredients	6 portions		24 portions	
	U.S.	Metric	U.S.	Metric
Spinach, cooked	1 lb.	450 g	4 lb.	1.8 kg
Butter	2 oz.	50 g	8 oz.	225 g
Garlic Clove, crushed	1	1	4	4
Salt	½ tsp.	½ tsp.	2 tsp.	2 tsp.
Pepper	¼ tsp.	¼ tsp.	1 tsp.	1 tsp.
Fillets of Sole	12	12	48	48
Parsley, chopped	1 tbsp.	1 tbsp.	4 tbsp.	4 tbsp.
Fresh Bread Crumbs	2 oz.	50 g	8 oz.	225 g
Lemon Wedges	6	6	24	24

Chop the spinach. Saute in butter. Add garlic and season with half of the salt and pepper. Flatten the fillets. Season with remaining salt and pepper. Spread spinach over each fillet. Starting with the thickest end, roll the fillets and hold them with toothpicks. Arrange in a buttered baking dish. Sprinkle with the bread crumbs and some melted butter. Bake at 350°F (180°C) for 20 to 25 minutes. Serve hot. Garnish with parsley and lemon.

Gougeonnettes of Sole

Ingredients	6 portions		24 portions	
	U.S.	Metric	U.S.	Metric
Fillets of Sole	2 lb.	900 g	8 lb.	3.6 kg
Salt	½ tsp.	½ tsp.	2 tsp.	2 tsp.
Pepper, ground	¼ tsp.	¼ tsp.	1 tsp.	1 tsp.
Whole Eggs	4	4	16	16
Flour	3 oz.	85 g	12 oz.	340 g
Fresh Bread Crumbs	12 oz.	340 g	3 lb.	1.360 kg
Lemon Wedges	6	6	24	24
Tartare Sauce	1 cup	2.5 dl	1 qt.	1 l

Cut the fillets. Season with salt and pepper. Roll the strips in flour, dip in beaten eggs, and coat in bread crumbs. Deep fry at 375°F (190°C) for 2 to 3 minutes. Arrange on a warm serving platter covered with a napkin. Garnish with lemon wedges. Serve the tartare sauce separately.

Grilled Dover Sole, Bearnaise

Ingredients	6 portions		24 portions	
	U.S.	Metric	U.S.	Metric
Dover Soles (whole)	6—7 oz.	6—200 g	24—7 oz.	24—200 g
Salt and Pepper, to taste				
Thyme, crushed	¼ tsp.	¼ tsp.	1 tsp.	1 tsp.
Lemon, sliced	1	1	4	4
Oil	½ cup	1.2 dl	2 cups	5 dl
Lemons and Parsley, for garnish				
Butter, melted				
Bearnaise Sauce	1½ cups	4 dl	1½ qt.	1.5 l

Prepare the sole as described on page 105. Wash under cold water and dry well. Arrange the fish on a sheet pan. Season with salt, pepper, thyme, and lemon slices. Sprinkle with the oil and refrigerate while preparing the bearnaise sauce.

Cook the whole fish on a hot grill or charcoal broiler. Give the fish a quarter turn to obtain a checkered pattern. Turn the sole over and repeat the same process until fully cooked. Arrange the sole on a warm serving platter. Garnish with lemon baskets filled with parsley. Brush melted butter over the fish before serving. Serve the bearnaise sauce separately.

Lemon Sole Tart

Ingredients	6 portions		24 portions	
	U.S.	Metric	U.S.	Metric
Whiting Fillets	2	2	8	8
Fish Fumet	2 cups	5 dl	2 qt.	2 l
White Wine	1 cup	2.5 dl	1 qt.	1 l
Fresh Mushrooms, chopped . .	7 oz.	200 g	1¾ lb.	800 g
Shallots, chopped	1 tbsp.	1 tbsp.	4 tbsp.	4 tbsp.
Butter	1 oz.	25 g	4 oz.	110 g
Fillets of Lemon Sole	6	6	2 doz.	2 doz.
Butter	2 oz.	50 g	8 oz.	225 g
Flour	2 oz.	50 g	8 oz.	225 g
Heavy Cream	¼ cup	0.6 dl	1 cup	2.5 dl
Cooked Pie Crust Shell(s), 8 in. (20 cm)	1	1	4	4
Small Artichoke Bottoms	6	6	24	24
Cooked Shrimp	5 oz.	140 g	1¼ lb.	560 g

Poach the whiting fillets in fish fumet and white wine. Drain and flake the fillets. Saute the shallots in butter. Add the mushrooms. Mix in the flaked whiting.

Flatten and roll the sole fillets, holding them with toothpicks.

Poach in the fumet. Drain and reserve in a warm place.

Prepare a roux with the butter and flour. Add the fumet. Bring to a boil. Stir in the cream. Season to taste with salt and pepper.

Spread the bottom of the pie shell(s) with the whiting mixture. Arrange the artichoke bottoms on top. Top each artichoke with a fillet of sole, removing the toothpicks. Strain the sauce. Add the shrimp, and coat the fillets. Heat for 5 to 10 minutes before serving.

Pate of Fillet of Sole

Ingredients	6 portions		24 portions	
	U.S.	Metric	U.S.	Metric
Fillets of Sole	1 lb.	450 g	4 lb.	1.8 kg
Salt and Pepper, to taste				
Salmon Quenelle Forcemeat (chapter 9)	12 oz.	340 g	3 lb.	1.4 kg
Black Truffles, diced	1 oz.	25 g	4 oz.	110 g
Pistachio Nuts	2 oz.	50 g	8 oz.	225 g

Flatten the fillets of sole. Season with salt and pepper. Spread each fillet with some of the prepared quenelle forcemeat. Set into a suitable pate

mold, alternating with leftover forcemeat, truffles and pistachios. Cover the mold. Bake in a waterbath at 350°F (180°C) for 45 minutes. Cool, then re-

frigerate. Slice onto a serving platter and serve with a cold sauce.

Sole Colbert

Ingredients	6 portions		24 portions	
	U.S.	Metric	U.S.	Metric
Medium Dover Sole	6	6	24	24
Eggs	3	3	12	12
Oil........................	1 tbsp.	1 tbsp.	2 oz.	0.6 dl
Salt	½ tsp.	½ tsp.	2 tsp.	2 tsp.
Pepper	¼ tsp.	¼ tsp.	1 tsp.	1 tsp.
Flour.....................	3½ oz.	100 g	14 oz.	400 g
Fresh Bread Crumbs........	10 oz.	280 g	2½ lb.	1.2 kg
Oil, for frying				
Lemons	3	3	12	12
Maitre d'Hotel Butter	6 oz.	170 g	1½ lb.	680 g

Wash the sole. Cut off the fins and skin both sides. Clean and butterfly the fish (see illustration in chapter 5). Mix eggs and oil, and season with salt and pepper. Dip the dry fish lightly in the flour, egg mixture, and bread crumbs.

Fry in a deep fryer at 360°F (185°C) for 6 to 8 minutes. Drain the sole and remove the center bones. Serve with lemon wedges and maitre d'hotel butter.

Stuffed Fillets of Sole with Quenelles

Ingredients	6 portions		24 portions	
	U.S.	Metric	U.S.	Metric
Fillets of Sole	12	12	48	48
Small Quenelles of Salmon, Bass, et cetera	12	12	48	48
Fish Fumet	2 cups	5 dl	2 qt.	2 l
White Wine	½ cup	1.2 dl	2 cups	5 dl
Mushrooms	3 oz.	85 g	12 oz.	340 g
Butter	2 oz.	50 g	8 oz.	225 g
Flour.....................	1 oz.	25 g	4 oz.	110 g
Salt and Pepper, to taste				
Heavy Cream	½ cup	1.2 dl	2 cups	5 dl
Cooked Shrimp, peeled and deveined	2 oz.	50 g	8 oz.	225 g

Flatten the fillets of sole. Roll each fillet around a quenelle. Secure with a toothpick. Poach in the fumet and wine.

Saute the sliced mushrooms in a small amount of butter. Prepare a roux with remaining butter and flour. Stir in the fumet to make a veloute.

Arrange the stuffed fillets on a serving platter. Season the sauce to taste. Add the cream and reduce for 5 to 10 minutes. Strain the sauce. Garnish the fish with the mushrooms and shrimp. Coat the fish with the sauce. Heat before serving.

Turban of Sole with Red Snapper Mousse

Ingredients	6 portions		24 portions	
	U.S.	Metric	U.S.	Metric
Fillets of Sole	1 lb.	450 g	4 lb.	1.8 kg
Mousse of Red Snapper, page 229	1 recipe	1 recipe	4 recipes	4 recipes
White Wine Sauce or Sauce Cardinal	2 cups	5 dl	2 qt.	2 l

Butter ring mold(s) and line with the boneless, trimmed fillets of sole. Fill the mold with the mousse. Cover with foil. Bake in a waterbath at 350°F (180°C) for 30–35 minutes. Unmold on a round serving platter. Coat with the hot sauce. Serve immediately.

Turban of Sole with Salmon Mousse

Ingredients	6 portions		24 portions	
	U.S.	Metric	U.S.	Metric
Salmon, boneless and skinless	1 lb.	450 g	4 lb.	1.8 kg
Egg Whites	2	2	8	8
Heavy Cream	1 cup	2.5 dl	1 qt.	1 l
Salt	½ tsp.	½ tsp.	1½ tbsp.	1½ tbsp.
White Pepper	¼ tsp.	¼ tsp.	1 tsp.	1 tsp.
Nutmeg	¼ tsp.	¼ tsp.	1 tsp.	1 tsp.
Dill, chopped	1 tsp.	1 tsp.	1½ tbsp.	1½ tbsp.
Sole Fillets	1½ lb.	680 g	6 lb.	2.7 kg
Glazing Wine Sauce	2 cups	5 dl	2 qt.	2 l
Fleurons	6	6	24	24

Prepare a mousse with the salmon, egg whites, cream, salt, pepper, nutmeg, and dill. (For details, see chapter 9.) Line the bottom and sides of a buttered ring mold(s) with the fillets of sole. Season with salt and pepper. Fill the mold(s) with the salmon mousse. Cover with parchment paper. Bake in a waterbath at 400°F (200°C) for 40 to 45 minutes. Invert mold onto a serving platter. Coat with sauce and quickly glaze under a broiler. Garnish with fleurons and serve immediately.

Mousse of Sole Pavillon

Prepare a mousse of sole (see chapter 9). Cover with a champagne sauce made with fish veloute and champagne. Garnish with truffles.

Mousse of Sole Joinville

Prepare a mousse of sole. Coat with sauce Americaine. Garnish with cooked, diced bay scallops, shrimp, crabmeat, mushrooms, and truffles.

Delices of Sole Laperouse

Poach fillets of sole in fumet, white wine, and shallots. Poach scallops in same fumet. Reduce the cooking liquid. Whip in fresh butter. Garnish fillets of sole with scallops. Pour the light sauce over the fish.

Fillets of Sole with Cucumbers

Simmer fillets of sole in lemon butter. Cut peeled cucumbers into large olive shapes. Cook in fish fumet. Saute in lemon butter. Garnish the fillets of sole with cucumbers.

Fried Fillets of Sole with Tartare and Cocktail Sauce

Bread the fillets of sole according to standard technique. Deep fry, and serve with tartare and cocktail sauce.

Spot (Lafayette, Goody)

For preparation, refer to Croaker.

Striped Bass (Rockfish, Striper)

Cold Striped Bass, Mayonnaise Sauce

Ingredients	6 portions		24 portions	
	U.S.	Metric	U.S.	Metric
Whole Striped Bass, dressed ..	1—4½ lb.	1—2 kg	4—4½ lb.	4—2 kg
Court Bouillon no. 1 to cover fish				
Mayonnaise Sauce	2 cups	5 dl	2 qt.	2 l
Radishes and Green Leeks, to garnish				
Hard-boiled Eggs, stuffed	6	6	24	24
Aspic Jelly	2 cups	5 dl	2 qt.	2 l
Parsley, to garnish				

Fillet the clean bass. Remove backbones. Poach in court bouillon, following directions described in chapter 6. Lift cold fillets out of court bouillon. Slice crosswise into portions. Glaze each piece of fish with aspic jelly. Decorate with radish fish cutouts and blanched green leeks.

Arrange slices on round platter(s) or on a mirror (if a buffet presentation). Garnish with stuffed eggs, chopped aspic jelly, and parsley. Serve mayonnaise sauce separately.

Fillet of Striped Bass Amandine

Saute meuniere. Top with toasted sliced almonds.

Fillet of Striped Bass Bonne Femme

See Fillets of Sole Bonne Femme.

Fillet of Striped Bass Jacals

Ingredients	6 portions		24 portions	
	U.S.	Metric	U.S.	Metric
Fillets of Striped Bass	2 lb.	900 g	8 lb.	3.6 kg
Crabmeat	6 oz.	170 g	1½ lb.	680 g
Anchovy Fillets	6	6	24	24
Heavy Cream	½ cup	1.2 dl	2 cups	5 dl
Mayonnaise	½ cup	1.2 dl	2 cups	5 dl
Salt	½ tsp.	½ tsp.	2 tsp.	2 tsp.
Pepper, ground	¼ tsp.	¼ tsp.	1 tsp.	1 tsp.
Lemon Juice	1 tbsp.	1 tbsp.	¼ cup	0.6 dl

Skin and bone the fish fillets. Arrange the fillets on buttered baking pan(s). Top with the crabmeat. Chop the anchovies. Combine with the heavy cream, mayonnaise, salt, pepper, and lemon juice. Pour the sauce over the fish fillets. Bake at 350°F (180°C) for 15 to 20 minutes, or until fish flakes when tested.

Poached Striped Bass Bercy

Ingredients	6 portions		24 portions	
	U.S.	Metric	U.S.	Metric
Whole Striped Bass, dressed ..	1—4½ lb.	1—2 kg	4—4½ lb.	4—2 kg
Court Bouillon no. 1 to cover fish				
Parisianne Potatoes, boiled ...	1 lb.	450 g	4 lb.	1.8 kg
Parsley, to garnish				
Sauce Bercy	2 cups	5 dl	2 qt.	2 l

Note the presentation of the whole fish. Cut the dressed striped bass at 1½-in. (4-cm) intervals until the knife meets the back bone. Do not cut through the bones. Cut off the head and save to prepare the fumet for sauce bercy.

The fish should be poached in a curled position and presented whole, on a platter. (If fish was poached straight, it would not fit a standard size platter.) Poach in court bouillon no. 1. (See chapter 6 for technique and timing.) Lift the fish out of the court bouillon. Skin and transfer to a serving platter. Garnish with Parisianne potatoes and parsley. Serve with sauce bercy.

Striped Bass en Croute

Skin striped bass fillets. Spread with a quenelle forcemeat. Wrap in puff pastry dough (see chapter 7). Bake at 450°F (230°C) allowing 10 minutes per inch thickness. Serve with a hot sauce.

Striped Bass in Brioche

Ingredients	6 portions		24 portions	
	U.S.	Metric	U.S.	Metric
Whole Striped Bass, 4 lb. (1.8 kg)	1	1	4	4
Butter	4 oz.	110 g	1 lb.	450 g
Shallots, chopped	4 oz.	110 g	1 lb.	450 g
Vermouth	½ cup	1.2 dl	2 cups	5 dl
Onion, chopped	2 oz.	50 g	8 oz.	225 g
Fresh Mushrooms	4 oz.	110 g	1 lb.	450 g
Fresh Bread Crumbs	4 oz.	110 g	1 lb.	450 g
Hard-boiled Eggs, chopped	4	4	16	16
Parsley, chopped	1 tbsp.	1 tbsp.	4 tbsp.	4 tbsp.
Brioche Dough	1 recipe	1 recipe	4 recipes	4 recipes
Beurre Blanc (chapter 11)	½ cup	1.2 dl	2 cups	5 dl

Fillet the fish. Saute in butter with half of the shallots to stiffen the flesh. Deglaze with vermouth. Cool the fillets. Saute remaining shallots with onion in butter. Add chopped mushrooms. Cook until onion is tender. Stir in the bread crumbs and the cooking liquid from the fillets. Season to taste with salt and pepper. Add the eggs and parsley.

Spread the stuffing over each fillet. Assemble fillets by twos with stuffing in the middle. Wrap each in rolled out brioche dough. Seal edges. Brush with egg. Allow to rise for 30 minutes. Brush again. Bake at 350°F (180°C) for 40 minutes. Arrange on serving platter(s). Serve with beurre blanc.

Striped Bass Italienne

Ingredients	6 portions		24 portions	
	U.S.	Metric	U.S.	Metric
Striped Bass Fillets	2 lb.	900 g	8 lb.	3.6 kg
Salt	½ tsp.	½ tsp.	2 tsp.	2 tsp.
Pepper	¼ tsp.	¼ tsp.	1 tsp.	1 tsp.
Flour	2 oz.	50 g	8 oz.	225 g

	12	12	48	48
Cherrystone Clams	12	12	48	48
Cleaned Mussels	12	12	48	48
Tomatoes, chopped and seeded	1 lb.	450 g	4 lb.	1.8 kg
Garlic Cloves, minced	2	2	8	8
Parsley, chopped	1 tbsp.	1 tbsp.	4 tbsp.	4 tbsp.
Fresh Basil or	2 tbsp.	2 tbsp.	½ cup	45 g
Dried Basil	1 tsp.	1 tsp.	1 tbsp.	1 tbsp.
Clam Juice	¾ cup	2 dl	3 cups	8 dl

Cut fillets into 5-oz. (140-g) portions. Season with salt and pepper. Dredge in flour. Deep fry at 360°F (185°C) for 5 minutes, or until half cooked. Drain well. Arrange fish on greased baking pan(s). Surround with clams and mussels. Spoon tomatoes and garlic over fish. Sprinkle with herbs and pour clam juice over.

Bake at 350°F (180°C) for 10 to 15 minutes, or until shellfish open. Arrange fish and shellfish on serving platter(s). Pour cooking liquid over. Serve hot.

Striped Bass Royale
See Mousseline of Salmon Royale.

Striped Bass Sainte Alliance

	6 portions		24 portions	
Ingredients	U.S.	Metric	U.S.	Metric
Whole Striped Bass, 4 lb. (1.8 kg)	1	1	4	4
Fresh Salmon	1 lb.	450 g	4 lb.	1.8 kg
Heavy Cream	1 cup	2.5 dl	1 qt.	1 l
Egg Whites	3	3	12	12
Salt	½ tsp.	½ tsp.	2 tsp.	2 tsp.
Cayenne Pepper	⅛ tsp.	⅛ tsp.	½ tsp.	½ tsp.
Dry White Wine	1 cup	2.5 dl	1 qt.	1 l
Strong Fish Fumet	1 cup	2.5 dl	1 qt.	1 l
Fleurons	6	6	24	24
Mushroom Caps, cooked	6	6	24	24
Truffle Slices	6	6	24	24

Scale whole fish. Butterfly the fish, removing the backbone and leaving the two fillets attached to the belly flaps.

Make a fresh salmon mousse using the salmon, half of the heavy cream, and the beaten egg whites (see chapter 9). Season the bass. Spread the mousse over the fillets. Arrange fish on buttered baking pan(s). Add wine and fumet. Bake at 350°F (180°C) for 40 to 45 minutes.

Pour the cooking liquid into a saucepan. Add remaining cream. Reduce to one half. Arrange cooked fish on preheated serving platter(s). Pour sauce over. Garnish with fleurons and mushroom caps. Top with truffle slices.

Striped Bass with Fennel (Loup au Fenouil)

Ingredients	6 portions		24 portions	
	U.S.	Metric	U.S.	Metric
Whole Dressed Striped Bass, 4 lb. (1.8 kg)	1	1	4	4
Pernod	¼ cup	0.6 dl	1 cup	2.5 dl
Fennel, chopped	6 oz.	170 g	1½ lb.	680 g
Butter	1 oz.	25 g	4 oz.	110 g
Sauce Allemande	1 cup	2.5 dl	1 qt.	1 l
Mushroom Duxelle	4 oz.	110 g	1 lb.	450 g
Egg Yolks	2	2	8	8
Parsley, chopped	1 tbsp.	1 tbsp.	4 tbsp.	4 tbsp.
Pernod	2 tbsp.	2 tbsp.	½ cup	1.2 dl
Chablis Wine	1 cup	2.5 dl	1 qt.	1 l
Shallots, chopped	1 tbsp.	1 tbsp.	4 tbsp.	4 tbsp.

Bone the fish for stuffing, leaving head and tail attached to fillets. Sprinkle fillets with pernod. Prepare a fumet with the bones. Make the sauce allemande (see chapter 11).

Saute fennel in butter until tender. Add the duxelle, egg yolks, parsley, and remaining pernod. Stuff the fish with this mixture. Place the fish on baking pan(s). Cover with foil and bake at 350°F (180°C) for 35 to 40 minutes. Skin the fish and place on a serving platter. Reduce the cooking liquid to a glaze and add to the sauce allemande. Coat the fish with the sauce and serve immediately.

Striped Bass with Seaweed

Ingredients	6 portions		24 portions	
	U.S.	Metric	U.S.	Metric
Whole Striped Bass	1—4 lb.	1—1.8 kg	4—4 lb.	4—1.8 kg
Fresh Seaweed or	3 lb.	1.4 kg	12 lb.	5.4 kg
Dried Laver	1 lb.	450 g	4 lb.	1.8 kg.
Fish Fumet	¼ cup	0.6 dl	1 cup	2.5 dl
Lemon Juice	1 oz.	0.3 dl	½ cup	1.2 dl
Tomatoes, chopped and seeded	4 oz.	110 g	1 lb.	450 g
Dried Tarragon	1 tsp.	1 tsp.	1 tbsp.	1 tbsp.
Parsley, chopped	1 tbsp.	1 tbsp.	4 tbsp.	4 tbsp.

Clean, scale, and wash striped bass. If dried laver is used, soak it briefly. Arrange half of the seaweed over the bottom of a fish steamer or poacher. Place fish on top. Add remaining seaweed. Pour 1 inch (2.5 cm) of water into steamer or poacher. Steam fish until flaky. Arrange on a serving platter. Remove skin. Combine remaining ingredients. Spoon over fish. Serve at room temperature.

Swordfish

Swordfish is best when broiled. Serve with a sauce. It can also be used for Seafood Fondue or Seafood Brochettes (see Miscellaneous Seafood Recipes in this chapter).

Tilefish

Tilefish is used mainly for chowders and ground fish recipes (see Cod, Haddock).

Braised Fresh Tuna

Ingredients	6 portions		24 portions	
	U.S.	Metric	U.S.	Metric
Butter	4 oz.	110 g	1 lb.	450 g
Fresh Tuna	2 lb.	900 g	8 lb.	3.6 kg
Onion, chopped, ...	4 oz.	110 g	1 lb.	450 g
Flour.....................	1 oz.	25 g	4 oz.	110 g
White Wine	1 cup	2.5 dl	1 qt.	1 l
Tomato Puree	½ cup	1.2 dl	2 cups	5 dl
Salt and Pepper, to taste				
Fresh Mushrooms	3 oz.	85 g	12 oz.	340 g

Melt the butter in a braising pan. Brown the tuna on all sides. Remove from pan and set aside. Add the onions to color lightly. Stir in the flour to make a roux. Add the wine and to-mato puree. Season with salt and pepper.

Place the tuna in the sauce. Cover and braise at 350°F (180°C) for 45 to 60 minutes. Slice the mushrooms and add to the dish. Cook for 5 more minutes. Trim and slice the tuna. Arrange on a serving platter and add the sauce.

Curried Tuna Indienne

Ingredients	6 portions		24 portions	
	U.S.	Metric	U.S.	Metric
Curry Sauce	2 cups	5 dl	2 qt.	2 l
Canned Light Tuna	1 lb.	450 g	4 lb.	1.8 kg
Rice	1 cup	225 g	4 cups	900 g

Bring the curry sauce to a boil. Flake the tuna. Mix in the sauce. Cook the rice according to standard directions. Heat the tuna mixture. Serve the rice separately.

Fresh Tuna Italienne

Ingredients	6 portions		24 portions	
	U.S.	Metric	U.S.	Metric
Fresh Tuna Steaks	1⅝ lb.	750 g	6½ lb.	3 kg
Butter	2 oz.	50 g	8 oz.	225g
Onion, chopped	4 oz.	110 g	1 lb.	450 g
Flour.....................	1 oz.	25 g	4 oz.	110 g
White Wine	6 oz.	2 dl	3 cups	8 dl
Tomato Puree	6 oz.	2 dl	3 cups	8 dl
Water	2 cups	5 dl	2 qt.	2 l
Mushroom Buttons	8 oz.	225 g	2 lb.	900 g
Parsley, chopped	1 tsp.	1 tsp.	1½ tbsp.	1½ tbsp.

Wash tuna in cold water. Drain well and brown in butter on both sides. Transfer to a hot plate and reserve. Add onion to butter and brown lightly. Stir in the flour to make a roux. Add the white wine, tomato puree, and water. Mix well and bring to a boil.

Place the tuna in the sauce and bake at 325°F (165°C) for 45 to 60 minutes or until tuna is firm and fully cooked. Transfer tuna to a serving platter. Reduce the sauce until thickened. Add mushrooms and cook for 5 minutes. Slice the tuna, add the sauce, and sprinkle with chopped parsley. Serve hot.

Mousselines of Tuna in Lemon Shells

Ingredients	6 portions		24 portions	
	U.S.	Metric	U.S.	Metric
Whole Lemons	6	6	24	24
Solid White Tuna	10 oz.	280 g	2½ lb.	1.2 kg
Butter	2 oz.	50 g	8 oz.	225 g
Mayonnaise	½ cup	1.2 dl	2 cups	5 dl
Worcestershire Sauce	½ tsp.	½ tsp.	2 tsp.	2 tsp.
Salt	½ tsp.	½ tsp.	2 tsp.	2 tsp.
Lemon Juice	1 tbsp.	1 tbsp.	2 oz.	0.6 dl
White Pepper	⅛ tsp.	⅛ tsp.	½ tsp.	½ tsp.
Unflavored Gelatin	1 env.	1 env.	4 env.	4 env.
Hard-cooked Eggs	2	2	8	8
Parsley, chopped	1 tbsp.	1 tbsp.	4 tbsp.	4 tbsp.
Paprika	¼ tsp.	¼ tsp.	1 tsp.	1 tsp.

Cut off tops of lemons. Remove pulp without damaging the skin. Save pulp and juice for later use. Drain tuna and mix until smooth, in a food processor, with butter, mayonnaise, Worcestershire sauce, salt, pepper, and lemon juice. Dissolve gelatin in water (¼ cup or 0.6 dl for each envelope). Melt over low heat and mix into the tuna.

Surround each lemon shell with a piece of foil to make a 1-inch (2.5-cm) collar. Fill each shell with tuna to the top of the foil. Refrigerate for 1 hour or until set. Carefully remove foil. Chop half of the eggs with the parsley. Sprinkle over tuna. Shake paprika over eggs. Arrange tuna mousselines on a serving platter and surround with wedges of hard-boiled eggs and parsley.

Neptune's Burger

Ingredients	6 portions		24 portions	
	U.S.	Metric	U.S.	Metric
Light Tuna	1 lb.	450 g	4 lb.	1.8 kg
Mayonnaise	½ cup	1.2 dl	2 cups	5 dl
Scallions, chopped	1 tbsp.	1 tbsp.	4 tbsp.	4 tbsp.
Dijon or Dusseldorf Mustard ..	1 tsp.	1 tsp.	1 tbsp.	1 tbsp.
Garlic Salt	¼ tsp.	¼ tsp.	1 tsp.	1 tsp.
Cream Cheese	4 oz.	110 g	1 lb.	450 g
Toasted Buns, separated	6	6	24	24
Tomato Slices	6	6	24	24
Swiss Cheese, grated	2 oz.	50 g	8 oz.	225 g

Drain tuna. Blend together mayonnaise, scallions, mustard, and garlic salt. Fold in the tuna. Spread cream cheese on bottom halves of the buns. Top with 3⅓-oz. (90-g) portions of tuna mixture, a tomato slice, and cheese. Brown under a top broiler, 3 inches (8 cm) from the source of heat. Top with remaining bun halves.

Spaghetti with Tuna

Ingredients	6 portions		24 portions	
	U.S.	Metric	U.S.	Metric
Thin Spaghetti	12 oz.	340 g	3 lb.	1.3 kg
Olive Oil	2 oz.	0.6 dl	1 cup	2.5 dl
Medium Onion, chopped	1	1	4	4
Garlic Clove, minced	1	1	4	4
Tomatoes, seedless and chopped	1 lb.	450 g	4 lb.	1.8 kg
Tuna, flaked	8 oz.	225 g	2 lb.	900 g
Butter	2 oz.	50 g	8 oz.	225 g
Basil, chopped	½ tsp.	½ tsp.	2 tsp.	2 tsp.

Cook the spaghetti according to standard directions. Heat the oil. Add the onion and garlic and cook over medium heat for 10 minutes. Add the tomatoes and simmer for 10 to 15 minutes. Heat the tuna in its own juice. Drain the spaghetti and toss in the butter. Serve on a warm platter. Top with the tuna and spoon the sauce over. Sprinkle with basil and serve immediately.

Zucchini Stuffed with Tuna

Ingredients	6 portions		24 portions	
	U.S.	Metric	U.S.	Metric
White Bread, cubed	5 oz.	150 g	1¼ lb.	600 g
Milk	¾ cup	2 dl	3 cups	8 dl
Medium Zucchini	6	6	24	24
Light Tuna	1 lb.	450 g	4 lb.	1.8 kg
Eggs	2	2	8	8
Salt	½ tsp.	½ tsp.	2 tsp.	2 tsp.
Nutmeg	¼ tsp.	¼ tsp.	1 tsp.	1 tsp.
Chicken Bouillon	1 cup	2.5 dl	1 qt.	1 l
Tomato Sauce	1 cup	2.5 dl	1 qt.	1 l
Swiss Cheese, grated	2 oz.	50 g	8 oz.	225 g

Soak the bread in milk. Cut zucchini lengthwise. Scoop out the pulp and cook in salted boiling water. Drain well. Blanch the zucchini halves for 10 minutes. Squeeze excess milk out of bread. Mix with the cooked zucchini pulp. Flake the tuna. Combine with the bread mixture and beat in the eggs, salt, and nutmeg.

Arrange the zucchini halves in a buttered baking dish or sheet pan and fill with the tuna mixture. Pour the chicken bouillon around the zucchini. Cover the zucchini with tomato sauce. Sprinkle the cheese over and bake at 400°F (205°C) for 30 to 40 minutes.

Tuna Antiboise

Ingredients	6 portions		24 portions	
	U.S.	Metric	U.S.	Metric
Large Tomatoes	6	6	24	24
Oil and Vinegar Dressing	½ cup	1.2 dl	2 cups	5 dl
White Tuna	1 lb.	450 g	4 lb.	1.8 kg
Hard-boiled Eggs, chopped ...	2	2	8	8
Capers	1 oz.	25 g	4 oz.	110 g
Mayonnaise	4 oz.	1.2 dl	2 cups	5 dl
Anchovy Paste	1 tsp.	1 tsp.	1 tbsp.	1 tbsp.

Slice off the bottoms of the tomatoes. Scoop out the pulp. Season the insides of the tomatoes with the dressing. Drain and flake the tuna. Combine the tuna, eggs, capers, mayonnaise, and anchovy paste. Pour excess dressing out of tomatoes and fill with tuna mixture. Arrange on a round serving platter and garnish with parsley. Serve chilled.

Tuna Antipasto

Ingredients	6 portions		24 portions	
	U.S.	Metric	U.S.	Metric
Fresh or Frozen Asparagus	1 lb.	450 g	4 lb.	1.8 kg
Cucumber, seedless and sliced	2	2	8	8
Fresh Mushrooms, sliced	8 oz.	225 g	2 lb.	900 g
Basic French Dressing	1 cup	2.5 dl	1 qt.	1 l
Light or White Tuna	1 lb.	450 g	4 lb.	1.8 kg
Lettuce Leaves, to garnish				
Cherry Tomatoes	8 oz.	225 g	2 lb.	900 g
Hard-boiled Eggs, sliced	6	6	24	24

Cook asparagus in salted boiling water. Cool and drain. Marinate the cucumbers, mushrooms, and asparagus in separate containers, dividing the dressing between them. Refrigerate for 1 hour.

Place the tuna in the center of a round platter lined with lettuce leaves. Garnish the platter with the marinated vegetables, tomatoes, and sliced eggs. Pour remaining dressing over the tuna.

Tuna Casserole

Ingredients	6 portions		24 portions	
	U.S.	Metric	U.S.	Metric
Medium Egg Noodles	12 oz.	340 g	3 lb.	1.3 kg
Cooked Broccoli or Asparagus	8 oz.	225 g	2 lb.	900 g
Light Tuna, flaked	12 oz.	340 g	3 lb.	1.3 kg
Medium Cream Sauce	1½ cups	4 dl	1½ qt.	1.5 l
Dry Bread Crumbs	2 oz.	50 g	8 oz.	225 g
Butter	1 oz.	25 g	4 oz.	110 g

Cook the noodles in salted boiling water. Drain and arrange in buttered oven-proof serving dish(es). Top noodles with vegetables and tuna, and cover with the cream sauce.

Sprinkle with bread crumbs and drizzle with melted butter. Bake at 400°F (205°C) for 20 to 30 minutes or until bubbly and brown.

Tuna Nicoise

Ingredients	6 portions		24 portions	
	U.S.	Metric	U.S.	Metric
Medium Tomatoes	4	4	16	16
Salt	½ tsp.	½ tsp.	2 tsp.	2 tsp.
Pepper, ground	¼ tsp.	¼ tsp.	1 tsp.	1 tsp.
Cucumber	1	1	4	4
Green Peppers	2	2	8	8
Hard-boiled Eggs	2	2	8	8
White or Light Tuna	1 lb.	450 g	4 lb.	1.8 kg
Scallions, chopped	2	2	8	8
Olive Oil	¼ cup	0.6 dl	1 cup	2.5 dl
Fresh Basil or Parlsey, chopped	1 tbsp.	1 tbsp.	4 tbsp.	4 tbsp.
Anchovy Fillets	6	6	24	24
Ripe Olives	3 oz.	85 g	12 oz.	340 g
Cherry Tomatoes	6	6	24	24

Wash and cut the tomatoes into wedges. Season with salt and pepper. Cut cucumber lengthwise, remove seeds, and slice. Wash the green peppers. Cut in halves and remove seeds. Cut into strips. Cut the eggs into wedges. Flake the tuna in its juice.

Combine the tuna with the cucumber, green pepper, tomatoes, and scallions. Season with salt, pepper, and olive oil. Serve in a salad bowl. Sprinkle with parsley or basil, and garnish with anchovy fillets, olives, egg wedges, and cherry tomatoes.

Tuna Pate

Ingredients	6 portions		24 portions	
	U.S.	Metric	U.S.	Metric
Dill Pickles	1 oz.	25 g	4 oz.	110 g
Capers	1 tbsp.	1 tbsp.	4 tbsp.	4 tbsp.
Ripe Olives, pitted	½ cup	80 g	2 cups	320 g
Solid White Tuna	1 lb.	450 g	4 lb.	1.8 kg
Parsley, chopped	1 tbsp.	1 tbsp.	4 tbsp.	4 tbsp.
Fresh Dill, chopped	½ tbsp.	½ tbsp.	2 tbsp.	2 tbsp.
Mayonnaise	½ cup	1.2 dl	2 cups	5 dl
Salt	½ tsp.	½ tsp.	2 tsp.	2 tsp.
Pepper	¼ tsp.	¼ tsp.	1 tsp.	1 tsp.
Hard-boiled Eggs, sliced	2	2	8	8

Coarsely chop the pickles, capers, and olives. Drain and flake the tuna and combine with the chopped condiments. Add the parsley and dill and mix in the mayonnaise. Season with salt and pepper. Spoon the tuna into a spring mold. Chill for 2 hours. Unmold onto a serving platter and garnish with hard-boiled eggs.

Turbot

Poached Turbot, Champagne Sauce

Ingredients	8 portions	
	U.S.	Metric
Whole Turbot	8 lb.	3.6 kg
Parsley Stems	1 oz.	25 g
Mushroom Stems	4 oz.	110 g
Peppercorns	6	6
Shallots, chopped	1 tbsp.	1 tbsp.
Dry Champagne	2 cups	5 dl
Fish Stock	4 cups	1 l
Salt and pepper, to taste		
Butter, melted	4 oz.	110 g
Flour	4 oz.	110 g
Heavy Cream	1 cup	2.5 dl
Truffles, sliced		
Mushroom Heads	10	10
Fleurons	8	8

Wash and clean the fish. Place on a wire rack. Combine parsley stems, mushroom stems, peppercorns, shallots, and champagne in a turbotiere or suitable fish poacher. Immerse fish in poaching liquid; season with salt and pepper. Cover and braise in 350°F (180°C) over for 40 minutes, basting frequently. When fish is cooked, remove to a preheated serving platter. Skin the fish and keep warm.

Make a roux with butter and flour. Moisten with fish stock and boil to a thick consistency. Pour cooking stock into the veloute. Add heavy cream and cook to a medium consistency. Strain sauce and pour over the fish. Garnish with truffle slices, mushroom heads, and fleurons.

Poached Turbot Hollandaise

The fish can be cut into steaks, fillets, or poached whole in a turbotiere (see the poaching technique). Serve with hollandaise sauce. Turbot can also be broiled or pan fried.

Turbot Souffle Sauce Banquise

This souffle is a classic preparation that requires time and savoir faire, and represents the typical image of French classical cuisine.

To make the turbot souffle, the fish must be boned without separating the fillets to form a pouch for the stuffing. The boning process is laborious and requires patience (see the following instructions).

Ingredients	10–12 portions U.S.	Metric
Whole Turbot	10–12 lb.	4.5–5.4 kg

For the mousse:

White Fish (Dover sole, lemon sole, or pike)	3 lb.	1.2 kg
Egg Whites	6	6
Heavy Cream	1½ cups	3 dl
Salt	½ tsp.	½ tsp
Pepper	¼ tsp.	¼ tsp.
Nutmeg	⅛ tsp.	⅛ tsp.
Alaska King Crab, diced	6 oz.	150 g

For cooking the fish:

Bacon Slices	6	6
Dry White Wine	½ bottle	½ bottle
Bourbon	½ cup	1.2 dl
Fish Fumet	½ cup	1.2 dl

For the sauce:

Heavy Cream	1 qt.	1 l
Beurre Manie		
Salt and Pepper, to taste		

For assembling the turbot:

Fluted Mushrooms, cooked . . .	10–12	10–12
Heartshaped Croutons, fried . .	12	12
Truffle Stars		

Boning the fish   Trim off the fins with scissors, leaving tail intact. On the dark skin side, slit down the backbone of the turbot with a sharp flexible boning knife. Slice the flesh along the lateral bones, leaving fillet attached to the outer edge of the fish. Clip the end of the lateral bone. Proceed in the same manner on other side of the fish. Lift the backbone of the fish, starting with the end, cutting under the flesh. Remove the gills and wash the fish carefully.

Preparing   the   mousse Finely chop the fillets of selected fish, pass through a fine sieve for best results. Keep fish on ice and gradually stir in the egg whites and cream. Season to taste and mix in the diced crabmeat. Stuff the turbot with the mousse.

Cooking the fish A specially constructed pan (turbotiere) is used to cook the fish. Lay the turbot, stuffed side down, on the rack. Place in the pan. Cover the surface of the turbot with the bacon. Add the white wine and bourbon. Barely cover the fish with fumet. Bring the liquid to the boiling point on top of the stove. Cover the turbotiere and bake in a moderate oven for approximately 50 minutes. Lift the turbot out of the pan and slide it onto a serving platter or tray. Discard the bacon slices.

Sauce Banquise   Strain the cooking liquid and reduce to a glaze (about ¾). Add the heavy cream and reduce until sauce starts to thicken. Mix in a few dots of beurre manie; the sauce should be thick enough to coat the back of a spoon. Season to taste with salt and pepper.

Assembling   the   turbot Discard any cooking liquid on platter. Place a row of fluted cooked mushrooms down the center of the turbot. Cover with sauce. Serve the remaining sauce separately. Surround the platter with croutons and decorate with truffle stars. Serve hot.

Turtle

Turtle is used mostly for soup. See Boula Boula and Key West Turtle Soup in chapter 10.

Maryland Diamondback Terrapin Soup*

Ingredients	6 portions		24 portions	
	U.S.	Metric	U.S.	Metric
Butter	4 oz.	110 g	1 lb.	450 g
Flour	2 tbsp.	2 tbsp.	½ cup	60 g
Milk	1 qt.	1 l	1 gal.	4 l
Salt and Pepper				
Hard-boiled Eggs, separated	6	6	24	24
Terrapins, 5 to 7 inches or	3	3	12	12
small cans	2	2	8	8
Thick Cream	2 cups	5 dl	2 qt.	2 l
Sherry Wine	½ cup	1.2 dl	2 cups	5 dl

Melt butter in a saucepan. Blend in the flour and add the milk, salt, pepper, and hard-boiled egg whites, which have been chopped fine. Then add the terrapin meat, as is. Mash the egg yolks and add them to the soup mixture. Add the thick cream. Serve hot.

When the soup is served, pass the sherry to be added individually. Or, just before serving, add sherry to the soup.

*This recipe was supplied by the Maryland Department of Community and Economic Development.

Weakfish
(Gray Sea Trout, Squeteaques, Summer Trout)

Weakfish can be prepared following rainbow trout or salmon recipes.

Whiting
(Silver Hake, Silver Perch)

Deep-fried Whiting "in Anger"

Ingredients	6 portions		24 portions	
	U.S.	Metric	U.S.	Metric
Whole Dressed Whitings, 9 oz. (250 g)	6	6	24	24
Milk	3 oz.	1 dl	1½ cups	4 dl
Salt, to taste				
Flour.....................	3 oz.	85 g	12 oz.	340 g
Oil, for frying				
Parsley, fried				
Lemon Baskets	2	2	8	8
Lemon Wedges	6	6	24	24
Tomato Sauce	2 cups	5 dl	2 qt.	2 l

Cut off fins of whitings. Remove gills. Wash under cold water and drain well. Curl the fish and insert the caudal tails into the mouths. Tie heads and tail with string.

Season milk with salt. Dip whitings and roll in flour. Shake off excess flour. Deep fry at 350°F (180°C) for 5 to 8 minutes. When cooked, the fish will rise to the surface. Drain fish and remove string. Arrange on a warm platter. Garnish with fried parsley and lemon baskets and wedges. Serve hot with sauce separate.

Fried Fillets of Whiting

Ingredients	6 portions		24 portions	
	U.S.	Metric	U.S.	Metric
Eggs	2	2	8	8
Salt and Pepper				
Oil.......................	1 oz.	0.3 dl	4 oz.	1.2 dl
Whiting Fillets	2 lb.	900 g	8 lb.	3.6 kg
Flour.....................	3 oz.	85 g	12 oz.	340 g
Fresh Bread Crumbs	7 oz.	200 g	1¾ lb.	800 g
Oil.......................	3 oz.	1 dl	1½ cups	4 dl
Butter	2 oz.	50 g	8 oz.	225 g
Lemon Wedges	6	6	24	24
Maitre d'Hotel Butter	6 oz.	170 g	1½ lb.	680 g

Beat the eggs with salt, pepper, and oil (1 oz.). Dredge the fillets in flour, dip into egg mixture, and roll in bread crumbs. Fry in oil and butter until golden brown. Arrange on warm serving platter(s). Garnish with parsley and lemon wedges. Serve maitre d'hotel butter separately.

Paupiettes of Whiting

Ingredients	6 portions		24 portions	
	U.S.	Metric	U.S.	Metric
Whole Whitings	6	6	24	24
Salt	½ tsp.	½ tsp.	2 tsp.	2 tsp.
Pepper	¼ tsp.	¼ tsp.	1 tsp.	1 tsp.
Eggs	2	2	8	8
Fresh Bread Crumbs	6 oz.	170 g	1½ lb.	680 g
Fried Parsley, to garnish				
Tomato Sauce	1½ cups	4 dl	1½ qt:	1.5 l

Fillet the whitings leaving the fillets attached to fish heads. Cut off bone at base of head. Dredge the fish fillets in flour, dip in beaten egg, and roll in bread crumbs. Roll up each fillet and secure with small skewer or toothpicks. Deep fry at 360°F (185°C) for 3 to 4 minutes.

Arrange on preheated serving platter(s). Garnish with fried parsley. Serve tomato sauce separately.

Quenelles of Whiting au Gratin

Prepare a quenelle forcemeat with boneless fillets of whiting. Shape into quenelles (see chapter 9). Cover with mornay sauce (chapter 11) and bake at 350°F (180°C) until brown.

Whiting Lyonnaise

Ingredients	6 portions		24 portions	
	U.S.	Metric	U.S.	Metric
Whole Whitings	6	6	24	24
Small Potatoes	2 lb.	900 g	8 lb.	3.6 kg
Medium Onions	3	3	12	12
Butter	2 oz.	50 g	8 oz.	225 g
White Wine	1 cup	2.5 dl	1 qt.	1 l
Salt	1 tsp.	1 tsp.	1 tbsp.	1 tbsp.
White Pepper	¼ tsp.	¼ tsp.	1 tsp.	1 tsp.
Thyme Sprigs	2	2	8	8
Parsley, chopped	2 tbsp.	2 tbsp.	½ cup	20 g

Clean and dry the whitings. Boil the potatoes in their skins. Cool, peel, and slice thinly. Peel and slice the onions. Saute in butter until tender. Butter ovenproof serving dish(es). Line with potatoes and onions. Arrange whiting over the bed of potatoes and onions, and add the wine. Season with salt, pepper, and thyme. Dot with butter and bake at 350°F (180°C) for 15 to 20 minutes. Sprinkle with parsley and serve.

Note: For another use of Whiting, see Lemon Sole Tart recipe.

CHAPTER 13

Fresh-water Fish Recipes

This chapter contains recipes for the following:

Buffalofish	Fresh-water Sheepshead	Sturgeon
Carp	Frogs' Legs	Trout
Catfish	Lake Herring	Whitefish
Caviar	Lake Trout	Yellow Perch
Chub	Pike	

Buffalofish

All the preparations for carp are applicable to buffalofish.

Carp

Note: For Carp Gefilte Fish *see* Gefilte Fish, page 213.

Devilled Carp

	6 portions		24 portions	
Ingredients	*U.S.*	*Metric*	*U.S.*	*Metric*
Carp Fillets, skinned	2 lb.	900 g	8 lb.	3.6 kg
Chili Sauce	3 oz.	1 dl	1½ cup	4 dl
Catsup	3 oz.	1 dl	1½ cup	4 dl
Lemon Juice	1 tbsp.	1 tbsp.	2 oz.	0.6 dl
Horseradish	2 tsp.	2 tsp.	3 tbsp.	3 tbsp.
Worcestershire Sauce	1 tsp.	1 tsp.	1 tbsp.	1 tbsp.

Place fish in shallow, greased baking dish(es). Mix remaining ingredients together. Spread over fish. Bake 20 to 25 minutes at 350°F (180°C). Serve on preheated serving platter(s).

277

Hungarian Carp

Ingredients	6 portions		24 portions	
	U.S.	Metric	U.S.	Metric
Carp Fillets	2 lb.	900 g	8 lb.	3.6 kg
Salt and Pepper, to taste				
Onions, chopped	4 oz.	110 g	1 lb.	450 g
Oil	2 oz.	0.6 dl	1 cup	2.5 dl
Paprika	1 tsp.	1 tsp.	1 tbsp.	1 tbsp.
Fish Fumet	1 cup	2.5 dl	1 qt.	1 l
Green Peppers, diced	3 oz.	85 g	12 oz.	340 g
Tomatoes, peeled, seeded, and chopped	8 oz.	225 g	2 lb.	300 g

Cut fillets into 5-oz. (140-g) portions. Season with salt and pepper. Brown onions in oil. Sprinkle with paprika. Stir in the fumet, green peppers, and tomatoes.

Arrange fish in shallow baking pan(s). Pour the fumet and vegetables over. Bake at 350°F (180°C) for 20 minutes, basting occasionally. Serve hot on a preheated platter.

Poached Carp with Horseradish

Ingredients	6 portions		24 portions	
	U.S.	Metric	U.S.	Metric
Dressed Carp, 4 lb. (1.8 kg) . . .	1	1	4	4
Court Bouillon, no. 2				
Parsley, to garnish				
Potatoes, boiled	1 lb.	450 g	4 lb.	1.8 kg
Heavy Cream	¾ cup	2 dl	3 cups	8 dl
Horseradish, grated	2 oz.	50 g	8 oz.	225 g
Lemons	2	2	8	8

Poach the carp in court bouillon no. 2 (see poaching technique for more details). Drain and skin the fish. Arrange on serving platter(s). Garnish with parsley and potatoes.

Whip the heavy cream. Fold in the horseradish. Season with salt and pepper to taste. Serve separately.

Catfish

Arkansas Crispy Catfish

Ingredients	6 portions		24 portions	
	U.S.	Metric	U.S.	Metric
Pan-dressed Catfish Fillets, skinned, 8-oz. (225 g) portions	6	6	24	24
Salt	1 tsp.	1 tsp.	1 tbsp.	1 tbsp.
Pepper, ground	¼ tsp.	¼ tsp.	1 tsp.	1 tsp.
Flour	4 oz.	110 g	1 lb.	450 g
Yellow Corn Meal	2 oz.	50 g	8 oz.	200 g
Paprika	1 tsp.	1 tsp.	1 tbsp.	1 tbsp.
Evaporated Milk	½ cup	1.2 dl	2 cups	5 dl
Bacon Slices	12	12	48	48

Thaw fish, if frozen. Clean, wash, and dry fish and season with salt and pepper. Combine flour, cornmeal, and paprika. Dip fish in milk and roll in flour mixture. Fry bacon in a heavy pan until crisp. Remove bacon. Fry fish in hot bacon fat for 4 minutes. Turn carefully and fry 4 to 6 minutes longer, or until fish is brown and flakes easily. Drain on absorbent paper. Arrange on preheated serving platter. Serve with bacon.

Broiled Sesame Catfish

Ingredients	6 portions		24 portions	
	U.S.	Metric	U.S.	Metric
Pan-dressed Catfish Fillets, skinned, 8 oz. (225 g)	6	6	24	24
Oil	½ cup	1.2 dl	2 cups	5 dl
Sesame Seeds	2 oz.	50 g	8 oz.	225 g
Lemon Juice	2 oz.	0.6 dl	1 cup	2.5 dl
Salt	1 tsp.	1 tsp.	1 tbsp.	1 tbsp.
Pepper, ground	¼ tsp.	¼ tsp.	1 tsp.	1 tsp.
Parsley, for garnish				

Thaw fish, if frozen. Clean, wash, and dry. Place on hinged wire grills. Combine remaining ingredients and baste fish with sauce. Broil for 5 minutes on each side, or until fish flakes easily when tested with a fork. Arrange on serving platter and garnish with parsley.

Cajun Catfish

Ingredients	6 portions		24 portions	
	U.S.	Metric	U.S.	Metric
Pan-dressed Catfish, 8-oz. (225-g) portions	6	6	24	24
Tomato Sauce	½ cup	1.2 dl	2 cups	5 dl
Garlic Salt	¼ tsp.	¼ tsp.	1 tsp.	1 tsp.
Onion Powder	½ tsp.	½ tsp.	2 tsp.	2 tsp.
Parsley, chopped	1 tbsp.	1 tbsp.	4 tbsp.	4 tbsp.
Oil......................	2 oz.	0.6 dl	8 oz.	2.5 dl
Parmesan Cheese	2 oz.	50 g	8 oz.	225 g

Thaw fish, if frozen. Wash and dry fish. Combine remaining ingredients except cheese. Brush fish inside and out with sauce. Place on well-greased baking pan and brush with remaining sauce. Sprinkle with cheese.

Bake at 350°F (180°C) for 20 to 25 minutes. Brown under broiler. Arrange on serving platter and serve hot.

Kansas Fried Fish

Ingredients	6 portions		24 portions	
	U.S.	Metric	U.S.	Metric
Pan-dressed Catfish, 8-oz. (225-g) portions	6	6	24	24
Eggs	1	1	4	4
Milk	2 oz.	0.6 dl	1 cup	2½ dl
Salt	½ tsp.	½ tsp.	2 tsp.	2 tsp.
Pepper, ground	¼ tsp.	¼ tsp.	1 tsp.	1 tsp.
Lemon Juice	1 oz.	0.3 dl	½ cup	1.2 dl
Flour.....................	3 oz.	85 g	12 oz.	340 g
Dry Bread Crumbs	1 cup	110 g	4 cups	450 g
Tartare Sauce	1½ cups	4 dl	1½ qt.	1.5 l
Oil, for frying				

Thaw fish if frozen. Combine eggs and milk and mix well. Season fish with salt, pepper, and lemon juice. Roll fish in flour, dip in egg mixture, and coat with bread crumbs. Deep fry at 350°F (180°C) for 4 to 5 minutes. Drain well and serve with tartare sauce.

Note: Catfish can also be oven fried. See Oven-fried Fillets and Steaks or Deep-fat-fried Fillets or Steaks.

Caviar

Fine caviar should be eaten au naturel, with nothing more than a few drops of lemon juice and a little ground black pepper. Members of the very exclusive Beluga Club consider it a sacrilege to sprinkle caviar with chopped onions, egg white, or egg yolks, a practice that is de rigueur in the most expensive restaurants in the United States. The ultimate arbiters of the Beluga Club suggest that if you must have an accompaniment with caviar, the only thing permissible is a baked potato. Indeed, a freshly baked potato split in half, seasoned with salt and freshly ground pepper, and topped with sour cream (only if you must have it) and the precious caviar is a delightful experience. Another method favored by creative gourmets is to serve a heaping teaspoon of Beluga over a soft boiled egg with the top portion of the shell removed. Gently blend the caviar with the egg and savor it with buttered toast.

Blinis with Caviar

Ingredients	25 portions	
	U.S.	Metric
Active Dry Yeast	1 package	1 package
Milk	¾ cup	2 dl
Sugar	1 tsp.	1 tsp.
Bread Flour or Buckwheat		
Flour	2 cups	240 g
Soft Butter	4 oz.	110 g
Egg Yolks	3	3
Salt	½ tsp.	½ tsp.
Egg Whites, stiffly beaten	3	3

Dissolve yeast in ¼ cup (0.6 dl) of warm milk. Add the sugar. Mix the remaining milk and the flour to make a paste. Cover and allow to rise until doubled in volume.

Cream together the butter, egg yolks, and salt. Beat in the yeast mixture. Allow to rise in a warm place for an hour. Fold in the egg whites.

Cook small pancakes, about 2 to 3 inches (5 to 7.5 cm) in diameter, in a buttered pan or a griddle. Serve with caviar and sour cream, or with smoked salmon and salmon caviar.

Chub
(Bluefin, Blackfin, Tullibee)

Chub can be prepared meuniere, grilled with maitre d'hotel butter, or fried with sauce remoulade or tartare.

Fresh-water Sheepshead
(Fresh-water Drum, White Perch, Gasperou, Gray Bass)

Sheepshead can be prepared like red snapper.

Frogs' Legs

Batter-fried Frogs' Legs

Ingredients	6 portions		24 portions	
	U.S.	Metric	U.S.	Metric
Small Frogs' Legs	2 doz.	2 doz.	8 doz.	8 doz.
Lemon Juice	2 oz.	0.6 dl	1 cup	2.5 dl
Parsley, chopped	1 tbsp.	1 tbsp.	4 tbsp.	4 tbsp.
Salt	½ tsp.	½ tsp.	2 tsp.	2 tsp.
Pepper	¼ tsp.	¼ tsp.	1 tsp.	1 tsp.
Garlic, minced	½ tsp.	½ tsp.	2 tsp.	2 tsp.
Beer Batter (see chapter 7)	1 recipe	1 recipe	4 recipes	4 recipes
Flour	2 oz.	50 g	8 oz.	225 g
Oil, for deep frying				
Tomato Sauce	1½ cups	4 dl	1½ qt.	1.5 l

Trim and wash frogs' legs, and marinate in lemon juice, parsley, salt, pepper, and garlic.

Mix batter ingredients. Fold in egg whites at last minute. Flour frogs' legs. Dip into batter, and deep fry at 350°F (180°C) until golden brown. Arrange on preheated serving platter(s). Serve with tomato sauce.

Frogs' Legs Paprika

Ingredients	6 portions		24 portions	
	U.S.	Metric	U.S.	Metric
Small Frogs' Legs	2 doz.	2 doz.	8 doz.	8 doz.
Onion, chopped	2 oz.	50 g	8 oz.	225 g
Butter	3 oz.	85 g	12 oz.	340 g
Paprika	1 tsp.	1 tsp.	4 tsp.	4 tsp.
Tomatoes, peeled and chopped	4 oz.	110 g	1 lb.	450 g
Flour	1 tbsp.	1 tbsp.	4 tbsp.	4 tbsp.
Heavy Cream	5 oz.	1.5 dl	2½ cups	6 dl

Trim and clean frogs' legs. Saute onion in butter until tender. Sprinkle with paprika, add tomatoes, and cook for 10 minutes. Season the frogs' legs and add to the tomato mixture. Cook for 5 minutes.

Stir flour into heavy cream and add to the sauce. Allow to simmer for 3 to 4 minutes. Arrange frogs' legs on serving platter. Cover with sauce.

Frogs' Legs Poulette

Ingredients	6 portions		24 portions	
	U.S.	Metric	U.S.	Metric
Medium Frogs' Legs	12	12	48	48
Salt and Pepper				
Mushrooms, sliced	2 oz.	50 g	8 oz.	225 g
Shallots, chopped	1 tbsp.	1 tbsp.	4 tbsp.	4 tbsp.
Dry White Wine	¾ cup	2 dl	3 cups	8 dl
Heavy Cream	¾ cup	2 dl	3 cups	8 dl
Butter	2 oz.	50 g	8 oz.	225 g
Flour	1 oz.	25 g	4 oz.	110 g
Lemon Juice, to taste				
Parsley, chopped	1 tbsp.	1 tbsp.	4 tbsp.	4 tbsp.

Trim and wash frogs' legs, and season with a little salt and pepper. Sprinkle the mushrooms and shallots in a suitable pan. (Pan should not be too large for the frogs' legs.) Arrange frogs' legs on top.

Add wine and heavy cream to cover. If not enough, add a little water. Cover and poach 10 minutes or until frogs' legs are done. Transfer frogs' legs to a serving platter.

Bring sauce to a boil and reduce to desired consistency. Blend butter with flour and drop small dots into boiling sauce until it thickens. Season with lemon juice and parsley and pour over frogs' legs.

Frogs' Legs Saute with Pecans

Saute frogs' legs meuniere (see cooking technique in chapter 6). Garnish with pecan nuts.

Lake Herring (Cisco, Blueback)

This can be prepared in the same manner as Whitefish.

Lake Trout (Mackinaw, Toque, Lonque)

Note: All the methods of preparing salmon and trout are applicable to lake trout.

Lake Trout Mexicaine

Ingredients	6 portions		24 portions	
	U.S.	*Metric*	*U.S.*	*Metric*
Whole Dressed Lake Trout ...	1—4½ lb.	1—2 kg	4—4½ lb.	4—2 kg
Court Bouillon no. 2 to cover fish				
Small Ripe Avocados	3	3	12	12
Lemon Juice	1 oz.	0.3 dl	4 oz.	1.2 dl
Crabmeat..................	6 oz.	170 g	1½ lb.	680 g
Cocktail Sauce	¾ cup	2 dl	3 cups	8 dl
Cherry Tomatoes and Parsley, to garnish				
Sauce Antiboise	2 cups	5 dl	2 qt.	2 l

Poach the trout in court bouillon following directions for the poaching technique. Cut the avocados in half, lengthwise. Remove pits. Peel and sprinkle with lemon juice. Combine the crabmeat with cocktail sauce, and garnish the avocado halves.

Lift the cool poached fish from the court bouillon, drain, and partly skin. Arrange on a serving platter. Garnish with avocados, cherry tomatoes, and parsley. Serve sauce antiboise separately.

Pike
(Lake Pickerel, Grass Pike)

Baked Pike with Sour Cream

	6 portions		24 portions	
Ingredients	U.S.	Metric	U.S.	Metric
Butter	2 oz.	50 g	8 oz.	225 g
Salt	½ tsp.	½ tsp.	2 tsp.	2 tsp.
Shallots, minced	1 tbsp.	1 tbsp.	4 tbsp.	4 tbsp.
Carrots, diced	2 oz.	50 g	8 oz.	225 g
Pike Fillets	2 lb.	900 g	8 lb.	3.6 kg
Parsley, minced	1 tbsp.	1 tbsp.	4 tbsp.	4 tbsp.
Fish Stock	1 cup	2.5 dl	1 qt.	1 l
Dry White Wine	½ cup	1.2 dl	2 cups	5 dl
Sour Cream	½ cup	1.2 dl	2 cups	5 dl
Eggs, beaten	1	1	4	4
Swiss Cheese, grated	2 oz.	50 g	8 oz.	225 g

Butter baking dish(es) with half of the butter. Sprinkle salt, shallots, carrots, and parsley over bottom. Place the fish in one layer over the vegetables and dot with remaining butter. Add stock and wine, cover with foil, and bake at 350°F (180°C) for 10 to 15 minutes.

Beat eggs and sour cream together and spoon over fish. Sprinkle with cheese. Brown under a broiler and serve with the cooking stock.

Pickerel Meuniere
Follow directions for Dover Sole Meuniere.

Poached Pike with White Butter
Poach the whole clean pike in court bouillon no. 2, following the poaching cooking technique. Serve with white butter (chapter 11).

Quenelles of Pike Nantua
Prepare a pike quenelle forcemeat with panada, following the recipe in chapter 9. Poach the quenelles in water. Serve with nantua sauce (chapter 11).

Quenelles of Pike Sauce Normande
Prepare quenelles as in previous recipe. Serve with sauce normande (chapter 11).

Sturgeon

Smoked Sturgeon a la Russe

Carve smoked sturgeon into thin slices. Arrange
on serving platter with lemon wedges. Serve with
caviar and blinis. (See under Caviar.)

Sturgeon in White Wine

Ingredients	6 portions		24 portions	
	U.S.	Metric	U.S.	Metric
Sturgeon Fillet	2 lb.	900 g	8 lb.	3.6 kg
Salt and Pepper, to taste				
Bacon, diced	5 oz.	140 g	1¼ lb.	560 g
White Wine	1½ cup	4 dl	1½ qt.	1.5 l
Butter	1 oz.	25 g	4 oz.	110 g
White Wine Sauce	1½ cup	4 dl	1½ qt.	1.5 l
Sour Cream	½ cup	1.2 dl	2 cups	5 dl

Skin the fillets. Season with salt and pepper. Arrange fillets on buttered baking pan(s). Sprinkle bacon pieces over fish. Pour the wine in bottom of pan.

Bake at 360°F (185°C) for 10 to 15 minutes, or until bacon is crisp and fish flaky. Arrange fish on preheated platter(s).

Reduce the cooking stock to a glaze. Add to the white wine sauce. Stir in the sour cream. Pour sauce over fish. Serve hot.

Trout
(Rainbow, Steelhead)

Broiled Trout Tournedos, Sauce Choron

Ingredients	6 portions		24 portions	
	U.S.	Metric	U.S.	Metric
Trout Fillets	2 lb.	900 g	8 lb.	3.6 kg
Salt	1 tsp.	1 tsp.	4 tsp.	4 tsp.
Pepper	¼ tsp.	¼ tsp.	1 tsp.	1 tsp.
Oil	2 oz.	0.6 dl	1 cup	2.5 dl
Parsley, to garnish				
Sauce Choron	1½ cups	4 dl	1½ qt.	1.5 l

Flatten the fillets. Season with salt and pepper. Cut lengthwise and roll each piece to resemble a fillet mignon. Secure with toothpicks. Brush with oil. Broil on a grill until fully cooked.

Serve on a warm platter. Garnish with parsley. Coat the fish with the hot sauce:

Fillet of Trout Grenobloise

See directions for Mullet Grenobloise.

Fillets of Trout Key West

Ingredients	6 portions		24 portions	
	U.S.	Metric	U.S.	Metric
Boneless Trout Fillets	12—3 oz.	12—85 g	48—3 oz.	48—85 g
Stone Crab Claws	6	6	24	24
Small Shrimp Quenelles	6	6	24	24
Fish Fumet	2 cups	5 dl	2 qt.	2 l
White Wine Sauce	1½ cups	4 dl	1½ qt.	1.5 l

Poach the fillets in simmering fish fumet. Poach the shrimp quenelles in fumet. Arrange the trout fillets on a warm serving platter(s). Garnish with the shrimp quenelles and crab claws. Pour the hot sauce over the fish. Serve hot.

Fillets of Trout Maltaise

Ingredients	6 portions		24 portions	
	U.S.	Metric	U.S.	Metric
Anchovy Butter	1 tbsp.	1 tbsp.	4 tbsp.	4 tbsp.
Tarragon Leaves, chopped ...	1 tbsp.	1 tbsp.	4 tbsp.	4 tbsp.
Fresh Mint, chopped	1 tsp.	1 tsp.	1 tbsp.	1 tbsp.
Parsley, chopped	1 tbsp.	1 tbsp.	4 tbsp.	4 tbsp.
Fresh Basil, chopped ....,....	1 tbsp.	1 tbsp.	4 tbsp.	4 tbsp.
Salt	½ tsp.	½ tsp.	2 tsp.	2 tsp.
White Pepper	¼ tsp.	¼ tsp.	1 tsp.	1 tsp.
Lemon Juice	1 tbsp.	1 tbsp.	2 oz.	0.6 dl
Trout Fillets	2 lb.	900 g	8 lb.	3.6 kg
Tomatoes, peeled and sliced ..	3	3	12	12

Mix the anchovy butter with all the herbs. Season with salt, pepper, and lemon juice. Spread the anchovy mix over each fillet. Place sliced tomatoes on top. Bake at 350°F (180°C) for 10 to 15 minutes.

Fillet of Trout Meuniere

See directions for Dover Sole Meuniere.

Fried Trout

Ingredients	6 portions		24 portions	
	U.S.	Metric	U.S.	Metric
Boneless Butterfly Trout, breaded	6—8 oz.	6—225 g	24—8 oz.	24—225 g
Oil, for frying				
Parsley, fried	2 oz.	50 g	8 oz.	225 g
Lemon Wedges	6	6	24	24
Tartare Sauce	1½ cups	4 dl	1½ qt.	1.5 l

Deep fry the trout at 360°F (185°C) until crisp. Arrange on serving platter(s). Garnish with fried parsley and lemon wedges. Serve with tartare sauce.

Gougeonnettes of Trout Kakou

Ingredients	6 portions		24 portions	
	U.S.	Metric	U.S.	Metric
Fillets of Seatrout or Weakfish	2 lb.	900 g	8 lb.	3.6 kg
White Pepper	¼ tsp.	¼ tsp.	1 tsp.	1 tsp.
Lemon Juice	2 oz.	0.6 dl	1 cup	2.5 dl
Flour.....................	3 oz.	85 g	12 oz.	340 g
Salt......................	½ tsp.	½ tsp.	2 tsp.	2 tsp.
Whole Eggs	3	3	12	12
Almonds, ground	8 oz.	225 g	2 lb.	900 g
Fresh Bread Crumbs........	8 oz.	225 g	2 lb.	900 g
Seasoned Salt	½ tsp.	½ tsp.	2 tsp.	2 tsp.
Parsley, fried				
Lemon Wedges.............	6	6	24	24
Mustard Sauce	1½ cups	4 dl	1½ qt.	1.5 l

Wash and skin fish fillets. Cut into strips about 3 inches (7.5 cm) long. Season with salt, pepper, and lemon juice. Toss the fish and marinate for 2 to 3 hours in the refrigerator.

Roll fish in seasoned flour, dip in beaten eggs, and cover with mixture of bread crumbs and ground almonds. Deep fry at 350°F (180°C) for 3 to 5 minutes. Serve on warm platter(s) covered with napkins. Top gougeonnettes with fried parsley. Surround with lemon wedges. Serve sauce separately.

Marinated Rainbow Trout en Escabeche

Ingredients	6 portions		24 portions	
	U.S.	Metric	U.S.	Metric
Whole Rainbow Trout	6—10 oz.	6—280 g	24—10 oz.	24—280 g
Salt	1 tsp.	1 tsp.	1 tbsp.	1 tbsp.
Black Pepper, ground	½ tsp.	½ tsp.	2 tsp.	2 tsp.
Olive Oil	1 cup	2.5 dl	1 qt.	1 l
Pimentos, thinly sliced	2 oz.	50 g	8 oz.	225 g
Onion, thinly sliced	8 oz.	225 g	2 lb.	900 g
Wine Vinegar	1 cup	2.5 dl	1 qt.	1 l
Black Peppercorns	1 tsp.	1 tsp.	4 tsp.	4 tsp.
Bay Leaves	2	2	8	8

Season the whole cleaned fish with salt and pepper. Heat the oil in a large skillet and fry the fish 3 minutes on each side and until brown. Arrange in one layer in shallow pan(s). Add the onion and pimentos to the oil and cook over low heat for 5 minutes. Cool. Combine vinegar and spices. Mix into the cooled oil and vegetables. Heat up the marinade and pour over fish.

Cool and refrigerate 2 to 3 days before using. The fish will keep for a week and is usually served cold as an entree or hors d'oeuvre.

Mousse of Salmon Trout

Ingredients	6 portions		24 portions	
	U.S.	Metric	U.S.	Metric
Smoked Salmon	1 lb.	450 g	4 lb.	1.8 kg
Smoked Trout	1 lb.	450 g	4 lb.	1.8 kg
Mayonnaise	¾ cup	2 dl	3 cups	8 dl
Aspic Jelly	1 cup	2.5 dl	1 qt.	1 l
Lemon Juice	1 tbsp.	1 tbsp.	2 oz.	0.6 dl
White Wine	½ cup	1.2 dl	2 cups	5 dl
White Pepper	¼ tsp.	¼ tsp.	1 tsp.	1 tsp.
Salt, to taste				
Heavy Cream	1 cup	2.5 dl	1 qt.	1 l

Remove bones and skin from salmon and trout. Put through a fine meat grinder. Mix in the mayonnaise and run through a food mill. Add the liquid aspic jelly, lemon juice, white wine, and seasonings. Whip the cream and fold into the fish mixture.

Spoon the mousse into decorated molds. Allow to set in refrigerator for about two hours before unmolding onto serving platter(s). Surround with chopped aspic jelly.

Mousse of Smoked Trout

See directions for Mousse of Salmon Trout.

Pate of Trout with Salmon Caviar

Ingredients	6 portions		24 portions	
	U.S.	Metric	U.S.	Metric
Boneless Trout Fillets	1 lb.	450 g	4 lb.	1.8 kg
Fresh Bread Crumbs	3½ oz.	100 g	14 oz.	400 g
Heavy Cream	1 cup	2.5 dl	1 qt.	1 l
Salt and Pepper, to taste				
Truffle, chopped	½ oz.	12 g	2 oz.	50 g
Fish Jelly	1 qt.	1 l	1 gal.	4 l
Salmon Caviar	6 oz.	170 g	1½ lb.	680 g
Artichoke Bottoms	6	6	24	24
Salmon Mousse	8 oz.	225 g	2 lb.	900 g

Puree the boneless, skinless fish in a food processor. Add the bread crumbs and heavy cream to obtain a thick paste. Season with salt and pepper. Fold in the truffle. Butter suitable mold(s). Carefully spoon the mixture into the mold. Cover with parchment paper. Bake in a waterbath at 350°F (180°C) for about 35 to 40 minutes. Cool in mold and turn onto a rack.

Glaze with the fish jelly and spread top with salmon caviar. Slice the pate, leaving a piece for display. Arrange the slices on a cold serving platter. Garnish with the uncut piece. Stuff the artichoke bottoms with the salmon mousse. Place around the platter. Decorate with chopped jelly.

Paupiettes of Trout Maitre d'Hotel

Ingredients	6 portions		24 portions	
	U.S.	Metric	U.S.	Metric
Trout Fillets, 3 oz. (85 g) each	12	12	48	48
Salt	½ tsp.	½ tsp.	2 tsp.	2 tsp.
Pepper	¼ tsp.	¼ tsp.	1 tsp.	1 tsp.
Lemon Juice	1 tbsp.	1 tbsp.	2 oz.	0.6 dl
Maitre d'Hotel Butter	6 oz.	170 g	1½ lb.	680 g
Lemon Butter	4 oz.	110 g	1 lb.	450 g

Flatten the boneless trout fillets. Season with salt, pepper, and lemon juice. Spread a small amount of maitre d'hotel butter over each fillet and roll. Secure with toothpicks. Saute in lemon butter until cooked. Transfer to a warm serving platter and serve hot.

Poached Fillets of Trout Hollandaise

Poach boneless fillets of trout in court bouillon, no. 2. Serve with hollandaise sauce and parsleyed potatoes.

Smoked Trout Moscovite

Ingredients	6 portions		24 portions	
	U.S.	Metric	U.S.	Metric
Smoked Trout Fillets	12	12	48	48
Stuffed Deviled Eggs	6	6	24	24
Iranian Caviar	4 oz.	110 g	1 lb.	450 g
Cucumber Salad	8 oz.	225 g	2 lb.	900 g
Aspic Jelly	1 cup	2.5 dl	1 qt.	1 l
Horseradish Sauce	½ cup	1.2 dl	2 cups	5 dl

Bone and skin the trout fillets. Arrange on serving platter. Garnish with the stuffed eggs, topped with caviar, alternated with cucumber salad and chopped aspic jelly. Serve the sauce separately.

Steelhead Napa Valley

Ingredients	6 portions		24 portions	
	U.S.	Metric	U.S.	Metric
Whole Steelhead, 4½ lb. (2 kg)	1	1	4	4
California Chablis Wine	1½ cups	4 dl	1½ qt.	1.5 l
Fish Fumet	1½ cups	4 dl	1½ qt.	1.5 l
Heavy Cream	1 cup	2.5 dl	1 qt.	1 l
Beurre Manie	2 oz.	50 g	8 oz.	225 g
Mushroom Buttons	8 oz.	225 g	2 lb.	900 g
Pearl Onions, peeled	8 oz.	225 g	2 lb.	900 g
Butter	1 tbsp.	1 tbsp.	2 oz.	50 g
Parsley, chopped	1 tbsp.	1 tbsp.	4 tbsp.	4 tbsp.
Dill, chopped	1 tbsp.	1 tbsp.	4 tbsp.	4 tbsp.
Fresh Sage, chopped	1 tbsp.	1 tbsp.	4 tbsp.	4 tbsp.
Asparagus, cooked	10 oz.	300 g	2½ lb.	1.2 kg

(cont.)

Clean the trout. Place in a fish poacher. Add the fish fumet and the wine. Cover and bring the fumet to 180°F (83°C). Time 10 minutes per inch thickness of the fish. Remove fish from cooking liquid. Skin and arrange on serving platter(s).

Reduce the strained liquid to one half. Add the cream. Reduce for 5 minutes over medium heat. Stir in the beurre manie and simmer the sauce for 10 minutes. Season with salt and pepper to taste. Saute mushrooms in butter until

done. Cook onions in salted boiling water. Combine mushrooms and onions with sauce. Pour over trout. Sprinkle the herbs over the fish and garnish with asparagus. Serve hot.

Stuffed Trout Fernand Point

Ingredients	6 portions		24 portions	
	U.S.	Metric	U.S.	Metric
Carrots, chopped	2 oz.	50 g	8 oz.	225 g
White Celery Hearts, chopped	2 oz.	50 g	8 oz.	225 g
Truffle, chopped	2 tbsp.	2 tbsp.	2 oz.	50 g
Mushrooms, chopped	2 oz.	50 g	8 oz.	225 g
Flour.....................	1 oz.	25 g	4 oz.	110 g
Egg Yolks	5	5	20	20
Whole Boneless Trout, 8 oz. (225 g)	6	6	24	24
Butter, melted	2 oz.	50 g	8 oz.	225 g
Carrots, sliced	2 oz.	50 g	8 oz.	225 g
Onions, sliced	2 oz.	50 g	8 oz.	225 g
Red Port Wine	2 cups	5 dl	2 qt.	2 l
Heavy Cream	1½ cups	4 dl	1½ qt.	1.5 l
Butter	2 oz.	50 g	8 oz.	225 g
Flour.....................	2 oz.	50 g	8 oz.	225 g

Boil carrots and celery for 5 minutes. Drain. Butter suitable saucepan and combine cooked carrots, celery, truffles, and mushrooms. Cook over brisk fire until cooked and quite dry. Add flour and cook 1 minute longer. Remove from fire and add egg yolks. Season with salt and pepper. Cool.

Bone trout and stuff with vegetable mixture. Secure stuffing

with twine or cheesecloth. Put melted butter in suitable baking dish. Add carrots and onions and season with a little thyme. Cook a few minutes without browning the vegetables. Place fish on top, add wine, and cover with foil. Bake at 300°F (155°C) for about 30 minutes. Remove skin from cooked fish. Put on serving platter. Keep warm.

Strain fish fumet into saucepan. Add heavy cream and bring to a boil. Combine flour and fresh butter and drop tiny lumps into the boiling sauce. Stir well, but do not allow to boil any longer. Pour sauce over fish.

Note: The customary garnish is mushroom heads and tiny shrimp.

Trout au Bleu

Ingredients	6 portions		24 portions	
	U.S.	Metric	U.S.	Metric
Live Trout 8 oz. (225 g) each ..	6	6	24	24
Court Bouillon, no. 2				
Parsley, to garnish				
Sauce Mousseline	1½ cups	4 dl	1½ qt.	1.5 l

Follow directions for the au bleu cooking technique. Arrange trout on a serving platter(s). Garnish with parsley. Serve with sauce mousseline.

Truite au Chablis
(Trout with Chablis Wine)

Ingredients	6 portions		24 portions	
	U.S.	Metric	U.S.	Metric
Whole Cleaned Trout, 8 oz. (225 g) each	6	6	24	24
Butter	6 oz.	170 g	1½ lb.	680 g
Salt and Pepper, to taste				
Shallots, chopped	1 oz.	25 g	4 oz.	110 g
Chablis Wine	5 oz.	1.5 dl	2½ cups	6 dl
Heavy Cream	1½ cups	4 dl	1½ qt.	1.5 l
Cream Sauce	5 oz.	1.5 dl	2½ cups	6 dl
Mushroom Caps, fluted	6	6	24	24
Fleurons	6	6	24	24

Arrange the cleaned trout on buttered baking pan(s). Season with salt and pepper. Sprinkle with the shallots. Pour the wine over the fish. Cover with parchment paper. Bake trout at 375° F (190°C) for 15 to 20 minutes. Skin both sides and arrange on serving platter(s).

Reduce the cooking liquid. Add the heavy cream and cream sauce. Bring to a boil. Reduce to medium thick consistency. Strain sauce over the trout. Top with mushroom caps. Garnish with fleurons. Serve hot.

Truite au Vert
(Trout with Green Vegetables)

Ingredients	6 portions		24 portions	
	U.S.	Metric	U.S.	Metric
Whole Trout, 8 oz. (225 g)	6	6	24	24
Fish Fumet	2 cups	5 dl	2 qt.	2 l
Fresh Tarragon Leaves	1 tbsp.	1 tbsp.	4 tbsp.	4 tbsp.
Spinach Leaves	4 oz.	110 g	1 lb.	450 g
Sorrel Leaves	2 oz.	50 g	8 oz.	225 g
Butter	3 oz.	85 g	12 oz.	340 g
Flour	2 oz.	50 g	8 oz.	225 g
Egg Yolks	4	4	16	16

Fillet and skin the trout. Poach in the fumet. Blanch all vegetables and puree in a blender. Prepare a roux with the butter and flour. Add strained fumet to obtain a thick sauce. Stir in the pureed vegetables and egg yolks. Heat the sauce to a boiling point.

Arrange trout fillets on serving platter(s). Coat with a small amount of sauce. Serve remaining sauce separately.

Truite Farcie Bretonne
(Stuffed Trout Bretonne)

Ingredients	6 portions		24 portions	
	U.S.	Metric	U.S.	Metric
Whole Trout, 8 oz. (225 g)	6	6	24	24
Salt and Pepper, to taste				
Fish Forcemeat (chapter 9) . . .	10 oz.	300 g	2½ lb.	1.2 kg
Butter	4 oz.	110 g	1 lb.	450 g
Sauce Bretonne	1½ cups	4 dl	1½ qt.	1.5 l

Clean and bone the trout. Season with salt and pepper. Fill with forcemeat. Insert small skewers in belly flaps to hold the forcemeat. Saute the trout in butter to brown lightly. Bake at 350°F (180°C) for 15 minutes or until forcemeat is done. Skin both sides of the fish and remove skewers. Arrange trout on a hot serving platter(s). Pour the hot sauce over.

Trout Amandine

Saute trout meuniere. Garnish with toasted sliced almonds.

Trout Doria

Saute meuniere, and serve with olive-shaped stewed cucumbers.

Trout Coulibiac

See directions for Salmon Coulibiac.

Mousseline of Idaho Trout Royale

See directions for Mousseline of Salmon Royale.

Note: The following are cold trout preparations.

Au Bleu

Cook according to the technique in chapter 6. Serve cold with a cold sauce.

Mousse of Trout Ondine

Prepare a standard salmon mousse. Mix in a few tiny cooked shrimp. Spoon into a fish mold decorated with aspic sheets. Unmold on oval platter. Decorate with shrimp and aspic jelly.

Stuffed Trout Mongolfier

Stuff whole trout with fish forcemeat (see Stuffed Trout Bretonne). Poach in fish fumet. Cool and skin. Coat with mayonnaise collee that has tomato puree in it. Serve with tomato salad and Russian salad.

Whitefish

Broiled Whitefish Fillets Amandine

Ingredients	6 portions		24 portions	
	U.S.	Metric	U.S.	Metric
Whitefish Fillets	2 lb.	900 g	8 lb.	3.6 kg
Melted Butter or Fat	2 oz.	0.6 dl	1 cup	2.5 dl
Salt	½ tsp.	½ tsp.	2 tsp.	2 tsp.
Paprika	¼ tsp.	¼ tsp.	1 tsp.	1 tsp.
Butter	3 oz.	85 g	12 oz.	340 g
Almonds, sliced	2 oz.	50 g	8 oz.	225 g
Lemon juice	1 oz.	0.3 dl	½ cup	1.2 dl
Parsley, chopped	1 tbsp.	1 tbsp.	4 tbsp.	4 tbsp.

Cut the fillets into 5-oz. (140-g) portions. Arrange on greased baking pan(s). Brush with melted butter or fat, and broil, without turning, 3 to 4 inches (8 to 10 cm) from source of heat, until fillets are done. Transfer to heated serving platter(s). Season with salt and paprika.

Brown almonds in butter over low heat. Stir in the lemon juice. Spoon over fish. Sprinkle with parsley.

Cold Whitefish, Sauce Andalouse

Ingredients	6 portions		24 portions	
	U.S.	Metric	U.S.	Metric
Whole Whitefish, dressed	1—3 lb.	1—1.4 kg	4—3 lb.	4—1.4 kg
Court Bouillon no. 2 to cover fish				
Cucumbers	2	2	8	8
Aspic Jelly, chopped	1 cup	2.5 dl	1 qt.	1 l
Stuffed Eggs	6	6	24	24
Sauce Andalouse	2 cups	5 dl	2 qt.	2 l

Wash and drain the whole fish. Tie on the rack of a fish poacher (poissonniere) in an upright position. Secure with cheesecloth to hold fish firmly. Poach in the court bouillon, following directions for poaching technique in chapter 6. Lift fish from court bouillon and remove skin.

To decorate, slice whole cucumbers lengthwise, then crosswise into paper-thin slices. Arrange slices on fish, starting from the tail, overlapping each slice to resemble fish scales. Glaze fish with cold liquid jelly. Place on serving platter(s). Garnish with stuffed eggs and serve cold. Serve sauce separately.

Poached Whitefish Mousseline

Poach whole whitefish in court bouillon no. 2, following poaching technique in chapter 6. Serve with mousseline sauce.

Note: All methods of trout preparation are applicable to whitefish.

Yellow Perch

Perch des Gourmets

Ingredients	6 portions		24 portions	
	U.S.	Metric	U.S.	Metric
Perch Fillets	2 lb.	900 g	8 lb.	3.6 kg
Salt and Pepper, to taste				
Lemon Juice	1 oz.	0.3 dl	½ cup	1.2 dl
Eggs	2	2	8	8
Flour	2 oz.	50 g	8 oz.	225 g
Butter	4 oz.	110 g	1 lb.	450 g
Potatoes, boiled	1 lb.	450 g	4 lb.	1.8 kg
Bearnaise Sauce	1 cup	2.5 dl	1 qt.	1 l
Tomatoes, cooked and diced . .	2	2	8	8

Marinate fillets in lemon juice, salt, and pepper. Dip fillets in flour, coat with beaten egg, and fry in butter until brown on both sides. Arrange cooked fish on preheated serving platter(s). Garnish with boiled potatoes. Serve with the bearnaise sauce combined with the tomatoes.

Perch Fish Fry

Ingredients	6 portions		24 portions	
	U.S.	Metric	U.S.	Metric
Dressed Perch	6	6	24	24
Cornmeal	2 oz.	50 g	8 oz.	225 g
Flour	2 oz.	50 g	8 oz.	225 g
Salt	1 tsp.	1 tsp.	1 tbsp.	1 tbsp.
Oil	½ cup	1.2 dl	2 cups	5 dl
Lemon Juice	1 tbsp.	1 tbsp.	2 oz.	0.6 dl
Parsley, to garnish				

Dip perch in water. Coat with mixture of cornmeal, flour, and salt. Fry in hot oil, browning on both sides, until fish flakes easily when tested with a fork. Arrange on serving platter(s). Sprinkle with lemon juice and garnish with parsley.

Fillets of Perch Amandine
See directions for Trout Amandine.

Fillets of Perch Hollandaise
Poach in court bouillon no. 2. Serve with hollandaise sauce.

CHAPTER 14

Shellfish Recipes

This chapter contains recipes for the following:

1. Salt-water Crustaceans
   American Lobster
   Crab
   Norway (Icelandic) Lobster
   Shrimp
   Spiny Lobsters

2. Fresh-water Crustaceans
   Crayfish

3. Mollusks
   Abalone
   Clams
   Mussels
   Octopus
   Oysters
   Scallops
   Snails

American Lobster

Broiled Lobster Windsor

Ingredients	6 portions		24 portions	
	U.S.	Metric	U.S.	Metric
Live Lobsters, 2 lb. (900 g) ...	6	6	24	24
Clarified Butter	4 oz.	110 g	1 lb.	450 g
Cognac	2 oz.	0.6 dl	1 cup	2.5 dl
Shallots, chopped	1 tbsp.	1 tbsp.	4 tbsp.	4 tbsp.
Dry White Wine	1 cup	2.5 dl	1 qt.	1 l
Fresh Tomatos, cooked ...... and chopped	4 oz.	110 g	1 lb.	450 g
Lobster Coral (if available)				
Basil, chopped	1 tsp.	1 tsp.	4 tsp.	4 tsp.
Tarragon, chopped	1 tsp.	1 tsp.	1 tbsp.	1 tbsp.
Bearnaise Sauce	¾ cup	2 dl	2 cups	5 dl

Cook lobster in boiling water for 3 to 4 minutes. Split in half and remove veins and stomach. Pour butter over. Broil for 5 minutes. Pour cognac over and ignite. Season with salt and pepper.

Cook shallots in wine. Add tomatoes, chopped coral, and herbs and reduce to half. Stir in the bearnaise sauce. Pour sauce over lobsters and heat for 5 minutes. Serve hot on pre-heated serving platters.

Lobster Flambeed with Pernod

Ingredients	6 portions		24 portions	
	U.S.	Metric	U.S.	Metric
Live Lobsters, 1½ lb.				
(680 g)	6	6	24	24
Olive Oil	½ cup	1.2 dl	2 cups	5 dl
Butter	4 oz.	110 g	1 lb.	450 g
Onion, chopped	1 oz.	25 g	4 oz.	110 g
Shallots, chopped	1 oz.	25 g	4 oz.	110 g
Garlic Cloves, minced	1	1	4	4
Cognac	1 oz.	0.3 dl	½ cup	1.2 dl
Tomatoes, chopped and seeded	4 oz.	100 g	1 lb.	450 g
Tomato Puree	2 oz.	50 g	8 oz.	200 g
Thyme Leaves	¼ tsp.	¼ tsp.	1 tsp.	1 tsp.
Bay Leaf	1	1	4	4
Dry White Wine	¾ cup	2 dl	3 cups	8 dl
Heavy Cream	5 oz.	1.5 dl	2½ cups	6 dl
Lemon Juice (whole lemons) ..	1	1	4	4
Pernod	1 oz.	0.3 dl	½ cup	1.2 dl

Split lobsters in half. Remove coral and the creamy parts from head and save. Crack the claws. Saute lobster halves in oil until shells turn red. Remove oil from the pan. Add half of the butter, onion, shallots, and garlic. Brown lightly. Deglaze with cognac and ignite. Add the puree, tomatoes, and seasonings. Bring to a boil. Remove lobster pieces. Extract meat from tails and claws. Cut into chunks and save the shells. Strain cooking liquid and boil to reduce by half. Stir the coral and creamy parts of the lobsters with the remaining butter. Stir in the cream, lemon juice, and pernod. Combine with the reduced cooking liquid. Mix in the lobster pieces. Fill the shells with the mixture. Brown under a broiler and serve hot with rice.

Lobster Fra Diavolo

Ingredients	6 portions		24 portions	
	U.S.	Metric	U.S.	Metric
Whole Boiled Lobsters,				
2 lb. (900 g)	6	6	24	24
Salt and Pepper, to taste				
Garlic Cloves, minced	2	2	8	8
Parsley, chopped	1 tbsp.	1 tbsp.	4 tbsp.	4 tbsp.
Olive Oil	2 oz.	0.6 dl	1 cup	2.5 dl
Butter	1 oz.	25 g	4 oz.	110 g
Tomatoes, chopped and seedless	1 lb.	450 g	4 lb.	1.8 kg

Cut lobsters in half lengthwise and crack claws. Season with salt and pepper. Arrange in baking pans. Saute the garlic and parsley in olive oil and butter. Add tomatos and cook over medium heat for 5 to 10 minutes. Spoon tomato mixture over lobster. Heat in oven. Arrange on a serving platter. Garnish with parsley.

Lobster Newburg

Ingredients	6 portions		24 portions	
	U.S.	Metric	U.S.	Metric
Cooked Lobster	2 lb.	900 g	8 lb.	3.6 kg
Butter	2 oz.	50 g	8 oz.	200 g
Dry Sherry Wine	¾ cup	2 dl	3 cups	8 dl
Heavy Cream	1 cup	2.5 dl	1 qt.	1 l
Egg Yolks	3	3	12	12
Salt	¼ tsp.	¼ tsp.	1 tsp.	1 tsp.

Cut lobster meat into large chunks. Cook slowly in butter about 5 minutes. Deglaze with wine. Simmer to reduce wine. Beat cream into egg yolks, add to lobster, and season. Heat to the boiling point, stirring continuously until thickened. Serve immediately in timbales or on hot toast.

Lobster Souffle

Ingredients	6 portions		24 portions	
	U.S.	Metric	U.S.	Metric
Butter	2 oz.	50 g	8 oz.	200 g
Lobster Butter	1 oz.	25 g	4 oz.	110 g
Flour	2 oz.	50 g	8 oz.	200 g
Cornstarch	1 oz.	25 g	4 oz.	110
Paprika	½ tsp.	½ tsp.	2 tsp.	2 tsp.
Milk	2 cups	5 dl	2 qt.	2 l
Egg Yolks	7	7	28	28
Cooked Lobster Meat, minced	1 lb.	450 g	4 lb.	1.8 kg
Fresh Bread Crumbs	1 oz.	25 g	4 oz.	110 g
Salt	1 tsp.	1 tsp.	4 tsp.	4 tsp.
Pepper, ground	¼ tsp.	¼ tsp.	1 tsp.	1 tsp.
Nutmeg, ground	⅛ tsp.	⅛ tsp.	½ tsp.	½ tsp.
Dry Sherry	2 oz.	0.6 dl	1 cup	2.5 dl
Egg Whites	8	8	32	32

Melt butter and lobster butter. Add flour, cornstarch, and paprika. Cook for 5 minutes over low flame. Boil milk and stir in, whipping until smooth. Cook 10 minutes, stirring occasionally. Grease and flour 10-inch souffle dish(es). Mix in egg yolks, one by one. Add lobster meat, bread crumbs, seasonings, and sherry. Beat egg whites to stiff peaks and fold into mixture. Bake about 45 minutes at 365°F (185°C).

Lobster Thermidor

Ingredients	6 portions		24 portions	
	U.S.	Metric	U.S.	Metric
Butter	2 oz.	50 g	8 oz.	200 g
Shallots	1 oz.	25 g	4 oz.	110 g
Mushrooms, diced	6 oz.	170 g	1.5 lb.	680 g
White Wine	½ cup	1.2 dl	2 cups	5 dl
Lobster Meat, diced	2 lb.	900 g	8 lb.	3.6 kg
Salt and Pepper, to taste				
Dry Mustard	½ tsp.	½ tsp.	2 tsp.	2 tsp.
Bechamel Sauce	1.5 cups	4 dl	1.5 qt.	1.5 dl
Heavy Cream	¾ cup	2 dl	3 cups	8 dl
Chives, chopped	1 tbsp.	1 tbsp.	4 tbsp.	4 tbsp.
Parsley, chopped	1 tbsp.	1 tbsp.	4 tbsp.	4 tbsp.
Lobster Shells	6	6	24	24

Glazing Sauce

Bechamel Sauce	½ cup	1.2 dl	2 cups	5 dl
Whipped Cream	½ cup	1.2 dl	2 cups	5 dl
Hollandaise Sauce	½ cup	1.2 dl	2 cups	5 dl

Saute shallots and mushrooms in butter. Deglaze with wine. Simmer for 5 minutes. Add lobster and seasonings. Stir in bechamel sauce, cream, chives, and parsley. Bring to a boil and season to taste. Fill lobster shells with mixture. Top with glazing sauce and brown under the broiler.

Mousseline of Lobster Americaine

	6 portions		24 portions	
Ingredients	U.S.	Metric	U.S.	Metric
Mousseline				
Raw Lobster Meat (save shells)	1 lb.	450 g	4 lb.	1.8 kg
Heavy Cream	2 cups	5 dl	2 qt.	2 l
Egg Whites	3	3	12	12
Salt	½ tsp.	½ tsp.	2 tsp.	2 tsp.
White Pepper	¼ tsp.	¼ tsp.	1 tsp.	1 tsp.
Nutmeg, ground	⅛ tsp.	⅛ tsp.	½ tsp.	½ tsp.
Truffle Slices	6	6	24	24
Fleurons				
Sauce				
Oil	2 oz.	0.6 dl	½ cup	1.2 dl
Butter	2 oz.	0.6 dl	½ cup	1.2 dl
Garlic Clove, minced	1	1	4	4
Shallots, chopped	1 tbsp.	1 tbsp.	4 tbsp.	4 tbsp.
Brandy	2 oz.	0.6 dl	1 cup	2.5 dl
White Wine	2 cups	5 dl	2 qt.	2 l
Fish Fumet	2 cups	5 dl	2 qt.	2 l
Tomato Paste	1 tbsp.	1 tbsp.	4 tbsp.	4 tbsp.
Heavy Cream	1 cup	2.5 dl	1 qt.	1 l
Butter	2 oz.	50 g	8 oz.	200 g
Flour	1 tbsp.	1 tbsp.	4 tbsp.	4 tbsp.
Salt and Pepper, to taste				
Pinch of Cayenne				

Mousseline Keep lobster meat very cold and chop finely in a chopping bowl. Gradually add cream, egg whites, and seasonings. Butter a 7-inch ring mold and fill with the mousseline. Cover with wax paper and bake in a waterbath for 30 to 40 minutes in a 325°F (165°C) oven. Unmold on a suitable platter, mask with the following sauce, and garnish with truffle slices and fleurons.

Sauce When cutting lobster, set coral aside. Saute lobster shells in oil and butter until shells are red. Pour off excess fat. Add garlic and shallots. Cook briefly. Pour brandy over lobster shells and ignite. Add wine, fish stock, and tomato paste. Add water to cover shells. Simmer for ½ hour, then strain. Reduce to half. Add cream and reduce again.

Mix coral, butter, and flour. Add to boiling sauce. Simmer for 2 minutes and strain. Season to taste. Pour over fish mousseline.

Homard a la Nage

Cook live lobsters in court bouillon no. 3. Split warm lobsters in half lengthwise. Crack the claws. Serve with lemon butter.

Curried Lobster

Saute cooked lobster meat in butter. Combine with curry sauce. Serve with saffron rice.

Lobster Hollandaise

Split boiled lobsters in half lengthwise. Crack claws. Serve warm lobster with Parisienne potatoes and hollandaise sauce.

Lobster Savannah

Follow the recipe for Lobster Thermidor. Use minted bearnaise sauce for glaze. Garnish with strips of green pepper, red pimentos, and anchovies.

Crab

Aspic of Crabmeat

Ingredients	6 portions		24 portions	
	U.S.	Metric	U.S.	Metric
Crabmeat	8 oz.	225 g	2 lb.	900 g
Unflavored Gelatin	2 tbsp.	2 tbsp.	8 tbsp.	8 tbsp.
Cold Water	½ cup	1.2 dl	2 cups	5 dl
Tomato Juice	2 cups	5 dl	2 qt.	2 l
Salt	½ tsp.	½ tsp.	2 tsp.	2 tsp.
Worcestershire Sauce	½ tsp.	½ tsp.	2 tsp.	2 tsp.
Onion Salt	½ tsp.	½ tsp.	2 tsp.	2 tsp.
Celery, chopped	4 oz.	110 g	1 lb.	450 g
Lemon Juice	1 tbsp.	1 tbsp.	4 tbsp.	0.6 dl
Salt	¼ tsp.	¼ tsp.	1 tsp.	1 tsp.
Mayonnaise	¼ cup	0.6 dl	1 cup	2.5 dl

(cont.)

Remove any shell from crabmeat, keeping the meat intact. Soften gelatin in water. Bring tomato juice to the boiling point. Add gelatin, stirring well to dissolve. Stir in the salt and Worcestershire sauce. Place in a suitable ring mold. Chill until firm.

Combine onion salt, celery, lemon juice, salt, mayonnaise, and crabmeat. Unmold aspic ring mold onto a serving dish. Fill center with crabmeat salad.

Aspic of Crab with Russian Salad

Ingredients	6 portions		24 portions	
	U.S.	Metric	U.S.	Metric
Liquid Jelly	1 cup	2.5 dl	1 qt.	1 l
Crabmeat	1 lb.	450 g	4 lb.	1.8 kg
Cocktail Sauce	1 cup	2.5 dl	1 qt.	1 l
Black Olives	3 oz.	85 g	12 oz.	240 g
Russian Salad	8 oz.	225 g	2 lb.	900 g

Pour the jelly into a decorative mold. Allow to set in the refrigerator. Combine crabmeat and sauce. Arrange the olives on the top of the jelly. Pack the mold with the crabmeat. Cool in the refrigerator for 1 to 2 hours. Dip in hot water to unmold. Serve with Russian salad.

Boiled Dungeness Crab

Ingredients	6 portions		24 portions	
	U.S.	Metric	U.S.	Metric
Live Dungeness Crabs	3	3	12	12
Boiling Water	10 qt.	10 l	10 gal.	40 l
Salt	½ cup	110 g	1 lb.	450 g
Butter or	12 oz.	340 g	3 lb.	1.306 kg
Mayonnaise	1 cup	2.5 dl	1 qt.	1 l

Dress crabs by prying off the top shell. Remove spongy parts underneath the shell (gills, stomach, intestines), and wash body cavity. Place in salted boiling water. Return to boiling and simmer for 15 minutes. Drain. Crack the claws and legs. Serve hot with butter, or chill and serve with mayonnaise.

Boiled Maryland Blue Crab

Ingredients	6 portions		24 portions	
	U.S.	Metric	U.S.	Metric
Boiling Water	6 qt.	6 l	6 gal.	25 l
Vinegar	2 cups	5 dl	2 qt.	2 l
Cayenne Pepper	1 tbsp.	1 tbsp.	4 tbsp.	4 tbsp.
Celery Salt	2 tsp.	2 tsp.	3 tbsp.	3 tbsp.
Mace	1 tbsp.	1 tbsp.	4 tbsp.	4 tbsp.
Ginger, ground	1 tbsp.	1 tbsp.	4 tbsp.	4 tbsp.
Hard-shell Blue Crabs	2 doz.	2 doz.	8 doz.	8 doz.

Add the seasonings to the boiling water. Cover and simmer for 5 minutes. Add crabs, return to boiling, and simmer for 15 minutes. Drain. Serve hot or cold.

Crab Cakes

Ingredients	6 portions		24 portions	
	U.S.	Metric	U.S.	Metric
Butter, melted	3 oz.	85 g	12 oz.	340 g
Onion, chopped	2 oz.	50 g	8 oz.	225 g
Mushrooms, chopped	6 oz.	170 g	1½ lb.	680 g
Flour	2 oz.	50 g	8 oz.	225 g
Dry Mustard	1 tsp.	1 tsp.	1 tbsp.	1 tbsp.
Paprika	½ tsp.	½ tsp.	2 tsp.	2 tsp.
Cayenne Pepper	$1/6$ tsp.	$1/6$ tsp.	¼ tsp.	¼ tsp.
Heavy Cream	½ cup	1.2 dl	2 cups	5 dl
Crabmeat	1 lb.	450 g	4 lb.	1.8 kg
Fresh Bread Crumbs	1 cup	50 g	4 cups	200 g
White Wine	2 oz.	0.6 dl	1 cup	2.5 dl
Chopped Parsley	1 tbsp.	1 tbsp.	4 tbsp.	4 tbsp.
Worcestershire Sauce	½ tsp.	½ tsp.	2 tsp.	2 tsp.
Whole Egg	1	1	4	4
Salt, to taste				

Saute onion and mushrooms in butter. Add flour, mustard, paprika, and pepper. Mix in the cream. Flake the crabmeat and add to the sauce. Mix in remaining ingredients. Allow the mixture to cool.

Portion into 2 cakes per person. Shape into patties and dredge in flour. Fry in butter until golden brown.

Crabmeat Imperial

Ingredients	6 portions		24 portions	
	U.S.	Metric	U.S.	Metric
Crabmeat	1 lb.	450 g	4 lb.	1.8 kg
Butter	2 oz.	50 g	8 oz.	225 g
Green Pepper, chopped	4 oz.	110 g	1 lb.	450 g
Heavy Cream	½ cup	1.2 dl	2 cups	5 dl
Fresh Mayonnaise	1½ cups	4 dl	1½ qt.	1.5 l
Salt and Pepper, to taste				

Remove any pieces of shell or cartilage from crabmeat. Saute the green pepper in butter until wilted. Set aside. Beat the cream until stiff. Fold in the mayonnaise. Add the crab-meat, salt, pepper, and green pepper. Stir until well blended.

Arrange crab mixture in individual small casserole dishes. Bake at 425°F (220°C) until bubbly and lightly browned.

Crabmeat Crunch

Ingredients	6 portions		24 portions	
	U.S.	Metric	U.S.	Metric
Crabmeat	2 lb.	900 g	8 lb.	3.6 kg
Butter or Margarine	4 oz.	110 g	1 lb.	450 g
Celery, diced	4 oz.	110 g	1 lb.	450 g
Cornstarch	1 oz.	25 g	4 oz.	110 g
Chicken Stock	2 cups	5 dl	2 qt.	2 l
Sliced Almonds, toasted	4 oz.	110 g	1 lb.	450 g
Lemon Juice	1 tbsp.	1 tbsp.	2 oz.	0.6 dl
Chow Mein Noodles	1—5 oz. can	140 g	4—5 oz. cans	550 g

Thaw crabmeat if frozen. Drain and remove any shell or cartilage. Melt butter or margarine in a skillet or saute pan. Add celery and crabmeat. Cook over low flame for 5 to 10 minutes, stirring frequently. Dis-solve cornstarch in chicken stock. Add to crabmeat, stirring constantly till thick. Add almonds and lemon juice. Adjust seasonings and serve with the noodles.

Crabmeat Orientale

Ingredients	6 portions		24 portions	
	U.S.	Metric	U.S.	Metric
Olive Oil	1 cup	2.5 dl	3 cups	8 dl
Soy Sauce	2 tbsp.	2 tbsp.	3 oz.	1 dl
Vinegar	3 tbsp.	3 tbsp.	4½ oz.	1.3 dl
Tabasco Sauce	¼ tsp.	¼ tsp.	¾ tsp.	¾ tsp.
Dijon Mustard	1 tsp.	1 tsp.	3 tsp.	3 tsp.
Rice, cooked	3 cups	900 g	6 lbs.	2.7 kg
Raw Mushrooms, sliced	8 oz.	225 g	1½ lb.	680 g
Water Chestnuts, thinly sliced	4 oz.	110 g	12 oz.	340 g
Green Pepper, finely chopped	4 oz.	110 g	12 oz.	340 g
Pimentos, chopped	3	3	9	9
Crabmeat, flaked	1 lb.	450 g	3 lb.	1.36 kg
Parsley, chopped	1 tbsp.	1 tbsp.	3 tbsp.	3 tbsp.
Chives, chopped	1 tbsp.	1 tbsp.	3 tbsp.	3 tbsp.

Prepare a dressing with the oil, vinegar, soy sauce, tabasco, and mustard. Combine remaining ingredients, except parsley and chives. Mix in the dressing. Arrange in a salad bowl. Sprinkle with parsley and chives.

Crabmeat Ravigotte

Ingredients	6 portions		24 portions	
	U.S.	Metric	U.S.	Metric
Crabmeat	1 lb.	450 g	4 lb.	1.8 kg
Sweet Pickles, chopped	2 tbsp.	2 tbsp.	3 oz.	85 g
Lemon Juice	2 tbsp.	2 tbsp.	½ cup	1.2 dl
Salt	¼ tsp.	¼ tsp.	1 tsp.	1 tsp.
Hard-boiled Eggs, chopped . . .	1	1	1	1
Parsley, chopped	1 tbsp.	1 tbsp.	4 tbsp.	4 tbsp.
Mayonnaise	¼ cup	0.6 dl	1 cup	2.5 dl
Stuffed Green Olives, chopped	2 tbsp.	2 tbsp.	3 oz.	85 g
Paprika	¼ tsp.	¼ tsp.	1 tsp.	1 tsp.
Pimento Strips				

Remove any shell or cartilage from crabmeat. Combine pickles, lemon juice, salt, eggs, parsley, and crabmeat. Arrange on a serving platter. Combine mayonnaise, olives, and paprika. Spread over the top of the crabmeat. Chill. Garnish with pimento strips.

Curried Crabmeat Omelette

Ingredients	6 portions		24 portions	
	U.S.	Metric	U.S.	Metric
Eggs	12	12	4 doz.	4 doz.
Salt and Pepper, to taste				
Butter	3 oz.	85 g	12 oz.	340 g
Crabmeat, flaked	7 oz.	200 g	1¾ lb.	800 g
Cream Sauce	1 cup	2.5 dl	1 qt.	1 l
Curry Powder	1 tsp.	1 tsp.	4 tsp.	4 tsp.

Beat the eggs. Season with salt and pepper. Melt the butter in an omelette pan. Pour in the eggs. Cook over brisk flame. Combine the crabmeat, cream sauce, and curry powder, and spoon into the middle of the omelet. Fold the omelet and arrange on a warm serving platter. Make 4 omelettes for 24 portions.

Golden Fried Soft-shell Crabs

Ingredients	6 portions		24 portions	
	U.S.	Metric	U.S.	Metric
Live Soft-shell Crabs, spiders or hotel prime	1½ doz.	1½ doz.	6 doz.	6 doz.
Salt	¾ tsp.	¾ tsp.	1 tbsp.	1 tbsp.
Pepper, ground	¼ tsp.	¼ tsp.	1 tsp.	1 tsp.
Lemon Juice	2 oz.	0.6 dl	1 cup	2.5 dl
Soy Sauce	1 oz.	0.3 dl	½ cup	1.2 dl
Flour	3 oz.	85 g	12 oz.	340 g
Whole Eggs, beaten	3	3	12	12
Fresh Bread Crumbs	2 cups	110 g	8 cups	450 g
Fried Parsley and Lemon Baskets, for garnish				
Remoulade or Green Sauce . .	2 cups	5 dl	2 qt.	2 l

Clean soft crabs according to instructions on page 104. Rinse under cold water. Arrange crabs on sheet pan. Season with salt, pepper, lemon juice, and soy sauce. Refrigerate for 2 hours.

Roll crabs in flour, dip in eggs, and coat lightly with bread crumbs. Deep fry at 375°F (190°C) for 1½ to 2 minutes. Arrange on a heated platter, lined with folded napkins. Garnish with the parsley and lemon baskets and serve hot. Serve the sauce separately.

Key Lime Stone Crab

Ingredients	6 portions		24 portions	
	U.S.	Metric	U.S.	Metric
Butter	2 oz.	50 g	8 oz.	200 g
Flour	2 oz.	50 g	8 oz.	200 g
Milk . . . . : .	1 cup	2.5 dl	1 qt.	1 l
Lime Rind, grated	1	1	4	4
Lime Juice	2 tbsp.	2 tbsp.	½ cup	1.2 dl
Butter	2 oz.	50 g	8 oz.	200 g
Stone Crabmeat	1 lb.	450 g	4 lbs.	1.8 kg
Cognac	2 tbsp.	0.3 dl	½ cup	1.2 dl

Make a cream sauce with the butter, flour, and milk. Season with salt. Add the grated rind and lime juice. Heat remaining butter and add crabmeat. Add cognac and ignite. Fold in the cream sauce. Serve with rice.

King Crab Salad

Ingredients	6 portions		24 portions	
	U.S.	Metric	U.S.	Metric
Sour Cream	½ cup	1.2 dl	2 cups	5 dl
Horseradish, grated	1 tbsp.	1 tbsp.	4 tbsp.	4 tbsp.
Cocktail Sauce . . . . : . .	1 cup	2.5 dl	1 qt.	1 l
King or Queen Crabmeat	1 lb.	450 g	4 lb.	1.8 kg
Seedless Grapes	6 oz.	170 g	1½ lb.	680 g

Combine the sour cream, horseradish, and cocktail sauce. Fold in the crabmeat and grapes. Arrange on a shallow serving dish. Chill before serving.

Stone Crab au Gratin

Ingredients	6 portions		24 portions	
	U.S.	Metric	U.S.	Metric
Stone Crab Claws	2 lb.	910 g	8 lb.	3.6 kg
Butter	2 oz.	50 g	8 oz.	200 g
Shallots, chopped	2 oz.	50 g	8 oz.	200 g
Dry White Wine	1 cup	2.5 dl	1 qt.	1 l
Cream Sauce	2 cups	5 dl	2 qt.	2 l
Hollandaise Sauce	½ cup	1.2 dl	2 cups	5 dl
Salt and Pepper, to taste				
Fleurons	6	6	24	24

(cont.)

Crack the crab claws to remove the meat. Save one claw per serving as garnish. Saute the shallots in butter over low heat. Add the flaked crabmeat and deglaze with the wine.

Combine an equal volume of cream sauce with the hollandaise. Stir remaining cream sauce into crab. Season with salt and pepper. Transfer crab into oven-proof serving dish(es). Cover with the hollandaise cream sauce and glaze under a broiler. Garnish with warm crab claws and fleurons. Serve hot.

Norway (Icelandic) Lobster

Icelandic Lobster Cocktail

Ingredients	6 portions		24 portions	
	U.S.	Metric	U.S.	Metric
Icelandic Lobster Tails, cooked, shelled, and deveined	12	12	48	48
Orange Sections	12	12	48	48
Mango Chutney	1 tbsp.	1 tbsp.	4 tbsp.	4 tbsp.
Lemon Juice	2 oz.	0.6 dl	1 cup	2.5 dl
Fresh Dill, chopped	1 tsp.	1 tsp.	1 tbsp.	1 tbsp.
Fresh Horseradish, grated	1 tsp.	1 tsp.	1 tbsp.	1 tbsp.
Whipped Cream	1 cup	2.5 dl	1 qt.	1 l
Boston Lettuce	1 head	1 head	4 heads	4 heads
Lemon Wedges, to garnish ...				

Combine lobster tails with orange sections. Add chutney, lemon juice, dill, and horseradish. Marinate for ½ hour. Fold in the whipped cream.

Shred cleaned lettuce leaves in cocktail glasses. Arrange a layer of lettuce and two lobster tails in each glass. Spoon over the sauce. Garnish with lemon wedges.

Langoustines au Gratin (Icelandic Lobster au Gratin)

Ingredients	6 portions		24 portions	
	U.S.	Metric	U.S.	Metric
Frozen Icelandic Lobsters	3 lb.	1.360 kg	12 lb.	5.4 kg
Butter	2 oz.	50 g	8 oz.	200 g
Fresh Mushrooms	8 oz.	225 g	2 lb.	900 g
Cognac	3 oz.	1 dl	1½ cups	4 dl
Sauce Cardinal	1½ cups	4 dl	1½ qt.	1.5 l

Cook the Icelandic lobsters in court bouillon no. 3. Drain, cool, shell, and devein the lobs- ter tails. Saute the lobster tails in butter. Add mushrooms cut in quarters. Deglaze with cognac. Stir in the cardinal sauce. Simmer for 5 minutes. Brown under a broiler. Serve with rice.

Langostinos Omelette Americaine

Ingredients	6 portions		24 portions	
	U.S.	Metric	U.S.	Metric
Eggs	12	12	48	48
Salt and Pepper, to taste				
Butter	3 oz.	85 g	12 oz.	340 g
Icelandic Lobster, diced and cooked	7 oz.	200 g	1¾ lb.	800 g
Sauce Americaine	1 cup	2.5 dl	1 qt.	1 l

Beat the eggs. Season with salt and pepper. Melt butter in an omelette pan. Pour in half (⅛) of the eggs. Cook over brisk flame. Combine lobster meat with sauce Americaine. Spoon half (⅛) into the middle of the omelette. Fold omelette and arrange on preheated serving platter. Repeat with remaining eggs and filling. Serve hot.

Deep-fried Lobsterette Sauce Remoulade

See the directions for Deep-fried Shrimp Sauce Remoulade.

Langoustines Meuniere

See the cooking technique for saute meuniere.

Shrimp

Aspic of Shrimp, Sauce Antiboise

Ingredients	6 portions		24 portions	
	U.S.	Metric	U.S.	Metric
Shrimp Mousse	10½ oz.	300 g	2 lb. 6 oz.	1.2 kg
Medium to Large Shrimp, in shells	12	12	48	48
Seafood Spice Mix, in small sachet	1	1	4	4
Lemon Juice	1 tbsp.	1 tbsp.	4 tbsp.	4 tbsp.
Tiny Shrimp, cooked	3½ oz.	100 g	14 oz.	400 g
Aspic Jelly, flavored with white wine	3 cups	8 dl	3 qt.	3 l
Sauce Antiboise	1½ cups	4 dl	6 cups	1.2 l

(cont.)

Prepare the shrimp mousse, omitting the truffles. Do not allow the mousse to set.

Cook the shrimp in salted boiling water with spice mix. Bring to a boil and simmer for 5 minutes. Drain and cool the shrimp. Shell and devein, and marinate in lemon juice.

Pour the lukewarm aspic jelly into a suitable decorative mold. Set on ice. As soon as jelly starts to set against the mold, pour out and reserve the rest. Arrange the large shrimp over the set jelly. Pour in a small amount of jelly to seal them. Combine the tiny shrimp with the mousse and spoon in to fill the mold. Pour small amount of jelly to cover. Refrigerate for 2 hours or more.

To unmold, dip mold in lukewarm water. Invert on chilled serving dish. Garnish with chopped jelly. Serve sauce separately.

Bouquet of Shrimp Boca Grande

Ingredients	6 portions		24 portions	
	U.S.	Metric	U.S.	Metric
Small Fresh Green Shrimp* ...	2 lb. 6 oz.	1.2 kg	10½ lb.	4.8 kg
Salt	2 tsp.	2 tsp.	2 tbsp.	2 tbsp.
Peppercorns	1 tsp.	1 tsp.	1 tbsp.	1 tbsp.
Seafood Spice Mix, in sachet bag	1	1	4	4
Large Grapefruit	1	1	4	4
Avocados	3	3	12	12
Lime Wedges	6	6	24	24
Cocktail Sauce	1½ cups	4 dl	1½ qt.	1.5 l

Boil enough water to cook shrimp. Add salt, pepper, and spice mix. Simmer for 5 minutes, then add the shrimp. Bring to a quick boil and simmer for 2 minutes. Drain shrimp. Peel and devein while warm. Take a few whole shrimp and arrange in a bouquet, inserting the pointed ends of heads into the grapefruit.

Cut avocados in half, lengthwise Remove stone. Peel and slice. Arrange the avocado slices on a serving platter, alternating with small bunches of shrimp. Place the bouquet of shrimp in center of platter. Garnish with lime wedges. Serve cocktail sauce separately.

Note: Do not store any cooked shrimp in water, as they lose their flavor.

*Green shrimp are freshly caught shrimp, with the heads on. They are often available in Southern and Gulf States and sometimes in fish markets.

Brochettes of Shrimp, Curry Sauce

Ingredients	6 portions		24 portions	
	U.S.	*Metric*	*U.S.*	*Metric*
Medium or Jumbo Shrimp, in shells	2 lb. 6 oz.	1.2 kg	10½ lb.	4.8 kg
Lemon Juice	1 tbsp.	1 tbsp.	2 oz.	0.6 dl
Chili Sauce	½ cup	1.2 dl	2 cups	5 dl
Soy Sauce	2 oz.	0.6 dl	1 cup	2.5 dl
Salt	½ tsp.	½ tsp.	2 tsp.	2 tsp.
Curry Sauce	1½ cups	4 dl	1½ qt.	1.5 l
Flour	2 oz.	50 g	8 oz.	225 g
Butter	2 oz.	50 g	8 oz.	225 g
Steamed Rice				

Shell and devein shrimp in "fantail" fashion (see chapter 5). Wash and drain and marinate in mixture of lemon juice, chili sauce, soy sauce, and salt for ½ hour. Prepare the curry sauce.

Thread shrimp through head and tail on skewers. Roll in flour. Saute in butter until shrimp turn pink and are slightly brown. Serve on a bed of steamed rice and top with curry sauce.

Broiled Jumbo Spanish Shrimp

Ingredients	6 portions		24 portions	
	U.S.	*Metric*	*U.S.*	*Metric*
Jumbo Spanish Scarlet Shrimp, U.10	2 doz.	2 doz.	8 doz.	8 doz.
Salt	1 tsp.	1 tsp.	1 tbsp.	1 tbsp.
White Pepper	¼ tsp.	¼ tsp.	1 tsp.	1 tsp.
Lemon Juice	1 tbsp.	1 tbsp.	2 oz.	0.6 dl
Butter, melted	4 oz.	1.2 dl	2 cups	5 dl
Lemon Wedges	6	6	24	24
Parsley				

Peel and fantail shrimp. Devein and butterfly (see chapter 5). Arrange shrimp on a baking dish. Season with salt, pepper, and lemon juice. Pour the melted butter over and broil about 4 inches (10 cm) from source of heat, for 10 minutes. Transfer to a serving platter. Garnish with lemon wedges and parsley.

Variation: For garlic broiled jumbo shrimp, use garlic butter.

Crevettes en Coquille
(Glazed Shrimp en Coquille)

Ingredients	6 portions		24 portions	
	U.S.	Metric	U.S.	Metric
Scallop Shells	6	6	24	24
Duchess Potatoes	10 oz.	300 g	2½ lb.	1.2 kg
White Wine Sauce	2½ cups	6 dl	4 cups	1 l
Mushroom Buttons	5 oz.	150 g	1¼ lb.	600 g
Butter	1 oz.	25 g	4 oz.	100 g
Lemon Juice	1 tsp.	1 tsp.	1 tbsp.	1 tbsp.
Shrimp, cooked and diced	1¾ lb.	800 g	7 lb.	3.2 kg
Truffle Slices (optional)	6	6	24	24

Select scallop shells of the same size. Spoon the duchess potatoes into a pastry bag fitted with a star tube. Pipe the potatoes using an up and down motion around the edges of the shells. Spoon a tablespoon of sauce into each shell. Wash the mushrooms, drain, and saute over a brisk fire in butter and lemon juice. Season with salt.

Combine the shrimp with remaining sauce and mushrooms. Garnish the shells. Glaze under the broiler. Place a slice of truffle in the center of each shell. Serve hot.

Note: Mornay sauce can be substituted for the white wine sauce.

Deep-fried Shrimp Sauce Remoulade

Ingredients	6 portions		24 portions	
	U.S.	Metric	U.S.	Metric
Medium Shrimp, raw	2¼ lb.	1 kg	9½ lb.	4 kg
Lemon Juice	1 tbsp.	1 tbsp.	½ cup	1.2 dl
Salt	½ tsp.	½ tsp.	2 tsp.	2 tsp.
White Pepper	⅛ tsp.	⅛ tsp.	½ tsp.	½ tsp.
Whole Eggs, beaten	3	3	12	12
Flour.....................	3 oz.	85 g	12 oz.	340 g
Fresh Bread Crumbs	2 cups	110 g	8 cups	440 g
Oil, for frying				
Parsley, deep fried				
Remoulade Sauce	1½ cups	4 dl	1½ qt.	1.5 l

Shell and devein the shrimp. Rinse under cold water and drain. Butterfly the shrimp (see chapter 5). Arrange on a tray. Season with salt, pepper, and lemon juice. Marinate for ½ hour or more.

Dip each shrimp in flour and egg, and roll in bread crumbs. Deep fry for 2 to 4 minutes, according to size. Arrange on a platter covered with a napkin. Surround with the fried parsley. Serve sauce separately.

Flambeed Shrimp Suedoise with Wild Rice

Ingredients	6 portions		24 portions	
	U.S.	Metric	U.S.	Metric
Minute Wild Rice	8 oz.	225 g	2 lb.	900 g
Medium to Large Shrimp	2 lb.	900 g	8 lb.	3.6 kg
Butter	2 tbsp.	25 g	4 oz.	100 g
Shallots, chopped	1 tbsp.	1 tbsp.	4 tbsp.	4 tbsp.
Brandy	2 oz.	0.6 dl	1 cup	2.5 dl
Veloute Sauce	4 oz.	1.2 dl	2 cups	5 dl
Sour Cream	3 oz.	1 dl	1½ cups	4 dl
Heavy Cream	3 oz.	1 dl	1½ cups	4 dl
Dill Weed	1 tsp.	1 tsp.	1 tbsp.	1 tbsp.
Salt	½ tsp.	½ tsp.	2 tsp.	2 tsp.
Pepper	¼ tsp.	¼ tsp.	1 tsp.	1 tsp.

Cook the rice according to directions on package. (Brown or regular rice can be substituted for wild rice, but the dish will lose in appearance and originality.)

Shell and devein shrimp. Rinse under cold water and drain. Melt butter in a saute pan. Add the shallots and cook over low heat for 5 minutes. Add shrimp and cook over high heat for 2 minutes. Pour in the brandy and ignite. Add the veloute sauce, sour cream, heavy cream, dill, salt, and pepper.

Stir to combine and bring to a boil. Do not overcook. Pack rice in buttered ring mold(s). Invert onto serving platter. Spoon shrimp suedoise in middle. Sprinkle with dill and serve hot.

Jumbo Red Shrimp Cap Ferrat

Ingredients	6 portions		24 portions	
	U.S.	Metric	U.S.	Metric
Jumbo Spanish Red Shrimp . .	2 doz.	2 doz.	8 doz.	8 doz.
Salt	1 tsp.	1 tsp.	1 tbsp.	1 tbsp.
Butter	2 tbsp.	2 tbsp.	4 oz.	110 g
Shallots, chopped	2 tbsp.	2 tbsp.	4 oz.	110 g
Roux	2 oz.	50 g	8 oz.	225 g
White Wine	1 cup	2.5 dl	1 qt.	1 l
Tomatoes, chopped, peeled, and seeded	1 lb.	450 g	4 lb.	1.8 kg
Heavy Cream	1 cup	2.5 dl	1 qt.	1 l
Parsley				
Cooked Rice (optional)				

(cont.)

Butterfly the unshelled shrimp (see chapter 5). Remove the sand veins. Rinse under cold water and drain. Sprinkle with salt.

Melt butter in a skillet. Stir in the shallots and cook over low heat for 5 minutes. Add roux and wine and whip until smooth. Add tomatoes and cream, and simmer until sauce is thick.

Place shrimp in a baking dish. Spoon a small amount of sauce over each shrimp. Bake at 400°F (200°C) for 10 to 15 minutes. Transfer to a serving platter. Garnish with parsley. Rice is the best accompaniment.

Jumbo Shrimp Louisiana

Ingredients	6 portions		24 portions	
	U.S.	Metric	U.S.	Metric
Jumbo Shrimp, in shells	2¼ lb.	1 kg	9½ lb.	4 kg
Olive Oil	½ cup	1.2 dl	2 cups	5 dl
Scotch Whiskey	2 oz.	0.6 dl	1 cup	2.5 dl
Dry Sherry Wine	¾ cup	2 dl	3 cups	8 dl
Fish Fumet	2½ cups	6 dl	2½ qt.	2.5 l
Onion, finely chopped	3½ oz.	100 g	14 oz.	400 g
Flour	1 oz.	25 g	4 oz.	110 g
Canned Tomatoes, diced and seedless	14 oz.	400 g	3 lb.	1.2 kg
Salt	½ tsp.	½ tsp.	2 tsp.	2 tsp.
White Pepper	¼ tsp.	¼ tsp.	1 tsp.	1 tsp.
Cayenne Pepper	pinch	pinch	⅛ tsp.	⅛ tsp.
Lemon Juice	1 tbsp.	1 tbsp.	4 tbsp.	4 tbsp.

Shell and devein the shrimp. Rinse under cold water and drain. Heat the oil to the smoking point in a saute or frying pan. Add the shrimp and stir continuously to color slightly. Pour off the oil and save for later use.

Pour the whiskey over the shrimp. Ignite, then deglaze with the wine. Add half of the fish fumet, bring to a boil, and simmer for a minute.

Heat up the oil in a frying pan. Add the onion and stir until golden brown. Sprinkle with the flour and stir to mix. Cook over low heat for 2 minutes. Add the tomatoes, moisten with remaining fumet, and bring to a boil. Combine the sauce with the shrimp. Season with salt, peppers, and lemon juice. Simmer until shrimp are cooked. Serve in a timbale with rice.

Omelette Souffle with Shrimp

Ingredients	6 portions		24 portions	
	U.S.	Metric	U.S.	Metric
Whole Eggs	1 doz.	1 doz.	4 doz.	4 doz.
Salt	½ tsp.	½ tsp.	2 tsp.	2 tsp.
White Pepper	¼ tsp.	¼ tsp.	1 tsp.	1 tsp.
Small Cooked Shrimp, shelled and deveined	9 oz.	250 g	2 lb. 2 oz.	1 kg
Shrimp Sauce	1¼ cup	3 dl	5 cups	1.25 l

Separate half of the eggs. Mix the yolks with the remaining whole eggs, salt, and pepper. Beat lightly. Whip the egg whites to a soft peak. Fold into the whole egg mixture.

To make one (3-portion) omelette melt some of the butter in a medium omelet pan. Pour in half (⅛) of the omelet mix. Stir with a fork over medium heat. Before the eggs set completely, spoon half (⅛) of the shrimp over half of the omelette and fold in two. Transfer to a serving platter and keep warm. Make other omelettes. Coat each omelette with shrimp sauce and serve remaining sauce separately.

Quenelles de Crevettes (Shrimp Quenelles)

Ingredients	6 portions		24 portions	
	U.S.	Metric	U.S.	Metric
Raw Shrimp, in shells	9 oz.	250 g	2¼ lb.	1 kg
Sole or Flounder Fillet	3½ oz.	100 g	14 oz.	400 g
Egg Whites	2	2	8	8
Heavy Cream	1 cup	2.5 dl	1 qt.	1 l
Salt	¾ tsp.	¾ tsp.	1 tbsp.	1 tbsp.
White Pepper	¼ tsp.	¼ tsp.	1 tsp.	1 tsp.
Cayenne Pepper	⅛ tsp.	⅛ tsp.	½ tsp.	½ tsp.
Shrimp Sauce	1½ cups	4 dl	1½ qt.	1.5 l

Peel and devein shrimp. Cut fish fillet into 1-inch (2.5-cm) pieces. Grind both in a meat grinder or, preferably, a food processor. Slowly add the egg whites and heavy cream, mixing continuously. Season with salt and peppers. To shape the quenelles, see chapter 9.

Butter a flame-proof cooking dish large enough to accommodate the quenelles. Cover the quenelles with salted boiling water or fish fumet, if available. Simmer, covered, for 3 minutes. Turn the quenelles over and let stand 3 more minutes. Drain on absorbent paper, arrange on a serving dish, and cover each quenelle with shrimp sauce.

Shrimp Americaine

Ingredients	6 portions		24 portions	
	U.S.	Metric	U.S.	Metric
Raw Shrimp, in shells	2 lb.	900 g	8 lb.	3.6 kg
Butter	3 oz.	85 g	12 oz.	340 g
Salt	½ tsp.	½ tsp.	2 tsp.	2 tsp.
Paprika	¼ tsp.	¼ tsp.	1 tsp.	1 tsp.
Cooked Rice	11 oz.	300 g	2¾ lb.	1.2 kg
Americaine Sauce	1 recipe	1 recipe	1 recipe	1 recipe

Shell and devein shrimp. Rinse under cold water and drain. Melt half of the butter in a saute pan. Cook the shrimp over low heat until pink and tender. Season with salt and paprika. Add the Americaine sauce and simmer for 5 minutes. Butter ring mold(s). Pack in the hot rice. Invert onto a serving platter. Spoon the shrimp in the center and serve hot.

Shrimp and Avocados, Sauce Verte

Ingredients	6 portions		24 portions	
	U.S.	Metric	U.S.	Metric
Seafood Spice Mix, in sachet bag	1 tbsp.	1 tbsp.	4 tbsp.	4 tbsp.
Salt	2 tsp.	2 tsp.	2½ tbsp.	2½ tbsp.
Small Shrimp, peeled and deveined	1¼ lb.	600 g	5 ½ lb.	2.5 kg
Ripe Avocados	3	3	12	12
Oil and Vinegar Dressing	3 oz.	1 dl	1½ cups	4 dl
Lettuce Leaves				
Lemon Wedges	6	6	24	24
Sauce Verte	1½ cups	4 dl	1½ qt.	1.5 l

Bring water, spice mix, and salt to a boil. Add shrimp. Bring to a boil and simmer for 2 minutes. Drain and cool. Split avocados in half, lengthwise. Remove pits. Marinate the avocado halves in oil and vinegar dressing for 15 minutes or more.

Cover round serving dish(es) with lettuce leaves. Fill avocado halves with shrimp and arrange on platter. Garnish with lemon wedges. Serve with sauce verte.

Shrimp au Gratin

Ingredients	6 portions		24 portions	
	U.S.	Metric	U.S.	Metric
Shrimp, in shells	2 lb.	900 g	8 lb.	3.6 kg
Butter	1 oz.	25 g	4 oz.	110 g
Onion, chopped	2 oz.	50 g	8 oz.	225 g
Sauce Allemande	1½ cups	4 dl.	1½ qt.	1.5 l
Cheese, grated	2 oz.	50 g	8 oz.	225 g
Dry Bread Crumbs	1 oz.	25 g	4 oz.	110 g
Butter, melted	1 tbsp.	1 tbsp.	2 oz.	50 g

Peel and devein shrimp. Cut large shrimp in half. Saute in butter until pink. Do not over-cook. Remove the shrimp and set aside. Add onion to pan, and cook over low heat for 10 min-utes. Add sauce allemande and heat to boiling point. Mix in the shrimp.

Transfer to an oven-proof serving dish. Combine cheese, bread crumbs, and melted but-ter, and sprinkle over the shrimp. Bake at 400°F (200°C) for 10 to 15 minutes, or until golden brown.

Shrimp Cardinal in Patty Shells

Ingredients	6 portions		24 portions	
	U.S.	Metric	U.S.	Metric
Medium Shrimp, in shells	2 lb.	900 g	8 lb.	3.6 kg
Lobster Butter	2 oz.	50 g	8 oz.	225 g
Brandy	1 oz.	0.3 dl	½ cup	1.2 dl
Dry White Wine	1 cup	2.5 dl	1 qt.	1 l
Fish Fumet	¾ cup	2 dl	3 cups	8 dl
Heavy Cream	1 cup	2.5 dl	1 qt.	1 l
Beurre Manie	1 oz.	25 g	4 oz.	110 g
Hollandaise Sauce	½ cup	1.2 dl	2 cups	5 dl
Baked Patty Shells, small oval or round	6	6	24	24
Salt and Pepper, to taste				

Shell and devein the shrimp. Rinse under cold water and drain. Heat the lobster butter in a saute pan. Toss in the shrimp and cook over medium heat for 5 minutes. Pour in the brandy and ignite. Deglaze with wine and cook an additional 5 min-utes. Remove the shrimp and keep warm.

Pour the fish fumet and cream into the liquid. Reduce by one quarter over high heat. Whip in the beurre manie in small pieces. Bring the sauce to a quick boil. Add the hollan-daise sauce. Combine the shrimp with the sauce and heat thoroughly. Season with salt and ground pepper, to taste. Heat the patty shells and fill with the shrimp mixture. Serve at once.

Shrimp Cocktail

Ingredients	6 portions		24 portions	
	U.S.	Metric	U.S.	Metric
Lettuce Leaves				
Grapefruit	1	1	4	4
Cocktail Sauce	2 cups	5 dl	2 qt.	2 l
Whole Shrimp, cooked in shells, for garnish				
Small Shrimp, cooked, peeled, and deveined	2 lb.	900 g	8 lb.	3.6 kg
Lemon Wedges	6	6	24	24

Cover the round serving platter(s) with lettuce leaves. Make a four-petal tulip flower with grapefruit. Pour the sauce into the grapefruit. (For individual servings, use lemons.)

Place the filled grapefruit in center of platter. Decorate with the whole unshelled shrimp. Surround with cooked shrimp. Garnish with lemon wedges.

Shrimp Egg Foo Yung

Ingredients	6 portions		24 portions	
	U.S.	Metric	U.S.	Metric
Bean Sprouts	4 oz.	110 g	1 lb.	450 g
Shrimp, peeled and deveined	8 oz.	225 g	2 lb.	900 g
Peanut Oil	¼ cup	0.6 dl	1 cup	2.5 dl
Whole Eggs	3	3	12	12
Raw Mushrooms, diced	2 oz.	50 g	8 oz.	200 g
Sauce				
Cornstarch	1 tbsp.	1 tbsp.	4 tbsp.	4 tbsp.
Chicken Stock	¾ cup	2 dl	3 cups	8 dl
Soy Sauce	1 tbsp.	1 tbsp.	¼ cup	0.6 dl
Salt	½ tsp.	½ tsp.	2 tsp.	2 tsp.

For Sauce Dissolve cornstarch in half of the stock. Boil remaining stock, add soy sauce and salt, and mix in the cornstarch. Stir until thick. Set sauce aside and keep warm.

For Pancakes Rinse and strain the bean sprouts. Dice the shrimp. In a skillet or wok, heat half of the oil. Stir fry shrimp for 1 minute (4 minutes for 24 servings). Set aside.

Beat the eggs lightly. Add shrimp, bean sprouts, and mushrooms. Heat a little oil in a skillet. Pour in ¼ cup (0.6 dl) of mixture. Cook until light brown. Turn pancake over and cook one more minute. Transfer to a platter. Make more pancakes using remaining mixture. Stack two by two and pour hot sauce over. Serve hot.

Shrimp Mousse

Ingredients	6 portions		24 portions	
	U.S.	Metric	U.S.	Metric
Butter	1 oz.	25 g	4 oz.	110 g
Onion, finely chopped	1 oz.	25 g	4 oz.	110 g
Carrots, finely chopped	1 oz.	25 g	4 oz.	110 g
Medium Shrimp, in shells	1¼ lb.	600 g	5½ lb.	2.5 kg
Cognac	3 oz.	1 dl	1½ cups	4 dl
Dry White Wine	3 oz.	1 dl	1½ cups	4 dl
Veloute Sauce	¾ cup	2 dl	3 cups	8 dl
Shrimp Butter	2 oz.	50 g	8 oz.	225 g
Cold Liquid Jelly	1½ cups	4 dl	1½ qt.	1.5 l
Heavy Cream, whipped	1 cup	2.5 dl	1 qt.	1 l
Salt and Pepper, to taste				
Truffle Slices	6	6	24	24

Melt the butter in a saute pan. Add onion and carrots and cook over low heat for 5 minutes. Combine shrimp with the vegetables and cook over high heat until shrimp are pink. Pour in the cognac and ignite. Deglaze with white wine. Cover and simmer for 5 minutes. Remove shrimp from pan, shell and devein.

In a food processor or blender, puree the shrimp with the vegetables and cooking liquid. Blend in the veloute sauce and shrimp butter. Fold in half of the jelly and all of the cream. Season with salt and pepper.

Pour the mousse into a decorative mold(s). Refrigerate for 2 hours.

To unmold, dip mold in lukewarm water. Invert onto a chilled serving platter. Decorate with truffle slices, and glaze with remaining cold liquid jelly.

Note: Test a teaspoon of the prepared mousse to determine its firmness when chilled. Add dissolved unflavored gelatin to liquid mousse if necessary to obtain a firm light-to-medium cold mousse.

Shrimp Orientale

Ingredients	6 portions		24 portions	
	U.S.	Metric	U.S.	Metric
Onion, chopped	4 oz.	110 g	1 lb.	450 g
Butter	4 oz.	110 g	1 lb.	450 g
Tomatoes, peeled, seeded, and chopped	1 cup	2.5 dl	1 qt.	1 l
Rice	1 cup	225 g	4 cups	900 g
Saffron Threads	½ tsp.	½ tsp.	2 tsp.	2 tsp.
Water	2½ cups	6 dl	10 cups	2.5 l
Raw Shrimp, in shells	2 lb.	900 g	8 lb.	3.6 kg
Salt	½ tsp.	½ tsp.	2 tsp.	2 tsp.
White Pepper	¼ tsp.	¼ tsp.	1 tsp.	1 tsp.
White Wine Sauce	1½ cups	4 dl	1½ qt.	1.5 l

Saute the onion in half of the butter, until transparent. Stir in the tomatoes. Cook for 5 minutes. Add the rice, saffron, and water. Stir well, cover, and bake for 20 minutes in a 350°F (180°C) oven. Pack the rice in a buttered ring mold(s). Keep warm.

Shell and devein shrimp. Rinse in cold water and drain. Melt the remaining butter in a skillet. Add the shrimp and cook over high heat until pink. Season with salt and pepper. Add the white wine sauce and simmer for 5 minutes. Unmold the rice on a round serving platter(s). Spoon shrimp and sauce in the middle. Serve hot.

Shrimp Quiche

Ingredients	6 portions		24 portions	
	U.S.	Metric	U.S.	Metric
Pie Crust Dough	½ recipe	½ recipe	double recipe	double recipe
Butter	2 oz.	50 g	8 oz.	225 g
Shallots, chopped	1 tbsp.	1 tbsp.	4 tbsp.	4 tbsp.
Dry White Wine	3 oz.	1 dl	1½ cups	4 dl
Raw Shrimp, diced	8 oz.	225 g	2 lb.	900 g
Whole Eggs	4	4	16	16
Half and Half	1½ cups	4 dl	1½ qt.	1.5 l
Salt	½ tsp.	½ tsp.	2 tsp.	2 tsp.
White Pepper	¼ tsp.	¼ tsp.	1 tsp.	1 tsp.
Nutmeg	⅛ tsp.	⅛ tsp.	½ tsp.	½ tsp.

Roll out the dough and line a 9-inch (22.5-cm) pie plate(s). Cover the bottom and sides with foil so that the dough keeps its original shape while baking. Bake at 350°F (180°C) for 15 to 20 minutes, or until brown. Remove foil.

Melt the butter, add the shallots, and cook over low heat for 5 minutes. Deglaze with the wine. Stir in the shrimp and cook for 5 minutes, or until shrimp turn pink. Beat remaining ingredients together. Mix in the slightly cooled shrimp, and fill the crust(s). Bake at 350°F (180°C) for 25 to 30 minutes, or until set and golden brown.

Shrimp Salad Roscoff

Ingredients	6 portions		24 portions	
	U.S.	Metric	U.S.	Metric
Mayonnaise	1 cup	2.5 dl	1 qt.	1 l
Tomato Ketchup	2 tbsp.	2 tbsp.	1 cup	2.5 dl
Cognac	1 tbsp.	1 tbsp.	½ cup	1.2 dl
Tabasco Sauce	1 drop	1 drop	4 drops	4 drops
Medium Shrimp, peeled and deveined	8 oz.	225 g	2 lb.	900 g
Lettuce Leaves	6	6	24	24
Fresh Tomatoes	2	2	8	8
Hard-boiled Eggs	2	2	8	8
Artichoke Hearts, marinated ..	6	6	24	24
Small Capers	1 oz.	25 g	3½ oz.	100 g
Black Olives	6	6	24	24

Combine the mayonnaise, ketchup, cognac, and tabasco sauce. Fold in the shrimp. Arrange lettuce leaves on a serving platter. Spoon on the shrimp mixture.

Blanch and peel the tomatoes, and cut into wedges. Arrange around the shrimp, alternating with slices of hard-boiled eggs and artichoke hearts. Sprinkle capers over the shrimp and decorate with olives.

Shrimp-stuffed Eggplant

Ingredients	6 portions U.S.	Metric	24 portions U.S.	Metric
Large Eggplants	2	2	8	8
Onion, chopped	4 oz.	110 g	1 lb.	450 g
Celery, chopped	2 oz.	50 g	8 oz.	225 g
Butter	2 tbsp.	25 g	4 oz.	110 g
Garlic Cloves, minced	1 tsp.	1 tsp.	1 tbsp.	1 tbsp.
Tomatoes, peeled, seeded, and chopped	1 lb.	450 g	4 lb.	1.8 kg
Salt	1 tsp.	1 tsp.	1 tbsp.	1 tbsp.
Pepper	¼ tsp.	¼ tsp.	1 tsp.	1 tsp.
Raw Shrimp, peeled and deveined	1¼ lb.	600 g	5 lb.	2.3 kg
Dry Bread Crumbs	1 cup	110 g	4 cups	450 g
Butter	1 oz.	25 g	4 oz.	110 g

Trim off ends of eggplants. Cut in half lengthwise. Scoop out pulp and set aside, leaving shells about ½ inch (1.25 cm) thick. Place the shells on baking pans, open side down. Add a little water and bake at 400°F (200°C) for 20 minutes.

Chop the pulp. Saute onion and celery in butter until transparent. Add garlic, tomatoes, and eggplant pulp. Simmer for 10 to 15 minutes. Season with salt and pepper. Mix in the shrimp and half of the bread crumbs.

Fill the eggplant shells. Sprinkle with the remaining crumbs. Sprinkle with melted butter, and bake at 350°F (180°C) for 15 to 20 minutes, or until shrimp are pink and firm.

Shrimp Tempura, Sushi Sauce

Ingredients	6 portions U.S.	Metric	24 portions U.S.	Metric
Cottonseed Oil, Peanut Oil, or Sesame Oil, for frying				
Uncooked Shrimp, in shells ...	3 lb.	1.4 kg	12 lb.	5.4 kg
Tempura Batter	1 recipe	1 recipe	4 recipes	4 recipes
Sushi Sauce				
Soy Sauce	2 oz.	0.6 dl	1 cup	2.5 dl
Sherry or Sake	2 oz.	0.6 dl	1 cup	2.5 dl
Chicken Bouillon	1 cup	2.5 dl	1 qt.	1 l

Heat the oil in deep fryer to 365°F (185°C). Shell and devein shrimp, leaving the tails attached. Dip shrimp into tempura batter. Drop in oil and cook for 3 to 4 minutes. Drain on absorbent paper. Arrange on a warm serving platter. Serve with sushi sauce.

Stir-fried Shrimp with Peas

Ingredients	6 portions		24 portions	
	U.S.	Metric	U.S.	Metric
Shrimp, peeled and deveined	1½ lb.	600 g	5½ lb.	2.5 kg
Small Frozen Peas	12 oz.	340 g	3 lb.	1.350 kg
Cornstarch	2 tsp.	2 tsp.	3 tbsp.	3 tbsp.
Egg Whites, lightly beaten	1	1	4	4
Dry Sherry	2 oz.	0.6 dl	1 cup	2.5 dl
Salt	1 tsp.	1 tsp.	1 tbsp.	1 tbsp.
Vegetable or Peanut Oil	2 oz.	0.6 dl	1 cup	2.5 dl
Scallions, cut into 2-in. pieces .	2	2	8	8
Ginger Slices	3	3	12	12

Wash shrimp, split in half lengthwise, then cut each half in two crosswise. Defrost peas and blanch for 5 minutes.

Toss the shrimp in cornstarch until lightly coated, then dip into mixture of egg whites, sherry, and salt. Heat the oil in a large skillet to the smoking point. Add the scallions and ginger and stir for 30 seconds to flavor. Remove with a slotted spoon and discard.

Add the shrimp to the oil and stir fry for about 2 minutes. Stir in the peas and heat for a few seconds. Transfer to a warm platter and serve at once.

Spiny Lobster

All the preparations for lobster are applicable to spiny lobster.

Crayfish (Crawfish)

Boiled Crawfish

Ingredients	6 portions		24 portions	
	U.S.	Metric	U.S.	Metric
Whole Crawfish	4 lb.	1.8 kg	16 lb.	7.2 kg
Salt, rock or Cayenne Pepper				
Lemons	1	1	4	4
Onions, preferably red	1	1	3	3
Garlic Cloves	1	1	3	3
Seafood Spice Mix, liquid or dry				

First wash the fish in large tub of water, making sure to remove all twigs, dead crawfish, or vegetation that may be mixed in with the crawfish. Then purge the crawfish by placing them in a strong salt-water solution for about 5 minutes. Wash once more in plain water making sure that the water remains clear.

Fill a large pot with enough water to cover the crawfish and the seasonings that will be added. Then salt the water well. Add cayenne pepper to taste. Add the cut lemon, onion, and garlic, along with the seafood mix.

Bring to a good boil, add the crawfish, and bring to a boil again. Boil for 3 to 5 minutes. Turn off the fire and let soak for about 20 to 30 minutes. Remove a few crawfish to sample.

Crawfish au Gratin

Ingredients	6 portions		24 portions	
	U.S.	Metric	U.S.	Metric
Whole Crawfish	3 doz.	3 doz.	12 doz.	12 doz.
Butter	2 oz.	50 g	8 oz.	225 g
Dry White Wine	1 cup	2.5 dl	1 qt.	1 l
Salt	½ tsp.	½ tsp.	2 tsp.	2 tsp.
Thyme Leaves	¼ tsp.	¼ tsp.	1 tsp.	1 tsp.
Bay Leaves	1	1	4	4
Veloute Sauce	1 cup	2.5 dl	1 qt.	1 l
Mushroom Duxelle	8 oz.	225 g	2 lb.	900 g
Parsley, chopped	1 tbsp.	1 tbsp.	4 tbsp.	4 tbsp.
Bread Crumbs	2 oz.	50 g	8 oz.	225 g

Saute the crawfish in butter until shells turn red. Deglaze with white wine. Add salt, thyme leaves, and bay leaves. Cook, covered, for 10 minutes.

Remove crawfish and shell them.

Reduce the cooking liquid. Add veloute sauce and mushroom duxelle. Combine with crawfish and parsley.

Arrange in a casserole baking dish. Sprinkle with bread crumbs. Brown under a broiler and serve hot.

Crawfish Tails Nantua

Ingredients	6 portions		24 portions	
	U.S.	Metric	U.S.	Metric
Crawfish Tails, shelled	3 doz.	3 doz.	12 doz.	12 doz.
Butter	2 oz.	50 g	8 oz.	225 g
Fresh Mushrooms	8 oz.	225 g	2 lb.	900 g
Nantua Sauce	¾ cup	2 dl	3 cups	8 dl
Truffle Slices	6	6	24	24

Saute the crawfish tails in butter. Cut the mushrooms into quarters and add to fish. Stir in the sauce nantua. Simmer for 5 to 10 minutes. Spoon into casserole serving dish(es). Top with truffle slices. Serve hot.

Mousselines of Crawfish Mornay

Ingredients	6 portions		24 portions	
	U.S.	Metric	U.S.	Metric
Butter	3 oz.	85 g	12 oz.	340 g
Truffle Slices	6	6	24	24
Crawfish Tails	12	12	48	48
Crawfish Mousse (see chapter 9)	1 lb.	450 g	4 lb.	1.8 kg
Mornay Sauce	1½ cups	4 dl	1½ qt.	1.5 l
Asparagus Tips	8 oz.	225 g	2 lb.	900 g

Butter 6 (24) individual molds. Garnish with a truffle slice and two crawfish tails. Fill

molds with crawfish mousse. Poach in a 350°F (180°C) oven, in a waterbath. Turn out onto

warm serving platter(s). Coat with mornay sauce. Garnish with asparagus tips.

Abalone

Abalone Chowder
See Clam Chowder.

Abalone Meuniere

Ingredients	6 portions		24 portions	
	U.S.	Metric	U.S.	Metric
Abalone Steaks	6	6	24	24
Salt	½ tsp.	½ tsp.	2 tsp.	2 tsp.
Pepper	¼ tsp.	¼ tsp.	1 tsp.	1 tsp.
Flour	2 oz.	60 g	8 oz.	240 g
Olive Oil	3 oz.	1 dl	1½ cups	4 dl
Unsalted Butter	4 oz.	110 g	1 lb.	450 g
Lemon Juice	1 tbsp.	1 tbsp.	2 oz.	0.6 dl
Parsley, chopped	2 tbsp.	2 tbsp.	8 tbsp.	8 tbsp.
Lemon Wedges	6	6	24	24

Tenderize abalone steaks and flatten to ¼ inch (½ cm) thickness. Cut into halves and season with salt and pepper. Dredge with flour and shake off the excess. Heat the oil and half of the butter in a heavy skillet or saute pan. Brown the abalone steaks about 30 seconds on each side. Remove steaks to a serving platter. Pour off the fat from the skillet. Melt the remaining butter and brown the butter until foamy. Add the lemon juice and chopped parsley. Pour over the abalone steaks and serve at once. Garnish with lemon wedges.

Marinated Abalone

Ingredients	6 portions		24 portions	
	U.S.	Metric	U.S.	Metric
Abalone Steaks or Canned Abalone	1½ lb.	680 g	6 lb.	2.270 kg
Fresh Tomatoes, peeled, seeded, and diced	1 lb.	450 g	4 lb.	1.8 kg
Onion, diced	2 oz.	50 g	8 oz.	200 g
Lemon Juice	½ cup	1.2 dl	2 cups	5 dl
Olive Oil	2 oz.	0.6 dl	1 cup	2.5 dl
Cucumbers, diced	2 oz.	50 g	8 oz.	200 g
Green Chili Peppers, minced . .	1 tbsp.	1 tbsp.	4 tbsp.	4 tbsp.
Green or Red Peppers, diced . .	2 oz.	50 g	8 oz.	200 g

Pound abalone steaks, if fresh, and cut into small cubes. Combine all ingredients in a mixing bowl. Marinate in the refrigerator for 1 to 2 hours.

Stir-fried Abalone and Oyster Sauce

Ingredients	6 portions		24 portions	
	U.S.	Metric	U.S.	Metric
Canned Abalone	2 lb.	900 g	8 lb	3.6 kg
Cornstarch	2 tbsp.	2 tbsp.	2 oz.	50 g
Soy Sauce	2 tbsp.	2 tbsp.	½ cup	1.2 dl
Oyster Sauce	4 oz.	1.2 dl	2 cups	5 dl
Vegetable Oil	3 oz.	1 dl	1½ cups	4 dl
Smoked Ham, minced	2 oz.	50 g	8 oz.	200 g

Drain abalone and cut in 1-inch (2.5-cm) cubes. Reserve liquid. Blend cornstarch into liquid, and stir in soy sauce and oyster sauce. Stir fry abalone in oil, to heat. Blend in cornstarch mixture to thicken. Add the ham. Heat and serve hot.

Note: Prolonged heating will toughen the abalone.

Clams

Clam Chowder
See chapter 10.

Clam Loaf

Ingredients	6 portions		24 portions	
	U.S.	Metric	U.S.	Metric
Bread, unsliced (1-lb. (450 g))	1	1	4	4
Butter	2 oz.	50 g	8 oz.	200 g
Onion, chopped	2 oz.	50 g	8 oz.	200 g
Garlic Clove, minced	1	1	4	4
Celery, chopped	4 oz.	110 g	1 lb.	450 g
Butter	2 oz.	50 g	8 oz.	200 g
Flour	1 oz.	25 g	4 oz.	110 g
Salt	½ tsp.	½ tsp.	2 tsp.	2 tsp.
Pepper	¼ tsp.	¼ tsp.	1 tsp.	1 tsp.
Thyme Leaves	¼ tsp.	¼ tsp.	1 tsp.	1 tsp.
Chili Sauce	1 tbsp.	1 tbsp.	4 tbsp.	4 tbsp.
Clams, chopped	1 qt.	1 l	4 qt.	4 l
Eggs	2	2	8	8
Bread Crumbs	8 oz.	200 g	2 lb.	800 g
Parsley, chopped	1 tbsp.	1 tbsp.	4 tbsp.	4 tbsp.

(cont.)

Slice a 1-inch (2½ cm) thick crust horizontally off the bread loaf. Hollow out the loaf, leaving a 1-inch (2½ cm) edge. Brush the inside with butter. Toast with the top crust in 350°F (180°C) oven for 10 minutes.

Cook onion, garlic, and celery in butter until tender. Stir in flour and seasonings, including chili sauce. Add clams and cook until thick, stirring constantly. Beat in the eggs. Add the bread crumbs and parsley.

Place mixture into toasted loaf. Cover with top crust. Bake at 350°F (180°C) for 35 to 40 minutes. Serve plain or with a sauce.

Clam Sauce for Egg Noodles

Ingredients	6 portions		24 portions	
	U.S.	Metric	U.S.	Metric
Clams, chopped	1 lb.	450 g	4 lb.	1.8 kg
Butter	4 oz.	110 g	1 lb.	450 g
Clam Liquor	½ cup	1.2 dl	2 cups	5 dl
Worcestershire Sauce	1 tsp.	1 tsp.	1 tbsp.	1 tbsp.
Paprika	¼ tsp.	¼ tsp.	1 tsp.	1 tsp.
Pepper, ground	¼ tsp.	¼ tsp.	1 tsp.	1 tsp.
Egg Yolks	2	2	8	8
Egg Noodles	8 oz.	225 g	2 lb.	900 g

Drain and save the liquor from the clams. Melt butter and add liquor and seasonings. Stir a little of the hot liquid into the beaten egg yolks, then add to remaining liquid, stirring constantly. Add clams. Heat again and serve with cooked noodles.

Clam Souffle

Ingredients	6 portions		24 portions	
	U.S.	Metric	U.S.	Metric
Clams, shucked	2 cups	5 dl	2 qt.	2 l
Clam Juice	1 cup	2.5 dl	1 qt.	1 l
Butter	2 oz.	50 g	8 oz.	200 g
Flour	2 oz.	50 g	8 oz.	200 g
Salt	½ tsp.	½ tsp.	2 tsp.	2 tsp.
Pepper	¼ tsp.	¼ tsp.	1 tsp.	1 tsp.
Nutmeg, ground	⅛ tsp.	⅛ tsp.	½ tsp.	½ tsp.
Eggs, separated	3	3	12	12

Simmer clams in their own juice until edges curl. Drain and save the liquor. Chop clams.

Make a roux with butter and flour. Add clam juice, and seasonings. Stir until sauce thickens and becomes smooth. Stir a little hot sauce into the beaten egg yolks, and add to remaining sauce. Add the clams. Fold in the stiffly beaten egg whites. Butter and flour souffle dish(es). Fill mold ¾ full. Bake at 350°F (180°C) for 40 minutes. Serve immediately, plain or with a sauce.

Clam Fritters
Clam Oregonati

See chapter 15, Nibbling On Seafood.

Mussels

Marinated mussels

	6–8 portions	
Ingredients	U.S.	Metric
Mussels, in shells	48	48
Garlic Cloves	2	2
Olive Oil	2 oz.	0.6 dl
Anchovy Fillets, chopped	10	10
Dry White Wine	1½ cups	4 dl
Wine Vinegar	1½ cups	4 dl
Parsley, chopped	2 tbsp.	2 tbsp.

Scrub and debeard mussels. Brown the garlic cloves in oil. Discard garlic. Add mussels in shells, anchovies, white wine, and vinegar. Cover pot and steam until mussels open. Discard shells, and arrange mussel meats in an earthenware crock or casserole. Sprinkle with parsley. Reduce cooking liquid by half. Pour over mussels and marinate for 2 to 3 days. Serve chilled as appetizers.

Mussels in Mustard Sauce

	6 portions		24 portions	
Ingredients	U.S.	Metric	U.S.	Metric
Mussels, cleaned and poached	1½ lb.	680 g	6 lb.	2.7 kg
Mayonnaise	5 oz.	1.5 dl	2½ cup	6 dl
Dijon Mustard	1 tsp.	1 tsp.	1 tbsp.	1 tbsp.
Celery, finely diced	6 oz.	170 g	1½ lb.	680 g
Lemon Juice	1 tsp.	1 tsp.	1 tbsp.	1 tbsp.
Radish Roses	6	6	24	24

Combine the mussels, mayonnaise, mustard, celery, and lemon juice. Serve in a shallow dish. Decorate with radish roses.

Mussels Mariniere

Ingredients	6 portions		24 portions	
	U.S.	Metric	U.S.	Metric
Mussels, in shells	5 lb.	2.270 kg	20 lb.	9 kg
Butter	2 oz.	50 g	8 oz.	225 g
Shallots, chopped	2 oz.	50 g	8 oz.	225 g
Parsley, chopped	2 tbsp.	2 tbsp.	8 tbsp.	8 tbsp.
Pepper, ground	¼ tsp.	¼ tsp.	1 tsp.	1 tsp.
Dry White Wine	1½ cup	4 dl	1½ qt.	1.5 l

Clean and wash mussels under cold running water and debeard. Heat the butter in a kettle. Add shallots and cook for 5 minutes. Add half of the parsley, and the pepper, wine, and mussels. Cover and steam until mussels open. Serve in soup bowls with the cooking liquid. Sprinkle with chopped parsley.

Mussels in White Wine Sauce

Ingredients	6 portions		24 portions	
	U.S.	Metric	U.S.	Metric
Mussels, in shells	3 qt.	3 l	12 qt.	12 l
Parsley, chopped	1 tbsp.	1 tbsp.	4 tbsp.	4 tbsp.
Dry White Wine	¾ cup	2 dl	3 cups	8 dl
Shallots, chopped	2 oz.	50 g	8 oz.	225 g
Onions, chopped	2 oz.	50 g	8 oz.	225 g
Egg Yolks	3	3	12	12
Salt and Pepper, to taste				
Lemon Juice, to taste				

Scrub and debeard mussels. Combine parsley, white wine, shallots, and onions. Bring to a boil. Steam the mussels in the boiling liquid until opened. Drain and save the cooking stock. Remove only top shells of mussels. Arrange mussels in oven-proof serving casserole.

Strain cooking liquid. Reduce by half. Pour a little liquid into egg yolks. Mix well and stir into remaining stock. Season to taste with salt, pepper, and lemon juice. Pour sauce over the hot mussels. Serve immediately.

Paella of Mussels

Ingredients	6 portions		24 portions	
	U.S.	Metric	U.S.	Metric
Mussels, in shells	3 qt.	3 l	12 qt.	12 l
Onions, chopped	2 oz.	50 g	8 oz.	225 g
Garlic Cloves, minced	1	1	4	4
Olive Oil	½ cup	1.2 dl	2 cups	5 dl
Rice	10 oz.	300 g	2½ lb.	1.2 kg
Saffron	½ tsp.	½ tsp.	2 tsp.	2 tsp.
Red Pimentos, cooked	1	1	4	4

Clean and scrub mussels. Steam in a kettle containing a small amount of water until all mussels are opened. Drain them and retain the cooking liquid. Remove top shells of mussels.

Brown the onion and garlic in oil. Stir in the rice and saffron.

Pour the strained cooking liquid (2½ cups, 6 dl, for 6) over rice. Add mussels in their half shells. Bake covered at 350°F (180°C) for 20 minutes. Stir in the cooked pimentos. Serve the paella in a preheated casserole dish.

Tomatoes Stuffed with Mussels

Ingredients	6 portions		24 portions	
	U.S.	Metric	U.S.	Metric
Ripe Tomatoes	6	6	24	24
Salt	¼ tsp.	¼ tsp.	1 tsp.	1 tsp.
Pepper, ground	⅛ tsp.	⅛ tsp.	½ tsp.	½ tsp.
Mussels, cleaned and poached	1½ lb.	680 g	6 lb.	2.7 kg
Mayonnaise	¾ cup	2 dl	3 cups	8 dl
Dill, chopped	1 tsp.	1 tsp.	1 tbsp.	1 tbsp.
Lemon Wedges	6	6	24	24

Wash tomatoes. Cut off the tops, scoop out insides, and sprinkle cavities with salt and pepper. Combine mussels with mayonnaise and fill tomatoes. Sprinkle with dill. Arrange tomatoes on a serving platter. Garnish with lemon wedges.

Octopus

Octopus Salad

Ingredients	12 portions U.S.	Metric
Baby Octopus, dressed	5 lb.	2.270 kg
Garlic Cloves, minced	3	3
Celery, diced	4 oz.	110 g
Ripe Olives, pitted	4 oz.	110 g
Olive Oil	½ cup	1.2 dl
Lemon Juice	½ cup	1.2 dl
Parsley, chopped	¼ cup	10 g
Fresh Basil or	1 tbsp.	1 tbsp.
Dried Basil	1 tsp.	1 tsp.

Blanch octopus in salted boiling water. Drain and cook in fresh water for 20 to 30 minutes, or until tender. Drain and cool the octopus. Cut into bite-sized pieces, discarding any non-fleshy parts. Combine remaining ingredients in a bowl. Mix in the octopus. Refrigerate for an hour or more before serving.

Oysters

Fried Oysters

Ingredients	6 portions U.S.	Metric	24 portions U.S.	Metric
Oysters, shucked	2 cups	5 dl	2 qt.	2 l
Eggs	2	2	8	8
Milk	1 tbsp.	1 tbsp.	2 oz.	0.6 dl
Fresh Bread Crumbs	2 cups	110 g	2 qt.	450 g
Dried Tarragon Leaves	½ tsp.	½ tsp.	2 tsp.	2 tsp.
Chives, chopped	1 tsp.	1 tsp.	1 tbsp.	1 tbsp.
Parsley, chopped	1 tsp.	1 tsp.	1 tbsp.	1 tbsp.
Salt and Pepper, to taste				
Oil, for frying				
Lemon Wedges	6	6	24	24

Pat oysters dry. Beat the eggs and milk. Combine the bread crumbs, tarragon, chives, and parsley. Dip the oysters into the beaten egg mixture. Coat with bread crumbs and deep fry for 3 to 4 minutes until brown and crisp. Drain and serve hot with lemon wedges and a cold sauce.

Oysters Florentine

Ingredients	6 portions		24 portions	
	U.S.	Metric	U.S.	Metric
Oysters, shucked	2 cups	5 dl	2 qt.	2 l
Spinach Leaves, blanched	10 oz.	300 g	2½ lb.	1.2 kg
Butter	2 oz.	50 g	8 oz.	200 g
Salt and Pepper, to taste				
Mornay Sauce	1½ cups	4 dl	1½ qt.	1.5 l
Swiss Cheese, grated	2 oz.	50 g	8 oz.	200 g

Poach the oysters in their own juice. Saute chopped spinach in butter, and season with salt and pepper. Put a small amount of spinach in oyster shells. Top with oysters, one on each shell. Coat with mornay sauce. Sprinkle with cheese and brown in a hot oven.

Note: If oyster shells are not available, the dish can be prepared in individual casseroles.

Oysters Rockefeller

Ingredients	2 dozen	
	U.S.	Metric
Shallots, chopped	1 tbsp.	1 tbsp.
Celery, chopped	1 oz.	25 g
Fennel, chopped	1 oz.	25 g
Parsley, chopped	1 tbsp.	1 tbsp.
Butter, melted	6 oz.	170 g
Watercress Leaves	2 cups	5 dl
Dry Bread Crumbs	⅓ cup	25 g
Pernod	2 oz.	0.6 dl
Salt and Cayenne Pepper, to taste		
Oysters, on the half shell	2 doz.	2 doz.
Rock Salt		

Saute shallots, celery, fennel, and parsley in half of the butter. Add the watercress to wilt. Combine the mixture with remaining butter, bread crumbs, and pernod, and blend in a food processor. Season to taste with salt and cayenne pepper.

Loosen the oysters in the half shells. Spoon a teaspoon of the mixture on top of each oyster. Place oysters on a bed of rock salt. Bake at 450°F (230°C) for 4 to 5 minutes. Serve hot.

Oyster Stew

Ingredients	6 portions		24 portions	
	U.S.	Metric	U.S.	Metric
Oysters, shucked	1 cup	60 g	1 qt.	1 l
Butter	4 oz.	110 g	1 lb.	450 g
Worcestershire Sauce	1 tsp.	1 tsp.	1 tbsp.	1 tbsp.
Hot Milk	1 qt.	1 l	4 qt.	4 l
Butter	1 oz.	25 g	4 oz.	110 g
Flour	1 oz.	25 g	4 oz.	110 g
Salt and Pepper, to taste				
Parsley or Chives, chopped . . .	1 tbsp.	1 tbsp.	4 tbsp.	4 tbsp.
Paprika	¼ tsp.	¼ tsp.	1 tsp.	1 tsp.
Oyster Crackers				

Gently heat the cleaned oysters in their own juice until the edges start to curl. Heat the butter, Worcestershire sauce, and milk. Mix the flour and butter, and add to the milk mixture to thicken. Just before serving, add the oysters. Season to taste with salt and pepper, herbs, and paprika. Serve hot with oyster crackers.

Oyster Omelette

Prepare omelette in usual fashion. Fold in oysters and veloute sauce, or use fried oysters.

Oysters on the Half Shell

See chapter 5 for for instructions on how to open oysters. Connoisseurs prefer to eat oysters raw on the half shell. They are usually served with brown bread, wine vinegar with chopped shallots, and lemon wedges.

Mushrooms Stuffed with Oysters

Cook medium mushroom caps in lemon juice and white wine. Poach shucked oysters in their own juice and a small amount of port wine. Drain mushrooms and oysters, reserving liquids. Stuff mushrooms with oysters. Reduce both cooking liquids together. Add heavy cream and boil to a syrupy consistency. Spoon the sauce over oysters. Sprinkle with parmesan cheese. Brown under a broiler and serve hot.

Scallops

Coquilles St. Jacques au Gratin
(Scallops au Gratin)

Ingredients	6 portions		24 portions	
	U.S.	Metric	U.S.	Metric
Dry White Wine	1 cup	2.5 dl	1 qt.	1 l
Shallots, chopped	1 tbsp.	1 tbsp.	4 tbsp.	4 tbsp.
Sea Scallops	2 lb.	900 g	8 lb.	3.6 kg
Duchess Potato Mix	10 oz.	300 g	2½ lb.	1.150 kg
Scallop Shells	6	6	24	24
Mushroom Buttons	8 oz.	225 g	2 lb.	900 g
Butter	1 oz.	25 g	4 oz.	110 g
Veloute Sauce	1½ cups	4 dl	1½ qt.	1.5 l
Parmesan Cheese	2 oz.	50 g	8 oz.	225 g

Combine wine and shallots. Poach scallops in the simmering liquid for a short time, 3 to 4 minutes. (Overcooked scallops are rubbery and tough.) Remove scallops from wine. Cut in halves and reserve.

Pipe duchess potato mix around edges of shells using a pastry bag fitted with a star tube. Saute mushrooms in butter until firm. Combine scallops and mushrooms and divide between shells.

Reduce the wine and shallots to three-quarters. Add the veloute sauce. Bring to a boil and simmer to a medium consistency. Pour sauce over scallops. Sprinkle with parmesan cheese. Brown scallops under a hot broiler and serve hot.

Coquille St. Jacques Parisienne
(Scallops Parisienne)

Ingredients	6 portions		24 portions	
	U.S.	Metric	U.S.	Metric
Duchess Potato Mix	1 lb.	450 g	4 lb.	1.8 kg
Scallop Shells	6	6	24	24
Scallops	2 lb.	900 g	8 lb.	3.6 kg
Fish Fumet	½ cup	1.2 dl	2 cups	5 dl
White Wine	½ cup	1.2 dl	2 cups	5 dl
White Wine Sauce, for glazing	1½ cups	4 dl	1½ qt.	1.5 l

(cont.)

Pipe the duchess potatoes around the edges of scallop shells, using a pastry bag fitted with a star tube.

Poach the clean scallops in fumet and white wine. Do not overcook. Arrange scallops in shells. Mask with the white wine sauce. Brown under a broiler. Serve hot.

Note: Similar recipes can be created by adding mushrooms to the above recipe or using mornay sauce instead of white wine sauce. Poached fish is also a good substitute for scallops.

Scallop Tartlets

Ingredients	6 portions		24 portions	
	U.S.	Metric	U.S.	Metric
Bay Scallops	1½ lb.	680 g	6 lb.	2.7 kg
Salt	½ tsp.	½ tsp.	2 tsp.	2 tsp.
Pepper	¼ tsp.	¼ tsp.	1 tsp.	1 tsp.
White Wine	1 cup	2.5 dl	1 qt.	1 l
Dry Vermouth	½ cup	1.2 dl	2 cups	5 dl
Small Fresh Mushrooms	1 lb.	450 g	4 lb.	1.8 kg
Butter	2 oz.	50 g	8 oz.	225 g
Flour	2 oz.	50 g	8 oz.	225 g
Heavy Cream	½ cup	1.2 dl	2 cups	5 dl
Tartlets (see chapter 7)	12	12	24	24

Season scallops with salt and pepper. Poach in white wine and vermouth. Do not overcook. Saute mushrooms in butter and lemon juice. Prepare a roux with butter and flour. Moisten with the poaching liquid, stirring continuously until sauce thickens. Add cream. Reduce sauce for 5 minutes. Add mushrooms and scallops. Heat and spoon mixture into preheated tartlets. Serve hot.

Seviche of Scallops

See recipe for Seviche on page 211.

Broiled Scallops en Brochette

See Seafood Brochettes on page 313.

Scallops Florentine

Prepare like Scallops Au Gratin. Cover bottom of scallop shells with creamed spinach.

Fried Scallops

Scallops can be purchased frozen and breaded. Deep fry at 360°F (185°C) for 3 to 4 minutes. Serve with a cold sauce. If using fresh scallops, bread according to the standard procedure.

Featured large, above, **Bouquet of Shrimp Boca Grande** makes a colorful and irresistible buffet showpiece: a mouth-watering bouquet of tiny pink shrimp adorned with slivers of green avocado and lime wedges. An enchanting way to serve the accompanying cocktail sauce is in a tulip-shaped grapefruit rind.

An elegant, eye-catching presentation of **Mousse of Salmon Trout,** upper inset, lends an additional touch of class to a dish always highly prized among seafood connoisseurs. This cold mousse of smoked salmon and trout is a delicate, creamy pink appetizer. It is served here with a refreshing border of chopped aspic jelly, and a decorative garnish.

Fresh Tuna Italienne, lower inset, gives your can opener a rest! Try high-protein *fresh* tuna meat braised, served in a sauce flavored with rich tomatoes and wine. Fresh tuna meat is firm and lean; it looks and tastes rather like veal.

At top left, **Marinated Shrimp** makes for little shrimp with big flavor. After being cooked and shelled, the shrimp are marinated for several hours, then served on a bed of crisp lettuce, garnished with sliced onions, stuffed hard-boiled eggs, radish roses, and mushroom flowers.

The black-tipped claws of the stone crab are hard to crack, but the sweet, tender meat—in a class with lobster—is worth the effort! **Stone Crab au Gratin,** top center, is topped and glazed with hollandaise sauce, and surrounded with fleurons. This splendid dish is the author's own creation.

Homard Froid a la Francaise makes a stunning, if short-lived, spectacle on any smorgasbord or buffet. The display at top right shows a large, boiled lobster with medallions, garnished to taste and guarded by its peers.

Simple decor adds drama to **Cold Striped Bass, Mayonnaise Sauce,** above left. This arrangement of poached, cold, boneless fillets of striped bass, also known as rockfish or "striper" with chopped jelly reflects elegantly upon itself in a mirror.

The fresh-water trout is a noble fish of exceptional quality—and **Cold Lake Trout Mexicaine,** above right, enhances its potential. A 3–4 lb. whole trout is poached and served cold, accompanied by avocado wedges stuffed with crabmeat, and cocktail sauce and antiboise.

Malossol is the caviar of lowest salt content and highest quality—it is dubbed "black gold fit for kings." **Blinis with Caviar,** top, presents the "black gold" in a most regal manner with small buckwheat pancakes (blinis) and various garnishes served in endive leaves for handling ease.

Broiled Jumbo Spanish Shrimp is heaven on earth for the seafood lover. Just *sitting* before this exquisitely arranged trio of jumbo Spanish scarlet shrimp that have been broiled in lemon butter, complimented by a glass of chilled, crisp, white wine (perhaps a *Pouilly Fuisse?*), is *almost* heaven.

Voila! **Homard a la Parisienne,** above is the French way to enjoy our freshly boiled lobster, cooled to room temperature and shelled, served with fresh tomatoes, lemon wedges, hard-boiled eggs, and a home-made mayonnaise.

Cherished among seafood dishes is the **Coulibiac,** top left: thin slices of pink, flavorful salmon are wrapped in a rich brioche crust together with a layer of mushrooms, egg slices, rice of kashe, and a veloute sauce will enhance flavor.

Although squid dishes are relatively new to American palates, European diners have long appreciated the likes of **Stuffed Squid Nicoise,** top right. Fresh squid mantles are stuffed with a mixture of rice, sauteed tentacles, tomatoes, and onions, then baked in a rich tomato sauce, and adorned with ripe olives.

Magnificent **Cold Whitefish, Sauce Andalouse,** above left, is most deserving of its silver platter.

The whitefish is noted for its exceptional eating quality. Here the whole, poached fish, slightly curved to follow the graceful contour of the platter, has been carefully decorated "au naturel" with paper-thin slices of crisp cucumber, glazed with a delicate, clear jelly.

Long recognized as a delicacy in their native Maryland, Atlantic blue crab "peelers" are relatively rare. After cleaning, the soft-shell crabs are best gently fried, whole—the entire crabs are edible. **Golden Fried Soft-Shell Crabs,** above right, repose on a napkin gondola, garnished with lemon, fried fresh parsley, and offered with a creamy sauce.

Snails

How to Cook Fresh Snails. Deprive the live snails of food for about two weeks. Put them in small cages or baskets in a well-aerated place, out of drafts. In a large container, mix 1 pound (450 g) of coarse salt with a small amount of flour. Stir the snails in this mixture and leave them for two hours. Then wash them thoroughly in cold running water to eliminate sliminess. Plunge them into boiling water for 5 minutes. Drain and cool. Remove the snail from its shell using a needle or toothpick. *Cooking:* Boil the snails in half dry white wine and half water. Season with salt and crushed peppercorns. Add thyme, bay leaves, parsley stems, and 1 to 2 cloves. Simmer the snails for 1½ to 3 hours, depending on the size of the snails. Remove the skim frequently. When they are cooked, let them cool in the cooking liquid.

Wash and boil the shells for ½ hour in boiling water containing a small amount of baking soda. Carefully rinse the shells in running water, drain, and dry them. To save time and guarantee cleanliness, tiny round crocks, big enough to hold a large snail, are replacing real shells. They are favored in establishments serving a high volume of Escargots Bourguignonne or similar recipes.

As a rule, snails are at their best when eaten with a special butter called escargot butter.

The following recipe is unquestionably a triumphal contribution to the Grande Cuisine of France. It was developed by René Lamarche, Executive Chef of the Paris Hotel School, Paris, France.

Escargots Bourguignonne

Ingredients	U.S.	*1 dozen* Metric
Butter	6 oz.	170 g
Garlic Cloves, peeled and crushed	2	2
Shallot, peeled	1	1
Almonds, sliced	1 tbsp.	1 tbsp.
Pernod	1 tbsp.	1 tbsp.
Parsley Sprigs, loose	1 cup	25 g
Salt	½ tsp.	½ tsp.
Pepper, ground	¼ tsp.	¼ tsp.
Snails, canned or freshly cooked	1 doz.	1 doz.
Shells	1 doz.	1 doz.

Combine the butter, garlic, shallot, almonds, pernod, parsley, salt, and pepper in a food processor. Mix thoroughly for about one minute. Drain the snails. Place a small amount of butter mixture in the bottom of each shell. Insert a snail in each shell, then fill shell with butter mixture. Lay the shells, butter side up, on a snail pan. Heat in 375°F (190°C) oven until the butter is bubbling. Serve at once with French bread.

CHAPTER 15

Nibbling on Seafood

Canapes, also called *zakuski*, are very popular tidbits consumed as appetizers at cocktail parties or before dinner. Their presentation is left to the imagination of the preparer. Essentially dinner hors d'oeuvres, their presentation and preparation are the basis for the guests' expectations of dinner.

Canapes do not have to be made from costly foods like caviar, foie gras, or smoked salmon, unless specifically requested. In that case, the overall cost of the meal obviously is expected to be higher. Excellent canapes can be created easily from a large variety of seafoods that are canned, pickled, or smoked. Many leftover poached fish and shellfish can also be used. Spreads can be made from leftover tuna, salmon, sardines, et cetera. Individual small mousses heighten the presentation of canape trays.

The base of a canape can range from a plain paper-thin toast to sophisticated rice or seaweed crackers. There are also various imported wafers and wheat crackers available in all sizes and shapes. Bread, plain or toasted, is also a popular base for canapes. A wide selection of breads is available commercially; white, whole wheat, rye, and pumpernickel are used most often. The recent emphasis on eating healthy and wholesome food has popularized such breads as wheat germ, cracked wheat, oatmeal, brown bread, and granola, just to name a few. These may also be used for canapes.

Butter mixtures (see chapter 11) that are used to mask the base of canapes, add a definite flavor to the finished products.

Canapes

Anchovy Canapes

Mask rectangular canapes with anchovy butter. Garnish with fillets of anchovies and chopped egg mimosa.

Caviar Canapes

Spread canapes with caviar butter. Top with a layer of caviar and a squeeze of lemon juice.

Caviar Cigarettes

Roll out thin slices of bread. Mix caviar and sour cream and spread over bread. Roll in the shape of cigarettes and cut to desired size.

Shrimp Canapes

Mask canapes with shrimp butter. Garnish with whole, tiny cooked shrimp or diced leftover shrimp. Top with a touch of mayonnaise or cocktail sauce.

Canapes Danoise

Spread rye canapes with horseradish butter. Top with smoked salmon and marinated herring slices.

Lobster Canapes

Butter round canapes with lobster butter. Top with sliced American or spiny lobster and sprinkle with egg mimosa.

Fish Canapes

Use any poached fish (bass,

flounder, sole, pike, salmon, snapper, or grouper, etc.). Spread canapes with mayonnaise, and top with slices of fish or fish salad. Spoon some aspic jelly over, and garnish with capers or small diced lemon pieces.

Canapes Cancalaise

Mask canapes with tunafish butter. Top with poached or smoked mussels.

Canapes of Smoked Salmon

Mask rectangular canapes with mayonnaise or horseradish butter. Top with rolled slices of smoked salmon. Or, spread cream cheese over salmon slices and roll and place on canapes.

Sardine Canapes

Spread triangular canapes with sardine butter. Top with bristling boneless sardines. Pipe anchovy butter over sardines to decorate.

Canapes of Lobster Coral

Spread canapes with lobster cheese. Top with lobster butter. Decorate with piped mayonnaise.

Canapes of Trout Anne-Lise

Mask round canapes with anchovy butter. Top with slices of poached paupiettes of trout. Top with a light mayonnaise and chopped parsley.

Canapes Paulette

Mask round canapes with anchovy butter. Sprinkle one half with chopped egg whites, and the other half with chopped egg yolks. Lay a row of tiny shrimp between white and yolks.

Hot Appetizers

Angels on horseback

Ingredients	2 dozen U.S.	Metric
Oysters, shucked	2 doz.	2 doz.
Parsley, chopped	1 tbsp.	1 tbsp.
Paprika	¼ tsp.	¼ tsp.
Bacon Slices, cut in thirds	8	8

Drain oysters. Sprinkle with parsley and paprika. Wrap bacon around oysters and secure with a toothpick. Place oysters on a sheet pan. Broil about 4 inches (7.5 cm) from source of heat for 8 to 10 minutes, or until bacon is crisp. Turn carefully and broil 3 to 4 minutes longer.

Clam Fritters

Ingredients	3 dozen U.S.	Metric
Clams, chopped	2 cups	5 dl
Clam Juice	1 cup	2.5 dl
Eggs	2	2
Flour	8 oz.	220 g
Baking Powder	2 tsp.	2 tsp.
Salt	1 tsp.	1 tsp.
White Pepper	¼ tsp.	¼ tsp.

Combine the chopped clams with the juice. Beat in the eggs, flour, baking powder, salt, and pepper. Drop teaspoonfuls of batter on a griddle or into a deep fryer. If using griddle, cook 2 minutes on each side; if deep frying, cook 3 to 4 minutes at 360°F (185°C).

Crab Appetizer

Ingredients	U.S.	4 dozen Metric
Crabmeat.................	½ lb.	225 g
Onion, grated	1 tbsp.	1 tbsp.
Butter.....................	2 oz.	55 g
Flour......................	2 oz.	55 g
Milk	½ cup	1.2 dl
Egg Yolk	1	1
Worcestershire Sauce	½ tsp.	½ tsp.
Salt.......................	¼ tsp.	¼ tsp.
Dry Bread Crumbs	½ cup	25 g

Remove any shells or cartilage from crabmeat. Cook onion in butter and blend in the flour. Add milk gradually to make a cream sauce, stirring constantly. Add egg yolk and seasonings. Add crabmeat and blend into a paste. Cool.

Portion crabmeat with a teaspoon. Shape into small balls and roll in bread crumbs. Deep fry at 375°F (190°C) for 2 minutes. Drain on absorbent paper. Serve on toothpicks.

Crabmeat Balls

Ingredients	U.S.	2 dozen Metric
Crabmeat.................	7 oz.	200 g
Fresh Bread Crumbs........	1 cup	50 g
Dry Sherry Wine	2 oz.	0.6 dl
Lemon Juice	1 tbsp.	1 tbsp.
Onion Salt	½ tsp.	½ tsp.
White Pepper	¼ tsp.	¼ tsp.
Prepared Mustard	2 tsp.	2 tsp.
Bacon Slices, halved	12	12
Lemon Wedges	24	24

Flake the crabmeat and combine with remaining ingredients, except the bacon. Mix well and shape into two dozen small balls. Wrap with bacon slices. Broil under medium heat until bacon is crisp, turning to brown evenly. Serve with lemon wedges.

Crab Puffs

Ingredients	U.S.	3 dozen Metric
Scallions, chopped	2 tbsp.	2 tbsp.
Celery, minced	2 tbsp.	2 tbsp.
Peanut Oil, for frying........		
Cream Cheese, softened	8 oz.	225 g
Clean Crabmeat	8 oz.	225 g
Fresh Bread Crumbs.........	2 tbsp.	2 tbsp.
Red Pepper Sauce	2 drops	2 drops
Egg Roll Wrappers	9	9

Cook the scallions and celery in a small amount of peanut oil until tender. Cream the cheese and stir in crabmeat, scallions, celery, bread crumbs, and red pepper sauce.

Cut each egg roll wrapper into four squares. Divide mixture between the 3 dozen wrappers. Moisten edges and seal. Deep fry at 350°F (180°C) for 2 to 3 minutes.

Barquettes of Shrimp

Ingredients	6 portions		24 portions	
	U.S.	Metric	U.S.	Metric
Raw Shrimp, in shells	2 lb.	900 g	8 lb.	3.6 kg
Mornay Sauce	1 cup	2.5 dl	1 qt.	1 l
Small Barquette Shells	12	12	48	48
Parmesan Cheese, grated	2 oz.	50 g	8 oz.	225 g

Shell and devein the shrimp. Rinse under cold water. In a medium saucepan, heat the mornay sauce and mix in the shrimp. Fill the barquettes with the shrimp mixture. Sprinkle with parmesan cheese and glaze under a broiler. Serve immediately.

Escargot Pastries

Spread escargot butter on rolled out puff pastry dough. Cut dough with a 2-inch (5-cm) round cutter. Place a snail on center of each circle. Brush dough with water and carefully seal the escargots by bringing the edges of dough together. Bake at 360°F (185°C) for 10 to 15 minutes.

Hot Tuna Canapes

Ingredients	8 portions	
	U.S.	Metric
Albacore White Tuna	7 oz.	200 g
Capers	1 tbsp.	1 tbsp.
Mayonnaise	1 oz.	0.3 dl
Paprika	1 tsp.	1 tsp.
Onion Juice	1 tsp.	1 tsp.
Lemon Juice	1 tsp.	1 tsp.
Egg Whites, stiffly beaten	3	3

Flake the tuna. Combine with capers, mayonnaise, paprika, onion juice, and lemon juice. Fold in the egg whites. Spread mixture on fingers of toast. Place on a sheet pan and broil 3 inches (7.5 cm) from source of heat, until lightly brown.

Sardine Pizza

Prepare pizza following directions for Anchovy and Cheese Pizza in chapter 12. Top with sardines. Bake at 425°F (220°C) for 15 to 20 minutes. Cut into bite-sized pieces.

Shrimp Fritters

Ingredients	24 portions	
	U.S.	Metric
Cooked Shrimp, peeled and deveined	1 lb.	450 g
Parsley, chopped	1 cup	85 g
Dill, chopped	1 tbsp.	1 tbsp.
Flour	1 cup	120 g
Salt	½ tsp.	½ tsp.
Baking Powder	3 tsp.	3 tsp.
Eggs, beaten	2	2
Milk	½ cup	1.2 dl
Tabasco	dash	dash
Oil, for frying		
Tuna-Anchovy Sauce	2½ cups	6 dl

Chop the shrimp and mix with parsley and dill. Prepare a batter with flour, salt, baking powder, eggs, milk, and tabasco. Mix in the shrimp. Drop shrimp mixture by small teaspoonfuls into deep fryer at 375°F (190°C). Fry for 2 minutes or until crisp and golden brown. Drain on absorbent paper. Serve with tuna-anchovy sauce.

Shrimp Pastries (Feuilletes de Crevettes)

Ingredients	24 pastries	
	U.S.	Metric
Olive Oil	2 tbsp.	2 tbsp.
Onion, chopped	2 oz.	50 g
Tomatoes, peeled, seeded, and chopped	4 oz.	110 g
Cooked Shrimp, diced	9 oz.	250 g
Hard-boiled Egg, chopped	1	1
Parsley, chopped	1 tbsp.	1 tbsp.
Salt	¾ tsp.	¾ tsp.
Puff Paste Dough	14 oz.	400 g
Egg Yolk, lightly beaten	1	1

Heat the oil in a skillet. Stir in the onion and cook over low heat for 5 minutes. Add tomatoes and simmer for 10 minutes to remove excess moisture. Stir in the shrimp, egg, parsley, and salt.

Roll out the dough, ⅛-inch (3-mm) thick. Cut into circles, 2½ inches (7 cm) in diameter. Brush the edges with water. Place a heaping teaspoon of shrimp mixture in center. Fold one half over and seal, pressing edges together. Brush with egg yolk. Bake at 400°F (200°C) for 10 minutes or until golden brown. Serve hot.

Shrimp Ravioli Pastries

Ingredients		24 pastries	
	U.S.	Metric	
Onion, chopped	2 oz.	50 g
Butter	2 oz.	50 g
White Wine	¼ cup	0.6 dl
Cooked Shrimp, diced	8 oz.	225 g
Heavy Bechamel Sauce	½ cup	1.2 dl
Salt	½ tsp.	½ tsp.
White Pepper	¼ tsp.	¼ tsp.
Puff Paste Dough	1 lb.	450 g

Saute the onion in butter until transparent. Add the wine and shrimp, and cook over high heat for 5 minutes. Stir in the bechamel sauce. Season with salt and pepper. Cool the mixture before using.

Divide the puff paste dough into 2 pieces and roll into two rectangles of same size, ⅛-inch (3-mm) thick. Using one sheet, place 1 teaspoonful of the shrimp mixture every 2 inches (5 cm) across and down the dough. Brush the dough with water all around the fillings. Carefully place the second rectangle over the first and press down around the fillings to seal the dough. With a ravioli cutter or pastry wheel, cut into squares between the fillings. Deep fry the pastries at 360°F (185°C) for 4 to 5 minutes. Drain on absorbent paper. Arrange on a serving platter and serve at once.

Stuffed Clams Oregonati

Ingredients	U.S.	Metric
Littleneck Clams	4 doz.	4 doz.
Shallots, chopped	1 tbsp.	1 tbsp.
Garlic Cloves, minced	1 tsp.	1 tsp.
Fresh Basil Leaves, chopped	1 tbsp.	1 tbsp.
Parsley, chopped	1 tbsp.	1 tbsp.
Tomato, chopped and seeded	1	1
Mushrooms, sliced	4	4
Parmesan Cheese, grated	¾ cup	2 dl
Lean Bacon Slices	3	3
Chives, chopped	1 tbsp.	1 tbsp.
Olive Oil	¼ cup	0.6 dl
Dry White Wine	½ cup	1.2 dl

Open clams (see chapter 5). Discard top shells and loosen clams on bottom shell. Combine shallots, garlic, basil, parsley, tomato, mushrooms, and one-half of the cheese and the bacon. Mix well in a food processor. Add chives. Spoon mixture over the clams and smooth the top. Arrange clams on a baking dish. Sprinkle with remaining cheese, olive oil, and wine. Bake until golden brown at 400°F (205°C).

Tuna Fritters

Ingredients	U.S.	24 portions Metric
Bread Slices	4	4
Canned Tuna	7 oz.	200 g
Hard-boiled Egg, chopped	1	1
Capers, chopped	1 tbsp.	1 tbsp.
Beer Batter	1 recipe	1 recipe
Oil, for frying		

Cut the crust off the bread slices. Combine the flaked tuna with the egg and capers. Spread over the bread, and cut into 24 portions. Dip into the beer batter. Deep fry at 350°F (180°C) until golden brown. Drain on absorbent paper. Serve with tomato sauce or other cold sauce.

Spiedini Alla Romana

Spread melba toast rounds with anchovy paste. Alternate a melba toast and slice of mozzarella cheese on bamboo skewers and bake lightly in oven.

Lobster or Shrimp Bouchees

Fill bouchees (see Puff Pastry in chapter 7) with mousse of lobster, shrimp, et cetera.

Shrimp Puffs

Prepare profiteroles with cream puff dough (see chapter 7). Fill with creamed diced shrimp.

Cold Appetizers

Barquettes of Tuna

Ingredients	U.S.	24 barquettes Metric
Solid White Tuna	9 oz.	250 g
Mayonnaise	½ cup	1.2 dl
Lemon Juice	1 tsp.	1 tsp.
Cooked Barquettes (see chapter 6)	24	24
Fillets of Tuna, imported	12	12
Parsley, chopped	1 tbsp.	1 tbsp.
Hard-boiled Eggs, chopped . . .	2	2

Drain and flake the tuna. Mix in the mayonnaise and lemon juice. Season with salt and pepper to taste. Fill the barquette shells with the tuna mixture. Top with the tuna fillets. Sprinkle with parsley and eggs.

Barquettes Marivaux

Ingredients	6 portions U.S.	Metric	24 portions U.S.	Metric
Cooked Shrimp, diced	7 oz.	200 g	1¾ lb.	800 g
Cooked Mushrooms, diced ...	3½ oz.	100 g	14 oz.	400 g
Mayonnaise Sauce	1 cup	2.5 dl	1 qt.	1 l
Small Barquette Shells	12	12	48	48
Hard-boiled Eggs, chopped ...	2	2	8	8

Combine the shrimp and mushrooms with the mayonnaise sauce. Garnish the barquettes. Sprinkle with eggs.

Boston Dip

Ingredients	2 cups U.S.	Metric
Canned Minced Clams	8 oz.	225 g
Cream Cheese, softened	8 oz.	225 g
Lemon Juice	1 tbsp.	1 tbsp.
Parsley, chopped	1 tbsp.	1 tbsp.
Salt	¼ tsp.	¼ tsp.
Hot Sauce	⅛ tsp.	⅛ tsp.
Assorted Chips, Crackers or Raw vegetables		

Drain clams and reserve liquor. Cream the cheese. Add seasonings and clams and mix thoroughly. Chill for an hour. Thin dip if necessary with clam juice. Serve with chips, crackers, or vegetables.

Crab Canapes

Ingredients	2 dozen U.S.	Metric
Crabmeat, chopped	6 oz.	170 g
Cheese, shredded	2 oz.	50 g
Mayonnaise	2 tbsp.	0.3 dl
Chives, chopped	1 tsp.	1 tsp.
Liquid Hot Pepper	1 drop	1 drop
Salt	¼ tsp.	¼ tsp.
Egg Whites	2	2
Cooked Baking Powder Biscuits	2 doz.	2 doz.

Combine crabmeat with cheese, mayonnaise, chives, liquid pepper, and salt. Beat the egg whites until stiff and fold into crab mixture. Split biscuits in half. Top each half with a teaspoon of the crabmeat mixture. Bake at 450° F (230° C) for 5 to 6 minutes until golden brown.

Cucumbers Stuffed with Smoked Salmon

Ingredients	20 appetizers	
	U.S.	Metric
Cucumbers	3	3
Smoked Salmon, skinless and boneless	8 oz.	225 g
Cream Cheese, softened	4 oz.	110 g
Butter	4 oz.	110 g
English Mustard	1 tsp.	1 tsp.
Lemon Juice	2 oz.	0.6 dl
Pumpernickel Bread Slices		

Wash cucumbers and trim the ends. With a lemon peeler, cut V-shaped grooves lengthwise, spacing grooves equally. Cut in half crosswise. Extract all seeds.

Combine remaining ingredients in a food processor. Mix into a smooth paste. Fill cavities of the cucumber halves with the salmon mixture. Chill for one hour. Slice into ¼-inch (½-cm) pinwheels. Serve on slices of buttered pumpernickel bread. bread.

Marinated Mussels
See Mussels in chapter 14.

Marinated Shrimp

Ingredients	6 portions		24 portions	
	U.S.	Metric	U.S.	Metric
Medium Shrimp, in shells	2 lb.	900 g	8 lb.	3.6 kg
Medium Onions, sliced	2	2	8	8
Vegetable Oil	1½ cups	4 dl	1½ qt.	1½ l
White Vinegar	1½ cups	4 dl	1½ qt.	1½ l
Salt	1 tsp.	1 tsp.	1 tbsp.	1 tbsp.
Dill Weed	½ tsp.	½ tsp.	2 tsp.	2 tsp.
Celery Salt	½ tsp.	½ tsp.	2 tsp.	2 tsp.
Tiny Capers	1 tbsp.	1 tbsp.	4 tbsp.	4 tbsp.
Garnish				
Stuffed eggs	6	6	24	24
Radish Roses	6	6	24	24
Lemon Wedges	6	6	24	24

Peel and devein shrimp. Cook in salted boiling water for 3 to 5 minutes. Drain and rinse under cold water. In a sealable container, alternate layers of onion slices and shrimp. Mix remaining ingredients and pour over shrimp. Cover to seal. Marinate in refrigerator for 24 hours, basting shrimp with marinade 2 or 3 times.

Arrange on a serving platter and garnish with stuffed eggs, radish roses, butter balls, and lemon wedges.

Sardine Dip

Ingredients	2 cups U.S.	Metric
Canned Sardines	4 oz.	110 g
Cream Cheese	8 oz.	225 g
Milk	1 tbsp.	1 tbsp.
Parsley, chopped	2 tbsp.	2 tbsp.
Lemon Juice	1 tbsp.	1 tbsp.
Worcestershire Sauce	1 tsp.	1 tsp.
Assorted Cheese or Crackers, or Raw Vegetables		

Combine all ingredients except crackers and vegetables. Mix well to a smooth paste.

Shrimp Bouquet Boca Grande

See Shrimp in chapter 14.

Smoked Fish Dip

Ingredients	2 cups U.S.	Metric
Smoked Salmon, Whitefish, et cetera	8 oz.	225 g
Sour Cream	½ cup	1.2 dl
Mayonnaise	½ cup	1.2 dl
Lemon Juice	1 tbsp.	1 tbsp.
Chives, chopped	1 tbsp.	1 tbsp.
Onion Powder	½ tsp.	½ tsp.
Salt	½ tsp.	½ tsp.
Dried Rosemary	¼ tsp.	¼ tsp.
Parsley to taste		
Assorted Crackers, Potato Chips		

Skin, bone, and flake the smoked fish. Combine all ingredients except parsley and crackers. Mix thoroughly. Chill for at least one hour. Sprinkle parsley over dip. Serve with chips and crackers.

Stuffed Tomato Surprise

Ingredients	U.S.	3 dozen Metric
Canned Tuna	7 oz.	200 g
Cream Cheese, softened	3 oz.	85 g
Medium Avocado	1	1
Lemon Juice	1 tbsp.	1 tbsp.
Salt	½ tsp.	½ tsp.
Hot Pepper Sauce	¼ tsp.	¼ tsp.
Worcestershire Sauce	½ tsp.	½ tsp.
Cherry Tomatoes	3 doz.	3 doz.

Drain and flake the tuna. Mix with cream cheese and the avocado pulp to a smooth paste. Season with lemon juice and seasonings. Wash tomatoes and hollow out centers. Fill each tomato with a heaping teaspoon of the tuna mixture.

Tartelettes Arkangel

Cover the bottom of small cooked tartlet shells (see chapter 7) with caviar and fill to level with puree of smoked salmon. Top with a piece of anchovy fillet.

Tartelettes of Shrimp a la Russe

Ingredients	U.S.	12 portions Metric
Tiny Whole Cooked Shrimp ..	1 lb.	450 g
Horseradish, grated	1 oz.	25 g
Mayonnaise	½ cup	1.2 dl
Salt	½ tsp.	½ tsp.
Sugar	½ tsp.	½ tsp.
Paprika	1 tsp.	1 tsp.
Lemon Juice	1 tsp.	1 tsp.
Tartlets	12	340 g
Caviar	1 oz.	25 g

Combine the shrimp with the horseradish, mayonnaise, salt, sugar, paprika, and lemon juice. Spoon mixture into tartlets. Garnish with caviar.

Tuna Bites

	3 dozen	
Ingredients	U.S.	Metric
Solid White or Light Tuna	14 oz.	400 g
Cream Cheese, softened	4 oz.	110 g
Blue Cheese	2 oz.	50 g
Chives, finely chopped	1 tbsp.	1 tbsp.
Lemon Juice	½ tsp.	½ tsp.
Salt, to taste		
Parsley, chopped	½ cup	25 g

In a food processor, combine tuna, cream cheese, blue cheese, and chives. Add lemon juice and season to taste with salt. Form into small balls and roll in parsley. Chill for an hour or more before serving.

Tuna Puffs

	6 portions		24 portions	
Ingredients	U.S.	Metric	U.S.	Metric
Cream Puff Dough	1 recipe	1 recipe	4 recipes	4 recipes
Canned Tuna	7 oz.	200 g	1¾ lb.	800 g
Mayonnaise	¼ cup	0.6 dl	1 cup	2.5 dl
Cream Cheese	2 oz.	50 g	8 oz.	225 g
Lemon Juice	1 tsp.	1 tsp.	1½ tbsp.	1½ tbsp.
Ginger, ground	¼ tsp.	¼ tsp.	1 tsp.	1 tsp.

Make bite size cream puffs with the dough. Flake the tuna and combine with the remaining ingredients. Split the puffs, fill with one-half of the tuna mixture, and top with the other half.

CHAPTER 16

The Decorative Power of Cold Fish and Shellfish

In addition to cooking seafoods with precision and care, the decorative aspect of cold fish and shellfish presents a challenge. Colorful fish and shellfish, in various sizes and shapes, are easily adapted to decorative work. The pink color of salmon, the pure white of bass, cod, and haddock, and the coral red of several crustaceans provide numerous color contrasts when used with other ingredients. However, regardless of the motif or theme selected for a specific occasion, simplicity is the rule for seafood decorations. Moreover, these decorations should not be time consuming. Fish and shellfish are perishable, and elaborate ornaments will spoil any dish kept too long at room temperature.

The great challenge is to decorate seafood platters that reflect today's marketing conditions and economics. The methods described and illustrated in this book fulfill both these requirements and still please the eyes and whet the appetite.

Decorative Approaches to Seafoods

Probably one of the most revolutionary decorative methods ever developed is the aspic sheet. The possibilities of these colorful sheets are innumerable. The following is the basic recipe; the main ingredient determines the final color.

Orange Aspic Sheet

Ingredients	U.S.	Metric
Canned Pimentos	3½ oz.	100 g
Water	¾ cup	2 dl
Salt	pinch	pinch
Unflavored Gelatin	1 oz.	25 g

Combine pimentos and warm water in an electric blender and puree to a fine paste. Add salt and gelatin and mix together well. Transfer mixture to a small saucepan and place in a hot waterbath for 5 minutes to remove any air bubbles. Then pour onto a slightly oiled 14-by-17-inch (35-by-42.5-cm) pan. Spread the mixture evenly over the whole surface of the pan. Refrigerate until firm.

For other color sheets, use the above recipe, substituting one of the following for the pimentos:

red sheet—use ½ pimentos and ½ tomato paste

yellow sheet—use hard-boiled egg yolks

white sheet—use hard-boiled egg whites

green sheet—use spinach or watercress

black sheet—use truffle peelings

How to Use Aspic Sheets

The very thin, gelatinized colorful sheets are now ready for use. A set of small cutters, specially designed for minute decorations, is necessary. Some cutters are geometric shapes, others are alphabet, animal, or leaf shapes. Freehand decorations can also be very effective.

After pressing a selected cutter against an aspic sheet, the shape can be lifted with a toothpick and placed on the cold seafood. Cold mousses, whole fish, pates and galantines of fish, fish steaks, and many other preparations are much more appealing when decorated. A smoked salmon mousse becomes a conversation piece when decorated with orange cutouts depicting small fish. Strips of green scallions or leeks make the decor even more attractive. Floral arrangements and geometric ornamentations can be executed easily with a selection of aspic sheets and cutters. Any leftover aspic can be remelted, poured into' smaller trays or plates, and frozen for future use.

Other Decorative Approaches

There are basically eleven ingredients that can be used efficiently and economically for seafood decorations. They are:

fresh raw vegetables
fresh cooked vegetables
canned or marinated vegetables
fresh raw fruit
canned fruit
fresh herbs
aspic sheets
hard-boiled eggs
fish roe
baked goods
dairy products

Fresh vegetables The following vegetables are used primarily in food decorations: carrots, celery, cucumbers, leeks, potatoes, radishes, tomatoes, and turnips. Depending on the imagination and experience of the decorator, other vegetables can also be used.

The decorations that can be created with these vegetables are numerous. They can be carved into flowers, sliced (raw or blanched), and cut into many different designs. Carrots can be used raw or cooked; cucumbers, cut lengthwise and sliced very thin, make perfect fish scales for decorating a whole fish. Leeks are usually blanched and cut into flower stems or leaves. Cooked firm potatoes are sliced and cut with various decorative cutters; when raw, they can be turned into roses or turnips, but their use as flowers for seafood decorations is not recommended. Paper-thin sliced radishes are beautiful when simply arranged into flowers.

The skin of tomatoes can be curled or rolled to resemble flowers. Whole round tomato slices or half slices, alternated with sliced cucumbers, are always attractive for a quick, colorful presentation. Red cabbage, marinated in vinegar, can be shredded or sliced around a variety of cold seafood dishes. And turnips, yellow or white, can yield simple unique arrangements, classified as decorations or the new cuisine. A vase of white turnip flowers, adorned with delicate pink carrot buttons, will turn a seafood centerpiece into a showpiece.

How to make a flower vase with a butternut squash.

Remove the top of a medium butternut squash. Scoop out the inside. Decorate the outside of the squash using turnip or carrot balls.

To make the turnip daisies:

1. Peel the turnip and cut into ¼-inch (6-mm) thick slices.

2. Using star cookie cutters in graduated sizes, cut stars from turnip slices. Cut two stars for each flower.

3. Use a small Parisian scoop to form carrot center for daisies.

4. Put an 8-to-10-inch (20-to-25-cm) Chinese skewer through larger star, then the smaller. Top with carrot center.

5. Push a green scallion stem over the skewer.

6. Arrange stems and daisies in the butternut squash vase. Use skewers of varying length for the bouquet.

7. Cut leaves out of green leek stems. Arrange attractively in the vase, using as many as needed to accompany the flowers.

How to carve a fisherman's net from a turnip.

A fisherman's net is an innovation in the art of seafood decoration. Although it is a time-consuming preparation, it is certainly worthwhile for the dedicated pro or amateur alike.

1. Select a large rhutabaga.

2. Trim and shape into a square.

3. Insert a ⅜-inch (1-cm) dowel into the center of the turnip square. (Sharpen one end for easy penetration.)

4. Soak turnip in a strong solution of salt and water to soften its texture. This will take 2 to 3 days.

5. Place the turnip flat on the working surface. Starting at one end of the turnip, carve a ¼-inch slice until the knife reaches the dowel. A meat slicer is the

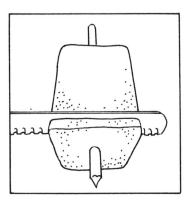

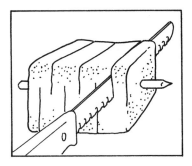

best carving implement. Keep the knife horizontal to the working surface. Give the rhutabaga a half turn and make a similar cut.

6. Give the turnip a quarter turn and carve a ¼-inch slice, in the same fashion as above. Give the vegetable a half turn and make a similar cut. Continue this procedure until the turnip is sliced from end to end.

7. Soak turnip for 12 hours in the salted water to soften the core.

 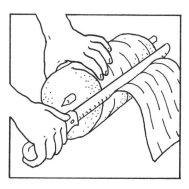

8. Round the turnip as shown.

9. Holding the turnip with one hand, slice the turnip in a continuous piece about ¼-inch (6-mm) thick. Special care

should be exercised not to break the continuous cut.

10. Stretch the net as shown. Use this original creation as a base on a platter. Arrange cold seafood on top. The turnip net

can be kept in salted water for several days and reused many times.

Hard-boiled Eggs Hard-boiled eggs are often used as a focal point in seafood decoration. They can be sliced, whole, wedged, stuffed, or chopped. Chopped egg yolks and egg whites, mixed with chopped parsley (a colorful garnish called *mimosa*) are sprinkled over many seafood dishes to add color.

To slice hard-boiled eggs, always use an egg slicer. For a simple decoration, alternate egg slices with tomato and cucumber slices around any cold seafood platter. To cut eggs into wedges, an egg wedger is recommended for a clean cut. Remove the yolks, stuff with a mousse, and use as appetizers. Hard-boiled eggs, cut in half lengthwise or crosswise, are usually stuffed, using the egg yolks in the stuffing.

The most eye-catching decorations can be made with whole eggs. Penguins, frogs, and other fancy decorations are easily done with a little imagination.

Baked Goods and Dairy Products As described in chapter 7, pie crust can be baked into barquettes (little boats) or tartelettes (little tarts); puff pastry is made into patty shells, bouchees, fleurons, et cetera. All of these can be decorative parts of seafood displays. Barquettes or tartelettes are usually filled with such colorful mixtures as mousses, Russian salad, and fish or shellfish salads, and arranged around seafood platters as accompaniments. Whole sandwich bread can be carved into a boat to contain appetizers or seafood salads.

The dairy product that is most adaptable to shaping and patterns is cream cheese. Cream cheese is usually applied with the help of a pastry bag, fitted with different sizes and shapes of metal tubes. Cream cheese roses are easily prepared with a rose tube. Softened cream cheese is also used to make mushroom clumps.

Fish Roe Colorful fish roe especially that of salmon (red caviar), sturgeon, lumpfish, or other fish (black caviar), or lobster coral, are great favorites in food decoration. Fish roe is used mostly as garnish for a variety of seafood products. A smoked salmon mousse is best garnished with salmon caviar. Stuffed eggs, barquettes, and other individual garnishes can be topped with black or red caviar. Fish roe is also used in forming designs or patterns of all kinds.

Fresh Herbs Generally, leeks are used to add to the design, color, or texture (relief) of the surface to be decorated. Whole leaves of various herbs can be used, but for seafood designs dill is the most suitable along with the blanched green part of leeks and parsley stems. Fresh herbs work well in the design of trees, flower stems, leaves, seaweed, and other floral motifs.

Homard a la Parisienne

The illustration (see color plate) shows an arrangement of cold lobster, with the meat taken out of the shells, garnished with lemons and parsley, and topped with a carrot spider mum.

Carrot Spider Mum

1. Wash, trim, and peel a thick carrot about 5 to 6 inches (12.5 to 14 cm) long; slice lengthwise into ⅛ inch thick slices (an electric slicer or a manual potato slicer is necessary to achieve the best results).

slices, leaving ½ inch uncut at both ends of carrot.

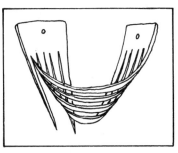

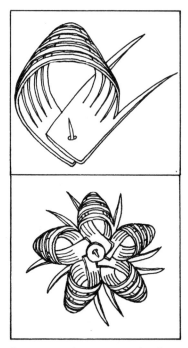

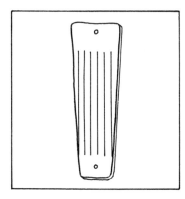

2. To make one flower, use 5 carrot slices. Make cuts at ¼-inch intervals the length of the

3. Note in second diagram that the two outside slices are cut free at the narrow end of the carrot.

4. Place one end of a carrot slice onto a toothpick. Fold the slice and place other end onto the same toothpick with a twist.

5. Arrange remaining slices into an attractive five petal

flower on the same pick. Conceal the tip of toothpick with a piece of ripe olive in the center of the flower to accent the color of the carrot spider mum.

Cold Fish Displays

Cold fish is best if poached whole or in one sizable piece. (See poaching technique in chapter 6). The fish will remain tender, flaky, and moist.

Such cold fish as salmon, whitefish, striped bass, and red snapper can be presented on a buffet table and attractively decorated using some of the ideas described in this section. A cold sauce should always be served with cold fish. Several garnishes may accompany cold fish to enhance their presentation. Some of these garnishes are:

cherry tomatoes stuffed with egg salad
Russian salad aspic mold
slices of eggs, tomatoes, and cucumbers overlapping around fish
stuffed deviled eggs

small boats (barquettes) filled with several types of foods
cucumber salad
marinated tomato salad
stuffed artichoke bottoms
mushroom caps stuffed with caviar
cooked shrimp
carrots and celery sticks
anchovy fillets
ripe and green olives
lettuce hearts
capers
green and white asparagus tips
smoked oysters
tomato wedges, quartered cooked eggs, and parsley sprigs

Cucumber Salad

Ingredients	6 portions		24 portions	
	U.S.	Metric	U.S.	Metric
Cucumbers	1 lb.	450 g	4 lb.	1.8 kg
Salt	1 tsp.	1 tsp.	1 tbsp.	1 tbsp.
Oil and Vinegar Dressing	½ cup	1.2 dl	2 cups	5 dl
Parsley, chopped	1 tsp.	1 tsp.	1 tbsp.	1 tbsp.

Peel cucumbers. Cut lengthwise and remove seeds. Slice thin and add salt. Allow to set for one-half hour. Squeeze cucumbers in a clean towel to remove all water. Mix in the dressing. Sprinkle with chopped parsley. Serve cold.

Marinated Tomato Salad

Ingredients	6 portions		24 portions	
	U.S.	Metric	U.S.	Metric
Fresh Firm Tomatoes	1 lb.	450 g	4 lb.	1.8 kg
Oil......................	3 tbsp.	0.5 dl	¾ cup	2 dl
Wine Vinegar..............	1 tbsp.	1 tbsp.	¼ cup	0.6 dl
Onion, chopped	1 oz.	25 g	4 oz.	110 g
Chives, chopped	1 tsp.	1 tsp.	1 tbsp.	1 tbsp.
Salt	½ tsp.	½ tsp.	2 tsp.	2 tsp.
Pepper, ground	¼ tsp.	¼ tsp.	1 tsp.	1 tsp.
Oregano..................	¼ tsp.	¼ tsp.	1 tsp.	1 tsp.

Blanch and peel tomatoes. Slice thinly. Combine oil and vinegar. Add the seasonings. Arrange tomatoes on a platter and pour dressing over. Allow to marinate for one hour before serving.

Russian Salad Aspic Mold

Ingredients	6 portions		24 portions	
	U.S.	Metric	U.S.	Metric
Potatoes, cooked and diced ...	4 oz.	110 g	1 lb.	450 g
Carrots, cooked and diced	4 oz.	110 g	1 lb.	450 g
Canned Baby Peas	4 oz.	110 g	1 lb.	450 g
Green Beans, cooked and diced	4 oz.	110 g	1 lb.	450 g
Mayonnaise	½ cup	1.2 dl	2 cups	5 dl
Salt and Pepper, to taste				
Instant Aspic Jelly, liquid	½ cup	1.2 dl	2 cups	5 dl

Combine the vegetables with the mayonnaise. Season to taste with salt and pepper. Mix in the instant aspic jelly. Spoon into small individual molds. Allow to set in refrigerator for one hour. Dip the molds in hot water and unmold around the cold fish.

Stuffed Artichoke Bottoms

Ingredients	6 portions		24 portions	
	U.S.	Metric	U.S.	Metric
Anchovy Fillets	3 oz.	85 g	12 oz.	340 g
Fresh, Tomatoes, blanched and peeled	4 oz.	110 g	1 lb.	450 g
Celery Stalks	2	2	8	8
Artichoke Bottoms, fresh or canned	6	6	24	24
Green Goddess Dressing (recipe follows)	½ cup	1.2 dl	2 cups	5 dl
Green Pepper	1	1	4	4

Cut the anchovy fillets into small pieces. Dice the tomatoes and the celery. Mix anchovies, tomatoes, celery, and dressing.

Stuff the artichokes with the mixture. Decorate with rings or strips of green peppers.

Green Goddess Dressing

Ingredients	6 portions		24 portions	
	U.S.	Metric	U.S.	Metric
Garlic Clove	1	1	4	4
Anchovy Fillets	2	2	8	8
Mayonnaise	5 oz.	1.5 dl	2½ cups	6 dl
Sour Cream	2 oz.	0.6 dl	1 cup	2.5 dl
Tarragon Vinegar	1 tsp.	1 tsp.	1 tbsp.	1 tbsp.
Lemon Juice	1 tsp.	1 tsp.	1 tbsp.	1 tbsp.
White Pepper, ground	⅛ tsp.	⅛ tsp.	½ tsp.	½ tsp.
Salt	¼ tsp.	¼ tsp.	1 tsp.	1 tsp.
Parsley Juice	1 tsp.	1 tsp.	1 tbsp.	1 tbsp.
Chopped Chives	1 tsp.	1 tsp.	1 tbsp.	1 tbsp.

Mince the garlic with the anchovies and combine with the remaining ingredients. Chill for half an hour before serving.

Stuffed Deviled Eggs

Ingredients	6 portions		24 portions	
	U.S.	Metric	U.S.	Metric
Hard-boiled Eggs	3	3	12	12
Mayonnaise	1 oz.	25 g	4 oz.	110 g
Cream Cheese, softened	2 oz.	50 g	8 oz.	225 g
Salt	¼ tsp.	¼ tsp.	1 tsp.	1 tsp.
Pepper, ground	⅛ tsp.	⅛ tsp.	½ tsp.	½ tsp.
Tabasco Sauce	dash	dash	⅛ tsp.	⅛ tsp.
Parsley, chopped	1 tsp.	1 tsp.	1 tbsp.	1 tbsp.

Cut eggs in half and remove yolks. Combine yolks, mayonnaise, and cream cheese in a food processor. Mix to a smooth paste. Add the seasonings.

Stuff the eggs with the mixture using a pastry bag fitted with a decorative star tube. Sprinkle with chopped parsley. Chill before serving.

Cold Lobster a la Francaise
(Used as a buffet display.)

Ingredients	12 portions		24 portions	
	U.S.	Metric	U.S.	Metric
Live Lobsters, 1¼ lb. (560 g) each	12	12	24	24
Live Lobster, 10–15 lb. (4.5–6.8 kg)	1	1	2	2
Stuffed Deviled Eggs	12	12	24	24
Aspic Jelly, chopped	2 cups	5 dl	1 qt.	1 l
Lemon Wedges	12	12	24	24
Cherry Tomatoes	12	12	24	24
Mayonnaise Sauce	1 qt.	1 l	2 qt.	2 l

Tie large live lobsters on a board as described in chapter 6. Boil in boiling salted water for 40 to 45 minutes. Boil the small lobsters in boiling salted water for 10 to 15 minutes. To display the large lobsters:

1. Remove tail meat by cutting under the shell with scissors, being careful not to damage the meat.

2. Extract the claw meat by cutting out a 2-inch, (5-cm) square piece of shell with a meat saw.

3. Cut the lobster tail(s) into small medallions. Pipe a small row of cream cheese on back of lobster carcass and arrange each medallion over the lobster carcass in an overlapping position. Decorate with truffles or pimento pieces.

4. Glaze the lobster by brushing with cold liquid jelly. Place on a large platter or, preferably, a mirror.

Remove tail and claw meat from small lobsters. Discard shells. Arrange around large lobster display, along with large lobster meat. Garnish platter or mirror with stuffed eggs and tomatoes, and serve with mayonnaise on the side.

Lobster a la Parisienne
(For buffet.)

Ingredients	15 portions U.S.	Metric
Live Lobsters, 4–5 lbs. (1.8–2.270 kg)	4	4
Russian Salad	2.5 lb.	1.140 kg
Liquid Aspic Jelly	1 qt.	1 l
Pimento Aspic Sheet	1 recipe	1 recipe
Truffle Aspic Sheet	1 recipe	1 recipe
Mayonnaise	2 cups	5 dl
Lemon Wedges	15	15
Cherry Tomatoes	15	15
Hard-boiled Eggs, sliced	6	6
Parsley, to garnish		
Sauce Vincent	3 cups	8 dl

Tie lobsters on small rectangular boards to prevent tails from curling while cooking. Cook in court bouillon no. 3 for 25 to 30 minutes. Cool at room temperature. To extract the tail meat, cut the carapace underneath with scissors. Remove tails. Cut a 2-to-3-inch square piece of shell under each claw. Extract the claw meat and dice. Mix diced lobster meat with Russian salad.

Coat a suitable mold with aspic jelly. Decorate with designs cut out of truffle and pimento sheets. Blend 1 cup (2.5 dl) of cold liquid jelly with the Russian salad. Fill decorated mold with the salad.

Slice lobster tails into medallions. Decorate with truffle cutouts and glaze with cold liquid jelly.

Pipe a row of mayonnaise collee along the back of each lobster. Arrange lobster medallions on top, overlapping each slice. Brush with cold liquid jelly.

To present, dip Russian salad mold in lukewarm water. Unmold in center of tray. Arrange whole lobsters around tray. Decorate with lemon wedges, hard-boiled egg slices, parsley sprigs, and tomatoes. Serve sauce Vincent separate.

Quenelles of Pike and Lobster Chaud Froid a l'Americaine

This is one of the most appetizing buffet dishes if executed with the utmost care. The pike quenelles covered with a light green chaud froid, and the lobster quenelles coated with a rich pink lobster chaud froid, provide an unusual and attractive contrast.

Quenelles of Pike

Ingredients	U.S.	8 portions Metric
Flour	4 oz.	110 g
Butter	3 oz.	85 g
Milk, heated	2 cups	5 dl
Egg Yolks	6	6
Salt	½ tsp.	½ tsp.
White Pepper	¼ tsp.	¼ tsp.
Nutmeg, ground	⅛ tsp.	⅛ tsp.
Fillets of Pike	1 lb.	450 g
Beef Kidney Suet	1 lb.	450 g
Egg Whites	2	2

Melt butter, add flour, and mix. Pour in the milk and work to make a paste. Remove from heat and add the egg yolks. Season with salt, pepper, and nutmeg. Set aside to cool.

Finely grind the chilled pike fillet with the suet. Add the flour panada and gradually mix in the egg whites. The mixture should remain cold and thick.

Shape oval dumplings with two tablespoons and simmer in salted boiling water for 10 to 12 minutes. Drain the quenelles and allow to cool for one hour.

Quenelles of Lobster

Ingredients	U.S.	8 portions Metric
Raw Lobster	10 oz.	280 g
Sole or Flounder Fillets	6 oz.	170 g
Egg	1	1
Heavy Cream	1 cup	2.5 dl
Salt	½ tsp.	½ tsp.
Pepper, ground	¼ tsp.	¼ tsp.
Cayenne Pepper	⅛ tsp.	⅛ tsp.
Nutmeg, ground	⅛ tsp.	⅛ tsp.

Peel and devein lobster. Wash and drain. Cut fish fillets into pieces. Place the lobster and fish into a chopper and grind finely. Add the egg, cream, and seasonings and stir well.

Shape the quenelles following the procedure used for quenelles of pike. Poach for 10 minutes.

Presentation   Alternate the two quenelles on a mirror. Garnish with small round carrot and turnip balls poached in water. Stuff small tomatoes with cucumber salad and garnish platter.

Green Chaud Froid Sauce

Ingredients	U.S.	Metric
Veloute Sauce	1 qt.	1 l
Fresh Spinach Leaves	1 oz.	25 g
Watercress Leaves	1 oz.	25 g
Dill	½ oz.	15 g
Unflavored Gelatin	1 oz.	25 g

In a blender, puree spinach, watercress, and dill with a little veloute sauce. Bring the pureed mixture to a boil. Strain through a fine strainer and add the remaining sauce. Dissolve the gelatin in water. Stir in the hot sauce. Cool the sauce and coat the pike quenelles.

Americaine Chaud Froid Sauce

Ingredients	U.S.	Metric
Americaine Sauce	1 qt.	1 l
Heavy Cream	½ cup	1.2 dl
Unflavored Gelatin	2 oz.	50 g

Heat up the sauce Americaine. Stir in the cream. Dissolve the gelatin in a small amount of water. Stir in the hot sauce. Cool the sauce and coat the lobster quenelles.

CHAPTER 17

Aquaculture and the Underutilized Marine Species

Aquaculture

We are facing a growing demand for our traditional fish products. It is expected that the per capita consumption of seafood in the United States will rise dramatically, if the supply does not dwindle.

Water farming or aquaculture may help alleviate the formidable demands on our favorite seafoods. Throughout the United States, tests and studies are being conducted to determine the feasibility of farming various types of fish and shellfish. Many projects have been successful, and fish farms could be major protein sources by 1990.

However, growing fish is not as simple as growing potatoes. There are problems regarding substantial investments, the length of time necessary to build up a prosperous operation, the knowledge of competition and market prospects, and many other factors related to the effective production of these new crops. Despite the problems, aquaculture already provides more than half of the nation's catfish, 40 percent of the oysters, nearly all of the commercial trout, and more than 15 percent of the salmon.

The maintenance of water quality (free of pollutants), the prevention of diseases, and the selection of feeds are controllable factors that should guarantee public acceptance of water-farmed seafoods, providing the cost is competitive with the "wild" fish products. The questions of taste and flavor will certainly be raised as the production of new farmed species increases.

A sharp growth in the production of trout, catfish, oysters, and salmon has occurred in recent years. According to the National Marine Fisheries Service, an arm of the Commerce Department's National Oceanic and Atmospheric Administration, more than 100 private ventures are involved in the marine aquaculture of oysters, clams, shrimp, and salmon. In addition, there are 2000 to 4000 commercial ventures based on rearing catfish, trout, crawfish, and other fresh-water species.

Since lobster production has reached its maximum sustainable yield, considerable effort is being made to determine whether lobster can be produced economically in intense culture systems. John Hughes, Director of the Massachusetts State Lobster Hatchery and Research Station at Oak Bluffs, has spent many years studying lobsters. He has developed lobster cultures and worked on the problems of raising lobsters successfully, quickly, and profitably in captivity. However, the number of problems to be overcome before full commercial farming of lobster becomes a reality are overwhelming. As the most valuable American seafood, lobster is the logical choice with which to attempt a commercial breakthrough. But what will the meat of farmed lobster, raised on artificial food and possibly in artificial sea water, and forced to grow at a gallop, taste like? Will their flesh still be "sweet, restorative, and innocent" as the writer R. Brookes once said? No one knows.

A plan for warm-water aquaculture of fast growing herbivorous fish (like carp, white amur, buffalo fish, tilapia), raised in a mass production, low energy system, could be feasible. The fish could be marketed in frozen boneless and skinless sticks, an economical process done mechanically by a bone and skin separator.

One fact is certain. Aquaculture will expand if encouraged at the federal level. In the Gulf States, about 2 million acres of low priced delta land would be suitable for fish farming.

Specialists estimate that aquaculture could account for the following annual levels of production by 1990:

oysters—200 million pounds
penacid shrimp—43 million pounds
Pacific salmon—226 million pounds
American lobster—10 million pounds
hard and soft shell clams—25 million pounds
bay scallops—5 million pounds
abalone—5 million pounds
mussels—25 million pounds
catfish—120 million pounds
pompano—3 million pounds
fresh-water trout—70 million pounds

sea-water trout—10 million pounds
crawfish—30 million pounds
low value fish (carp, buffalo fish, white amur, etc—400 million pounds

These estimates add up to a projected annual yield of nearly 1.2 billion pounds by aquaculture by 1990.

Shrimp Farming

For several years, biologists have been studying methods and techniques of raising shrimp in ponds. Latest reports indicate that shrimp farming is feasible, if worked on a large scale, and may become a very profitable business in the Southern and Gulf States. Results of studies show that shrimp do grow fatter in ponds, and have an excellent taste.

"The day of the fisherman, the hunter of the sea, is drawing to a close and the demand for pure protein is much higher than we can supply," said an optimistic director of a successful shrimp farm in Florida. But Mr. McAvoy of the NMFS in Gloucester, Massachusetts, is very cautious and does not see an immediate boom in aquaculture. "The protein of farmed fisheries is still too high and it will take several years to compete with the current prices of fish and shellfish caught by our fishermen."

The Underutilized Marine Species

Europeans and Asians consume a greater variety of fish and shellfish than Americans. We are too meticulous about taste when it comes to eating our astoundingly varied aquatic heritage. So, we trade squid for tuna, and the sea urchin for cash. Herring does not appeal to our finicky taste; we disdain the mussel, the American eel, and countless other species of fish.

Europeans dare to eat such bizarre, ugly monsters as the anglerfish, skate, lumpfish, and wolffish! The crucial question should be asked: In a hungry world, where thousands of people die of starvation, when are we going to lessen the terrible waste by learning to eat new species of fish that are profitable and accepted in other countries? In 1975 United States imports of edible fish products soared to 1,913.1 million pounds of mainly tuna, shrimp, salmon, and sardines. While depriving poor nations of badly needed protein, American deep sea trawlers threw back 25 to 30 percent of their hauls. In the United States, there is no market for so-called junkfish as there is in Europe. Most of these fish do not survive when released; rough handling, the change in pressure, and crushing under tons of other fish kill most of them. So, it is time for fish-marketing experts to test market the many underutilized species of fish that go to waste by the millions of pounds each year.

The National Marine Fisheries Service, and other Departments of Fisheries in the United States, are in constant touch with the needs and desires that surface in the market place. There is a growing demand for new seafood products from both institutional and retail buyers. We are becoming aware of the short supplies of traditional items and the need to develop new fish products. The Resource Utilization Office of the NMFS plays an important role in the initial research and development surrounding the introduction of new varieties or uses of seafood. Investigating the abundance of stocks of food fish is another contribution made by the NMFS Resource Office. When gathering data on a specific underutilized resource, such factors as behavior and the amount that can be harvested safely are taken into account.

Fishermen must be assured that there is a profitable market for the new catch, that the resource is plentiful, and that consumer interest exists. Then, the market will be wide open for the sale of a new fish product.

There are a number of marketable underutilized fish products, such as:

anglerfish, also known as monkfish
Jonah crab and red crab
krill
shark and dogfish
skate
squid
wolffish

Anglerfish (Monkfish, Goosefish)

Anglerfish Sauce Americaine

Ingredients	6 portions		24 portions	
	U.S.	Metric	U.S.	Metric
Anglerfish Fillets	2 lb.	900 g	8 lb.	3.6 kg
Oil	2 oz.	0.6 dl	1 cup	2.5 dl
Butter	2 oz.	0.6 dl	1 cup	2.5 dl
Onion, chopped	4 oz.	110 g	1 lb.	450 g
Garlic Cloves, minced	1	1	4	4
Carrots, chopped	4 oz.	110 g	1 lb.	450 g
Cognac	2 oz.	0.6 dl	1 cup	2.5 dl

Dry White Wine	1 cup	2.5 dl	1 qt.	1 l
Tomato Paste	2 tbsp.	2 tbsp.	½ cup	1.2 dl
Bay Leaf	1	1	4	4
Beurre Manie, to thicken				
Parsley, chopped	1 tbsp.	1 tbsp.	4 tbsp.	4 tbsp.
Tarragon, chopped	1 tbsp.	1 tbsp.	4 tbsp.	4 tbsp.

Brown the fillets in a mixture of oil and butter. Add the onions, garlic, and carrots and cook for a while. Add the cognac and ignite. Moisten with wine and stir in the tomato paste and bay leaf. Season with salt and pepper to taste. Cover and bake at 350°F (180°C) for 25 minutes. Remove the fish from the cooking liquid. Slice thinly. Thicken cooking stock with beurre manie. Bring to a boil. Strain sauce over fish. Sprinkle with chopped parsley and tarragon. Serve hot.

Anglerfish Nicoise

	6 portions		24 portions	
Ingredients	U.S.	Metric	U.S.	Metric
Anglerfish steaks, 5 oz. (140 g)	2 lb.	900 g	8 lb.	3.6 kg
Flour	1 oz.	25 g	4 oz.	110 g
Butter	4 oz.	110 g	1 lb.	450 g
Onion, chopped	4 oz.	110 g	1 lb.	450 g
Tomato Sauce	1 cup	2.5 dl	1 qt.	1 l
Dry White Wine	1 cup	2.5 dl	1 qt.	1 l
Salt	½ tsp.	½ tsp.	2 tsp.	2 tsp.
Pepper	¼ tsp.	¼ tsp.	1 tsp.	1 tsp.
Thyme	¼ tsp.	¼ tsp.	1 tsp.	1 tsp.
Bay Leaf	1	1	4	4
Rice	1 cup	225 g	4 cups	900 g
Beurre Manie, to thicken				

Roll fish steaks in flour. Saute in half of the butter until brown. Remove steaks from pan. Add the onion and cook until light brown. Stir in the tomato sauce, wine, salt, pepper, and herbs. Place fish steaks in sauce and simmer for 30 to 40 minutes. Cook rice according to standard directions. Remove cooked fish from sauce. Thicken with beurre manie. Remove bay leaf. Arrange fish steaks on serving platter; cover with sauce. Serve rice separately.

Antarctic Soup

Ingredients	U.S.	Metric
Fish Stock	1½ cups	4 dl
Cooked Krill Paste	7 oz.	200 g
Butter	2 oz.	50 g
Flour	1 oz.	25 g
Whipping Cream	1 oz.	0.3 dl
Dry Sherry Wine	1 oz.	0.3 dl
Salt and Pepper, to taste		

Blend the cooked krill paste with half of the cold fish stock. Prepare a roux from butter and flour; add to the remainder of the fish stock. Bring to a boil and remove from heat. Add the blended cooked krill paste and season with the remaining ingredients. Add salt and pepper to taste. Heat the soup but do not boil.

Albatross Krill Cream

Ingredients	U.S.	Metric
Butter	2 oz.	50 g
Cream Cheese, softened	3 oz.	1 dl
Cooked Krill Paste	14 oz.	300 g
Unflavored Gélatin	1 envelope	1 envelope
Water	1 oz.	0.3 dl
Pepper, ground	⅛ tsp.	⅛ tsp.
Seafood Spice	¼ tsp.	¼ tsp.
One Lemon (juice)		
Fresh Dill, chopped	1 tbsp.	1 tbsp.

Mix the butter until creamy. Add the cream cheese and cooked krill paste. Combine well in an electric mixer. Dissolve gelatin in water. Melt over low heat, and stir in krill mixture. Stir in the seasonings, lemon juice, and dill. Spoon krill mixture into a mold. Refrigerate to set.

Walther Herwig Vol-au-Vent

Ingredients	U.S.	Metric
Fish Paste (cod, haddock, or lean fish)	5 oz.	150 g
Salt	1 tsp.	1 tsp.
Cooked Krill Paste	14 oz.	300 g
Bacon, chopped	2 oz.	50 g
Pepper, ground	⅛ tsp.	⅛ tsp.
Chives, chopped	1 tbsp.	1 tbsp.

Thoroughly mix fish paste with salt, krill paste, and chopped bacon. Stir well. Fill the pastry vol-au-vent, fully cooked, with krill mixture and bake at 325°F (165°C) until cooked.

Krill Sticks

Shape the same filling used for vol-au-vent into sticks. Dip in beer batter, and deep fry for a short time. Do not overcook.

2000 Sauce

Ingredients	U.S.	Metric
Plain Yogurt	1 cup	2.5 dl
Mayonnaise	1 cup	2.5 dl
Cooked Krill Paste	1 lb.	450 g
Whipping Cream	½ cup	1.2 dl
Fresh Dill, chopped	2 tbsp.	2 tbsp.
Chives, Parsley, Capers, and Pickles, chopped	1 tbsp. each	1 tbsp. each
Lemons (juice)	2	2
Sild (canned herring), chopped	4 oz.	4 oz.
Ground Pepper, Chili, Sugar . .	1 pinch each	1 pinch each

Mix all ingredients thoroughly.

Shark
(Dogfish)

Barbecued Shark Steaks

Ingredients	6 portions		24 portions	
	U.S.	Metric	U.S.	Metric
Shark Steaks	6—5 oz.	6—150 g	24—5 oz.	24—150 g
Oil	¼ cup	0.6 dl	1 cup	2.5 dl
Onion, chopped	2 oz.	50 g	8 oz.	225 g
Green Peppers, chopped	2 oz.	50 g	8 oz.	225 g
Garlic Cloves	1	1	4	4
Tomato Sauce	1 cup	2.5 dl	1 qt.	1 l
Lemon Juice	1 tbsp.	1 tbsp.	2 oz.	0.6 dl
Worcestershire Sauce	1 tbsp.	1 tbsp.	2 oz.	0.6 dl
Salt	1 tsp.	1 tsp.	4 tsp.	4 tsp.
Pepper	¼ tsp.	¼ tsp.	1 tsp.	1 tsp.

Thaw steaks if frozen. Heat the oil in a frying pan. Add the onion, green pepper, and garlic, and cook until tender. Add remaining ingredients except for steaks. Simmer for 10 minutes and cool. Arrange steaks in baking pans. Pour the cold sauce over and marinate for 30 minutes.

Broil the steaks on a grill, basting with the marinade. Turn, and cook until fish is flaky and tender. Arrange on a warm serving platter. Pour the heated marinade over.

Billingsgate Fish and Chips

See Miscellaneous Seafood Recipes in chapter 12.

Curried Shark

Ingredients	6 portions		24 portions	
	U.S.	Metric	U.S.	Metric
Shark Fillets, fresh or frozen . . .	1½ lb.	680 g	6 lb.	2.7 kg
Butter	2 oz.	50 g	8 oz.	225 g
Curry Sauce	1½ cups	4 dl	1½ qt.	1.5 l
Sour Cream	¾ cup	2 dl	3 cups	8 dl
Curry Powder	1½ tsp.	1½ tsp.	2 tbsp.	2 tbsp.
Parsley, chopped	1 tbsp.	1 tbsp.	4 tbsp.	4 tbsp.

Cut the shark fillets into 1-inch (2.5-cm) cubes. Saute in butter for 3 to 5 minutes. Stir in the remaining ingredients and simmer for 5 minutes. Serve over rice.

Jaw's Burger

Ingredients	6 portions		24 portions	
	U.S.	Metric	U.S.	Metric
Fresh Dogfish Fillets	1½ lb.	680 g	6 lb.	2.7 kg
Eggs, beaten	1	1	4	4
Salt	1 tsp.	1 tsp.	1 tbsp.	1 tbsp.
White Pepper	¼ tsp.	¼ tsp.	1 tsp.	1 tsp.
Hamburger Buns	6	6	24	24
American Cheese, sliced	6	6	24	24

Skin the fillets. Wash in cold water and drain. Cut into cubes and grind coarsely. Combine with egg. Season with salt and pepper. Shape the ground fish into 4-oz. (110-g) patties. Fry on a hot griddle about 3 min-utes on each side. Place on toasted bun half and top with cheese slice. Melt cheese under broiler. Cover with other bun half. Serve with French fries, tartare sauce, and ketchup.

Shark Marseillaise

Ingredients	6 portions		24 portions	
	U.S.	Metric	U.S.	Metric
Fresh Shark Fillets	2 lb.	900 g	8 lb.	3.6 kg
Oil	3 tbsp.	3 tbsp.	¾ cup	2 dl
Onion, chopped	4 oz.	110 g	1 lb.	450 g
Tomatoes, peeled, seedless, and chopped	1 lb.	450 g	4 lb.	1.8 kg
Garlic Clove, minced	1	1	4	4
Parsley, chopped	1 tbsp.	1 tbsp.	4 tbsp.	4 tbsp.
Salt and Pepper, to taste				
Dry White Wine	½ cup	1.2 dl	2 cups	5 dl

Cut shark into serving portions. Heat the oil in a skillet. Add onions and cook over low heat for 5 minutes. Stir in the tomatoes, garlic, and parsley. Arrange the fish portions over the vegetables. Season with salt and pepper. Pour wine over. Bake at 350°F (180°C) for 15 minutes. Transfer the fish onto preheated platter(s). Pour the sauce over and serve hot.

Shark Teriyaki

See Fish Kebab Teriyaki under Miscellaneous Seafood Recipes in chapter 12.

Squid
(Inkfish, Cuttlefish, Calamari)

Sauteed Squid

Ingredients	6 portions		24 portions	
	U.S.	Metric	U.S.	Metric
Whole Squid	3 lb.	1.4 kg	12 lb.	5.4 kg
Butter	3 oz.	85 g	12 oz.	340 g
Garlic Cloves, minced	2	2	8	8
Parsley, chopped	2 tbsp.	2 tbsp.	½ cup	40 g
Lemon Juice	1 tbsp.	1 tbsp.	2 oz.	0.6 dl
Salt	½ tsp.	½ tsp.	2 tsp.	2 tsp.
White Pepper	¼ tsp.	¼ tsp.	1 tsp.	1 tsp.

Clean squid and cut into pieces. Melt butter in a saute pan. Add garlic and cook for 1 minute. Stir in the squid and remaining ingredients and saute for 1 to 2 minutes over brisk fire. As soon as squid is white and curls up, it is cooked. Do not overcook or squid will be tough. Serve hot with rice and tomato sauce.

Sauteed Squid Meuniere

Ingredients	6 portions		24 portions	
	U.S.	Metric	U.S.	Metric
Squid, small to medium	12	12	4 doz.	4 doz.
Flour.....................	4 oz.	110 g	1 lb.	450 g
Salt	1 tsp.	1 tsp.	4 tsp.	4 tsp.
Pepper, ground	⅛ tsp.	⅛ tsp.	½ tsp.	½ tsp.
Oil.......................	2 oz.	0.6 dl	1 cup	2.5 dl
Chives, chopped	1 oz.	25 g	4 oz.	110 g
Butter	4 oz.	110 g	1 lb.	450 g
Lemon Juice	2 lemons	2 lemons	8 lemons	8 lemons
Lemon Slices	6	6	24	24

Clean squid. Cut mantle into medium pieces and tenacles into 1-inch (2.5-cm) pieces. Combine flour, salt, and pepper. Roll squid pieces in flour. Heat the oil in a skillet and fry the squid pieces for 3 to 5 minutes. Turn and fry until done. Drain on paper. Sprinkle with chives. Serve with lemon butter and garnish with lemon slices.

Squid Stuffed with Spinach and Cheese

Ingredients	6 portions U.S.	Metric	24 portions U.S.	Metric
Medium Squid	6	6	24	24
Olive Oil	2 tbsp.	2 tbsp.	4 oz.	1.2 dl
Onion, chopped	2 oz.	50 g	8 oz.	200 g
Savory	1 tsp.	1 tsp.	4 tsp.	4 tsp.
Nutmeg, grated	¼ tsp.	¼ tsp.	1 tsp.	1 tsp.
Salt	¼ tsp.	¼ tsp.	1 tsp.	1 tsp.
Pepper, ground	⅛ tsp.	⅛ tsp.	½ tsp.	½ tsp.
Egg Yolks	3	3	12	12
Swiss or Parmesan Cheese, grated	½ cup	100 g	2 cups	400 g
Frozen Spinach, 10-oz. (280-g) packages	2	2	8	8
Sauce				
Olive Oil	2 oz.	0.6 dl	1 cup	2.5 dl
Onion, chopped	4 oz.	110 g	1 lb.	450 g
Canned Seedless Tomatoes, chopped	2 cups	400 g	8 cups	1.6 kg
Dry White Wine	1 cup	2.5 dl	1 qt.	1 l
Bay Leaves	1	1	4	4
Thyme Leaves	¼ tsp.	¼ tsp.	1 tsp.	1 tsp.
Saffron	½ tsp.	½ tsp.	2 tsp.	2 tsp.
Salt	½ tsp.	½ tsp.	2 tsp.	2 tsp.
Pepper, ground	¼ tsp.	¼ tsp.	1 tsp.	1 tsp.
Parsley, chopped	2 tbsp.	2 tbsp.	½ cup	40 g

Clean the squid. Chop the tentacles finely. Heat the oil in a skillet. Add the tentacles, onion, savory, nutmeg, salt, and pepper, and cook slowly for 10 minutes. Beat the egg yolks in a large bowl. Add the cheese, the cooked, drained, and chopped spinach, and fried tentacles with seasonings. Stuff each squid cone with the filling.

Sauce Heat the oil in a large skillet or saute pan. Add the onions and cook over low heat for 5 minutes. Arrange the stuffed squid over the onion. Add the tomatoes, wine, bay leaves, thyme, saffron, salt, and pepper. Cover and simmer for 20 to 25 minutes. Transfer squid onto a warm serving platter. Reduce the sauce to desired consistency and pour over the squid. Sprinkle with chopped parsley and serve hot.

Squid Siciliano

Ingredients	6 portions		24 portions	
	U.S.	Metric	U.S.	Metric
Squid, cleaned	1½ lb.	680 g	6 lb.	2.7 kg
Fresh Bread Crumbs	½ cup	25 g	2 cups	100 g
Cooked rice	1 cup	225 g	4 cups	1 kg
Ground Beef	8 oz.	225 g	2 lb.	910 g
Salt and Pepper, to taste				
Garlic Clove, minced	1	1	4	4
Romano Cheese, grated	2 oz.	50 g	8 oz.	225 g
Parsley, finely chopped	2 tbsp.	2 tbsp.	½ cup	40 g
Oregano	1 tsp.	1 tsp.	4 tsp.	4 tsp.
Tomato Sauce	1 lb.	450 g	4 lb.	1.8 kg

Clean squid, leaving mantle in one piece. Set aside. Saute bread crumbs, cooked rice, and ground beef in butter. Season with salt, pepper, and garlic. Cool mixture. Add the grated cheese, parsley, and oregano. Stuff squid with filling. Place in a shallow baking dish and top with tomato sauce. Bake at 350°F (180°C) for 20 to 30 minutes.

Squid Tempura

Ingredients	6 portions		24 portions	
	U.S.	Metric	U.S.	Metric
Whole Squid, fresh or frozen . .	2 lb.	910 g	8 lb.	3.6 kg
Flour	4 oz.	110 g	1 lb.	450 g
Vegetable Oil, for frying				
Batter				
Flour	3 oz.	85 g	12 oz.	340 g
Cornstarch	1 tbsp.	1 tbsp.	2 oz.	50 g
Baking Powder	1 tsp.	1 tsp.	4 tsp.	4 tsp.
Egg Whites, slightly beaten	3	3	12	12
Water	½ cup	1.2 dl	2 cups	5 dl
Dipping Sauce				
Soy Sauce	2 oz.	0.6 dl	1 cup	2.5 dl
Sherry or Sweet Sake	2 oz.	0.6 dl	1 cup	2.5 dl
Chicken Bouillon	1 cup	2.5 dl	1 qt.	1 l
Sugar	1 oz.	25 g	4 oz.	110 g

Thaw frozen squid. Spread mantle open and tenderize with mallet. Cut in half across, then cut lengthwise into ¾-inch (2-cm) strips. Dredge in flour.

Combine the batter ingredients until smooth. Dip pieces of squid into batter and fry at 375°F (190°C) for 4 to 5 minutes.

Combine the sauce ingredients and heat over low fire. Arrange fried squid on a warm platter. Serve sauce separately.

Stuffed Squid in Tomato Sauce

Ingredients	6 portions		24 portions	
	U.S.	Metric	U.S.	Metric
Medium Squid	12	12	48	48
Olive Oil	½ cup	1.2 dl	2 cups	5 dl
Parmesan Cheese	2 oz.	50 g	8 oz.	225 g
Ricotta Cheese	1 cup	2.5 dl	1 qt.	1 l
Anchovy Fillets, chopped	2 oz.	50 g	8 oz.	225 g
Eggs, beaten	2	2	8	8
Fresh Bread Crumbs	4 cups	225 g	2 lb.	900 g
Black Pepper, ground	¼ tsp.	¼ tsp.	1 tsp.	1 tsp.
Tomato Sauce	2 cups	5 dl	2 qt.	2 l

Clean squid. Chop the tentacles finely. Heat the oil in a skillet. Add the tentacles and cook over low heat for 5 minutes. Transfer to a mixing bowl. Add the parmesan and ricotta cheese, anchovies, eggs, and bread crumbs. Season with pepper. Stuff the squid cones with the filling. Arrange on baking pan(s) in single layers. Cover with tomato sauce. Bake at 350°F (180°C) for 10 to 15 minutes. Serve on preheated serving dish(es).

Stuffed Squid Nicoise

Ingredients	6 portions		24 portions	
	U.S.	Metric	U.S.	Metric
Small Squid, whole	2 lb.	910 g	8 lb.	3.6 kg
Olive Oil	3 oz.	1 dl	1½ cups	4 dl
Large Onion, minced	1	1	4	4
Medium Garlic Cloves, minced	2	2	8	8
Canned Tomatoes, peeled, seedless and chopped	1 lb.	450 g	4 lb.	1.8 kg
White Wine	1 cup	2½ dl	1 qt.	1 l
Bay Leaves	1	1.	4	4
Salt	¾ tsp.	¾ tsp.	1 tbsp.	1 tbsp.
Pepper, freshly ground	¼ tsp.	¼ tsp.	1 tsp.	1 tsp.
Saffron Threads	¾ tsp.	¾ tsp.	1 tbsp.	1 tbsp.
Rice, cooked	1 cup	225 g	4 cups	900 g
Small Black Olives	2 oz.	50 g	8 oz.	225 g
Parsley, chopped	1 tsp.	1 tsp.	1 tbsp.	1 tbsp.

Prepare squid for stuffing. Cut the tentacles into small pieces and saute in hot oil. Add the onion and cook until transparent, stirring frequently. Add the garlic, tomatoes, white wine, bay leaves, salt, pepper, and saffron. Cook over medium heat for 10 minutes.

Combine the rice with one quarter of the sauce and stuff the squid mantles. Arrange in a baking dish. Pour the remaining sauce over and bake at 400°F (200°C) for 10 to 15 minutes. Transfer onto a serving platter. Sprinkle olives and parsley over squid. Serve hot.

Appendices

Going Metric

Our traditional system of weights and measures is slowly being replaced by the simpler metric system. Although the metric system is logical, and easy to learn and use, many people are perplexed by the new system. The following information on converting ounces into grams, quarts into liters, and degrees Fahrenheit into degrees Celsius or centigrade should help. As a basic guide, remember that: water freezes at 0 degrees C (Centigrade) and boils at 100 degrees C; that 1 meter equals 100 centimeters (cm); and 1 liter equals 100 centiliters (cl). We have to learn to live with C g, dl, l, et cetera. You can begin by thinking metric.

Weight Conversion

The metric system has the gram as its basic unit of weight, with decimal multiples. One-thousand grams equals 1 kilogram (kg). To convert avoirdupois ounces into grams, multiply the ounces by 28.35. For example: 6 oz. $\times$ 28.35 = 170.1 g. Table A.1 lists some commonly used weight conversions.

Table A.1 Weight Conversions

Avoirdupois Ounces	to	Grams	Grams	to	Avoirdupois Ounces
1 oz.		28.35 g	10 g		0.35 oz.
2 oz.		56.70 g	15 g		0.53 oz.
3 oz.		85.05 g	20 g		0.70 oz.
4 oz.		113.39 g	30 g		1.05 oz.
5 oz.		141.74 g	40 g		1.41 oz.
6 oz.		170.09 g	50 g		1.76 oz.
7 oz.		198.44 g	60 g		2.11 oz.
8 oz.		226.79 g	70 g		2.47 oz.
9 oz.		255.14 g	80 g		2.82 oz.
10 oz.		283.49 g	90 g		3.17 oz.
11 oz.		311.48 g	100 g		3.52 oz.

(cont.)

Table A.1   Weight Conversions

Avoirdupois Ounces	to	Grams	Grams	to	Avoirdupois Ounces
12 oz.		340.19 g	200 g		7.04 oz.
13 oz.		368.54 g	300 g		10.56 oz.
14 oz.		396.89 g	400 g		14.08 oz.
15 oz.		425.25 g	450 g		15.87 oz.
16 oz.		453.59 g	500 g		17.64 oz.
2 lb.		907.18 g	1000 g 1 kg		35.27 oz.
3 lb.		1360.77 g	2000 g 2 kg		70.54 oz.
4 lb.		1814.36 g	3000 g 3 kg		105.82 oz.
5 lb.		2267.80 g	4000 g 4 kg		141.09 oz.
6 lb.		2721.54 g	5000 g 5 kg		176.36 oz.

NOTE: Most recipes do not follow the above chart precisely. For convenience, a close equivalent conversion is widely used. For example: 7 oz. equals 200 g; 16 oz. equals 450 g; 100 g equals 3½ oz.; 230 g equals 8 oz.

Temperature Conversion

Table A.2 shows the conversion of degrees Farenheit to degrees Celsius or centigrade, ranging from deep-freeze temperatures to deep-frying temperatures. To convert degrees F to degrees C quickly, refer to the following example:

$$(F - 32) \times 5 \div 9 = C$$

In reverse, $(C \times 9 \div 5) + 32 = F.$

Table A.2   Temperature Conversion

Farenheit	Celsius or Centigrades
−0.4 F.	−20 C.
10.4 F.	−12 C.
21.2 F.	−6 C.
26.6 F.	−3 C.
32 F.	0 C. (freezing point
37.4 F.	3 C. of water)
42.8 F.	6 C.
48.2 F.	9 C.
53.6 F.	12 C.
59 F.	15 C.
64.4 F.	18 C.
69.8 F.	21 C.
75.2 F.	24 C.
80.6 F.	27 C.
86 F.	30 C.

Farenheit	Celsius or Centigrades
91.4 F.	33 C.
98.6 F.	37 C.
212 F.	100 C. (boiling point of water)
225 F.	110 C.
250 F.	120 C.
275 F.	135 C.
300 F.	155 C.
325 F.	165 C.
350 F.	180 C.
375 F.	190 C.
400 F.	205 C.
425 F.	220 C.
450 F.	230 C.

NOTE: Most recipes follow approximate conversions for oven and deep-frying temperatures. Examples below rule are approximate.

Volume Conversion

The liter is the basic unit of volume in the metric system. In this book, most recipes are converted into deciliters (dl) or centiliters (cl). One liter (1) equals 10 dl, 100 cl, or 1000 ml. Small amounts of liquid are measured in centiliters or milliliters. Table A.3 lists some common volume conversions.

Table A.3 Volume Conversions

U.S.	Metric	U.S.	Metric
1 tsp.	0.5 cl	64 oz. or ½ gal.	200 cl or 20 dl or 2 l
1 tbsp. or 3 tsp.	1.5 cl	128 oz. or 1 gal.	400 cl or 40 dl or 4 l
2 tbsp. or 1 oz. (fluid)	3 cl or 0.3 dl	2 gal.	800 cl or 80 dl or 8 l
2 oz. (fluid)	6 cl or 0.6 dl	3 gal.	1200 cl or 120 dl or 12 l
3 oz.	9 cl or 0.9 dl	4 gal.	1600 cl or 160 dl or 16 l
4 oz. or ½ cup	12 cl or 1.2 dl	5 gal.	2000 cl or 200 dl or 20 l
8 oz. or 1 cup	25 cl or 2.5 dl		
16 oz. or 2 cups	50 cl or 5 dl or 0.5 l		
32 oz. or 1 qt.	100 cl or 10 dl or 1 l		

NOTE: The above chart is used and accepted in the trade although the conversions are not exact. One quart equals 0.95 l, but this figure is rounded to 1 l. The final products are not affected by these slight adjustments.

French Translation of Common Species of Fish and Shellfish

French is known as the language of diplomacy, but it is also recognized as the official language in gastronomy. Expressions like *maquereau au vin blanc* (mackerel in white wine), *saumon fume d'Ecosse* (Scottish smoked salmon) and *homard a la nage* (boiled American lobster) are common on many hotel and restaurant menus. Exclusive food establishments generally list their menus in French.

The following lists of fish and shellfish is a translation of most species found commercially on the United States markets.

Salt-water Fish

Anglerfish, Monkfish	Baudroie or Lotte	Ocean Perch	Perche d'ocean
Anchovy	Anchois	Pollock	Colin
Cod (fresh)	Cabillaud	Pompano	Pompano
Cod (salted)	Morue	Salmon	Saumon
Dolphin	Dauphin	Sardine	Sardine
Eel	Anguille	Shad	Alose
Flounder	Plie	Sea Trout	Truite de mer
Frogs' Legs	Cuisses de grenouilles	Skate	Raie
Grouper	Merou	Shark	Requin
Haddock	Aiglefin	Smelt	Eperlan
Hake	Merluche, Merlu	Sole	Sole
Halibut	Fletan	Striped Bass	Bar, Loup de mer
Herring	Hareng	Swordfish	Espadon
Lingcod	Lingue bleue, Julienne	Tuna	Thon
Mackerel	Maquereau	Turtle	Tortue
Mullet	Mulet	Whiting	Merlan

Fresh-water Fish

Carp	Carpe	Sturgeon	Esturgeon
Catfish	Poisson chat	Rainbow Trout	Truite Arc-en-ciel
Lake Herring	Hareng de lac	Whitefish	Fera
Lake Trout	Truite de lac	Trout	Truite
Pike	Brochet		

Mollusks

Abalone	Ormeau	Scallops	Coquille St. Jacques
Octopus	Poulpe	Snails	Escargots
Oysters	Huitre	Squid	Calamare

Crustaceans

Crawfish	Ecrevisse	Lobsterette	Langoustine
Crab	Crabe	Spiny Lobster	Langouste
Lobster	Homard	Shrimp	Crevette

Glossary

Anadromous   Ascending rivers from the sea for breeding, such as shad and salmon.

Barnquette   A small, boat-shaped pie crust shell usually filled with hot or cold seafoods.

Beurre manie   A mixture of equal weight of flour and butter used to thicken sauces.

Breaded shrimp   Peeled shrimp coated with breading. The product may be identified as fantail (butterfly) and round, with or without tail fins and last shell segment. Also known as portions, sticks, steaks, et cetera when prepared from a composite unit of two or more shrimp pieces, whole shrimp, or a combination of both without fins and shells.

Breading   A commercial breading is a finely ground mixture, containing cereal products, flavorings, and other ingredients, that is applied to a product that has been moistened, usually with batter.

Brisling   A small herring, resembling a sardine, that is cured and tinned for food especially in Norway.

Butterfly fillets   The two skin-on fillets of a fish joined together by the belly skin.

Canape   An appetizer prepared on a base such as bread, crackers, or toast.

Canned fishery products   Fish, shellfish, or other aquatic animals packed in cans, jars, or other containers, which are hermetically sealed and heat sterilized. Most, but not all, canned fishery products can be stored at room temperature for an indefinite time without spoiling.

Catadromous   Living in fresh water and going to sea to spawn.

China cap   A cone-shaped strainer or sieve.

Consumption of fishery products   Estimated amount of commercially landed fish, shellfish, and other aquatic animals consumed in the United States. Estimates are on an edible weight basis.

Croutons   Small pieces of fried or toasted diced bread used as a garnish in soups and other seafood dishes.

Cured fishery products   Products preserved by drying, pickling, salting, and smoking. Does not include canned, frozen, irradiated, or pasteurized products. Dried products are cured by sun or air drying; pickled or salted products are preserved by applying salt, or by pickling (immersing in brine); smoked products are cured with smoke, sometimes in combination with drying or salting.

Duxelle   Finely chopped mushrooms cooked with chopped shallots. Used primarily as part of stuffing for seafood.

En brochette   On a skewer, like seafood en brochette.

Exvessel price   Price received by fishermen for fish, shellfish, and other aquatic plants and animals landed at the dock.

Finnan haddie   Smoked haddock.

Fish blocks   Regular fish blocks are frozen blocks or slabs of fillets, or pieces of fillets, cut or sliced from fish. Minced fish blocks are frozen blocks or slabs of minced flesh produced by a meat and bone separating machine.

Fish fillets   The sides of fish, either skinned or with skin on, cut lengthwise from the backbone. Most types of fillets are boneless or virtually boneless; some may be specified as "boneless fillets."

Fish portion   A piece of fish flesh, generally of uniform size with a thickness of ⅜ inch or more, that does not conform to the definition of a fish stick. A fish portion is generally cut from a fish block.

Fish steak   Cross section slices cut from large dressed fish. Steaks are usually ¾ inch thick.

Fish stick   An elongated piece of breaded fish flesh weighing not less than ¾ ounce and not more than 1½ ounces, with the largest dimension at least three times that of the next largest dimension. A fish stick is generally cut from a fish block.

Fleuron   Small, crescent-shaped baked puffed pastry used as garnish around prepared seafood dishes with sauces.

Forcemeat   Chopped meats and seasonings used for stuffing or to make quenelles (dumplings).

Groundfish   Broadly, fish that are caught on or near the sea floor. The term includes a wide variety of bottomfishes, rockfishes, and flatfishes. However, the National Marine Fisheries Service sometimes uses the term in a narrower sense. The term usually applies to cod, cusk, haddock, hake, pollock, and Atlantic ocean perch.

Julienne   A method of cutting vegetables and fruit into fine long strips.

Landings, commercial   Quantities of fish, shellfish, and other aquatic plants and animals brought ashore and sold. Landings of fish may be in terms of round (live) weight or dressed weight. Landings of crustaceans are usually on a live weight basis except for shrimp, which may be on a heads-on or heads-off basis. Mollusks are generally landed with the shell on, but in some cases only the meats are landed (as with scallops). Data for all mollusks are published on meat weight basis.

Liaison   A thickening agent composed of heavy cream and egg yolks.

Marine fishing   Fishing for finfish in oceans, bays, estuaries, and tidal portions of rivers. Marine fishing also includes the harvest of shellfish and other living aquatic organisms in these waters.

Matelote   Fish stewed with wine, vegetables, and seasonsings.

Mayonnaise collee   A mixture of mayonnaise and aspic jelly; used to glaze cold foods.

Mirepoix   A mixture of chopped onions, carrots, and celery.

Per capita consumption   Consumption of edible fishery products in the United States, divided by the total population. In calculating annual per capita consumption, estimates of the resident population of the United States on July of each year are used.

Retail price   The price of fish and shellfish sold to the final consumer by food stores and other retail outlets.

Round (live) weight   The weight of fish, shellfish, or other aquatic plants or animals as taken from the water; that is, the complete or full weight as caught.

Index

384